IS THIS WHAT FAITH LOOKS LIKE?

IS THIS WHAT FAITH LOOKS LIKE?

A CONVERSATIONAL JOURNEY

Keith W. Howard

A GoldSash Publishing Book

Buckeye, Arizona

PUBLISHING

23395 Cocopah Street

Buckeye, AZ 85326

Copyright 2012 by GoldSash Publishing

All rights reserved,

Including the right of reproduction

in whole or in part in any form

Manufactured in the United States of America

Howard, Keith, b. 1966

Inspirational
"A GoldSash Publishing Book"
Includes biographical references and index

ISBN
978-0615745046

To Stefanie

TABLE OF CONTENTS

FOREWORD 19

ACKNOWLEDGEMENTS 21

INTRODUCTION 23

BIBLE BOOK ABBREVIATIONS 26

BIBLE VERSION ABBREVIATIONS 27

GROUP 1: FAITH OF OUR PATRIARCHS 31
    Creation 31
    Teeming with Life 31
    Temptation 32
    Observations Early On 32
    The Nephilim 32
    Noah's Flood 33
    Shem 34
    Orientation 34
    Is This What Faith Looks Like? 35
    The Posture of Prayer 35
    The Hot Coals and the Knife 36
    Choose What's Right 37
    Right Where God Wants You to Be 37
    Missed It by That Much 38
    The Fun in Dysfunction 40
    Anointed and Annoyed 41
    Was It Right? 42
    A Super-Race? 44
    Immaculate Integrity 45

A Predestination of My Choosing 47
Close Family Bonds 48
Don't Let the Left Hand Know 49
Parting is Such Sweet Sorrow 49
This Way and That 50
O-M-T 51
Silence the Croakers 52
A Yellow Jersey 53
No Bones about It 54
God-Speak or Human Jibberish 56
Remember to Forget 56
Ghetto Spirituality 57
Keeper of the Flame 58
Limitless Mercy 59
Diamonds in the Rough 60
The Devil's Workshop 61
Something Different 61
Redeeming a Culture of Arts 63
The Apex of Human Experience 63

GROUP 2: LAW AND ALLEGIANCE 67

A Living Aroma 67
The Trickle Down of Leadership 68
Wired to Worship 69
Every Last Vestige 70
Capital Casualty 71
A True Social Security 73
Foreshadowing a Blessing 75
The Need to Be Needed 76
A Vow of the Heart 77
Can You Imagine? 78
You No Good Rapscallion 79
Caleb's Different Spirit 80
Glory Incognito 82
Donkeys, Dogs and Discernment 83

Audience of One 86
Arouse the Nostalgia of Almighty 87
The Purple Lineage 88
The Glory Hole 90
Golfers and Gates Giving Testimony 91
Reverent Worship 93
Not on My Watch 94
The Compassionate Heart of God 95
Loose Shoe, Loose Shoe! 96
Warfare 98

GROUP 3: TRUST IN WAR TIMES 103

The Scarlet Cord 103
Achan's Ache 104
Lumberjacks and Waterboys 106
Divine Intervention 107
Ponds and Prayer 108
A Sharp Attack on Dullness 109
Housewife Gone Covert 109
Deflected Accolades 111
He Intervenes 112
The Punch Lineage 113
Old Testament Theophany 114
The Blessing of Integrity 115
Remember Wally Pipp 117
You Are Alright 118
A Really Special Friend 118
Give Me a Sign 119
Common Sense Isn't Common 120
Irony of Two Desperate Kings 121
The Storyline of Humanity 122
The Bygones Backfired 123
I'll Run No Matter What 124
Dumb, Dumber and Dumbest 125
Steps of Trepidation 126

Singing the Blues 127
My, Oh My, Micaiah 128
Christian Voodoo? 131
Doubly Blessed.. 132
Elisha Room... 133
No Guarantees 134
What's in a Name?... 135
On Another Level 136
Be Careful Little Eyes What You See 137
Oh, the Music!... 138
A Tribute to My Friend Jap 139
Running Interference 141
In a Word 142
Hezekiah's Hesitation 142
Testing, Testing, 1, 2, 3... 143
A Slam on the Worship Wars 144
Open and Honest Prayer 145
No Easy Undertaking.. 146
Great Projects in Bite-Sized Chunks...................................... 147
A Sudden Flash of Inspiration 148
Such Reverence.. 149

GROUP 4: PROPHETS AND POETS BELIEVING 153
Nashty and Vashti... 153
Esther's Keen Sense 154
Holy Trinity Inferred 155
I Didn't Even Know... 155
Confessions of a Techie-Schizo 156
Beauty.. 158
A Hen and a Pig and a Sacrifice.. 159
The Instant Message God 160
Oh, I Get It... 160
The Absence of I 161
The First Mistletoe... 161
The Dis-ease of Disease.. 162

Fulcrum and Counterweights	163
Within	164
Code Talkers	165
Eat Mor Chikin	166
Unity	167
Hanging Harps and Hope	167
Impassioned Pleas	168
My Heart's Keeping	168
Bait Christian	169
My Friend's Advice	170
Five Mississippi	171
Disarming Antagonists	172
That's What Friends are For	173
Use It or Lose It	174
Coach	175
Thirty Second Tune-Up	175
Wordly Wisdom	176
Right in the Happy Middle	176
Praise to Whom Praise is Due	177
Fly a Kite	178
Save Some Kick	179
Boring!	181
Snow White and the Seven Grieves	181
Greatest Joy	182
Before the Ice Cream Melts	183
I Wait	185
Migration to Salvation	185
A Flood of Mercy	187
Interstate Isaiah	188
He's an Early Almond	190
Job Posting: Prophet	191
The Weeping Prophet	192
The Diaspora – Figs Gone Figurative	193
Creative Genius	194
Optical Omnipotent	195
The Silence of Madmen	196

New Morning, New Mercy 196
Second Addams Family 197
Insight on Predestination 198
Resolve Rests 201
Bethlehem Bakery 202
Trust and Timing 203
He Welcomes Our Wrestling 204
Up on the Camelback 205
Our Crooning Crown 206
The Desired of All Nations 206
Again, What's in a Name? 208
Last Joshua 209
Riders on the Storm 209
Jesus and Jimmy the Greek 211

GROUP 5: A NEW LIVING HOPE 215

Bethlehem Remembered 215
The Trellis of Your Faith 216
Stunning Beauty of Nature 217
A-S-K 219
Scariest Verse in the Bible 220
Healed Emphatically 220
Clarity of Assignment 221
Feather Light Burdens 222
Separation Stories 223
Eternity – What If? 224
The True You of You 226
And He Healed Them All 227
The Amazing Mind Reader 228
Catch and Release 229
Small Huddles 230
Keep Fiddling Away 231
Catcalling and Raucous Bellowing 231
A Very Taxing Burden 232
A Literal Underground Church 233

Do Well by God	234
Table Fellowship	235
Jesus Barabbas or Jesus Christ?	236
A Downpour in the Desert	238
A Really Clever Impostor?	239
Incompatible Capacities	241
Thread-Breadth Window	243
To Coin a Phrase	244
Mary Mother	245
He Has Staked His Claim	246
71 Mustang Fastback	247
What Does It Mean to Pray?	248
Fruitful Consequences	249
Listen to How You Listen	249
Afterlife	249
The Glory of Humility	250
To the Day	252
Living Logos	252
Eternal Wind	253
Seeker Sensitive Worshiper	254
Aching, Yearning, Longing	255
A Little Dirt Don't Hurt	257
Doubting Thomas, I Doubt It	258
Lazarus, a Mob Hit	259
Judas, Dine In or Carry Out?	260
Purely Incarnational	262
The High Priestly Prayer	263
Taser versus Transformer	264
The Symbol of the Cross	265
The Breath of God	266
Upwardly Mobile	267
Pneumatic Uplift	268
Heavenly Languages	269
The Holy Spirit's Prompting	270
Way	271
The Right Stuff	272

Shepherd Savior 274
This Was All a Misunderstanding 275
Shake the Snake 276

GROUP 6: LETTERS THAT SHOW LOYALTY 281

Luther's Gate 281
The Christian Hokey Pokey 282
The Golf Clap of Heaven 283
I've Stepped in the Sticker Patch 283
Devotion Stew 284
Rockabilly Red Boots 285
One Form of Identification 287
Real. Comforter. Genes. 288
Money and Love Growing Like Trees 289
Beauty in Diversity 289
No Air Boxing 290
Discernment 291
Unclean, Unclean! 292
Loyalty 293
Veritable Law Couriers 294
That's Just Wrong 295
Duped by the Mundane 295
The God-Filled Life 296
The Man in the Moon 297
Good Stock 297
Our Dream 298
Emptied Excellence 299
Further Up, Further In 300
Feature Presentation 301
Love Struck 302
A Really Happy Life 304
If Only 304
Good Use of the Time 305
Military Fatigues 306
It's All about You 307

Celestial Super-Band	308
Recipe for Zero Joy	310
A Nameless Verse	310
100% Pure	311
A Model on Mentoring	312
Investigative Journalism	313
Used and Amused	314
New Digs	315
From His Vantage Point	316
Pistachios, Profiles and Peace	317
Solid Food	318
New and Improved	319
This Can't Be Faith	319
Substantive Faith	320
Faith that Lives	320
The Courage to Encourage	321
Wavy Wishfulness	322
Nearness	323
How Valuable is Faith!	323
Open Heavens	324
Steady as She Goes	324
A Lamp Shining in a Dark Place	326
Is Salvation a Fixed Invitation List?	327
Disappearing Trick	328
God's Kids and the Devil's Kids	329
A Loving Father and a Willing Son	329
Gnostic Know-It-Alls	332
Exercise Inside and Out	333
Jester in the Holy Court	333
Attitude	335

GROUP 7: APOCALYPTIC ASSURANCE ... 339

Finiteness Hits a Wall	339
Generational Goodness	340
It's God's Fault	342

Dem Dry Bones 343
Gog Me with a Span 344
The Dead Sea Lives 345
Divided Land, Unified Hearts 346
Watch Out for the Freshman Fifteen 347
A Word on Hostile Environments 348
Determinant Resolve 349
Daniel's Deliverance 350
Literal Lions and Reverie Rams 350
Crossing the Delaware 351
Apocalyptic Endurance 352
Glorious Age 353
Hocus Pocus, Help Us Focus 353
A Hopeful Horn 354
A Tale of the Undoing of Death 355
Wormwood Words 357
Faithful to the End 358
And Nothing but the Truth 359
It's On like Donkey Kong 360
The Restoration of All Things 361
Alpha and Omega 362

APPENDIX A 364

APPENDIX B 368

GLOSSARY OF SELECTED TERMS 371

GENERAL INDEX 373

SCRIPTURE INDEX 393

END NOTES 403

FOREWORD

Readers will be blessed and challenged by Keith Howard's first book, "IS THIS WHAT FAITH LOOKS LIKE?" These devotional posts stir a variety of emotions, and are at times humorous, sometimes poetic and soaring, consistently scholarly and thought-provoking, but always practical and inspiring. It's noteworthy, that in each of these conversations there is a hook that grabs the reader's attention. By providing that hook, the author makes it easy to get a handle on Biblical perspectives that impact life where it matters most. These studies were fashioned first in the heart of the author before appearing in this format. Because these messages flowed from a personal spiritual pilgrimage these conversations pointedly engage the reader in the following ways.

First, this book engages the reader by demonstrating the value of a consistent devotional life. One cannot write a book like this without daily prayer and Bible reading as an absolute priority. The author read, reflected, and unpacked an astounding array of interesting and often complex real-life issues by viewing them through the lens of unchanging Biblical truth.

Second, this book engages the reader by modeling the outcomes and the residual effect of a consistent devotional life. Bible reading and prayer are gifts that keep on giving! The writer could not have produced this work without that residual dimension. By digesting again the journal entries produced by those daily appointments with the Divine, the writer relived those soulful encounters; and in turn, has encouraged others by putting these essays in written form.

Third, this book engages the reader through its broad appeal and practical utility. This is a devotional book for everyone. Ministers and recent converts, as well as those who came to faith decades ago, will benefit from these conversations. The division of the messages into seven categories or groups along with the inclusion of a general index and Scripture index at the end of the book makes this work user-friendly. These studies will enhance your spiritual sojourn as a companion piece to daily Bible reading. The language of the book is coherent and inviting, and the word images are well-chosen. Those word images represent ideas "well-expressed" and are "like a design of gold, set in silver." *Proverbs 25:11 GNT*

On a personal note, I met Keith Howard twenty seven years ago when he was a university student in Texas. I was introduced to him by my daughter Stefanie. I was anxious to meet this minister- in- training since he was dating my daughter. After that initial visit with this very pleasant young man I told my wife Mamie, "He rings true." That first impression has been reinforced repeatedly by his character and conduct through the years. I've known Keith Howard as my daughter's suitor, as a son-in-law, as the father of two awesome grandsons, and now as a colleague and ministry equal. He has served with distinction as a ministry staff person, a lead pastor, and a denominational leader on a state-wide level. Keith Howard clearly possesses the skill set of the pastor-teacher referenced in Ephesians 4:11. He is a diligent and tenacious student of Scripture, and a voracious reader of a wide range of authors from both sacred and secular sources. The broad scope of Keith Howard's reading and research is evident in his preaching and teaching, and in this book, "IS THIS WHAT FAITH LOOKS LIKE?"

Jerry R Roberts

Sun City West, Arizona

ACKNOWLEDGEMENTS

I want to thank individuals who moved this project from possibility to reality. God knew of my need for a meticulously-minded individual to proof my scribbling with an eye to detail. He blessed our church family with just such a one. Sharon Seilhymer spent many hours poring over the document suggesting better syntax, catching errors, and raising the overall competency of the work.

I am deeply honored to have the foreword written by the capable hand of Jerry R. Roberts. He is an accomplished writer, truly a wordsmith, and he has done yeoman's work here. The reader is directed to his work elsewhere. His exemplary study, in the process of discerning God's will from the models demonstrated in the book of Acts, is unequaled. He was the perfect choice for the foreword because, as I have often commented, Jerry Roberts is one of the best communicators I know, an unquestionably great conversationalist. He is knowledgeable of a vast array of subjects and ideas. He has served as a state-wide youth director; a sought-out itinerant evangelist; a successful pastor at the local church level; a presbytery board member of a large geographic district; and a missionary who had oversight of all Central America. He has been largely responsible for planned giving to Latin America ChildCare, which is a quality, Christian education program for underprivileged children. He juggles multiple family roles with incredible due diligence. My knees knocked when I went to his office to ask for the hand of his daughter in marriage. When I asked him to write the foreword I felt an eerily similar respect. It is very meaningful to me that he would grace these pages with his words.

I am grateful to the congregation of Buckeye First Assembly, the church I am privileged to lead. They provide the landscape for much of the content of this book. I am always amazed by the venues God arranges. Our congregation is becoming more like Jesus. May our church continue to wrestle and grapple with real faith lived out in the rough and tumble. We are growing together.

My wife, Stefanie, and our two boys, Zakary and Nicholas, are such an inspiration to me. Stefanie and I began ministry on staff at a church in Lake Worth, Texas, the lake at Fort Worth, a quarter of a century ago. This was shortly before we married. Our ministry career has paralleled our merger. This coming year we will celebrate twenty-five years of matrimony. Stefanie is my other self. I am dedicated to her, and so is this book. She has shouldered many burdens in ministry that allow me creative endeavors. She has subtle fingers on the ivory keys and the ten-key. Her pensive demeanor is well-rounded and grounds me. Zakary and Nicholas provide the greatest joy a father could hope for. Frighteningly similar, and uniquely individual, their gifts and abilities reciprocate exponentially on me in waves. Basketball beasts, intellect that is scary, and musical prowess that teaches – wow, these guys rock. They don't fit in my lap any more. The computer is there often. I turned around twice and they were grown. What I wouldn't give to play "Climb up Daddy Mountain" again like we used to.

For others who contributed without even realizing it, thanks. Many conversations with friends and family members prompted thoughts that rattled in my head and found their way into chicken scratch. I am grateful.

Most of all, I am thankful to our Lord Jesus Christ for the privilege of the journey. Spirit-prompted encounters have translated into practical object lessons. I wouldn't trade anything for this odyssey; although I do not wish to repeat parts of it. And yet, there are other blessed components of my sojourn for which I am amazed beyond belief. My life is touched by grace. For any mistakes in this work I am fully to blame. If any good emerges from it, credit belongs to our Lord.

INTRODUCTION

I participated in a one-day preachers' boot camp intended to assess, evaluate and give feedback. I signed up because I want to get better at public speaking. The response from the committee was so encouraging. I was told I have a delivery style that is warm and conversational. A few years later, when I was doing a lot of academic writing, I kept hearing from professors that I have a gift for writing. One of them, Stephen Rexroat, now with the Lord, went out of his way to encourage me to pursue writing. He said that I have a style that is, well, you guessed it, conversational.

Say, I've got an idea. Can you and I have a conversation? A long one? For, oh, I dunno', the next year or so?

To commemorate twenty-five years of ministry I decided to write a post each day. These pieces are the result of a one-year project in which I wrote daily a short, sometimes not so short, substantive post that was devotional in nature. I tried my very best to make it thoughtful and reflective. Each one has an accompanying Scripture, usually one verse. The entries were posted each day under the description "uplifting and encouraging posts, substantive and inspiring," and generated thousands of *likes* on Facebook, Twitter, Google+1 and Youversion.

Is This What Faith Looks Like? boasts a hodgepodge of literary styles: alliteration; song; narrative; history; biographical. On some occasions I engage the ancient art of storytelling. Also, there are warm anecdotes from life lessons and childhood experiences. Additionally, some of my poems are interspersed throughout the book where it seemed appropriate. When you get to these I would encourage you to pause, read reflectively, and ask what might be meant or implied. Every available literary mechanism is employed from stoicism to sarcasm. At times the posts are deeply theological. And at times my whimsical style of humor may not be at once obvious, and it may not be at thousandths funny; but it is real and relaxed, intoned, embedded and littered throughout. The posts are at times exhilarating and other times controversial, both transparent and nuanced. Sometimes the entries do not instruct, but are designed intentionally to cause one to think. The comment is made, the question is raised. It hangs in the atmosphere forcing one to grapple with it. There are times when this is most faith-building.

For more than a quarter of a century I have read through the Bible at least once each year. *Is This What Faith Looks Like?* was berthed in this framework of experiential prayer. It is arranged for optimal use in a variety of approaches.

First, if you choose to start in Genesis and read straight through, this devotional will track with your progress. You will find the entries approximate what you are reading throughout the course of the year. The order of the entries follows traditional canonical order, with the one exception that Ezekiel and Daniel are grouped with the Revelation. All three books are thought to be apocalyptic literature typically. The sequential way of reading may aid to spark some thoughts on what you have just read. Some themes of the Resurrection and the Incarnation, for instance, are unearthed from passages in which they may otherwise remain embedded, simply because my holy-day antenna was up, as the calendar-conveyor moved me in a direction.

Secondly, however, I recognize there are many valuable reading plans available to the contemporary Christian – whole Bible in a year; Chronological Bible; Jesus' Words; New Testament and Proverbs; Historical Plan and many others. One may employ any such approach and supplement her or his purposeful Bible reading with *Is This What Faith Looks Like?* The Scripture index in the back will indicate when I have written about a particular verse.

A third method may prove a healthy consideration for the reader. The posts have been grouped according to seven major literary divisions of Scriptural texts: patriarchs; law; war-times; poetry and prophecy; gospels and action; letters from apostles; and apocalyptic literature. Rather than read the posts in succession, one might alternate groups daily. Strategically there are seven groups; one for each day of the week. I must mention the groups do not have the same number of entries; however, with a little flexibility they will fit well into a strategy for the fifty-two week year. Appendix A, at the end of the book, will prove useful for this method. Checking off the entries may be helpful and could illicit other, endless, creative ideas and approaches.

One last approach merits a mention. You may wish to come to the posts by their literary genre. Appendix B will assist you at those times when you may have a hankering for a certain style. This could be just the ticket. Note this appendix is simply for categorization and does sometimes repeat post titles.

This conversation is intended to uplift and inspire. At all times be especially present to the backdrop and splash of faith on every page. It is also meant to stretch and challenge you. May this book exercise you in the same sense that spiritual leaders throughout the history of the Church have used the term *disciplines*. Of course *Is This What Faith Looks Like?* may be used independently, with each day providing a shot in the arm for the Christian wanting to be in communion with our Lord. However, I am quick to add a disclaimer. That was not its original intent. It was meant to accompany systematic Bible reading, for which there is no substitute.

This year I enjoyed the Contemporary English Version in my devotions. Its footnotes concur with study-helps for the Roman Catholic's "St Joseph Edition," and it meets criteria for Roman Catholic Imprimatur. And yet, I am not Roman Catholic. I read from a different version each year. The posts reflect nice subtleties that each version will unearth. When other translations are quoted they are noted in the text. I've avoided the temptation to number the entries or label them with dates. If you were to miss one day you would either race to catch up or get discouraged and quit. We don't want that, now do we? No, just relax. These posts are meant to be succulent, not fast food. No fries on the floorboard, okay?

A theme surfaced in my devotions this year and it was this: one component of faith is steadfast determination, wrestling with difficulties, finding a way to trust, even in the hard times. The reader should know I am not against believing faith. The solution to hyper faith is not less faith. I simply wish to highlight the dignity of struggling in the life of the Christian, and also in the eyes of our Lord. Take your time with the words, perhaps wrestle, you 'ole *Israel*, you. This next year, like your life, will move with ebb and flow. Find your happy pace that tracks with about one post per day. Some days you'll be hungrier than others. If you should miss a day every now and then, you'll still finish by year's end.

I am Evangelical, further, Pentecostal, using a Catholic version. You will notice my slant in the inclinations. If we differ, and we do, even if you are from my own tribe, don't let it throw you. Please keep the conversation rolling; don't let it lull. Save the meat, toss the bones. My hope is to encourage and lift you, for you to experience substance and be inspired.

Keith W. Howard
Buckeye, Arizona

BIBLE BOOK ABBREVIATIONS

Gen	Genesis	Nah	Nahum
Exod	Exodus	Hab	Habakkuk
Lev	Leviticus	Zeph	Zephaniah
Num	Numbers	Hag	Haggai
Deut	Deuteronomy	Zech	Zechariah
Josh	Joshua	Mal	Malachi
Judg	Judges	Matt	Matthew
Ruth	Ruth	Mark	Mark
1 Sam	1 Samuel	Luke	Luke
2 Sam	2 Samuel	John	John
1 Kgs	1 Kings	Acts	Acts
2 Kgs	2 Kings	Rom	Romans
1 Chr	1 Chronicles	1 Cor	1 Corinthians
2 Chr	2 Chronicles	2 Cor	2 Corinthians
Ezra	Ezra	Gal	Galatians
Neh	Nehemiah	Eph	Ephesians
Esth	Esther	Phil	Philippians
Job	Job	Col	Colossians
Ps	Psalms	1 Thess	1 Thessalonians
Prov	Proverbs	2 Thess	2 Thessalonians
Eccl	Ecclesiastes	1 Tim	1 Timothy
Sng	Song of Solomon	2 Tim	2 Timothy
Isa	Isaiah	Titus	Titus
Jer	Jeremiah	Phlm	Philemon
Lam	Lamentations	Heb	Hebrews
Ezek	Ezekiel	Jas	James
Dan	Daniel	1 Pet	1 Peter
Hos	Hosea	2 Pet	2 Peter
Joel	Joel	1 John	1 John
Amos	Amos	2 John	2 John
Obad	Obadiah	3 John	3 John
Jonah	Jonah	Jude	Jude
Mic	Micah	Rev	Revelation

BIBLE VERSION ABBREVIATIONS

AMP	Amplified Bible
CEV	Contemporary English Version
GNT	Good News Translation
GWT	God's Word Translation
HOL	Holman Christian Standard Bible
JBP	J.B. Phillips New Testament
KJV	King James Version
MES	The Message
NASB	New American Standard Bible
NIV	New International Version
NKJV	New Kings James Version
NLT	New Living Translation
NRSV	New Revised Standard Version

1

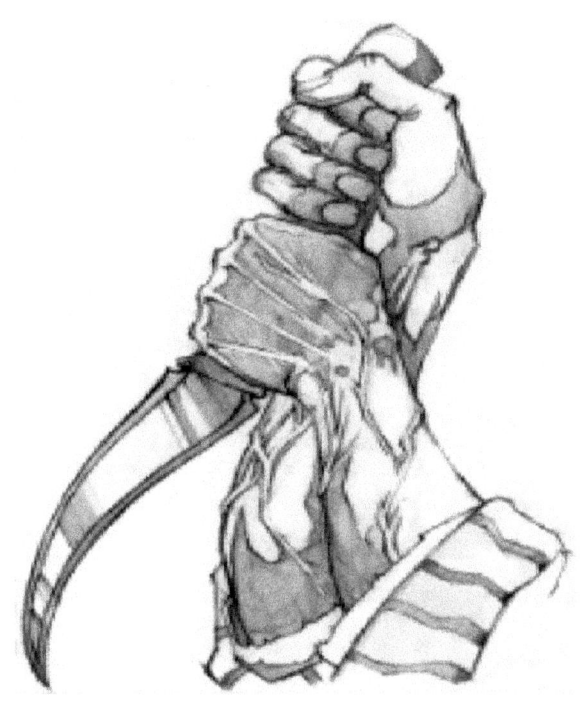

Faith of our Patriarchs

GROUP 1: FAITH OF OUR PATRIARCHS

Creation

> *Genesis 1:2*
>
> *The earth was barren, with no form of life; it was under a roaring ocean covered with darkness. But the Spirit of God was moving over the water.*

It is one of the most interesting discussions in Scripture that there was, in some sense, confusion in God's pre-creation universe. This is before Adam and Eve sinned. In a new universe with one privileged planet, named earth by God himself, there is a masterful, mystifying plan that involves a serpent in the paradise and the cognition of a Lamb, slain even from the foundation of the world.

Teeming with Life

> *Genesis 2:15*
>
> *The Lord God put the man in the Garden of Eden to take care of it and to look after it.*

As part of God's pre-sin world, humanity was instructed to care for the earth. We live in a world that is increasingly detached from agriculture. We simply buy beef and chicken at the refrigerated section of the super market with little concern for where it came from. It is the same with the produce aisle. After the Industrial Age we have vegetation trucked and treated. We tend not to think of the pesticides involved, or where it was grown. That is changing though. It is becoming part of a Christian ethic to insure that chickens are not caged but have space to cluck. Cattle that is desired is that which preserves the dignity of the animal. Grass-roaming, corn-fed beef is honorable. This does not even touch on the role of the Church on a planet going green. Perhaps we shall talk about that in our conversation. Suffice to say, a Christian is thankful for an atmosphere that sustains life. God did not place us on a cold, gray planet where we merely exist. Instead, since he abhors a culture of death, he has blessed us with surroundings teeming with life.

Temptation

Genesis 3:1

The snake was sneakier than any of the other wild animals that the LORD God had made. One day it came to the woman and asked, "Did God tell you not to eat fruit from any tree in the garden?"

"The snake was sneakier than any other wild animals." So the serpent was sneaki*est*, but others were sneaky too? The implication is left hanging there for us to wrestle with. Was God's pre-sin paradise riddled with land mines, and booby traps? If free-will exists then it must be embedded in the fabric of creation, otherwise it is imposed-will. Free-will plays out in church life every day. Pastors (I am one) make mistakes. Boards make mistakes. Leaders make mistakes. Members make mistakes. The Church is fraught with errors. It is part and parcel to this glorious mystery called freedom. So we stretch, are tested, tempted and tried. But there is One who faced every temptation and yet, was without sin. "For we have no superhuman High Priest to whom our weaknesses are unintelligible – he himself has shared fully in our experience of temptation, except that he never sinned" (Heb 4:15, JBP).

Observations Early On

Genesis 4:7

If you had done the right thing, you would be smiling. But you did the wrong thing, and now sin is waiting to attack you like a lion. Sin wants to destroy you, but don't let it!

Two observations are interesting here to say the least, early on in the quest of humanity. 1. Cain is one generation removed from Adam and Eve. Already murder has entered the human race. Notice there is no notion on Cain's part to claim a generational curse. 2. The concept of free-will is reinforced. Sin wants to destroy you, but don't let it! We have a say in the matter of behavior and belief.

The Nephilim

Genesis 6:1-8

More and more people were born, until finally they spread all over the earth. Some of their daughters were so beautiful that supernatural beings came down and married the ones they

> wanted. Then the LORD said, "I won't let my life-giving breath remain in anyone forever. No one will live for more than one hundred twenty years." The children of the supernatural beings who had married these women became famous heroes and warriors. They were called Nephilim and lived on the earth at that time and even later.
>
> The LORD saw how bad the people on earth were and that everything they thought and planned was evil. He was very sorry that he had made them, and he said, "I'll destroy every living creature on earth! I'll wipe out people, animals, birds, and reptiles. I'm sorry I ever made them."
>
> But the LORD was pleased with Noah.

There are endless fascinations with who the Nephilim are. And there are some pretty good observations. The writings of Ray C. Stedman are helpful. I side with him. The Nephilim were a demonic invasion into the human race. It is worth mentioning that if the Nephilim came down to earth, presumably they could go back up, go between back and forth. Perhaps wandering is a better description. One wonders about the populating of the planet. Were Adam and Eve the only ones? According to Thomas Kendall the marriage of cousins in the early, prehistoric world would have had no ill effects on their offspring. Where did all the people come from? In part, by these mysterious Nephilim. And after the flood, which I take at face value as worldwide in scope, they apparently intermingled with humanity again because the Bible references them later. When all races and people groups were wiped out and had to start again, the race of Nephilim is resurrected. How? Either the flood was not worldwide and catastrophic, or the Nephilim revisited the post-Noah world. How frequent and accelerated are their visits in our day?

Noah's Flood

> Genesis 7:1
>
> The LORD told Noah: Take your whole family with you into the boat, because you are the only one on this earth who pleases me.

Was Noah's flood world-wide in scope? Some have proposed it was only a flood of one geographic region. There are three points the text makes clear. 1. Noah is the only one on earth that pleases God. It is true the Hebrew word for earth, *eretz*, can mean land. However, if there were other survivors in other regions God would want to clarify that. He would certainly want to distinguish a smaller territory from the entire earth of Genesis 1:1, the same word, if that's what he had intended. 2. There is an intentional effort from God to preserve all animal-life. Why such a fuss if it is only a geographic flood? 3. The highest mountain peaks were covered. This statement would require clarification from the author had he intended the reader to interpret it as anything other than global in scope. Many cultures of the world have mention of a devastating, worldwide flood in their histories. It seems to me the text leaves no room for fanciful, anachronistic speculation.

Shem

> *Genesis 11:10*
>
> *Two years after the flood, when Shem was one hundred, he had a son named Arpachshad. He had more children and died at the age of six hundred.*

When Shem (from whom we derive the term Semite) had lived half of his six-hundred year life, the ninth generation after him was born, and that was Abraham's generation. Just think of the longevity. What's more, Noah was still alive for the first 58 years of Abraham's life too. Abraham could get first-hand accounts of the flood.

Orientation

> *Genesis 13:12, 13, 18*
>
> *Abram stayed in the land of Canaan. But Lot settled near the cities of the valley and put up his tents not far from Sodom, where the people were evil and sinned terribly against the LORD.*
>
> *Abram took down his tents and went to live near the sacred trees of Mamre at Hebron, where he built an altar in honor of the LORD.*

Lot pitched his tent in the proximity of wickedness. "Lot settled near the cities of the valley and put his tents not far from Sodom, where the people were evil and sinned terribly against the Lord." Abram, however, oriented himself toward righteousness. It says, "Abram took down his tent and went to live near the sacred trees of Mamre." In our culture individuals often claim exemption from responsibility based upon genetic disposition. This has important implications on the discussion of sexual orientation. However, orientation is not passive but active, not a mandate but a choice. May God assist us in spiritual decision-making.

Is This What Faith Looks Like?

Genesis 15:2-6

But Abram answered, "LORD All-Powerful, you have given me everything I could ask for, except children. And when I die, Eliezer of Damascus will get all I own. You have not given me any children, and this servant of mine will inherit everything." The LORD replied, "No, he won't! You will have a son of your own, and everything you have will be his." Then the LORD took Abram outside and said, "Look at the sky and see if you can count the stars. That's how many descendants you will have." Abram believed the LORD, and the LORD was pleased with him.

Abraham is filing a complaint, a courteous complaint, but a complaint nonetheless. *Father of nations, me? Hello? Count the stars in the heavens? Number the sand grains of the seashore? I just want one kid to call me Daddy.* However, once Abraham was sure he had heard from God, he believed and acted upon it. Serving the Lord in the rough and tumble is lived out painstakingly in real time. It seems like we're spinning our wheels and the servant is going to get the inheritance. Is this what faith looks like? Fleshing out my existence? Scratching and clawing? Pounding the beat? Sometimes, yes. Believe and act. Trust and obey.

The Posture of Prayer

Genesis 18: 27, 28

Abraham answered, "I am nothing more than the dust of the earth. Please forgive me, LORD, for daring to speak to you like this. But suppose there are only forty-five good people in Sodom. Would you still wipe out the whole city?"

We associate the word 'posture' typically with our physical position. And this is good. In an age in which there is such an emphasis on comfort and grace, I find it is good, periodically, to kneel intentionally, to close my eyes, to bow my head, to clasp my hands. There is also the posture of the heart, and this is what Abraham illustrates so well. It is a humble approach void of arrogance. It is appropriate self-degradation that stops short of poor self-image. It is a boldness very daring, clothed in apology. Dust must so posture itself to Spirit, not jockey for position.

The Hot Coals and the Knife

Genesis 22:6-8

Abraham put the wood on Isaac's shoulder, but he carried the hot coals and the knife. As the two of them walked along, Isaac said, "Father, we have the coals and the wood, but where is the lamb for the sacrifice?"

"My son," Abraham answered, "God will provide the lamb."

There are many comparisons between Abraham and Isaac with God the Father and Jesus Christ. The Danish philosopher, Soren Kierkegaard, may have had this in mind when he wrote one of his most important works, *Fear and Trembling*. In it he tries to enter the mind of Abraham to know the rumblings of his inner man, what he must have wrestled with. Kierkegaard imagines four scenarios in which morality is temporarily placed on the back burner for the greater good, what he calls the "teleological suspension of the ethical."[1] The age old discussion, does the end justify the means? What places this in a whole separate layer is that it happens at the initiation of God. But Genesis 22 begins to make sense when we realize this is a test intended to model the great love of God who provides his own Lamb. Jesus, Almighty God, exists in real eternity, outside the scope of real time, which is by definition temporary time. God never intended Abraham to sacrifice Isaac. Abraham was willing to give his only son. God did give his only Son. Isaac carried the wood up the mountain just as Jesus carried the wood of the cross up the mountain of Golgotha. Father Abraham carried the hot coals and the knife. Hmm. Did Father God carry hot coals and the knife for Jesus' death? I don't know. It leads to conversations about Penal Substitutionary Atonement, Ransom Theory and Christus Victor. I like to envision the holy finger of God stained by the charcoal his hand had placed in the grate. Fire judges sin as white-hot tears fill the eyes of God. Isaiah references hot coals that were taken from the altar to cleanse his lips. What altar? The Lamb was slain from the foundation of the world. Both John and Peter reference this. Is it possible the spear of the soldier that pierced Jesus' side mysteriously coincided with the perfect moment of eternity? Perhaps the same knife that God used to butcher the skins which covered Adam and Eve? So the sacrifice was actuated from creation but activated at Calvary. God wanted to see if Abraham was willing to do what he had already done in a future generation. We don't like to visualize a holy God dirtied by intervention; but he doesn't seem to define purity as not getting his hands soiled.

Choose What's Right

>*Genesis 24:49*
>
>*Now please tell me if you are willing to do the right thing for my master. Will you treat him fairly, or do I have to look for another young woman?*

"Will you choose to do what's right for my master?" The thought is repeated three times in the story of the servant securing a bride for Isaac, once at the beginning by Abraham to the servant, again at the retelling to Laban, and again, after family discussion, when Rebekah is asked what she will choose. It is repeated throughout the centuries too, "Will you choose to do what's right for my master?" Rebekah models Christian virtue so well. She trusts her father implicitly, follows a stranger on a long journey to marry a man she has only just now heard about, but never met. Faith on display. How about you? Will you follow? Will you be the true bride of Christ, spotless and without blemish? Will you take the long journey to meet the One you have never actually seen with your eyes? "Will you choose to do what's right for my master?"

Right Where God Wants You to Be

>*Genesis 26:1, 2*
>
>*Once during Abraham's lifetime, the fields had not produced enough grain, and now the same thing happened. So Isaac went to King Abimelech of the Philistines in the land of Gerar, because the LORD had appeared to Isaac and said:*
>
>*Isaac, stay away from Egypt! I will show you where I want you to go.*

A great deal of strategy went into the re-population of planet earth after the flood. In the Tower of Babel incident God created multiple language groups and separated them. As Abraham and his nephew Lot grew more powerful and dominant, they separated and created new territories. Before Father Abraham died, he granted a pre-death inheritance to both Hagar and Keturah and their sons, and sent them to land far to the east. And yet, it wasn't an aimless sending, as we shall see.

Isaac and his so-called big-brother rival, Ishmael, were actually on good terms. They took care of the burial arrangements of their father together, probably because there was enough money to go around and everybody was happy with the inheritance. What's more, Isaac then goes to live at Beer-Lahai-Roi (The well of The-Living-One-Who-Sees-Me), the place of the well that God provided for Ishmael and his mom when he was at the point of death, wandering in the wilderness. Water is a big deal.

Next, the Lord appears to Isaac and says to stay away from Egypt, the obvious choice for refuge. This is strange because his grandson Jacob will go there and become the mighty nation of Israel. They will occupy Egypt for 430 years and then pillage them when they leave. So, Isaac follows the direction of the Lord and has a rough go of it. He endures two different heated debates over water rights. But he keeps a good attitude and keeps digging wells. Finally, the third well he opens is free from dispute and he names it "Lots of Room."

All of what has just been described is the beginning of conflict in the Middle East between the Islamic nations and Israel. When Jesus comes on the scene there is strategic populating of the kingdom of God. He chooses his inner 3, Peter, James and John; then there are the 12 disciples. In time he will send out 72. Jesus was his most animated when rejoicing with them over the authority they experienced. The last written encounter of Jesus with his disciples is when he has breakfast with them on the seashore in John 21. It mentions the catch of 153 fish. Why? The great twentieth-century theologian, Arno Gaebelein, points out there were 153 nations in the world at the time Jesus was having breakfast with these fishers of men. In the beginning of the book of Acts we read numbers such as 3,000 and 5,000. And by the end of the book of Acts the kingdom was rapidly populating the known world. The expansion continues right up to our current time.

Could it be you are strategically avoiding your Egypt, working hard to dig wells seemingly with no success? Perhaps you are right where God wants you to be in the spread of the kingdom.

Missed It by That Much

Genesis 27:30-36

Right after Isaac had given Jacob his blessing and Jacob had gone, Esau came back from hunting. He cooked the tasty food, brought it to his father, and said, "Father, please sit up and eat the meat I have brought you, so you can give me your blessing."

"Who are you?" Isaac asked. "I am Esau, your first-born son."

Isaac started trembling and said, "Then who brought me some wild meat right before you came in? I ate it and gave him a blessing that cannot be taken back." Esau cried loudly and

> begged, "Father, give me a blessing too!" Isaac answered, "Your brother tricked me and stole your blessing."
>
> Esau replied, "My brother deserves the name Jacob, because he has already cheated me twice. The first time he cheated me out of my rights as the first-born son, and now he has cheated me out of my blessing." Then Esau asked his father, "Don't you still have any blessing left for me?"

In one sense my heart goes out to poor Esau who comes in with a nice meal, all set to receive the blessing of his father, Isaac. In the 60s TV sitcom *Get Smart*, Agent 86, otherwise known as Maxwell Smart, would say in shrill voice to Agent 99, "Missed it by that much." Esau actually did miss it by just that much. He had success in his hunt, we presume. He must have been excited to walk in with what he had prepared for his father. In a moment, however, it all changed. Without notice or warning, his twin is promoted, blessed and endowed; while he is demoted, impoverished and disinherited. That it was done craftily with deception makes the sting even worse. But in the other sense we get the idea that Esau was careless with his priorities. He devalued his birthright, sold it for a bowl of stew. And regarding his father's deathbed blessing, one wonders if he came about the meal honestly. Did he actually hunt and kill, or did he contrive, too, like his brother and mother? Did he take an animal out of the family flock? Is that how he "missed it by that much?" Speculation. to say the least.

In any event, the point is, Esau became very bitter about the way he was wronged, so angry, in fact, that he was ready to kill Jacob. Twenty years later, when Jacob returns, blessed abundantly, and bearing gifts, Esau has not exactly been deprived either. He says to Jacob, in essence, "What are all these flocks I met on the way? I don't need them." Was he mad still? Oh yeah. He didn't bring 400 men with him to escort his brother Jacob back home with a parade. He intended to bring him harm, even twenty years later. But his heart warmed at the lavish gifts of Jacob. Twenty years earlier, regarding the blessing, he had "missed it by that much." But now, potentially the biggest mistake of his life, he "missed by that much." Had he gone through with it and killed Israel, he would have been permanently cursed.

It's a fascinating study, "Jacob I have loved, and Esau I have hated." The words were never spoken during the lifetime of either. They were written a thousand years postmortem and intended to reference the nations Jacob and Esau had become. This verse, often touted as a foundation for predestination, actually bolsters a view in support of free will. We live in the land of consequences for decisions we have made. Do brothers still get angry and not speak for twenty years? Yes. Do children get estranged from their parents in strained relationships? Yes. If we could just trust the heart of God, and give up understanding every mystery, we would come to realize in his master plan it all works together for good. And when it comes to our eternal destinations we cannot claim we "missed it by that much." We can't point fingers. We can't claim exemption because of difficult circumstances. We must own up to our mistakes, confess our wrongdoing, and embrace a living faith in Christ that transforms all of our relationships.

The Fun in Dysfunction

Genesis 30:8

Rachel said, "I've struggled hard with my sister, and I've won!" So she named the boy Naphtali.

The premier Jewish family is openly vulnerable in the text; bordering at times on the comedic, they put the fun in dysfunction. Their struggles become the template of struggle that all persons can relate to in one way or another. The antics of Jacob and his wives and concubines are terse with apprehension and sometimes absurd. Leah is unloved, or at least, less loved. She's birthing children en masse, but is more notorious for the production of tension. Rachel is loved with unscrupulous bias; yet her yearning to have children lingers for quite a while. They both, in time, incorporate their handmaids in the tradition of Grandma Rebekah. All of this presents a tug of war with Jacob as the rope. Throughout the storied adventure Leah and Rachel name their respective children for their pain. The story unfolding from these families informs the intervention of God upon earth.

The escapades of the premier Jewish family speak to the dysfunction of God's chosen people. This serves as an inset on the map of humanity. God's selection of Israel as his chosen people continues the theme of Yahweh siding with the beggared, or the underdog of the earth. In the larger picture, what is happening to Israel mirrors the plight of humanity. God chooses them because of his love, not because of their exemplary status. The family difficulties are merely demonstrative of God's acceptance of all people. That there is hope for their common difficulties shows the potential for God's intervention of all human woe.

Anointed and Annoyed

> *Genesis 32:24-32*
>
> *Afterwards, Jacob went back and spent the rest of the night alone.*
>
> *A man came and fought with Jacob until just before daybreak. When the man saw that he could not win, he struck Jacob on the hip and threw it out of joint. They kept on wrestling until the man said, "Let go of me! It's almost daylight."*
>
> *"You can't go until you bless me," Jacob replied.*
>
> *Then the man asked, "What is your name?"*
>
> *"Jacob," he answered.*
>
> *The man said, "Your name will no longer be Jacob. You will be called Israel, because you have wrestled with God and with men, and you have won." Jacob said, "Now tell me your name."*
>
> *"Don't you know who I am?" he asked. And he blessed Jacob.*
>
> *Jacob said, "I have seen God face to face, and I am still alive." So he named the place Peniel. The sun was coming up as Jacob was leaving Peniel. He was limping because he had been struck on the hip, and the muscle on his hip joint had been injured. That's why even today the people of Israel don't eat the hip muscle of any animal.*

Jacob had the nighttime visitor cradled, hands locked, pinned – he's going nowhere. This is one of the most mysterious encounters in Scripture. The reader is left to grapple with it. Who is this "man" Jacob would not release from his hold until he had blessed him? The text drops clues for us. He didn't want the morning light to reveal his identity. He assumed authority to change Jacob's name. And what a name change, right? God-wrestler. Jacob believed he had the ability to offer a blessing. He felt he had seen the face of God and survived. In the end a good reading leaves one in wonderment. *Could it be? Is this God? Naw. Maybe. Hmm.* And we are left to wrestle with this wrestling. In a similar encounter, Judges 13:17-19, Manoah wants to know the identity of his messenger guest. In nearly identical wording he says, "Why do you want to know my name? It is wonderful." It is very Isaiah 9:6-esk language, "Wonderful Counselor." If this is not God tangled with Jacob, it is at least a high ranking official, one of his special emissaries. Remarkably, it is quite possibly a pre-incarnate appearance of Christ himself. How amazing that the entire identity of the nation God chose for himself is predicated upon wrestling! Historically, the Jewish people have scratched and clawed, eeked out an existence. Blessed bountifully, yes, but hated in the earth. From Haman to Hitler they have been manipulated. These scattered nomads were the only nation to exist without a physical land, and did so for two-thousand years until they received it again in 1948. One swath of land along the Mediterranean Sea, surrounded by five giant, angry neighbors, Israel (Wrestler) is God's privileged jewel, favored and fighting, anointed and annoyed, like Jacob, she walks with a limp. You and I must wrestle. Our faithful prayer rises like the smoke from torches in the huts on the back acres of plantations in the Antebellum South. Black spirituals gave hope to a hopeless people entrenched in the horrors of slavery. Freedom is worth the fight. Blessing is worth the beat down. "I will not let you go unless you bless me."

Was It Right?

Genesis 34:25-31

Three days later the men who had been circumcised were still weak from pain. So Simeon and Levi, two of Dinah's brothers, attacked with their swords and killed every man in town, including Hamor and Shechem. Then they took Dinah and left. Jacob's other sons came and took everything they wanted. All this was done because of the horrible thing that had happened to their sister. They took sheep, goats, donkeys, and everything else that was in the town or the fields. After taking everything of value from the houses, they dragged away the wives and children of their victims. Jacob said to Simeon and Levi, "Look what you've done! Now I'm in real trouble with the Canaanites and Perizzites who live around here. There aren't many of us, and if they attack, they'll kill everyone in my household."

They answered, "Was it right to let our own sister be treated that way?"

There is so much wrong with this story I don't even know where to start. Shechem is a wild stallion who is used to roaming the range, kicking up his hoofs, snorting hot air, and picking off victims one at a time, whoever tickles his fancy. He spots Dinah and rapes her. He is so in "love" with her he wants to marry her. Love has nothing to do with it. He finds her pleasurable and satisfying and he wants to have her anytime he wants without the inconvenience of having to rape her, because after all, as verse 19 says, he is "the most respected person in his family." Yikes!

In this extreme Patriarchal society the shortfalls are glaring. We don't get to hear any of the comments of Dinah's mother, Leah, anger, concerns or otherwise. Can you just imagine the conversations that took place in the tents with her and Aunt Rachel, and servants Bilhah and Zilpah? Family systems being the way they are, and given the dysfunctional nature of this particular family, it is conceivable that Mom, her Sis and maids influenced and incited the action of the sons, if they perceived hesitation by Father Jacob.

Now we come to Simeon and Levi. One time I went to a high school basketball tournament. There was a game on the floor between a team from a rural community and a team from the city. The heated contest went back and forth until finally the small town boys triumphed. The momentum seemed to swing in the game when one of the country boys had had enough of the hand-checking and verbal taunting. He shoved the other player and clinched his fist, ready to clean his clock. There was a well-dressed, sophisticated gentlemen sitting next to me in the stands. He wasn't for either team. It was at this moment he leaned over to me and said, "Out on the farm we have ways of taking care of problems like this."

In the village of Shechem, before there was any rule of law, it was much like the days of the Wild West. Simeon (which means God hears or to be heard), and Levi (harmony, govern, or guide), took matters into their own hands. The irony is spellbinding. The sin Shechem had committed was sexual, so the crafty strategy by Simeon and Levi was to lure them into cutting their sex organs. The one thing that defined Shechem as unruly and arrogant became the very thing that led to his downfall. Jacob can't be too angry at his two sons. They learned from the best, their own Pop. And is Jacob entirely innocent? Did he really believe the proposal? Mix and intermarry Israel with this ungodly, ruthless culture?

In our day we have law at all levels, municipal, county, state and federal. There is a system to take care of criminal behavior. However, in your spiritual development you are encouraged by Jesus to be "shrewd as snakes yet innocent as doves" (Matt 10:16). How might you outwit your enemy today if you listen carefully to the Holy Spirit?

The village of Shechem is bloody. Simeon and Levi are thundering back to camp with their sister Dinah in tow. There are joyful hugs of reassurance. Yet, fear embraces them all even more. *Now what do we do? We have to run for our lives!* As they hasten to break camp, the sons ask the pertinent question, "Was it right to let our sister be treated this way?" And Israel continues to wrestle.

A Super-Race?

> Genesis 38:24-26
>
> About three months later someone told Judah, "Your daughter-in-law Tamar has behaved like a prostitute, and now she's pregnant!"
>
> "Drag her out of town and burn her to death!" Judah shouted.
>
> As Tamar was being dragged off, she sent someone to tell her father-in-law, "The man who gave me this ring, this cord, and this walking stick is the one who got me pregnant."
>
> "Those are mine!" Judah admitted. "She's a better person than I am, because I broke my promise to let her marry my son Shelah." After this, Judah never slept with her again.

Every family has skeletons in the closet; but if you venture into the wardrobe of the godly, Jewish bloodline you will have to sift through the bones. This is what makes the Bible so refreshingly real. I venture to say, if you or I were writing the Scriptures, we would have tried to clean it up a little bit. You know, polish it, glamorize it somewhat. It needs some sparkle. Let's not have so many killings. And could you do something about all the jealousy, outright acts of retaliation, and deceptive half-truths? And oh my goodness, the sexual sins are glaring!

In a short span, the generations of Genesis, we have numerous misgivings. Granted their surroundings are not optimal. There are evil cities mentioned in the culture all around them, Sodom, Gomorrah, and Shechem. But there are several suspicious, borderline encounters. Did Noah's drunkenness hint at inappropriate behavior? Just what was Ham poking fun at that Shem and Japheth needed to cover up? When Lot was living in Sodom and Gomorrah, he threw his daughters under the bus, telling the evil men of the city they could rape them all night instead of violating his male, messenger guests. But, alas, the daughters would have the last laugh. After Lot's wife had experienced high sodium intake, to understate the obvious, there is the incestuous preservation of the lineage with both daughters.

It continues. Abraham takes an extreme "life-saving" measure and disowns Sarah as his wife, apparently a practice during his travels. Abraham's acceptance of Sarah's suggestion to have relations with Hagar is culturally acceptable but spiritually suspect. His son, Isaac, follows his Dad's example when traveling with Rebekah, calling her his sister too. But now wait a minute, she's technically not a sister, she's a cousin. So the truth is being stretched more as it passes down a generation. What's more, Jacob follows Grandfather Abraham's practice and expands on it as well, doubles it in fact. He has Leah, Rachel, Bilhah and Zilpah all four - two wives and two servants. We have Reuben involved with his father's servant. It follows him to his father's deathbed blessing turned curse. It is certainly not Dinah's fault that she was raped; but the whole encounter of revenge smacks of mistrust.

And Judah, oh, Judah tops them all. Judah, grieving the death of his son who the Bible says was evil, gives the obligatory second son to his widowed daughter-in-law, Tamar, for a husband. But he refused to father a child intentionally. It was displeasing to the Lord and he died for it. Judah, not wanting to lose his only remaining child, patronizes Tamar by telling her that his last son needs to grow up first. But in time it becomes apparent he has no intention of following through on this.

Tamar succeeds in tripping up her father-in-law by playing to his weakness. His visit to a prostitute is a disgraceful failure that exposes his deception. He avoids doing the right thing. He blurted out his displeasure with his harlot daughter-in-law until it backfired and exposed his own shortcoming. It is a stain on the national smock. Yet, the Bible moves forward the redemptive plan of God who intercepts sinful human history. We see the blemishes, warts and all. One thing about it, no one can insinuate this is some kind of super race that finally produced a superior product in Christ. No, this is a broken humanity in need of a Rescuer.

Immaculate Integrity

> *Genesis 40:20-22*
>
> *Three days later, while the king was celebrating his birthday with a dinner for his officials, he sent for his personal servant and the chief cook. He put the personal servant back in his old job and had the cook put to death. Everything happened just as Joseph had said it would, but the king's personal servant completely forgot about Joseph.*

Joseph interpreted the dreams of his two cellmates and it happened just exactly as he told them. Three days later the cup bearer was restored to his position in service of the king, and the baker was judged and executed. Fade to black, go to commercial break, the scene played out just like it was supposed to. Right? Only, we don't have the play by play commentary of Joseph's emotions in between the declaration and the fulfillment.

Once I played a round of golf with my brother-in-law. As he hovered over the ball that was teed up at the first hole, he looked up to the man we had just met and said, "So, tell me, how are things going with your marriage?" I gulped. This total stranger was a solo at the club house, and they tagged him along with our twosome. I was astounded when the gentleman became noticeably altered. It turns out he was right in the middle of divorce proceedings. He played the longest 18 holes of his life, stuck with two pastors. Keenan didn't hound him; but at key times throughout the three-and-a-half hours he was able to speak into his life in profound ways. When I asked him later how he knew, he said it was just a strong impression that he couldn't shake, and he was trying to develop a sensitivity to those kinds of Holy Spirit moments.

I wonder if Joseph lay in bed that night thinking, "Why did I say that? What if I'm wrong? What if nothing happens? Are the other prisoners going to be mad at me? Are they going to nail me in the yard?" To this point we haven't read anything about Joseph's dreams coming true, not yet. We haven't read of his interpretations being bat on. But what we do see is immaculate integrity that will not be shaken off course. He's been true to his studies. He's been true to his father's wishes. He's been honest with his conniving brothers. He's been faithful to his commitment of purity even though hounded by Potiphar's wife for days on end.

I wonder what the three days were like for Joseph between his interpretations and their fulfillment. Did the cup bearer wink and nod? Did the baker stare and grimace? Did Joseph fast and pray for the fulfillment? He had to get excited on the third day when he heard that it was the Pharaoh's birthday. Had he known that already? We don't know. We're not told. Maybe it was a clue to him that God was up to something. What's more impressive to me is the fact that Joseph remained faithful and true in the two years after the dream's fulfillment. He did not lose heart, even though forgotten again. When the moment arrived for him to be on the big stage, he was ready because he had conditioned his heart with countless episodes of prayer and devotion in his cell. In the tents of his family's camp; in the cistern, hearing his brothers' voices above; in the master's home resisting; in the jail cell falsely charged; in the governor's chariot heralded - in each instance, Joseph is a man of integrity.

A Predestination of My Choosing

> Genesis 42:6-9
>
> *Since Joseph was governor of Egypt and in charge of selling grain, his brothers came to him and bowed with their faces to the ground. They did not recognize Joseph, but right away he knew who they were, though he pretended not to know. Instead, he spoke harshly and asked, "Where do you come from?"*
>
> *"From the land of Canaan," they answered. "We've come here to buy grain."*
>
> *Joseph remembered what he had dreamed about them and said, "You're spies! You've come here to find out where our country is weak."*

In this moment, with his brothers bowed before him, Joseph did not gloat in vain victory, I'm sure of it. No man can be so arrogant in the face of Sovereignty. No, we have Joseph fighting back tears as the embedded backdrop of these chapters. Maybe as a kid he had the dream and tried to imagine it unfolding. It may be that in his youthfulness he pictured his rising to the top by impression, persuasion and outright skill. Now, though, *oh no*, that's not the case. He has endured the hardship of separation and false accusation. There were many lonely nights in servants' quarters, and many others in a cold jail cell. Now, his heart is warmed by a childhood memory like the food critic, Ego, in *Ratatouille*. His thoughts now must have traced mysteriously the lines of Providence. Standing erect, cloaked in governorship, wielding authority, his brothers curtsied before him, there is no jockeying for position. The famine has seen to that.

Joseph realizes it was never about him. No, the hand of God intercepted devastation. This is about rescue. Only God could pull this off. Praise God. This is another example of Almighty God getting his hands on human history for the good.

In my own life I have sensed his fingers, haven't you? I had a part to play. I chose this and that. My freedom of will has always been intact. Sometimes there were good choices, other times better. Sometimes there were bad choices, other times pure evil. Yet with repentance, humility and forgiveness, God kept me moving in a direction. As if there were raised bumper rails on the edge of my life's bowling lane, the Sovereign hand of God moved me forward, a predestination of my choosing. There are moments in life when it is good to come up for air, you know, breathe in the *pneuma*, the wind, breath, spirit of God. Sometimes it's good to stop and smell the roses. The aroma of the Rose of Sharon is spellbinding. Upon Him become transfixed. Thornton Wilder captured it with the character Emily in his play, *Our Town*. "Oh world, you are too beautiful to take in."

Close Family Bonds

> *Genesis 44:27-31*
>
> *Sir, our father then reminded us that his favorite wife had given birth to two sons. One of them was already missing and had not been seen for a long time. My father thinks the boy was torn to pieces by some wild animal, and he said, "I am an old man. If you take Benjamin from me, and something happens to him, I will die of a broken heart."*
>
> *That's why Benjamin must be with us when I go back to my father. He loves him so much that he will die if Benjamin doesn't come back with me. I promised my father that I would bring him safely home. If I don't, I told my father he could blame me the rest of my life.*

The deep emotional plea of Judah, for his baby brother Benjamin, is indicative of the interconnectedness of family bonds. He is recalling the hesitancy of his aging father to send Benjamin on this excursion in the first place. Responsibility settles upon him. He has put his neck on the line. So we have Jacob back home pacing the floor, Judah hurling himself before the second in command of all of Egypt, and Governor Joseph, loved-one incognito, choking back tears that would eventually flow like a river, all because of deep family bonds. There is a unique feeling triggered when you know your father is proud of you. There is a special warmth in Mom's affection that cannot be duplicated. There is a deep belly laugh brought on only by a brother. There is an intuition between sisters that no other relationship rivals. Grandparents imbue security and longevity. Grandchildren emit loyalty and lineage. Before there was ever a nation called Israel, before there was the Church of Jesus Christ, there was Adam and Eve, a family unit. A healthy church is the coming together of healthy families. God values the family concept very deeply. Jacob writhes uninformed, Judah pleads uncommonly, Joseph delights in anticipation, and God, oh, he has dreamt of this family moment coming to pass. Family bonds are deep, a gift from our maker.

Don't Let the Left Hand Know

Genesis 48:14

But before Jacob gave them his blessing, he crossed his arms, putting his right hand on the head of Ephraim and his left hand on the head of Manasseh.

Old Jacob has been savvy his whole life. Joseph has heard his father tell the story about the time Grandpa Isaac was on his deathbed and couldn't distinguish between his two sons, Jacob and Esau. It's only natural that Joseph would assume *his* Dad needs some assistance on his own deathbed. But Jacob has still got game. He has intentionally placed his right hand, the hand of blessing, on Joseph's younger son, Ephraim. The will of God is mysterious beyond our figuring out. Consider the fragile fraternals of Genesis. Jacob and Esau are twins. Esau is born first only by moments. Yet, in time, it is Jacob who receives the blessing. Rebekah was told two nations wrestled inside of her. Baby Zerah sticks his hand out of the womb first and they tie a scarlet thread around his wrist. But Perez pushes to the front and is born first. In Kindergarten they call that shortcutting. However, Perez is reckoned as the firstborn in the line of Judah which is now so distorted it resembles the comedy song by Ray Stevens, *I'm My Own Grandpa*.

Here, there is some reason in the mind of God that Ephraim received favored tribal status above his brother, Manasseh. Interestingly, Manasseh is the tribe that becomes divided physically, "Reuben, Gad, and the half-tribe of Manasseh." The tribe of Judah eventually would have a king named Manasseh. He was one of the most evil kings on record. Ephraim gains a reputation as faithful in battle, produces the great prophet Samuel, and is called "my dear son" by Jeremiah.

Jesus taught when you give to the needy don't let the left hand know what the right hand is doing (Matt 6:3). It was a teaching intended to show how good deeds should become second nature. Providentially, Jacob crossed his right hand over the left to bless Ephraim.

May the right hand of Providence reach across and bless you today.

Parting is Such Sweet Sorrow

Genesis 49:28-33

These are the twelve tribes of Israel, and this is how Jacob gave each of them their proper blessings.

Jacob told his sons:

Soon I will die, and I want you to bury me in Machpelah Cave. Abraham bought this cave as a burial place from Ephron the Hittite, and it is near the town of Mamre in Canaan. Abraham and Sarah are buried there, and so are Isaac and Rebekah. I buried Leah there too. Both the cave and the land that goes with it were bought from the Hittites.

When Jacob had finished giving these instructions to his sons, he lay down on his bed and died.

Jacob is going the way of all the earth. He calls his twelve sons to his side to give them his blessing. For some of them, Reuben, Simeon, and Levi, it is not truly a blessing but a judgment. For Judah it could have been very painful, but turned redemptive. For most of them, and especially Joseph, there is a sweet repose.

I recall, all too well, the bittersweet conclusion of my own father's life. Dad called all five boys to his side. When he was near comatose, suddenly there came a burst of energy. He rallied his strength, sat up in bed, and began to speak words to each of his five sons. This extraordinary pastor of more than four decades preached, possibly, his best sermon in that hospital room. We wept and embraced. He spoke words over us of affirmation, prophecy, and encouragement. For about sixteen minutes we captured priceless video of Dad pouring profound love upon his family. It is a treasure I carry with me. It is permanently etched upon my psyche. If you are blessed with a loving parent who has invested godliness in you, take time to express your gratitude. Don't squander the godly heritage you've been endowed with. It is truly the greatest inheritance you could ever hope for. Speak words of love now, before the parting, because parting is always sorrowful, even if at the same time sweet.

This Way and That

Exodus 2:12

Moses looked around to see if anyone was watching, then he killed the Egyptian and hid his body in the sand.

I wrote a children's tale that was birthed out of bedtime stories with my boys when they were little. It's called *The Cotton Candy Trees of Cottonwood Elementary*. In it, a gopher sneaks out of his hole and peers all around to make sure the coast is clear. Once he is convinced he's unnoticed he dashes to the Cotton Candy Trees and eats 'em all up! I would really get into character as I mimicked the gopher inching out of hiding place, and would say, "He looked this way and that." This kept the boys mesmerized in suspense.

Moses reminds me of the gopher as he looks all around to see if he's noticed before executing what he feels is stern justice toward the unsuspecting Egyptian. But, alas, someone else was watching. Someone's always watching, from the cheap seats, from the peanut gallery. And the next day his secret came back to haunt him. It's a threat of *National Enquirer* proportions, *Entertainment Tonight*. What if it hits Facebook? He personified flight risk, left Egypt running for his life, headed to Midian. Even if he had been undetected by human eyes there is an all-seeing eye watching. Whether we realize it, acknowledge it, or disregard it entirely, God is always observing and making notes. The Bible teaches we will be held accountable. "All things are open and laid bare before the eyes of him to whom we must give account" (Heb 4:13). This principle holds true for all humanity. It's true for Moses who became one of the greatest national leaders in history. It is true for you and me. Settle your accounts quickly, now, today, while there is time, before the day when the chandler calls for reconciliation of all accounts.

O-M-T

> *Exodus 3:14*
>
> *God said to Moses:*
> *I am the eternal God. So tell them that the Lord, whose name is "I Am," has sent you. This is my name forever, and it is the name that people must use from now on.*

A good interpretation of God's response to Moses' inquiry regarding his name would be, "I will be what I will be," or "I am the One who brings into being." The word God uses to define his name in verse 14 is very nearly related to YHWH in verse 15, a primitive root meaning "to become." Many Hebrew people do not speak the name of God when they read it in Scripture. Apparently, for a period of 2,600 years the name of the LORD was not spoken. The tetragrammaton Y-H-W-H has been variously pronounced by scholars. There are good reasons to believe the correct pronunciation of it would have been Yahweh; but there are equal arguments for thinking it would've been pronounced Jehovah. Still others argue it is neither, it is unpronounceable, and that is the whole point. Many reverent Jews also refuse to write the word 'God' and render it as G-d instead, and also Lord as L-rd. Orthodox Jews substitute the word Ha-Shem ("The Name") into their commentaries to avoid taking the name of the Lord in vain. Some claim the reason for this is that it cannot be written because that would be disrespectful, equivalent to taking his name in vain. Others say, no, the reason it isn't written is so that it can never be erased. The erasing would be the disrespectful part. Who's right? I don't know if we can say conclusively. But isn't it an amazing and interesting colloquy?

At the very least we may say God's name is respected. At least it has been historically. How antithetical is all of this discussion to our day. We live in a time and culture in which there is so little concern and respect for speaking out the Name of the LORD. His holy name is reduced to an abbreviated text message O-M-G. It is totally acceptable in our culture to exhale the surprised gasp, "Oh my God!" It covers every emotion from pleasure to disgust. It is verbalized in the most flippant manner by youths and aged alike. It is both trendy and fun to come across as unconcerned about it, as if it's no big deal. You know, you've seen it, the individual who blurts out God's name in such a manner that her disposition indicates she was totally unaware of any offense. We are supposed to gather that she has no stricken conscience by having just smacked the God of the Universe across her lips with no care whatsoever. Only, of course, she is aware of it; otherwise, it wouldn't be en vogue to do in public. C'mon, we're not that naive. Every expression means something. If there is no difference, then, what is the difference? *Seems like everybody does it and it's okay.* Only one problem, do you suppose the Bible is accurate when it claims that we will give account for every idle word we speak (Matt 12:36)? Perhaps a better interjection would be O-M-T! Oh my tongue!

Silence the Croakers

> *Exodus 8:9, 10*
>
> "All right," Moses answered. "You choose the time when I am to pray for the frogs to stop bothering you, your officials, and your people, and for them to leave your houses and be found only in the river."
>
> "Do it tomorrow!" the king replied.
>
> "As you wish," Moses agreed. "Then everyone will discover that there is no god like the Lord."

If you were given the chance to decide when the plague of frogs ended would you choose tomorrow? What is the Pharaoh thinking? I wonder, that night, did he pull the covers up over his head to screen out the intruders? Did he try to muffle the noise of their croaking with his pillow?

Did he roll on top of them in the night? Perhaps he was trying to outwit Moses. Since Moses asked him when he would like the plague to end, he probably thought it was a set-up. Of course any normal person would choose to stop the insanity immediately. So Pharaoh threw him a curve. Do it tomorrow.

Moses' words, "As you wish," lift and ring, waft through the air, and settle upon the stricken conscience of the Egyptian leader. I'll bet he didn't sleep any better the next night. As he lay in his royal suite, trying to make sense of this Israelite with the magic walking-stick who prayed to his God and caused the amphibians to be banished, the insomniac despot replayed the snakes, blood and frogs over and over again on the view screen of his mind. The silence was loud. God wasn't through with him yet, not by a long ways. Gnats, flies, dead animals, sores, hailstones, locusts and darkness all await. Instead of melting his heart like wax, Pharaoh allowed the experiences to harden his heart like clay. Eventually it would cost him the life of his own son, and all the firstborn males throughout all of Egypt. Imagine the horrible mourning and wailing. An entire military draft decimated by the angel of death. How could anybody be so stubborn?

Thank heavens we are not like that! Are we? Do you know any individuals who put off serving God until a later time? They are too busy. There's a checklist of activities that must be accomplished first. God is relegated to the last line on the bucket list. It's always tomorrow. I will tomorrow. Maybe tomorrow. What if tomorrow never comes? Or what if when your tomorrow gets here you just don't want to serve God? It's not appealing to you anymore? What then? What if you put him off so many times that you actually harden your own heart? You wouldn't even be sensitive to his voice any longer. You wouldn't even know that you were uncaring. How sad! Silence the croakers today! Don't spend one more night with the frogs.

A Yellow Jersey

> *Exodus 9:5-7*
>
> *Tomorrow is the day the LORD has set to do this. It happened the next day—all of the animals belonging to the Egyptians died, but the Israelites did not lose even one. When the king found out, he was still too stubborn to let the people go.*

There is a subtle shift from the incident of the frogs to this occurrence of the dead animals. Whereas Moses gave Pharaoh the opportunity to decide the timing on the ending of the plague of frogs, God now says he himself will end the dying tomorrow. It is a game changer in terms of momentum. It's the established pattern for the remaining plagues too. Keith Jackson, the beloved sports analyst, used to say, "The big M just put on a yellow jersey!" Momentum is a funny thing. It can rise and swell, and when it does you catch the wave and ride it a far as it will take you. A good coach will develop a keen eye to recognize momentum when it occurs. This is a huge swing in the favor of Moses and the Israelis. The Jews had been worried that Moses was really ticking off the Pharaoh; but the further it goes along, they are realizing, more and more, that God is in control. And Moses is gaining more and more credibility to boot. It is as if God says to the Pharaoh, *"I just let you think you were in control. Actually, you were playing into my hand."* We are now moments away from the Gatorade bath. It's in the books. It's all academic. Dandy Don Meredith is singing, "Turn out the lights, the party's over." Momentum is rising in Moses' camp. It's only a matter of time before they are departing from Egypt, and everybody knows it. They have endured beatings, reduction in the provision of straw for the bricks, increased workload to achieve the same quota, and countless other difficulties through oppression, mind-control, and manipulation. To be on the cusp of great victory following such mindless tactics for so long must have been very, very sweet.

No Bones about It

Exodus 12:46

The entire meal must be eaten inside, and no one may leave the house during the celebration. No bones of the Passover lamb may be broken.

Isn't it interesting that such a specific directive be given to the Israelites regarding the Passover Lamb. Don't break any of its bones. In fact, there are many, very targeted instructions. The lamb must be free from blemish, perfect, the best of the flock. Each family is required to raise it, domesticate it, get to know it for a minimum of two weeks ahead of time. Roast it entirely, everything, head, legs, and insides. Do not boil it or eat it raw, only roast it. And when the time came to eat it they were instructed to garnish the lamb with bitter herbs, take it with flat-bread that had no yeast in it so that it could not rise up. The instructions were to use a hyssop branch to paint the blood from the lamb over the doorposts and along the door jambs or crossbeams. They were to eat it in haste, symbolically, with their robes tucked in their belts, ready to run. This meal is a mixture of emotions. There is celebration because of the deliverance from Egypt, but possibly sadness for acquaintances that would be left behind under the rule of a harsh dictator. They are probably glad for the provision of food, but torn by the fact that they have known this animal. They are tasting savory meat, but it is mixed with bitterness in the herbs.

I am drawn to the guidelines about the bones, such attention to detail. Be sure not to break any bones. There's really not a lot of mention of bones in the Bible considering its volume. There are numerous references in the poetical books, Psalms, Proverbs, Job, and Song of Solomon. Apart from these, the references become more case specific. Adam mentions Eve is "bone of my bones, flesh of my flesh." Ezekiel sees a valley of dry bones that have the breath, wind, spirit enter them again and are revived into a mighty nation. It's a picture of hope for Israel.

There's one fascinating story of a young prophet who came to Bethel from Judah (1 Kgs 13), and prophesied over the altar there, saying that it would be broken in two and have ashes poured out on it. He said a ruler named Josiah would execute justice and human bones would be burned upon the altar in judgment. Because he didn't obey the specific directions he was killed by a lion on his way out of town and buried. Almost 300 years later the prophecy came true as Josiah initiated huge reforms (2 Kgs 23). He removed all the Asherah poles and Molech statues. In Bethel he removed all the tombs of false priests and had their bones burned. Then Josiah pointed to one tomb on the hillside and asked who it was. They told him that it was the actual prophet who had prophesied about all of this. Josiah said to leave his bones alone and let him rest. These are a few significant stories about bones.

The Israelites were told not to break any bones of the lamb. It is a foreshadowing of the prophecy that Jesus' death fulfilled, the apostle John says so (John 19:35-37). When the soldiers wanted a criminal to die quicker on the cross they would break his legs. This would accelerate the dying because the victim was unable to push up on the cross to gasp for breath, and so he would suffocate. However, when they came to Jesus he had already died, so the vengeful soldier, wanting to do something cruel and unruly, thrust his spear in Jesus' side instead. Blood and water flowed indicating a torn heart muscle. Jesus died, quite literally, of a broken heart. The fact that he died before his legs could be broken, thus fulfilling Exodus 12:46, is one of many miraculous prophecies completed by the perfect life of Christ. The apostle Paul said that Jesus is our Passover Lamb. Yes, perfect, the best of the flock. No blemish, sinless. He is the perfect sacrificial Lamb. His death was garnished with bitter herbs. The Bread of Life, Jesus, was truly flattened as if with no yeast; but this bread would rise. No bones about it.

God-Speak or Human Jibberish

Exodus 14:15

The Lord said to Moses, "Why do you keep calling out to me for help? Tell the Israelites to move forward."

What language will you choose? God-speak or human jibberish? It is impossible for us humans to realize the lengths divinity went to in order to interact with us. God says to Moses, "Why do you keep calling out to me for help?" The Egyptians are closing in on the children of Israel. They are backed up against the Red Sea. Seems like it would be a natural time to cry out for help. But God says, "Why do you keep calling out to me for help?" It comes across as, "Didn't we talk about this already, Moses? Don't you trust me?" What is to us a perfectly acceptable request is to the mind of God an alien inquiry. We cannot appreciate fully what it is like to never lack, fear or doubt.

In the gospel of Mark, Jesus is "amazed at their lack of faith" (Mark 6:6). He's only able to lay hands on a few sick people and see them recover. You or I might notify the denominational magazine if we experienced a few miracles in a church gathering. Some might call it an outbreak of revival. Jesus was just the opposite. He was amazed all right, but not like we would be. "He was amazed at their lack of faith." I can just see him pondering, "Hmm, isn't that something? Only a few people healed. What do you know about that?" It must be wonderful to never know lack, fear or doubt! On another occasion in the gospel of Mark Jesus "rebuked them for their lack of faith and their stubborn refusal to believe those who had seen him after he had risen" (Mark 16:14).

God intercepts our human frailty with divine sustenance. Is your back against the proverbial sea wall? Can you smell the aroma of salt water in the air? Do you fear your enemy is closing in on you so that you will drown? Nothing is impossible with God! What language will you choose today? God-speak or human jibberish?

Remember to Forget

Exodus 17:14-16

Afterwards, the Lord said to Moses, "Write an account of this victory and read it to Joshua. I want the Amalekites to be

> forgotten forever." Moses built an altar and named it "The Lord Gives Me Victory." Then Moses explained, "This is because I depended on the Lord. But in future generations, the Lord will fight the Amalekites again and again."

Do you catch the irony of this verse? I want you to make sure you forget the Amalekites. Make a big deal of it. Don't forget. Mark it. Remember to forget the Amalekites. The Amalakites represent the antithesis of holiness and purity. Idolatry, witchcraft, vileness, filth, violence, hatred, and other things like this - forget it. And don't you ever forget to forget it. It is similar to the logic that says it is impossible to forgive and forget. How can you forget the impressions that are permanently etched on your mind? Not happening. But you can prioritize the musings on the view screen of your mind. It requires active amnesia. Forget your Amalekites. Don't dwell on the pain of the past. Recall that you are a new creation in Christ. Remember to forget.

Ghetto Spirituality

> Exodus 22:6-8
>
> If you carelessly let a fire spread from your property to someone else's, you must pay the owner for any crops or fields destroyed by the fire.
>
> Suppose a neighbor asks you to keep some silver or other valuables, and they are stolen from your house. If the thief is caught, the thief must repay double.
>
> But if the thief isn't caught, some judges will decide if you are the guilty one.

The Israelites have left Egypt and now need rules to govern their affairs. In world history there had been Hammurabi's Code. He was a Babylonian king. But aside from this there had been few precious attempts at civil law. It would be many hundreds of years until the introduction of Justinian Law. Of course, the Ten Commandments Moses received on Mount Sinai, directly from God, are much to be preferred. They have an inspired sense of the holiness of God and carry the weight of Scripture. But it is interesting that all three, Hammurabi, Moses and Justin have reference to marriage responsibilities, treatment of the aging, and rules of justice in cases of crime. It appears that all humans have an innate understanding of responsibility.

These particular verses come under a section on property rights. They are very interesting in light of their context. "Carelessly," verse 6, that's the operative word. If you carelessly let the fire spread to your neighbor's land you are responsible for the damages it causes. Only, they don't have any land right now. Not yet, they are in the wilderness headed towards their Promised Land. If you are asked to watch over your neighbor's silver or other valuables and it gets stolen from your house you are responsible unless the thief is found out. You cannot be careless about another's treasure. Well, they did have valuables. They had just looted Egypt. But are there really any thugs bumming around the campground compound? And they didn't have houses to be robbed in the wilderness. No, they are planning for daily life in the land of milk and honey they are headed to. They are in the middle of the desert, but are actively participating in vision casting for the fulfillment of their collective dream.

Community is a huge part of God's plan. Stanley J. Grenz wrote a great deal about community in the economy of God. It was a major part of his theology. He believed we can only pursue theology from the faith community which we are grounded in. The whole human experience is always in community, never in isolation.[ii]

It is noteworthy that God's preparation for where the Israelites were headed included the treatment of one's neighbors. You will always have neighbors. Do you envision life on easy street? Lush lawns, an easier pace, so much better than the hectic hustle and bustle of your ghetto spirituality? Do you dream beyond the projects that imprison? Be that good neighbor now, in the desert, before you ever reach the Promised Land. Don't be careless about your neighbors. They are the one lasting entity in your environment today.

Keeper of the Flame

> *Exodus 27:20, 21*
>
> *Command the people of Israel to supply you with the purest olive oil. Do this so the lamp will keep burning in front of the curtain that separates the holy place from the most holy place, where the sacred chest is kept. Aaron and his sons are responsible for keeping the lamp burning every night in the sacred tent. The Israelites must always obey this command.*

The single most important part of service to the Lord is keeping the flame burning. Aaron and his sons had the responsibility of refilling the oil in the lamp. The instruction was an imperative statement. The lamp must burn continually. It must never go out. Ministry takes on various forms in each generation. Aaron & Sons routinely crushed olives to extract their oil for the lamp. It was someone's assignment in the family. I recall my parents, who were pastors for forty-two years, wrestling with mimeograph machines and getting ink all over the place. In my ministry I routinely get in arguments with copiers and computers. The danger for all of us is that special things can become routine simply because of their repeated occurrence. It is easy for me to forget the elders gathered around me in ordination prayer when I am wedged in the tight crawlspace rerouting mic cables, or playing plumber with an overflowing urinal. I wonder if Aaron's sons ever quipped, "Why do I have to break open and smash these olive bulbs day after day?"

I remember one episode of the Andy Griffith Show where Opie joined a secret club. His title was the keeper of the flame. It was his responsibility to bring the candle and match box to every meeting. He deemed it a high calling, almost a holy responsibility. He wouldn't let his fellow members down. He wouldn't rat out his gild even at the risk of jeopardizing his own standing.

In the broader sense all Christians are ministers. It is incorrect to ask a believer, "Are you in the ministry?" The correct question is, "What is your ministry?" And whatever your ministry may entail, the most important thing is that you are a keeper of the flame. You must continually provide oil for the lamp to burn. Don't let the holy become trivial. Don't mix mystery with mundane. The apostle Paul wrote, "Moreover, it is required in stewards that a man be found faithful" (1 Cor 4:2, NKV). You may not be able to leap over buildings in a single bound. You may not be able to stop a steaming locomotive. You do not have to wear an "S" on your chest. But can you tend to the candle today? Will you be a faithful keeper of the flame?

Limitless Mercy

Exodus 26:34

Inside the most holy place, put the sacred chest that has the place of mercy on its lid.

There is a lot of speculation and mystery surrounding the Ark of the Covenant. It is recorded in a Jewish Midrash that the chest had flames coming out of it to burn scorpions and snakes away from its path. Another Midrash records that the men didn't carry the ark, rather it carried them. It is actually written that they hovered a few inches off the ground. Recent speculation has the ark housed in the Dome of the Rock.

A space has been observed, through heat sensory, that has the exact dimensions of the ark, and supposedly in the spot legend says was the foundation of the world. Of course, many of these stories are exaggerated and glorified. But there is something substantive about the presence of Almighty God resident in the ark. Remember, it was God's idea for them to have this manmade object. It's ironic that they would have this chest because they were warned sternly against having any idols or relics. But this is no idol, it represents the very presence of God. Scripture records it brought victory to the Jews when carried into battle. Furthermore, it wreaked havoc on their enemies when they captured it. When an Israelite tried to steady the ark because the oxen stumbled, he was struck dead. But the same ark blessed its foster village so much after that, that David had it brought back to Jerusalem with a festive parade of worship to God. The ark is shrouded in mystery, but one thing is for sure. The holy of holies, where the ark resided inside Moses' traveling tabernacle, was a replica of the actual holy place in heaven. When Jesus died on the cross, the veil that separated us from the holy of holies was literally torn from top to bottom. This is according to the writer of Hebrews. "We may come boldly to the throne of grace to receive help in our time of need" (Heb 4:16). Limitless mercy exists for you and me at the Ark of the Covenant.

Diamonds in the Rough

Exodus 28:29

In this way Aaron will have the names of the twelve tribes of Israel written on his heart each time he enters the holy place, and I will never forget my people.

Aaron carries jewels on his breastplate, close to his heart. It occurs to me the instructions given by God to Aaron and his sons assume that there were jewels available to be placed on the fabric. Twelve exotic and rare jewels are secured to the vest of the high priest. They must have been pillaged from the Egyptians in the exit. These priceless jewels are redeemed from hedonistic ritual, possibly epicurean pleasure, and are now incorporated into the holy garment of intercession. In much the same way Jesus views his followers as treasures. This is a remarkable type of Christ, our high priest. He carries us close to his heart. In just the same way Aaron entered the holy place, Hebrews tells that Jesus ever lives to make intercession on our behalf. Hebrews also says he is a better priest of a better covenant serving in the true tabernacle. He has redeemed his jewels from a wasted life, we who are diamonds in the rough, and showcased us as his prized possession. How privileged are we to be secured to the fabric! We are carried right into the holy of holies, ushered in on the person of the high priest.

The Devil's Workshop

> *Exodus 32:24*
>
> *Then I asked them to bring me their gold earrings. They took them off and gave them to me. I threw the gold into a fire, and out came this bull.*

Oh c'mon Aaron, *"I just put the earrings in the fire and out came this golden bull."* Really? You expect us to believe that? But isn't that how a lot of things happen? A song starts as a clip of a melody that bounces around inside your head. What is that tune? Oh, wait. Is this a new song? Where'd that come from? A phrase rattles around inside your noggin, travels the neurons, across nerves to your fingertips, and suddenly types its way into literature. All creative endeavor, good or evil, leaves one with the sense that something mysterious took place. Was that in me? Where did that come from? The phenomenal artist, Bob Ross, would say, *"I see a tree and it lives right there in a meadow."* It was remarkable to watch the blank canvass come alive at his command. Something out of nothing. So I see how Aaron could be left with the impression that this golden calf just came out of the fire. I'll bet as he twirled the melted gold he thought, "Hey, doesn't that sort of look like a cattle head? Wait, I think I'm seeing a snout." The problem happened much sooner. It is not permissible to exempt oneself from responsibility on the basis of going with the flow. The old timers used to say an idle mind is the devil's workshop. The Israelites got bored. Where's Moses anyway? Aaron lost focus. He capitulated instead of capitalizing. He could have done any number of things differently. Call the people to prayer. Rebuke the indifference. Use delay tactics. Anything. Something! But instead, his idle mind led to an idol mind. And this grave misstep cost him dearly. Don't flirt with indifferent boredom. You were made for more creativity than that!

Something Different

> *Exodus 33:14-16*
>
> *The Lord said, "I will go with you and give you peace."*
> *Then Moses replied, "If you aren't going with us, please don't make us leave this place.*

But if you do go with us, everyone will know that you are pleased with your people and with me. That way, we will be different from the rest of the people on earth."

I was substitute teaching a high school class. The permanent teacher had left videos for the classes to watch in her absence. For the Freshmen class she had chosen a movie that I deemed inappropriate. It was rated PG-13 and had scenes in which sex acts were depicted. A fully clothed woman made very explicit advances toward a young man. The movie simulated that she was completely aroused. I was aghast. I turned it off. Having 30 minutes remaining, I had the students do an assignment. "Title your paragraph 'Appropriateness'," I said. "Write ten sentences on the subject. You can talk about sex scenes, profanity, rating systems. Just give your opinion." In the classroom of 39, only 6 handed it in. Each of the six was equally offended that I had turned the movie off. "Nothing happened" one wrote. "Nothing was going to happen," wrote another. "I know, I have this movie." Ah, but something did happen. It had already happened. In the name of plot and theme, through the disguise of appreciating fine arts, young minds were influenced. Young men with racing hormones were force fed deceptive practices that if followed could decimate their future families. Young women were reinforced subtly with the idea that sex is something manipulative. And culture moved a negligible degree further away from what is right. Lest I be viewed a fuddy duddy, I speak as one who values the arts. I have a degree in music. I have written two full score musicals. I'm a writer of theology, inspiration, and narrative. I am thrilled with young, talented minds, sold out Christians of unquestionable character, embracing the film industry redemptively. I have a deeply held conviction that creativity is of paramount importance. But this is not qualitatively educational. Something deeply spiritual occurs when impressionable minds are tacitly brainwashed.

I stood in the second floor classroom, now empty, looking out over the sprawling campus crawling with young people. I prayed for them. The view felt a little like what it must be from God's vantage point. Some of them know I'm a pastor. I don't want them to think I was imposing my spirituality on them, though they have had many other spiritualties imposed on them. I imagined them saying, "He thinks he's so holy." I know better about myself. All of us humans are sinners. We are awash with sin. Grace alone differentiates the few among the masses, the sinner from the saint. Our stains are gone.

Here's the deal. There must be something that makes the Christian stand out as different. If there is no difference, what is the difference?

"That way we will be different from the rest of people on earth." I don't like the way it felt being the spoil sport. But I do know, agree or disagree, thirty-nine freshmen left that classroom knowing there was something different about me.

Redeeming a Culture of Arts

Exodus 35:30-35

Moses said to the people of Israel: The Lord has chosen Bezalel of the Judah tribe. Not only has the Lord filled him with his Spirit, but he has given him wisdom and made him a skilled craftsman who can create objects of art with gold, silver, bronze, precious stones, and wood. The Lord is urging him and Oholiab from the tribe of Dan to teach others. And he has given them all kinds of artistic skills, including the ability to design and embroider with blue, purple, and red wool and to weave fine linen.

Bazalel has been gifted with the ability to create as an artisan, a worker with precious metals, embroidered materials and master of color combinations. The Scripture mentions he is filled with the Holy Spirit. How important is the inspiration and anointing of the Holy Spirit in our lives for the fulfillment of vision! And some are especially gifted like Bazalel. I hope for a Christianity that redeems culture: film making, screen plays and play writes; all genres of music and literature; expressive arts of paint, sculpture, dance, and drama - all intertwined in a creativity that is God-breathed. All talent is talent. All cultures of humanity have gifted persons, Christ-followers and non-followers alike. Talent is a tool. When that talent is devoted purely to God a new dimension emerges. The language of Scripture is that "the things of God are spiritually discerned" (1 Cor 2:14). In other words, godly matters are intuited on a spiritual level. The spirit that is not alive in Christ yet, does not pick up things that the Christ-centered heart does. Pentecostals speak of anointing. Mainliners are fond of the word transcendence. Call it what you will, it is real. It is very real. Would that God immerse our abilities with a real measure of his presence!

The Apex of Human Experience

Exodus 40:34-38

Suddenly the sacred tent was covered by a thick cloud and filled with the glory of the Lord. And so, Moses could not enter the tent. Whenever the cloud moved from the tent, the people would

> *break camp and follow; then they would set up camp and stay there, until it moved again. No matter where the people traveled, the Lord was with them. Each day his cloud was over the tent, and each night a fire could be seen in the cloud.*

It is interesting to study the instances in the Bible that speak of the manifest presence of God. When he appears to Moses the first time it is mysteriously a bush on fire that doesn't burn up. Only God could consume an object without consuming it. You and I are consumed without being consumed. Moses had the unique experience of interchange with God as one would with a friend, face to face. And yet we are left with the feeling that it is not quite the same thing because even after this statement we find Moses in an encounter in which he is blocked from the manifest glory of God, covered, squeezed into the crack of a rock, only allowed to see his departure. Apparently the fading presence of God is all Moses could handle. This diminishing radiance, God's glory on the downslope, is the apex in terms of human experience. Did you ever think about the fact that Scripture mentions Moses going up Mount Sinai to meet with God, then describes God coming down to the top of the mountain? There is no high like the Most High. Moses was certainly the best candidate of his day for entertaining the divine, the holiest, most humble man on earth.

A careful reading shows the cloud is not itself the presence of God, but conceals the presence. The presence of God was manifest clearly in the tent. The tent was "covered" by God's presence. It was "filled." But when God was ready to move, it required human effort to keep pace. The tent had to be moved. To coin C.S. Lewis, He's not "a tame lion."[iii] The apostle Paul goes to great lengths describing our earthly bodies as tents. When God is ready to move, he just moves. His glory is traveling.

It is at night time in Moses' camp that we understand God has clothed himself with a cloud, and his presence glows through, like the embers of a fire. Imagine the hues of red-orange, mysteriously hazy and foggy, a veritable sunset happening at the tent of meeting. Psalm 93 describes God as "robed in majesty." Whenever Moses would leave from *the leaving presence,* he would be left with a sunset happening on his face. He had to cover it up or else the people couldn't gaze upon him. Post-resurrection Paul tells us to remove the veil and let out the treasure from within these earthen vessels. Oh for that complexion that invites stares! Be in his presence today. Let his Spirit "cover" and "fill" your tent. And when he roams, pull up the tent stakes and go. Keep pace with his presence.

2

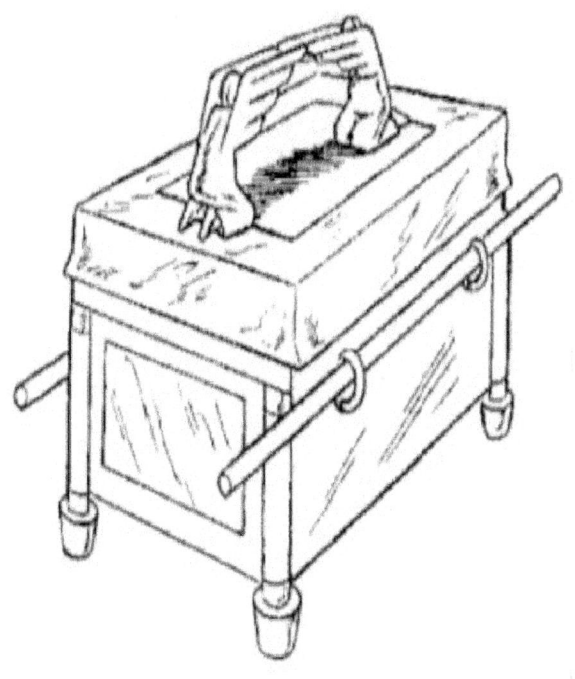

Law and Allegiance

GROUP 2: LAW AND ALLEGIANCE

A Living Aroma

> *Leviticus 3:16*
>
> *One of the priests will put these pieces on the altar and send them up in smoke as a food offering with a smell that pleases me.*

Seven times in three short chapters we have the Lord giving his preference that the sacrifice should be offered "with a smell that pleases me." In the coming chapters there will be references to this as well, though not as many. Why does the smell matter to God? It could be that the Scripture is speaking, in these instances, with what is called anthropomorphism. This is when we attribute human characteristics to God in order that we may have a handle with which to understand concepts of God that, otherwise, would be lost on us. For instance, "Is the arm of the Lord shortened that he cannot reach?" But it is not meant to be taken that God, who is Spirit, has a literal arm; rather the concept to appreciate is that nothing can keep God from intervening. Or for another example, when it says the finger of God inscribed the Ten Commandments, the most important concept is that God communicated what is most important to him, not whether or not we should picture God with a finger. Personally, I do not struggle with Spirit God having some type of embodiment. We are made in his likeness, somehow like him. This doesn't mean God is reduced to our level in any way. He is on another dimension entirely. If he has an embodiment that allows for Omnipresence that is his business, he's God.

I am really intrigued by God being pleased with the smell of a sacrifice. For us humans the sense of smell is comprised of two small patches high in the nasal cavity that contain 5 to 6 million yellowish cells. By comparison rabbits have 100 million, and dogs 220 million. True, we are nothing like bloodhounds, but it is said that we have the ability to trace clean human tracks across a sheet of paper. The sense of smell makes up a large part of taste too. Taste is made up of only four components: sweet, sour, bitter and salt. Scents sort of mesh with taste to make the distinctions. If it were not for smell, taste would not be nearly as gratifying. A baby finds its mother's milk by the sense of smell. Poetically, the Bible tells us to desire the pure spiritual milk of the word.

I have an idea this text is not speaking anthropomorphically. Both

Hebrew (OT) and Greek (NT) have just one word that means spirit, breath, wind, air. I can't think of any of the senses that better bridges spirit and physical than the sense of smell. Hearing possibly. But just think of the interaction of wind, air, breath involved with the sense of smell. The line between the physical and spiritual realm is never thinner than when a pleasing, prayerful sacrifice is lifted up to the Lord, a sweet aroma.

We know from the Proverbs what displeases the Lord: a lying tongue; a prideful, arrogant look; shedding of innocent blood; and (for double impact) a mouth that puts out lies. The Proverbs tell us these are things the Lord hates. Hebrews, however, is definitive; "Without faith it is impossible to please God." May you offer a faithful sacrifice, your life, your very living, a sweet smelling aroma to the Lord.

The Trickle Down of Leadership

Leviticus 4:3

When the high priest sins, he makes everyone else guilty too. And so, he must sacrifice a young bull that has nothing wrong with it.

When the high priest sinned it caused guilt to come upon the whole community. There is a trickle-down effect of leadership. The successful modeling of authentic Christianity results in genuine discipleship. Equally, the misrepresentation of virtue not only indemnifies its purport, but has negative lasting effect on those impressionable minds the leader has led. It is true that we are very privileged to live in the New Testament era. Jesus is our faithful high priest. We don't ever have to worry that our high priest will falter. However, we all have experienced failed leaders in our lives to some degree. I have wept crocodile-sized tears when dear friends have been stripped of ministry credentials. I have questioned my own integrity at times when I have seen failures crop up in my life. It keeps me on my knees. When you become a spiritual leader you put a bright red target on your back.

There is responsibility for all levels of leadership in God's Church. This holds true for the missionary, administrative overseer, evangelist, Bible college or seminary professor, pastor, counselor or otherwise. It also carries implications for the Sunday School teacher, local church board member, office staff, and others as well. I will never forget the first Sunday I stepped to the pulpit as a newly elected Senior Pastor. From my chair on the platform I stood. Six steps, one - two - three - four - five -

six. Heart pounding, sweaty palms, lump in my throat. I had preached numerous times before. I wasn't nervous. That wasn't it. These people knew me. I was well prepared in terms of study, prayer, presentation. No, this was different. What was it? In that moment, I felt the full weight of responsibility settle upon me. That's what had just happened. Eleven years later I became convinced that God would have me relinquish the reins to this church I loved dearly. Having spent a year and a half praying about it, I sat at the piano bench and wept very hard. I felt something like a blanket lift off of me. I can't say it was a physical sensation, but a very real, heartfelt impression. I said out loud, "It's all over, isn't it, Lord?" It was two hours later an invitation was confirmed to visit the church I now lead.

The ministry motor is always idling. It never turns off completely. In one moment you can move from laughter and banter to the next moment of crisis and counsel. The engine revs, then it lulls. The ministry motor must stay tuned with prayer and reflection so that it doesn't stall. A leader must manage the chaos and the monotony. Maybe this is why James warned, "Not many of you should become teachers, my fellow believers, because you know that we who teach will be judged more strictly" (Jas 3:1). A good piece of advice was given to me years ago: Don't take too much blame when things go wrong; and don't take too much credit when things go well. The apostle Paul told a young pastor, Timothy, "Whoever aspires to be an overseer desires a noble task" (1 Tim 3:1). A noble task indeed. Today, pray for a leader.

Wired to Worship

Leviticus 9:24

The Lord sent fiery flames that burned up everything on the altar, and when everyone saw this, they shouted and fell to their knees to worship the Lord.

We are instinctively worshipers. I believe we each came wired from the factory that way. Interestingly, when humans do not worship God, they fill that slot with a replacement. We will worship someone or something. I have a personal view that this is the entire reason we were created, for worship. And this, not in a heavy handed totalitarianism, God desires relationship.

We are predisposed to respond to God when he calls. He sometimes has a flare for the dramatic. In this instance fire consumes the sacrifice. The crowd shouts, then they fall to their knees in worship. I would love to have been there... I think. In the next chapter we read of Aaron's sons dying as the same holy fire leaps out and strikes them because of their lack of protocol. They became comfortable with the holy One. Their worship became routine. They allowed mystery to become mundane.

Over the course of our lives there are multiple times when God's inquest demands response. Sometimes these opportunities are draped in the spectacular, other times simplicity. May our response to him be consistently reverent, engaged, and appropriate. Be especially present today to the Holy Spirit.

Every Last Vestige

Leviticus 10:5-7

So they dragged the dead men away by their clothes.

Then Moses told Aaron and his other two sons, Eleazar and Ithamar: Don't show your sorrow by messing up your hair and tearing your priestly clothes, or the Lord will get angry. He will kill the three of you and punish everyone else. It's all right for your relatives, the people of Israel, to mourn for those he destroyed by fire.

But you are the Lord's chosen priests, and you must not leave the sacred tent, or you will die.

Aaron and his two sons obeyed Moses.

Sometimes obedience will require every last vestige of strength and discipline. Let's be honest. There is a tremendous imbalance of fairness in the world. This inequity shows up in glaring ways when one considers the Christians dismembered, amputated, imprisoned, beaten and mistreated around the globe for the cause of Christ. This is so historically and currently. It is so in communist nations and, increasingly, in my own free nation. But my burdens pale in comparison to those of fellow Christians both worldwide and locally.

Possibly the greatest test comes when there is a pressing matter of the heart. Can you imagine Aaron and his other sons not being allowed to grieve the death of their loved-ones? This is never advised in our day. Or, what about Ezekiel being told ahead of time that his wife would die, but he must not weep? He preached in the morning and she died in the evening. That must have been a very troubling sermon. Again, an unheard of mandate. These requirements are unparalleled in our day but their pain is not unmatched. I have been with parents in the emergency room who handed me their dead child. I've stepped inside the curtain when the nurse told me, "Glad you're here. They don't realize Grandma just died. Would you break it to them?" I've responded to the family home for the death of an eleven-year-old by self-inflicted gunshot wound. There have been countless other immeasurable wounds too deep for words. Sometimes the pain of those wounds makes the separation of death seem preferable.

I'm amazed at the resilience of some Christians. The way they can bounce back is remarkable. Perseverance is one quality that cannot be understated. And if there is a true friend to share the journey, the pain and sorrow is shared and divided. I'm reminded of the line by Samwise to Mr. Frodo in *The Lord of the Rings*. They are on the side of the ashen mountain with debris all around. They are dirtied and tired. It is the point of no return. No holds barred, it will take sheer commitment and grit of determination. Sam, realizing the magnitude of the burden that has been placed on the shoulders of his dear friend, Frodo, says, "Come Mr. Frodo. I can't carry it for you. But I can carry you and it as well. So up you get. Come on." Then he lifts his friend and throws him over his shoulder and begins the long, exhausting trudge up the hill. If you are called to bear unimaginable burdens, take courage. If you are called to be a friend, take note. Sometimes obedience requires every last vestige of strength and discipline.

Capital Casualty

> *Leviticus 24:14*
>
> *This man has cursed me! Take him outside the camp and tell the witnesses to lay their hands on his head. Then command the whole community of Israel to stone him to death.*

This is a real tragedy from all respects. It's tragic for the young man who did the cursing, tragic for his mother who loses her son, tragic for Moses who must execute justice, and tragic for all the onlookers who must become the ones to carry out the sentence. The young man, whose mother is an Israelite and father is an Egyptian, dies because of his vulgar disregard for the holiness of God's name. He blasphemes God's name and the decision has to be made what to do about it. Capital punishment is meted out and it is a casualty.

It raises several questions. How is it that he survived the initial moment of blasphemy? Uzzah wasn't so fortunate. He steadied the ark when the oxen stumbled and the holiness of God struck him down for his disregard. Aaron's sons, Nadab and Abihu, were both killed for burning incense on a fire pan at the wrong time, or in the wrong way. In any event, it was unauthorized. So why isn't this unnamed young Israeli Egyptian struck down immediately for his brazen behavior? Well, you see, it may have to do with the price of leadership. Uzzah, Nadab, and Abihu are each leaders, at least tacitly, by their family line and responsibilities.

Another question comes to mind: What role, if any, does his being an Egyptian play into this? There are several scenarios to be considered, but each one involves speculation. One, it could be that the young man has resentment in his heart about the entire situation. He's angry because he's traveling through the wilderness and has lost everything. His entire life is back in Egypt. It's entirely possible that he was young when they left. He's grown up in a tent in Moses' camp living on manna that he didn't ask for.

Two, presumably the father is out of the picture. He is not mentioned in the text. Contemporary English Version gives a great deal of latitude and mentions "their son" but the original Hebrew has no such phrasing. Why is he absent? More speculation. All first born sons of Egypt had died in the tragic night of the Passover. Perhaps his father was one such victim. If so, why didn't this young man die? Perhaps he had an older brother who had also died and his mother fled in the aftermath with the Israelites. Or, more likely, his father died in the Passover because his grandfather was an Egyptian. It could be that his mother saved her son's life by painting the blood of the lamb over her doorpost. You see, when two opposing nationalities marry, one holy unto God and the other hedonistic, there are knots intertwined that cannot easily be untangled. If her husband had insisted on staying with his own nuclear family then he died in the Passover. Maybe the mother left him that night, taking the baby. We don't know. Or maybe the father died in any number of ways. Doesn't seem like divorce, there's no mention of that. It's speculation. We're not told.

In any event, resentment has grown for some time in this young man's heart. His mother's name is Shelomith. It is a variant of peace, *shalom*, similar to the name Solomon was given. But things are not peaceful in the home. We're not told the situation of this fight. One pictures that he's been an agitated kid, a trouble maker. He's in another fight. Again, speculation. *"What am I gonna' do with this kid?"* And in the intense moment of frustration, out spews the verbal hatred. He blasphemes

God's name. The definition for blaspheme means to pierce, to puncture, to perforate. The definition for curse, which accompanies blaspheme, is to be slight, swift or trifling. He cussed God's name repeatedly and blew it off as no big deal! *"Yeah, I said it. What are you gonna' do about it?"*

God's ability to be free from any sense of political correctness is astounding. He is not motivated by what someone can do or cannot do for him. He is pure. There is simply right and wrong, nothing more. It is instantly obvious to him. Nothing is hidden. When Moses seeks God's wisdom the directive is handed down. *He must die. This needs to be an example for everyone to see.*

How is it that people survive cursing God's name every day? They do it all day long, every day, in movies, songs, offices, schools, all over our nation, this one nation under God. But God does hear. And some day he will respond. May a holy respect and reverence for Almighty hover us reminding us to be extremely careful to honor his Name.

A True Social Security

> *Leviticus 25:10*
>
> *This fiftieth year is sacred—it is a time of freedom and of celebration when everyone will receive back their original property, and slaves will return home to their families.*

I've been reading the Bible a long time. I feel like I'm just now beginning to get a grasp on the Year of Jubilee. It has implications that have dawned on me slowly, steadily, over my forty-five years. I haven't even lived a fifty-year period yet, the time frame of the Jubilee. Close, but not yet. By the way, if estimates are correct, neither did many of the ancient Israelis. The value of the Jubilee is settling upon me like the aroma of a pleasant meal cooked low and slow.

In church-life ministers are familiar with a manual called *Robert's Rules of Order.* It is the Bible in terms of parliamentary procedure. One can study it from cover to cover and never understand every part of its scope and consequence; although the ones who become familiar with its nuances can excel in leadership. The basic premise of *Robert's Rules of Order* is that everyone, in a session of the meeting being conducted, has the right to be treated fairly, have opportunity to speak, and to be heard. It provides a system for protocol. To my understanding the Jubilee accomplishes the same thing economically. Every family is provided the opportunity for firm footing, an established financial base.

Bear in mind, when this declaration is written the nation is still travelling. They haven't made it to the Promised Land yet. While in transit, they already had been given the blueprint for the rule of law once they arrive. Now, they are given the national social security. It is as if they have the judicial branch, and a sort of mixture between executive and legislative branches combined.

Typically, various forms of government may be described as dictatorship, authoritarian, totalitarian, monarchy, republic or other. Theocracy means rule by religious leadership; but that doesn't really describe Israel which has God conversing directly with its leader. Philosophically there are approaches within systems that work dynamics economically, such as capitalism, socialism, laissez-faire, or feudalism. You won't hear the term jubilee used in Economy 101.

With the ancient Jewish Jubilee you have a system that allows for competitive markets. One may buy and sell property. And that property is evaluated for purposes of appraisal. For instance, a property in a walled city was valued higher, so voluntary exchange was at a premium. However, there would never be a real estate bust in ancient Israel. The avarice of Wall Street couldn't infiltrate it. Greed is sifted out because everyone knows all real estate reverts back to the original owners every fifty years. One could make money by fair market value, but couldn't charge unfair interest or squeeze out exorbitant gains.

On the other hand, there were no government hand-outs either. Families had vested interests in how their members performed. Inheritance was reckoned by sonship/fatherhood. Absentee fathers were unheard of. This system of checks and balances proved beneficial for the nation of Israel. Individuals could prosper but not to the detriment of the nation. And the nation could prosper but not to the detriment of the individual. It was a true security for society. And society is made up of secure individuals.

I live in America and I'm grateful for our triplicate governance that separates state from religion but doesn't squelch religious liberty, at least not to date. Our government by republic was founded upon biblical principle found in Isaiah 33:22 which says, "For the LORD is our judge (judicial branch), the LORD is our lawgiver (legislative branch), the LORD is our king (executive branch); he will save us." Consider pausing to pray for our national leaders today. "I urge, then, first of all, that petitions, prayers, intercession and thanksgiving be made for all people - for kings and all those in authority, that we may live peaceful and quiet lives in all godliness and holiness" (1 Tim 2:1, 2).

Foreshadowing a Blessing

Leviticus 26:33-35

After I destroy your towns and ruin your land with war, I'll scatter you among the nations. While you are prisoners in foreign lands, your own land will enjoy years of rest and refreshment, as it should have done each seventh year when you lived there.

What an amazing foreshadowing and prophecy of the seventy years in Babylonian captivity. Israel had been instructed to observe a sabbatical year every seventh year. God proclaimed spectacular blessings over them for their obedience. He also warned of dire consequences if they disobeyed. The Jews were to plant and harvest crops for six years. Every seventh year, though, was to be a sabbatical year in order to let the land rest. After seven complete seven-year periods came the big celebration. Jubilee marked the 50th year. This was to be an act of trust and obedience. God would bless them abundantly; but they did not trust and obey.

What is it about human nature? We cater to a sinister curiosity that always seems to push the envelope. Immediate convenience at the expense of long term discipline always results in difficulty.

This corrective punishment seems unbearable at first glance, seventy years in Babylonian captivity. There were people who were born, lived their entire lives, and died, all during this burdensome punishment. But pan back the zoom and see the panoramic view of Israel as a nation. It begins to make sense. If the Scripture is true when it says, "A day with the Lord is as a thousand years, and a thousand years is as a day" (2 Pet 3:9), then there is one sense in which, comparatively, seventy years is a little more than an hour and a half. Figuratively, to send Israel to Babylon is the equivalent of God saying to his stubborn daughter, Israel, "Go to your room and think about what you've done." Is it even grounding? She still gets to go to the mall on the weekend with her friends. Maybe she was sent to bed without her dinner. God has been more than fair with his obstinate daughter whom he has stretched his arms out to all day long while she refused to pay attention (Isa 65:2).

Time is like a rubber band that is stretched. It will eventually collapse back upon itself. When time is no more, God will be seen as right, fair and just. We will be without an excuse, whether in the wilderness, or the Promised Land, or even if he tells us to bless the city of Babylon, where we have been sent. Plant gardens there. Build houses. Raise children.

Whatever our context we may be blessed. He has foreshadowed it. We can choose to be blessed or to be cursed.

The Need to Be Needed

Numbers 1:49-51

When you count the Israelites, do not include those from the Levi tribe.

Instead, give them the job of caring for the sacred tent, its furnishings, and the objects used for worship. They will camp around the tent, and whenever you move, they will take it down, carry it to the new camp, and set it up again. Anyone else who tries to go near it must be put to death.

I recently went to have some repairs done on my car. The shop was one of those stereotypical old school garages, run down slump block building, an eye-sore sort of place, grease everywhere, tools galore. These kind of places have always intimidated me because I don't know a lot about cars, and I feel very much out of my element. But I was instantly won over by the winsome personality of a great, skilled mechanic. And the prices are noticeably cheaper than other places with new pristine buildings and many employees. Low overhead translated to low costs.

At the garage there was an adorable little Lhasa Apsa whose main job was to lay in the shade. I joked that he was a Spanish-speaking dog. The crew would yell at him in Spanish to get out of the way for an incoming car. He only responded when they spoke in Spanish. While waiting on the work I played with this pup I nicknamed Moppy because he looked just like a dirty mop. He loved to roll in the dirt and grease. He saw himself as a vital part of the crew. Moppy was so friendly and he loved to be petted. He needed me for something that morning. He would come up to where I was sitting and lick my hand until I noticed he wanted to gnaw on my finger. It was just the right size. Apparently, he was cutting a new tooth, or maybe his jaw was sore. For some reason he wanted to gum my ring finger right at the back of his molars. His relaxed response let me know when it was just the right spot. Little playful bites, careful not to pierce my skin. Such a simple act by one of God's creatures. He needed me. And it felt good to be needed.

We all have a need. It is the need to be needed. The Levites had a very special assignment. They were the carriers of the tabernacle. No one else could do it, struck down if they tried. I've never been involved with a church situation that involved a set up and tear down crew such as in a new church plant in rented facilities. I've got friends and family members who have, though. They tell me these individuals are indispensable. I think about significant ministry ventures we have conducted. The manual labor personnel are crucial to success. Every individual has a unique ability. It is crucial to match ministry with giftedness: sound, lighting, electrical, maintenance, landscaping, music, children, teaching, hospitality - we all need to be needed.

What do you need? What does your church need? Could there be a match? Find a need and meet it.

A Vow of the Heart

Numbers 6:9-11

If someone suddenly dies near you, your hair is no longer sacred, and you must shave it seven days later during the ceremony to make you clean. Then on the next day, bring two doves or two pigeons to the priest at the sacred tent. He will offer one of the birds as a sacrifice for sin and the other as a sacrifice to please me. You will then be forgiven for being too near a dead body, and your hair will again become sacred.

There was a special vow taken by individuals in Bible times who were called to a life of separation unto God. It was the vow of a Nazarite. There were three primary criteria of the Nazarite: 1.) to avoid alcohol in every form, even to the point of not eating grapes, raisins, or even the skins; 2.) to never have a haircut; and 3.) to avoid dead bodies, even in the deaths of nuclear family members.

The word *nazir*, from which Nazarite derives, means set apart for purposes of being holy, devoted. It's a word that is used to describe a branch, a winding vine. It plays a significant role in prophesy. It would be easy to chase *nazir* down a rabbit trail to a very interesting diversion. Let me just say, there are connections between prophecies of Jesus as the Branch, and the fulfillment of Matthew 2:23 which reads, "[Jesus] went and lived in a town called Nazareth. So was fulfilled what was said through the prophets, 'He will be called a Nazarene'" (Matt 2:23).

Tradition says Samuel was a Nazarite, as well as John the Baptist. It is said that James, the brother of Jesus, had taken the vow of a Nazarite, and possibly even Jesus himself. Absalom, the son of David, is thought to have been a Nazarite too. His hair grew so heavy he was allowed a special clemency, to clip it annually (2 Sam 14:26).

The most notorious Nazarite was Samson. You can read about him in the book of Judges, chapters 13 through 16. The requirements of the Nazarite played a vital role in Samson's story. He took a vow to avoid touching dead bodies, but he did. One of the encounters involves him reaching inside the dead body of a lion. There is no mention of Samson ever drinking alcohol; although he hangs out in environs where it would most likely be consumed, and this leaves him suspect. Most intriguing, though, is the fact that he allowed his hair to be cut off after toying with Delilah, giving her a series of hints about his strength being connected to his hair. The narrative hints regret on his part, and a sense of remorse for his sin. He is bound by bronze shackles and reduced to grinding meal at the prison. With his eyes gouged out and his strength gone we are told, "But the hair on his head began to grow again." In his dying act of valor he pulls down the pagan temple pillars and causes the death of 3,000 enemy Philistines.

The text implies that Samson died a hero's death, an act of war. He is buried with honor. Lay aside one's emotional feelings about the deaths of the Philistines, whether that was that right or wrong. What we should note is, here is an example in the Old Testament of an individual unable to go to the sons of Aaron to conduct the rite needed in which a Nazarite would shave his head in order to become clean. Samson is caught in sin, away from home. He is remorseful. The priest doesn't shave his head, the Philistine does. And yet, something took place inside, a vow of the heart. It mirrors the centurion in the New Testament saying to Jesus, "Just say the word and it will be done."

Call to him where you are. Come to him as you are. He will hear you and understand the sincerity of your heart.

Can You Imagine?

>Numbers 7:11
>
>*The Lord said to Moses, "Each day one leader is to give his offering for the dedication."*

What an amazingly somber, holy march it must have been, the family shepherds in the lead with the animals in tow. Can you imagine the little rams with their tiny horns just beginning to protrude through their scalps? A young bull sacrificed? Okay, two bulls, two full grown bulls being offered in sacrifice. How much time and strength would that take? Then the rams and goats. Do the other animals get skittish when they see the bulls get slaughtered? They have to know something is up, right? There is an amazing lot of discipline required with this covenant sacrifice. Each tribe has the mixed emotions of pride and sympathy. There's pride as the appointed tribal leader promenades before the nation's dignitaries. Dressed his best, new silver offering bowls to donate, filled with the finest flour and yeast. But there is sympathy at the thought of innocent animal-life discarded. Even in ancient times, free from animal rights activists and environmental proponents, these activities must have been emotional on a level. We have every reason to believe these animals were somewhat domesticated, at the very least loved, cared for, not merely quota. The children and the tender-hearted winced at the gory sight not fit for younger audiences. Blood smattered, the altar is a bath, awash in it. As the smoke ascended on the final day of sacrifice, the twelfth day, was there a sigh of relief? Finally, it's over. And as they watched it year, after year, after year, these people came to understand something about the cost of sacrifice.

Now the writer of Hebrews says, "Come let us offer the sacrifice of praise, that is lips that make confession to his name" (Heb 13:15). Do you recall verbal praise that really required something of you recently? I mean, vocal exhortation that cost you a great deal? I do not. Join me today in attempting to be over the top, extravagant, towards the One who sacrificed his all for you and me.

You No Good Rapscallion

Numbers 10:35, 36

Each day as the Israelites began their journey, Moses would pray, "Our Lord, defeat your enemies and make them run!" And when they stopped to set up camp, he would pray, "Our Lord, stay close to Israel's thousands and thousands of people."

I had the most colorful Algebra teacher in my freshman year of high school; though I didn't realize it at the time. He seemed ancient, honestly. Now, I'm his age. Whoa! Mr. Fortenberry was a godly man, a church-going, honest man in the trenches of public school. I heard that he went to the Baptist Church; although I never asked him. Someone said he was a Sunday School teacher. He loved kids, invested in them, but he had to fly under the radar on things like being cordial. I mean, after all, there is a code of ethics. The kids had to pretend that all teachers were absurdly lame, and teachers responded in kind by implying the students were entirely other-worldly. It was a delicate system of mutual respect that bore fruit as long as it was stringently adhered to. And Mr. Fortenberry brought balance to that harsh admiration society. He was a mixed bag of colloquialisms. If you came to class unprepared, lacking notebook paper, or needing to borrow a pencil, he would exclaim, "You no good rapscallion!" God forbid you ever didn't have your homework and claimed you would bring it tomorrow. Mr. Fortenberry had a rehearsed speech. "What is this! Know ye not that today is the day of salvation!"

Mr. Fortenberry drove my school bus too. I don't know of any teachers who also drive bus these days, but he did. He picked me up in the morning and dropped me off in the afternoon. He had a set routine that I heard, literally, thousands of times during that stretch of two years before I became part of the upper echelon, you know, the elite, who either drove or rode with a friend to school. Mr. Fortenberry would say the exact same words each time a student got on the bus. In classic southern drawl, that conveyed the warmth of hospitality, he would quip, "Mornin' Sunshine!" And at the end of the day when they climbed down those bus steps in the afternoon, "Evenin' Glory."

I was reminded of this when reading about Moses. He also had a set routine each time they broke camp. Can't you just envision him erect like a standard at the vanguard of the breaking camp, speaking out words that became a blessing over Israel as they followed in pursuit of the cloud of the presence, "Our Lord defeat your enemies and make them run!" And when they arrived at their destination a word was in order too. In my mind I have him standing at the mock gate until they have brought up the rear, watching over his massive flock. Maybe that isn't accurate, but it plays out that way on my view screen. "Our Lord, stay close to Israel's thousands and thousands of people." What comforting words, the power of his prowess in wartime, the proximity of his presence in camp. If you battle, he is with you. If you rest, he is also there.

Caleb's Different Spirit

> *Numbers 14:24*
>
> *But my servant Caleb isn't like the others. So because he has faith in me, I will allow him to cross into Canaan, and his descendants will settle there.*

I have done substitute teaching. I try to avoid the younger children's grades. They tend to be needy. They have to have someone "holding their hand," so to speak, throughout the day. I find it very draining. There are constant requests for approval and affirmation. So I will put up with the nonsense, sometimes, of the junior high and high school students, in exchange for more freedom in the day. One distinct thing I have noticed among the younger ages is a belief that life should be fair. Primary graders have an expectancy of justice and equity; though they would never describe it that way.

God also has an expectation that things should be fair, right, and equitable. First, God tells the Israelites that all of the firstborn of Egypt would be killed by the death angel. And they were, as the angel passed over on that last, fateful night before the Exodus began. Next, once they are in the wilderness, he clarifies that, actually, all the firstborn of the Israelites belong to him as well, it is just that he didn't require the death of them since the blood was applied to the doorposts. They still belong to him though. In exchange for the firstborn of all Israel, he would accept the Levites, who would serve at the tabernacle as the priestly tribe, and would not receive land allotments.

Now, he offers that the Levites can be bought back. You see, there is always this sense of fairness, rightness, being carried forward. It is embedded in the narrative of the Old Testament, the very backdrop for the New Testament gospel. If you were to research various theories on atonement you would notice how this lines up best with substitutionary atonement theory. That is to say, you did this, I responded this way. You took this, I will take that. There is a right. There is a wrong. All things being equal, there must be balance. A wrong must be righted. Life should be fair.

Ironically, God, who is fair, is often accused of being unfair. If there is a God, why is there evil in the world? If there were a God there wouldn't be poverty on the scale as we see it in our world. God could do something about it if he exists. The fact is he has done something about it. He made all things right in the death of his Son, Jesus, on the cross. It is actually very beautiful that he has made sure that consequences still stay in effect. We are responsible for our actions. There is a direct line between choice and result. But on the grander scale, all who genuinely put their faith in Christ notice how he makes all things new.

Today you may not be able to solve deep theological conundrums; but you can trust that God is fair and he has been falsely accused.

Glory Incognito

Numbers 20:1-11

The people of Israel arrived at the Zin Desert during the first month and set up camp near the town of Kadesh. It was there that Miriam died and was buried.

The Israelites had no water, so they went to Moses and Aaron and complained, "Moses, we'd be better off if we had died along with the others in front of the Lord's sacred tent. You brought us into this desert, and now we and our livestock are going to die!

Egypt was better than this horrible place. At least there we had grain and figs and grapevines and pomegranates. But now we don't even have any water."

Moses and Aaron went to the entrance to the sacred tent, where they bowed down. The Lord appeared to them in all of his glory and said, "Moses, get your walking stick. Then you and Aaron call the people together and command that rock to give you water. That's how you will provide water for the people of Israel and their livestock."

Moses obeyed and took his stick from the sacred tent. After he and Aaron had gathered the people around the rock, he said, "Look, you rebellious people, and you will see water flow from this rock!"

He raised his stick in the air and struck the rock two times. At once, water gushed from the rock, and the people and their livestock had water to drink.

There are interesting phrases in this passage. In verse 9, before Moses strikes the rock, we read, "Moses obeyed." There can only be one explanation. It is possible to obey partially, half-baked, because obviously he didn't obey in verse 11. And this act of negligent disobedience cost him entry into the Promised Land. Moses was frustrated to no end. He's stuck in the middle, the arbitrator, the go-between. On the one hand, he has the people complaining and murmuring. They're thirsty. We humans get mean and nasty when we feel deprived.

On the other hand, "God appeared in all his glory" in verse 6. In the midst of a drought? Glory? Impeccable timing! One pictures dirty, dry Israelites, smacking their chapped lips in the blistering desert. *Tada!* God appears with a light show, splashed by LEDs. If read wrongly, it leaves a bad impression of God, on the level of say, a Marie Antoinette who, hearing that the French populace had no bread to eat, quipped, "Let them eat cake." Or, possibly, it is like the Commander in Chief on the TV Sitcom, *Corey in the House*. The character, President Richard Martinez, would vainly blurt out at the most inopportune moments, "I'm the President of the United States." The minions are subjected to abject want, but not to fear, his majesty is frilled in pomp. But, no, that's not what's going on in any respect. Bear in mind, if God appears at all, it will be in "all" his glory. There is no such thing as his appearing in half glory, though we are prone to half obedience. Still, our disaster doesn't allow for diminishing his glory. He can't dumb it down. If he could he wouldn't be God.

No, this was God's plan for provision, if Moses would simply obey. After the event, I'll bet Moses thought a thousand times, why did I strike that rock? Why couldn't I just trust God and do it his way, fully obeying? It was disrespectful, what he did, striking that rock instead of speaking to it. The Psalms often speak of our Lord as a Rock. In the New Testament there is a very nice reference to Simon, renamed Peter, *Rock*. It sort of comes off as chip off the block. The chief cornerstone is Christ himself. Jesus Christ, our solid rock, was struck at Calvary. Blood and water flowed, the blood for the remission of sins, the water to quench our spiritual thirst. He told us he would give us living water so that we never thirst again.

Ironically, God Almighty, under the old covenant, could not appear any less than spectacular, even as he came down to the mountaintop and Moses went up to the heights, the neutral site. God-sightings were accounted to be in smoldering mountain fumes, clefts of rocks as he walked away, a cloud of presence, a pillar of fire, or in the tent of meeting leaving traces on Moses' face. But Jesus is Glory Incognito. The manger is his bassinet. The carpenter's chisel is his scepter. He is Splendor with skin on. Immanuel is Immortality Incarnated, God in all his glory.

Donkeys, Dogs and Discernment

> *Numbers 22:22-32*
>
> *Balaam was riding his donkey to Moab, and two of his servants were with him. But God was angry that Balaam had gone, so one of the Lord's angels stood in the road to stop him.*
>
> *When Balaam's donkey saw the angel standing there with a sword, it walked off the road and into an open field. Balaam had to beat the donkey to get it back on the road.*

> *Then the angel stood between two vineyards, in a narrow path with a stone wall on each side.*
>
> *When the donkey saw the angel, it walked so close to one of the walls that Balaam's foot scraped against the wall. Balaam beat the donkey again.*
>
> *The angel moved once more and stood in a spot so narrow that there was no room for the donkey to go around.*
>
> *So it just lay down. Balaam lost his temper, then picked up a stick and whacked the donkey.*
>
> *When that happened, the Lord told the donkey to speak, and it asked Balaam, "What have I done that made you beat me three times?"*
>
> *"You made me look stupid!" Balaam answered. "If I had a sword, I'd kill you here and now!"*
>
> *"But you're my owner," answered the donkey, "and you've ridden me many times. Have I ever done anything like this before?"*
>
> *"No," Balaam admitted.*
>
> *Just then, the Lord let Balaam see the angel standing in the road, holding a sword, and Balaam bowed down. The angel said, "You had no right to treat your donkey like that! I was the one who blocked your way, because I don't think you should go to Moab."*

I find this passage about the talking donkey so humorous. Some more liberal thinkers might find it humorous because they believe the story is a farce; the idea of a talking donkey is absurd. That's not me. I am conservative in biblical interpretation. I have no problem believing a donkey could speak if God opens its mouth. The greater miracle is that God could open the eyes of a human to see what is happening in the spirit realm.

I have a friend who is a Spirit-filled, Licensed Marriage and Family Therapist. He is a respected Christian counselor who has been used of the Lord to help numerous couples in times of crisis. He told me once that his dog always lies on the rug in his office. It's part of the ambience of the room. Makes it feel more like home. Sets clients at ease. He swears that the dog, numerous times, has behaved erratically, seeing things that he himself didn't see in the natural. Only later, after numerous sessions, would he become aware of dark spiritual battles that were taking place. Over the years, he has begun to recognize cues from the dog when spiritual activity is occurring in the room.

So, why is the text humorous? It's funny because when the donkey talks Balaam doesn't retort, "You can talk!" Instead when the donkey asks, "What have I done to you that made you beat me three times?" Balaam, ticked off, retorts, "You made me look stupid!" Now, get this. Here's a guy carrying on conversation with a donkey and he's worried about looking stupid!

Balaam is respected as a spiritual advisor. Balak sought him out and was willing to pay big bucks to have his advice. In stereotypical fashion of the day he utilized animal sacrifices. He may have been aided by timbrel and dance. It wouldn't have been out of the ordinary for him to go into an ecstatic state. We don't know a lot about Balaam. He doesn't present his prophetic vitae and resume. We only know that in the New Testament, Peter, Jude and John the Revelator, all three condemn him as a false prophet of greed. He said the right things, used the right language about the Lord and all; but he may well have been syncretistic, blending lots of practices into a religious stew. Ironically, the one who was notorious for seeing things wasn't seeing very well at all. He had to have his eyes opened.

Similarly, Elisha and his servant, Gehazi, were in a village surrounded by an enemy army mounted on horses ready to attack. Gehazi could only see in the natural. But Elisha prayed for his eyes to be opened and they were. Now he realized there was a great ally host in the foothills surrounding them. They were riding chariots and horses of fire. This can only mean that some individuals are able to perceive spiritual things while others do not. I believe wholeheartedly the difference has to do with, to borrow Ephesians' language, walking in the Spirit, keeping pace with the Holy Spirit. You may never see aberrations of any kind. That's not the point. I believe we can open ourselves to direction from the Holy Spirit as we conscientiously seek his will.

Maybe you have sung the song by Paul Baloche before, *Open the Eyes of My Heart, Lord.* This may be one of the most important prayers you have prayed.

Audience of One

Numbers 27:17-23

Your people need someone to lead them into battle, or else they will be like sheep wandering around without a shepherd."

The Lord answered, "Joshua son of Nun can do the job. Place your hands on him to show that he is the one to take your place. Then go with him and tell him to stand in front of Eleazar the priest and the Israelites. Appoint Joshua as their new leader and tell them they must now obey him, just as they obey you.

But Joshua must depend on Eleazar to find out from me what I want him to do as he leads Israel into battle."

Moses followed the Lord's instructions and took Joshua to Eleazar and the people, then he placed his hands on Joshua and appointed him Israel's leader.

There is a subtle shift in the leadership structure upon Moses' death; but it is a very important one. Joshua will lead the people. He is not to have the same face to face direct instruction from God that Moses enjoyed. Eleazar, the priest, will be entrusted with keeping the purity of the Law. Joshua will consult with Eleazar and lead the people accordingly. So now we see shared responsibility. There is a progression from Moses exclusively, to Joshua as General and Eleazar as Priest. It's always moving forward. Israel will experience seasons of rule by various sources: judges, prophets and kings.

From that time to this continues a mode of ministry in which God works in a manner more dependent upon individual discernment. Leadership has looked differently since Moses. He communed directly with God. His face glowed. The firsthand delivery of God's message is generations removed, whatever we may say about experiencing the presence of God. I speak as one who values throne room experience and believes the ministry must flow from there. Still, there is a sense in which each generation loses a grain of quality like the old cassette tapes that were dubbed over repeatedly. That's why we read the Bible and wait, yearn, long, hope to understand. That's why we pray, pause, reflect, ponder.

There is one seismic shift with the death and resurrection of Christ. He is our High Priest. He is the very embodiment of the Priest, the Prophet and the King. We no longer need to go through a priest like Eleazar. We, instead, approach God's throne by our Joshua, Yeshua, our Savior, Jesus Christ. The priesthood of the believer is an important New

Testament concept realized by Martin Luther in the time of the Reformation, or at least he contributed. We may approach the throne of grace as individuals. Nonetheless, some individuals have hands laid on them by ordaining bodies. Ministers lead at the cost of great peril if they jeopardize their integrity. How crucial to have leadership that longs for the pure Word of God.

I'm Pentecostal. We are a restoration movement. That is to say, ministry is best when it resembles the activity demonstrated in the New Testament. So we try to practice it. That doesn't mean we have no value for church history and its lessons. Quite the contrary, we would say, each generation must have a pure experience with God or it risks repeating some of the same mistakes. I remember the night I was ordained into ministry. Elders gathered around me, spoke words of challenge, gave a charge, and laid their hands on me to pray. The voice that rang out loudest was my own father, a pastor himself for more than four decades. That night they told me they were recognizing with ceremony and paper what God was doing. They couldn't call me to ministry, only God could, and they would honor it. Church leadership is fraught with errors. We are prone to mistakes. We feel impressions, hunches, we follow. You are a leader. Who do you lead? May we seek earnestly to please our most important audience, an audience of One.

Arouse the Nostalgia of Almighty

Numbers 28:6

This sacrifice to please me was first offered at Mount Sinai.

God is reciting observances to the Israelites so they remember them when they enter the Promised Land. This involves the daily sacrifices; the weekly sacrifices on the Sabbath; the monthly new moon sacrifice; the annual Passover; the meal of thin bread; and the Harvest Festival. In the middle of this liturgical litany comes a verse softened by the nostalgia of Almighty God. He remembers the first time a sacrifice was offered on Mount Sinai. Just think of how beautiful this is, and all the implications it carries. It is something along the lines of remembering an anniversary. This is sweet recall for our Sovereign. Aromas are powerful triggers. We can easily recall walking into a home in which a meal was being prepared. Sautéed peppers and onions, or the scintillating zest of spices filling the air. Or, how about this? Most of us enjoy a good BBQ and are drawn magnetically to the grill.

The Jewish feasts draw upon the concept of rehearsal, similar to what we might think of for a wedding. Go through all the paces. Make sure everyone understands where to be, what to say and do. Understand the significance of what is happening. Mind you, all of the seven feasts are not listed here, but some are included in this reminder of routines. God has rehearsed his relationship with his chosen people, Israel, for millenniums. The Christian Church has been grafted in the vine and we benefit from the feasts. *Passover* points to Jesus, our sacrificial Lamb. *Unleavened Bread* speaks of Jesus' sinless life. *First Fruits* may be thought of as Jesus' resurrection. *Weeks*, or Pentecost, was all about the seven weeks after first fruits, or specifically the fiftieth day, which in the year Jesus died was marked by the outpouring of the Holy Spirit upon the Church. *Trumpets* hints at the rapture of the Church. *Atonement* could very well be when "they look upon the one they have pierced" as he returns to earth at the end of the tribulation. *Tabernacles* indicates he will again tabernacle with his people.

God hears every prayer. He remembers the benchmark moments of your life. The times you've knelt at an altar and lingered. The times you were alone in the car and had a few moments waiting for the light to change and a salty tear slid down your cheek that no one else saw. God recalls, and watches and listens for new prayers all the time. They are precious to him. Could it be that you arouse the nostalgia of Almighty today?

The Purple Lineage

> *Deuteronomy 4:41-43*
>
> *Moses said, "People of Israel, you must set aside the following three towns east of the Jordan River as Safe Towns: Bezer in the desert highlands belonging to the Reuben tribe; Ramoth in Gilead, belonging to the Gad tribe; and Golan in Bashan, belonging to the Manasseh tribe. If you kill a neighbor without meaning to, and if you had not been angry with that person, you can run to one of these towns and find safety."*

This verse marks the first reference in the Bible to what is known as the Golan Heights, originally one village meant to provide safety for those who had committed manslaughter in Israel. Today that village still exists and has a population of about 35,000 people. Most are of Syrian descent and have family and friends on the other side of the border. Who knew the serendipitous decision of half of the tribe of Manasseh to remain on the east side of the Jordan would reap such fruitful reward! The Golan Heights is very important to Israel providing a third of her water supply. It also gives Israel apple orchards, wineries, ski slopes and lush pastures for cattle.

The Golan Heights was an important hold-out in the Jewish Revolt of 67-73 A.D. As a fortress it earned the reputation Masada of the North because of its steep hills. For a few hundred years following this it was very popular in Israel. Then it ping ponged ownership for eighteen centuries. Recently, the Golan Heights is in the news again. Since the Six-Day War of 1967 it is a geographic area that has been occupied by Israel. International sentiment says it belongs to Syria; though this Scripture speaks of its occupation by Israel 1,400 years before the time of Christ. Metaphorically, a line was drawn in the sand in 1967 by the United Nations. Literally, it was called the Purple Line because of the way it was drawn on the UN's maps. It is a neutral zone that, for all practical purposes, serves as the boundary line between Israel and Syria. There has been a tug of war over the Golan Heights through recent years. In 1973 Syria launched a surprise attack on Israel during one of its holy days, Yom Kippur. They advanced until Israel launched a counter attack. Eventually Israel pushed back and beyond. Finally, the two nations agreed to revert to the Purple Line. Today it is supervised by the United Nations Disengagement Observer Force, a bigger Purple line that buffers Israeli and Hezbollah animosities.

God made a promise to Father Abraham, "I will bless those who bless you and curse those who curse you" (Gen 12:3). Abraham's son, Isaac, and grandson Jacob, renamed Israel, are the ones God chose as "his own people" (Exod 8:20). It is true Arabs trace their lineage to Abraham too. Yet the Bible also embeds carnage and turmoil prophetically between the Israelis and Arabs. The promise to Father Abraham has decided the rise and fall of nations and rulers historically. National securities have hinged upon their treatment of Israel. She is a small swath of land only a hundred and fifty miles from north to south, surrounded by five giant nations. She is as privileged in the Middle East as Earth is in the universe.

There is another line. Purple is the color of royalty. Jesus was draped in it in a mocking way previous to his cross. What the soldiers did in arrogance as a joke, ironically, was confirmed by the empty tomb. The Purple Lineage guards the borders of Israel and will continue to do so until he determines the times of the end. Israel's largely unrecognized King is my King too. I am grateful to live in the United States who has, to date, sided with Israel. I pray we never turn our back on her. On which side of the Purple Lineage do you reside?

The Glory Hole

Deuteronomy 9:21

It was a sin for you to make that idol, so I threw it into the fire to melt it down. Then I took the lump of gold, ground it into powder, and threw the powder into the stream flowing down the mountain.

I like to watch the reality show, *Gold Rush*. A half dozen down-on-their-luck workers from Oregon throw caution to the wind and head to Alaska trying their hand at gold mining. They come from all walks of life and meld together into a brash, unorthodox team, learning the trade on the fly. Their language is sometimes crude, their office demeanor is oft out of bounds; but you never doubt their friendship. Beards grow thick while professional relationships wear thin. Through all the heartaches and breakdowns, I find myself rooting for them to strike it big. In the first season they bet the farm on finding the glory hole, the legendary place where gold pooled up at the bottom of bedrock 65 feet beneath the contour of the creek.

This passage of Scripture elicits a lot of different responses from thinking minds. Some more liberal minds say it is proof positive that the Bible is contrived. Matching this verse with its companion passage in Exodus 32:20, they reason that once gold has been reduced by burning, one cannot then crush it and grind it into powder. It's impossible. Gold melts at 2000 degrees Fahrenheit. *What did Moses use for a crucible? Where did he get the tongs and container that wouldn't melt before the gold did? What about the dangers of loose and flammable clothing?* "No," chimes the postmodern sage, *"Simple, primitive experimenter. We are not that gullible!"* So they dismiss it as farce. These are the same minds that have our age as superior in intellect. All the ancient world is in black and white in their minds, and could not possibly know something that we don't know. They're the ones scratching heads in wonder at the Egyptian Pyramids, Stonehenge and The Hanging Gardens of Babylon.

Other approaches drift towards logical explanation. For instance, a popular rationale is that this Scripture intends us to know Moses burned the wooden stand the golden calf rested on, and the gold was only charred. There is precedence for this in Scripture. Another speculation says the golden calf was only wood overlaid with gold. That doesn't seem to bode well with the text though. Or, yet another explanation, there was a variant in the text, a transposition of the word order. The stone tablets from Moses' hands were the items that were burned. Separately, the gold was crushed and ground.

Still another camp of opinion says it was a miracle. God works miracles and he can do anything he wants. Well, amen to that. Once you believe "In the beginning God created the heavens and the earth," the rest is *easy peasy lemon squeezy*. I mean, c'mon, gold is just the asphalt of heaven. However, I tend to believe we just don't have all the details. It's like we're listening in on one end of a phone conversation. I think somehow or another these Israelites drank some kind of diluted gold lemonade. It wouldn't be toxic. Did you know there is actually an exquisite desert for the filthy rich which is a Sundae that has real gold in the toppings? And since gold is nineteen times heavier than water, I would imagine much of it is still trapped in an ancient glory hole in the river bed of the stream adjacent to Mount Sinai. How much do you think enough gold to form a calf goes for these days? Hey, let's get an exhibition together. Are you in?

Relationship with the living God: now that's the true glory! Let every other distraction be ground to powder and burned away in the process of Christian growth. Abandon it all in favor of climbing the mountain to the place where the presence of God speaks to you.

Golfers and Gates Giving Testimony

Deuteronomy 11:18-21

Memorize these laws and think about them. Write down copies and tie them to your wrists and your foreheads to help you obey them. Teach them to your children. Talk about them all the time-- whether you're at home or walking along the road or going to bed at night, or getting up in the morning. Write them on the door frames of your homes and on your town gates. Then you and your descendants will live a long time in the land that the LORD promised your ancestors. Your families will live there as long as the sky is above the earth.

Professional golfer, Payne Stewart, was notorious for his lavish, some would say outlandish, wardrobe. Stewart donned the old school ivy caps and knickers. He mixed and matched vibrant, bright colors in a wild cacophony for the eyes. Perhaps his most daring accessory was the wristband he wore toward the end of his career. He was poised on the green of hole number 18 in the 1999 U.S. Open at Pinehurst in North Carolina. Stewart was entrenched in a tight dual with another outspoken believer, Phil Mickelson. As the camera zoomed in on his hand grip, there it was, WWJD. What would Jesus do? Well, apparently if Jesus were a golfer he would sink the putt because Payne drained the cup to win his third major. What makes it more memorable is that it was only four months before his untimely death as his plane lost cabin pressure over the mid-western United States, before it crashed off course in South Dakota.

It is a wonderful idea to let the accessories of life speak of your faith. I saw a middle-school aged girl wearing a T-shirt recently. It was bright and attractive. It had the logo of her church where she had been baptized and read, "I took the plunge. Ask me about it."

Friends I know live in a small community of neighbors high in the mountains of western Colorado. At the entrance to each driveway is a beautiful, ranch style, gate with a Bible verse branded into the wood. "Holy to the Lord." "As for me and my house." "Unless the Lord builds the house." It must be pure release each time they enter.

Perhaps you know of church buildings with Scriptures painted under the flooring on the concrete. Or homes with verses painted decoratively on the walls. There are numerous buildings in Washington D.C. with cornerstones that speak of our Christian heritage. This is a wonderful testimony.

There are equally alarming etchings embedded in our history: marks of secret societies like Free Masonry in buildings; an Egyptian style obelisk that smacks of ancient occultism and the sun god Ra; a dollar bill that has what are at the very least suspicious markings and strangely spells out the word M-A-S-O-N in the form of a pentagram, the same dollar bill that reads, "In God We Trust"; and many say the angled streets of Washington D.C. form a Pentagram with the White House at one of the points. And, weirdly, it does, though it is not finished on one edge. Coincidence? Who's to say?

Brilliant minds have wrestled with these things. Martin Luther articulated his view in his *Doctrine of the Two Kingdoms*. It is his written opinion on the melding of government and spirituality. He taught God rules in two ways, through the secular government's rule of law and the Church's gospel of grace. Thomas Jefferson wrote a letter to the Danbury Baptists promising them that the government would not infringe on their right to freedom of worship. In the letter he referred to the separation of church and state. That phrase has been absolutely turned on its head in our day to mean something Jefferson never intended.

There are ways anchored in the fabric of our world that are not going to change. It is crucial that Christians let their lights shine. Admittedly, there are different opinions. Whatever your views on community involvement, if you lean more to the methods of a James Dobson or a Jim Wallace, find a way to let your life radiate. What does that look like for you? Bracelet brandishing, or bread giveaways, or both. Sharing Jesus, or social justice, or some mix of the two. What would Jesus do? What will you do to identify with him today?

Reverent Worship

Deuteronomy 13:4

You must be completely faithful to the LORD. Worship and obey only the LORD and do this with fear and trembling.

Piercing words. "Worship and obey only the Lord and do this with fear and trembling." The Contemporary English Version picks up on a particular wording that all other versions do not emphasize, "fear and trembling". It doesn't show up identically in the Hebrew text, but these translators seem to have honed in on an idiom of the language. So, CEV has nine more references to "fear and trembling" than do all the other translations, seven of them in Deuteronomy. Each of them speaks of worshiping the Lord. These verses have to do with a reverence for Almighty God.

In the New Testament times there was a woman who had been hemorrhaging for twelve years and couldn't find any help from doctors. She braved the crowd to reach out and touch the hem of Jesus' garment. Ray Vander Laan teaches that the five-knotted cord she would've grabbed on his rabbi garb signified the books of Torah, and was indicative of the fulfillment of Messiah. It wasn't something she did easily or took lightly. When Jesus singled her out in front of the entire crowd she "came and fell at his feet trembling with fear" (Mark 5:33). This was an act of reverent worship.

The apostle Paul used the phrase "fear and trembling" three times. The most notorious instance is to the church in Philippi where he writes, "Work out your plan of salvation with fear and trembling" (Phil 2:12). He is saying let your lifestyle speak of the reverence you have for Almighty God.

The fear we have for the Lord is not frightening but reverent. He is holy and we are awestruck. He has invited us into relationship. We need it, long for it, ache and yearn for it. And we accept it. But we never take it lightly. We fear him for he is holy. Let our very lifestyles speak of this reverent worship.

What might that look like for you today - reverent worship?

Not on My Watch

> *Deuteronomy 17:15-19*
>
> *Go ahead and appoint a king, but make sure that he is an Israelite and that he is the one the LORD has chosen. The king should not have many horses, especially those from Egypt. The LORD has said never to go back there again. And the king must not have a lot of wives--they might tempt him to be unfaithful to the LORD. Finally, the king must not try to get huge amounts of silver and gold. The official copy of God's laws will be kept by the priests of the Levi tribe. So, as soon as anyone becomes king, he must go to the priests and write out a copy of these laws while they watch. Each day the king must read and obey these laws, so that he will learn to worship the LORD with fear and trembling.*

This Scripture passage speaks of God's acquiescence to the wrongful desires of Israel. He gives them permission to have a king. But let's be straight; he didn't want Israel to have a king. He intended to be their King himself. "The Lord answered, 'Samuel, do everything they want you to do. I am really the one they have rejected as king'" (2 Sam 8:7).

It didn't take very long for the idea of monarchy to backfire. The first king, Saul, became so paranoid and self-righteous as to take his eyes off the Lord. He died a pitied death on the hillside in battle. King David, the second one, was a godly and righteous man, albeit he had glaring failures. He is the king of record regarding lineage. In particular, the Christ is the Son of David. The third king, Solomon, was the embodiment of this very disclaimer. Solomon did everything the Lord warned the Israelite kings not to do. Horses? Yes, quite an impressive fleet. Foreign wives? And how! Seven-hundred wives and three-hundred concubines. And as far as massive amounts of gold and silver? Well, let's just say, he could have opened the Jerusalem Mint. He was very wise in the early years, but gives every indication of slipping far away from the Lord in his waning years.

Interestingly, the single most important job of the king would be to have in his possession a copy of the Law and make sure it was adhered to.

The word Torah carries the implication of not just law in the sense of lines and precepts, but also instruction, or that is to say, what is preferable and beneficial. Perhaps this is why David is the greatest king in the history of Israel. He meditated on the Law day and night. He says as much in Psalm 1. Previously, at the exchange of leadership from Deliverer Moses to General Joshua, God reminded him of this. "Do not let this book of the Law depart from your mouth. Meditate on it day and night so that you may be careful to do everything written in it. Then you will be prosperous and successful" (Josh 1:8).

With the passage of time, eventually, the kings neglected the Law entirely. This atrocity continued unabated until the rise of one Josiah. Tradition says that when wicked King Ahaz had all copies of Torah burned, the priests hid one copy between the lines of bricks in the Temple wall. Years later when Josiah began to lead reforms, one of his objectives was to repair the breeches in the wall. That's when the scroll was discovered again in a fresh and new way. It didn't matter that Josiah had not been dealt the right cards in life. Josiah made no excuses. He could have become agitated. *"I'm held accountable by these texts? Okay, who forgot to tell me that? It was found where, in the duct work? Are you kidding me? What happened?"* Instead, the moment he became aware of his duties as a king he assumed responsibility for his actions. He called the people to repentance. Josiah's attitude was, *"Oh no! Israel is not going to the dogs. Not on my watch."*

Wouldn't it be wonderful if you and I could recapture a passionate love for Scripture? A holy zeal for the Law of the Lord? You have the power to effect change for your life. Don't sit idly by and watch your life go down the tubes while your Bible collects dust on the shelf. Don't let your Bible app get lost in a plethora of useless icons. NO. Not on my watch!

The Compassionate Heart of God

Deuteronomy 24:19-22

If you forget to bring in a stack of harvested grain, don't go back in the field to get it. Leave it for the poor, including foreigners, orphans, and widows, and the LORD will make you successful in everything you do.

When you harvest your olives, don't try to get them all for yourself, but leave some for the poor. And when you pick your grapes, go over the vines only once, then let the poor have what is left. You lived in poverty as slaves in Egypt until the LORD your God rescued you. That's why I am giving you these laws.

I'm impressed that God has a compassionate heart. At base he is moved with love to aid hurting ones. Often throughout these chapters you will read phrases that speak of his desire for Israel to be kind to runaway slaves, foreigners, poor, widows and orphans. And then it will be followed by a disclaimer that runs along these lines, *"Remember, you were slaves in Egypt. That's why I'm giving you these instructions."*

It is a fair accountability he calls for. Nationally, Moab and Ammon will not be allowed any mercy. They were party to attempting to kill Israel in the wilderness by not allowing them passage through their land. Edom, though, is tacitly part of the family line and is to receive gracious treatment, though in time they will be judged too for their poor treatment of Israel.

Individually, a man who marries a woman and makes false accusation about her virginity is beaten. Her just cause is upheld. If you see an oxen has stumbled under a heavy load, stop and assist. Help him get back on his feet. If you bring in your harvest and remember that you left one stack in the field don't go back and get it. Trust that God worked through your forgetfulness to bless the poor. God is at base compassionate.

Some people view God as a mean, vindictive father who is bent on a personal vendetta to take out his aggression on them. It is a horrible game of one-upmanship. For every good deed they do there are two bad deeds that weigh them down. Surely God is out to get them. He's going to prove his justice on them. But that's not the God revealed in the Bible.

The compassionate heart of God weaves through his people's history and winds into the Palestinian countryside to a village called Nazareth. In an era of evil, paranoid, tyrant thrones a King ascends who needs no accolades. His coronation? A cross on the hillside called the Place of the Skull. Why? The compassionate heart of God. "For God so loved the world that he gave his one and only Son that whoever believes in him shall not perish but have eternal life" (John 3:16).

Loose Shoe, Loose Shoe!

Deuteronomy 25:5-10

Suppose two brothers are living on the same property, when one of them dies without having a son to carry on his name. If this

> happens, his widow must not marry anyone outside the family. Instead, she must marry her late husband's brother, and their first son will be the legal son of the dead man.
>
> But suppose the brother refuses to marry the widow. She must go to a meeting of the town leaders at the town gate and say, "My husband died without having a son to carry on his name. And my husband's brother refuses to marry me so I can have a son."
>
> The leaders will call the living brother to the town gate and try to persuade him to marry the widow. But if he doesn't change his mind and marry her, she must go over to him while the town leaders watch. She will pull off one of his sandals and spit in his face, while saying, "That's what happens to a man who won't help provide descendants for his dead brother." From then on, that man's family will be known as "the family of the man whose sandal was pulled off."

Possibly no practice in the Bible is more confusing to American minds than this entirely other-culture act of the disgruntled sister-in-law removing the man's sandal and spitting in his face. But then, if someone time-traveled from there into our contemporary world and tried to comprehend a witness raising the right hand and swearing, it would be difficult to explain as well.

As a contacts-wearing, glasses-owning, RK surgery-needing American, I remember the taunts of *"Four Eyes, Four Eyes!"* No elementary grade jeering could rival the chants of ancient Israel, *"Loose Shoe, Loose Shoe!"* This ancient tradition may shed light on why an Iraqi threw his shoe at President George W. Bush while he made a speech in the Middle East. It was the same as heckling.

The reason a man in that culture would refuse to father a child with his dead brother's wife had nothing to do with morality. His temptation was money. If there was no child born to her then all the property became his. Greed was the issue.

The shoe, for some unknown reason, had to do with the exchange of property in ancient times. Boaz bought the rights to Ruth, her mother-in-law, Naomi, and all the property. The kinsman redeemer renounced his legal right to all of it. He took off his shoe and handed it to Boaz.

We can grasp the concept if we think hard about it. In the early days of our nation Americans who moved west were given the opportunity to stake their claim in uncharted territory. If they were willing to homestead it, the land was theirs. Ancient Israel had a similar type of homesteading. They called it "putting their foot" on the land that they wished to stake claim of. In Deuteronomy 11, Moses told the Israelites every place they set their feet would be theirs for inheritance. Certainly modern man understands the desire to have a place to put his feet up.

Psalm 60 parades a litany of nations God will triumph over. In verse 8 he indicates ownership metaphorically. It says he tosses his sandal over Edom. Conversely, the shoes of the righteous, when welcomed, bring peace. Isaiah 52:7 speaks of the missionary mind of God. "How beautiful on the mountain are the feet of him who brings good news."

The most significant thing about Deuteronomy 25 is verse 10, where the name of the family is changed. From now on he will be known as "Loose Sandal." Not just him, but his whole family line. It is the most derogatory of terms, all because he was greedy and wanted property that wasn't rightfully his. *"Loose Sandal, Loose Sandal."*

How amazing that John the Baptist instructed his listening crowd, there was one coming after him who was before him! "I'm not worthy to reach down and loose his sandal" (John 1:27). Perhaps it was idiomatic. Jesus has every right to the land. Jesus has not neglected his family, quite the opposite he has called us all brothers!

Warfare

> *Deuteronomy 32:30*
>
> *How could one enemy soldier chase a thousand of Israel's troops? Or how could two of theirs pursue ten thousand of ours? It can only happen if the LORD stops protecting Israel and lets the enemy win.*

The young general, Ulysses S. Grant, raced to the top of the hill. He writes in his autobiography that his heart was beating so fast, he could feel it all the way up in his throat, pounding. Now, the thing that happened next was truly amazing. And it defined the career of this brilliant war hero. He says that he peaked to the top of the hill with his soldiers in charge behind him. It was different from any of the battles he had faced in the Mexican War because he knew, now, that he was responsible for their lives. When he got to the top of the hill and looked over the ridge, his enemy, which was led at that time by a Lieutenant Thomas, had fled for their lives, running to get away from them. It was the first time that he ever realized the enemy was afraid of them too.

Deuteronomy speaks of the fact that when we trust in the Lord our God, who is our Rock, we can trust him wholly, and know that one warrior has the ability to set a thousand people running. It teaches that two, coming together in unison, have the ability to make 10,000 soldiers flee for their lives.

I pray for the same application to be true to you as a New Testament Christian. I know you face battles. I believe that the Lord your God will set your enemy running away from you. If you are godly, and righteous, and live a life of prayer and devotion, I just believe you're going to experience profound victories in your life. And I pray that for you today.

3

Trust in War Times

GROUP 3: TRUST IN WAR TIMES

The Scarlet Cord

Joshua 2:17-21

The spies said: You made us promise to let you and your family live. We will keep our promise, but you can't tell anyone why we were here. You must tie this red rope on your window when we attack, and your father and mother, your brothers, and everyone else in your family must be here with you. We'll take the blame if anyone who stays in this house gets hurt. But anyone who leaves your house will be killed, and it won't be our fault.

"I'll do exactly what you said," Rahab promised. Then she sent them on their way and tied the red rope to the window.

Careful observation shows this rope spoken of at Rahab's house was scarlet red. This blood-colored rope symbolizes the cord that ties the whole Bible together. The blood that Jesus shed on the cross purchased our salvation. In the same way Rahab's mother and father, brothers and sisters, and children were safe so long as they stayed inside the house with the red rope, you and I are safe as long as we are under the blood of Jesus.

I can just see Rahab in the coming days, her hometown under siege by Israel. They are marching around the outside perimeter. She's dangling the red rope, a visual reminder to the army below. Each time she spots the spies she had assisted there is excitement in her house. *"They're the ones, those two, right there. Remember?"* Winks and nods at first, and then waves and catcalls as the days give way to the inevitable. Around and around Joshua and the children of Israel march like vultures circling their prey. Perhaps fear sets in. *"Please don't forget our agreement. Remember how I helped you."* As the vanguard proceeds around the city, seven times on the final day, her kids call out, *"Mom, I see Joshua again. Should we dangle the red rope." "Yes,"* comes the reply. *"Shake the rope. Just make sure you are careful kids. Don't do anything to hurt the rope. Don't let it fall. Be very careful. That red rope must stay in the window. And you must stay in the house! Don't leave the house kids!"*

Each time the Israelites pass around they remember the branch of hyssop and the blood of the lamb applied to the doorposts the night of the Exodus from Egypt. Ancestors now dead had told them their whole lives in the wilderness about that night. *"That's the one. Right up there. That window. The one with the scarlet cord. See the lady waving. Don't harm that house."*

"Is the red rope important Mama? Is that why it's been in the window ever since those two men were here?" You know she would never risk taking it out of the window, not even for a moment. *"Yes children, the red rope is very important. It's important for you, for Mama, for Papaw and Grandma. The red rope is very, very important."*

On the seventh cycle of the seventh day when Joshua gave the signal and a mighty roar rose up, Rahab must have wondered and doubted. *"Will they honor the red rope? I'm a foreigner. They know my past. They know all the things I've done wrong. Will the scarlet cord hold?"* It held. Her home was built into the very wall. The walls of Jericho tumbled. Did she lose everything except for her life and the lives of her loved ones?

There is a scarlet cord that ties two Testaments together from beginning to end. That scarlet cord ties two millenniums together. It even reaches back to the earliest times. It is anchored around the foundation of the world. Children, trust the scarlet cord. The scarlet cord will hold. Trust the scarlet cord.

Achan's Ache

Joshua 7:20-22

"It's true," Achan answered. "I sinned and disobeyed the LORD God of Israel. While we were in Jericho, I saw a beautiful Babylonian robe, two hundred pieces of silver, and a gold bar that weighed the same as fifty pieces of gold. I wanted them for myself, so I took them. I dug a hole under my tent and hid the silver, the gold, and the robe." Joshua had some people run to Achan's tent, where they found the silver, the gold, and the robe.

Achan's heart was racing so fast he couldn't contain it. What a rush of adrenalin! The Israeli crowd was pumped sky high. Seven days of marching around Jericho; and today seven trips around. Now it was time. The trumpet blasted, the roar erupted from the crowd, some chants of praise, other sounds of indiscernible guttural groans and yells. The walls began to shift this way and that, swaying, and in an instant, a thunderous collapse. A mushroom cloud swelled upon the landscape. His comrades disappeared into the dust in front of him. He could hear their jubilant screams echoing and boomeranging. This was it. God was giving them their first city of many.

Achan raced forward, his sword drawn, wielding it wildly. Up over the massive pile of stones, canvassing the debris, through the settling soot to a landing where he peered right, opposite the ones before him. He lunged through a dark, natural tunnel created by the falling pattern of massive stones into a clearing where the sudden sunburst pierced his eyes. The chaos of slaughter was already settling by now. It was a fast annihilation. Out of his peripheral he caught an image of one family huddled, being escorted by Joshua's top men. *"That must be Rahab,"* he thought as he scampered. Distanced from the entrance now, the battalion was thinning out, flaring off in myriad of directions, scouring and sweeping, making sure. Achan wound deeper, farther, into the labyrinth of the city. *"Over there,"* he thought, *"I'll try over there."* A cluster of homes joined by block stone, ascending upward, simple one-room dwellings with roof-top parapets that stepped up the natural lay of the land.

Achan dashed in, through, around, up and over. Again and again. Room after room. The vanguard had done its job well. No one. Not a person left. One last sweep of these few high places and then he would join up with the victorious warriors to trade stories. His upright weapon pressed close to his chest, he girdled around the doorway opening into the airy room that allowed just a splash of sunlight from the roof line ducts. There it was, brilliant, beautiful. He hadn't expected this. Not at all. Maybe an angry, bewildered inhabitant, or a fearful, shaking child, that, yes he would expect, but not this. A treasure, an abandoned treasure. He sheathed his sword. Wedges of gold. *"This can't be."* But it was. Stacked in the corner, enveloped by a lake of coins. He dropped to his knees aghast. That's when he noticed the wardrobe. *"Just look at them. Woven robes. They must be from Babylon."*

It was in this moment he recalled the assignment, completely destroy the city of Jericho, everything. Every bit of it is devoted to destruction. *"Yeah, but this find?"* He rationalized. *"This is different. This is precious."* Then he conceived the plan. *"I'll wrap some of these coins in one of those robes. Maybe just one wedge of gold too. I can tuck it inside my armor. No one will ever know!"* He reasoned that he could bury it beneath the tent wherever he camped. *"Why, once we settle the land I can come back. It'll be my private stash."* He may have even convinced himself that it was God's good fortune, this forbidden fruit.

The thing that he didn't destroy destroyed him!

Whenever we attempt to replace relationship with God with anything or anyone else it is always because there is an ache inside of us. Something yearns. We long. We hurt. Nothing will scratch the itch. Only God can satisfy. Achan's Ache is a lesson to each one of us. Obey carefully.

Lumberjacks and Waterboys

Joshua 9:14

The Israelites tried some of the food, but they did not ask the LORD if he wanted them to make a treaty.

Joshua 9 gives the account of the deceptive Gibeonites who tricked the Israelites into a peace treaty that they definitely would not have honored had they known they were actually near neighbors. The Gibeonites put old, worn-out cargo bags on their pack mules, and toted old, crusty, moldy bread to intimate that they had traveled a long, hard journey. They said, *"Look here at our old shoes, worn clean through."* They duped Joshua and the leaders into a peace treaty because the Jews didn't consult the Lord for advice. One wonders what instructions the Israelites would've received if they had only prayed.

The Israelites should have been more discerning, and I'm convinced they would've been, had they prayed. When the Gibeonites claimed their bread had become moldy with the long journey, the Israelites should have remembered how God had given them manna every morning for forty years. When the Gibeonites claimed their shoes had worn out, the Israelites should have remembered how God sustained them in the wilderness and their shoes didn't wear out for forty years.

Once the truth came out many of the Israelites wanted to kill the Gibeonites; but Joshua wouldn't allow it. He honored his covenant to keep them safe even though they had lied. He relegated them to cutting wood and carrying water. Through the years these lumberjacks and water boys became pretty clandestine in the history of the Jews. Israel had to come to their defense against an alliance of five enemy kings. The land of the Gibeonites became the only kingdom the Israelites didn't conquer. The murder of Amasa was in response to it all. Gibeon was, in fact, the source of civil war for Israel. Gibeon became a field of daggers and hostility, a place of rebellion.

I have a very dear friend who was once pastor of a congregation that was thriving, and growing exponentially. When the congregation had outgrown the building it seemed a natural next step to expand. Without truly waiting before the Lord in prayer, he, along with the other leaders, hired the best architect in the city and aggressively pursued a massive building program. He openly admits that it wasn't sufficiently prayed over. They just simply sought the consultation of a brilliant, but ungodly business man. In short order the economy turned south and families pulled out and relocated. It was a very, very difficult stretch for my friend. He learned a valuable lesson through it all. His watchword became, "Blessed is the man who does not walk in the counsel of the ungodly; or stand in the way of sinners, or sit in the seat of the scornful; but his delight is in the law of the Lord, and on his law he meditates day and night." Psalm 1:1, 2.

Allow no lumberjacks and water boys to jump on your band wagon. Consult God before making any other consultations.

Divine Intervention

> *Joshua 10:42*
>
> *The Lord fought on Israel's side, so Joshua and the Israelite army were able to capture these kings and take their land.*

The White House was on fire and President Madison and his administration had already left. In fact, they were seriously considering abandoning Washington, D.C. entirely. No, I'm not rewriting history. I'm sharing factual accounts with you. The thing that happened next is nothing short of a miracle. A hurricane-force gale blew through. It brought a tremendous thunderstorm. The rain poured down and it put out the fire at the White House. It also caused the British to pull back from their advance. And that's how America was rescued.

Joshua 10 speaks about God Almighty fighting on behalf of Israel himself. I truly believe sometimes God intervenes in our situations to bring about his victory. You might be facing a fiery storm today. But I hope you will stay encouraged. Keep being faithful because at just the right time God will deliver you. Stay true to his Word. He might be planning to put out fires in your life in a remarkable way.

Ponds and Prayer

> *Judges 1:15*
>
> *She answered, "I need your help. The land you gave me is in the Southern Desert, so please give me some spring-fed ponds for a water supply."*

In these chapters we are not reading about individuals but tribes. Over and over we read descriptions of the tribes, their land, their inheritance. In this setting suddenly we have three individual names crop up. Caleb was a fine leader, a tested man of integrity, character and tenure. Cohort of Joshua, he was strong and faithful in his aging years, capable of taking enemy territory and settling it as his inheritance at eighty-five. His son-in-law, Othniel, captured the land of Kiriath-Sepher to win his bride, Achsah. He was later a judge of Israel, highly respected. Judges 3 describes him being filled with the Spirit in a season of real decline on the part of the Israelites. He led them into battle against their enemy Cushan Rithathaim. Othniel was a mighty warrior and deliverer for Israel. Achsah, Caleb's daughter, Othniel's bride, was opportunistic and seized the moment for a wedding gift. Caleb gave her the upper and lower streams. These were good people, really good people.

Steven A. Rosen and Gideon Avni, both have PhDs and have done extensive archaeological work in the Negev with Israeli Antiquities Authority. They paint a picture of arid desert in the southern parts with only nomadic peoples who would live there during the milder winters. But in the northern regions, where Achsah's ponds seem to have been, they see evidence of superstructures of rocks which were positioned to hold down tents, and of farmlands. This was possible because of primitive irrigation systems from the mountain runoff. With water supply at a premium Caleb's gift to his daughter was a spectacular wedding gift.

The great Baptist minister of the 19th Century, Charles Haddon Spurgeon, taught that this Scripture teaches us perseverance in prayer. Achsah was bold to ask for what she needed. She knew her father would meet her need. Caleb answered yes almost before she could get the request out of her mouth. Bob Deffinbaugh agrees with this logic because it is possible the ponds were in an area that had been taken but not occupied. It took great faith to ask for it, and action to acquire it once it was given.

A Sharp Attack on Dullness

Judges 3:15, 16

*The Israelites begged the L*ORD *for help, and the L*ORD *chose Ehud from the Benjamin tribe to rescue them. They put Ehud in charge of taking the taxes to King Eglon, but before Ehud went, he made a double-edged dagger. Ehud was left-handed, so he strapped the dagger to his right thigh, where it would be hidden under his robes.*

Ehud is a judge who serves in a time when Israel is very passive spiritually. Collectively, at a national level, they repeatedly drift in and out of fervor. It is clear the judges were far more than the image we contrive in an American stereotype, black robed dignitaries seated ceremonially and being approached at the bench. No, the judges of ancient Israel were not only judicial; they were generals who delivered Israel out of apostasy.

This story of Ehud is rich with symbolism. He had a double-edged sword. Centuries removed the writer of Hebrews draws upon this imagery using it to describe the Word of God. "The word of God is living and active, sharper than any double-edged sword" (Heb 4:12, NIV). John wrote a Revelation of Jesus Christ. In it twice he quoted Jesus, the living Word, as wielding a double edged sword. "I am the one who has the sharp double-edged sword! Listen to what I say" (Rev 2:12). The sword was hidden under Ehud's robe. Later King David gives the imagery of hiding God's Word in our hearts. "Thy Word have I hidden in my heart that I might not sin against God" (Ps 119:11). In the story Ehud buries his sword deep into the obese King Eglon. The narrative intends to portray Eglon's slothfulness as his downfall. Ehud uses his concealed sword to launch a sharp attack on dullness. This story can give us a real picture of the role God's Word has in our lives. We might tend to think of hiding God's Word in our hearts as a defensive maneuver; but the hidden sword of this story is quite offensive. Wield the Word as a tactical operation attacking all areas of lethargy, listlessness, and passivity of your life.

Housewife Gone Covert

Judges 4:9

*"All right, I'll go!" she replied. "But I'm warning you that the L*ORD *is going to let a woman defeat Sisera, and no one will honor you for winning the battle."*

The events of Judges 3 and 4 are about individuals stepping up to the plate and doing what was needed. It singles out women who did what men typically did in the culture, and honors their heroics. Deborah fulfills the role of judge, prophet and general. She conducted Torah classes under a large gathering tree. She prophesied to Barak that he should lead the army with 10,000 troops. When he hesitated she led the charge at his request. A key figure in the victory was Jael, a housewife gone covert, she lured the enemy general and carried out his execution making use of a tent peg and hammer. Any blunt object will do. Her name means mountain goat, not very endearing in our day, but in her time it signified ascent, climbing higher.

What is noticeable in Deborah's song is the absence of people who should've been there to help. Apparently there wasn't unanimity of purpose. The tribe of Reuben did not join the alliance in this important Battle of Jabin. "Gilead" references the tribes that stayed on the other side of the Jordan; that would mean not only Reuben, but Gad and East Manasseh as well. The tribes of Dan and Asher stayed out of the alliance too. The song may hint at the fact that they felt secure on the coast. But Zebulun and Naphtali risked their lives and God delivered them. So this ragtag bunch of soldiers, a mere 10,000 when it could've easily numbered into six digits if there was support of the entire nation, was led by one woman and delivered by another.

There is an ongoing hot button issue in God's Church, the role of women in ministry. It has steeped at a low grade for decades and is not likely to be resolved any time soon. In my particular tribe ladies were not allowed to carry a license for ministry, but could be evangelists, in the early years. Often women would go into a town that needed a new work and begin holding a revival. Since they could be evangelists, but not pastors, they would hold "revival meetings" for four or five years. I'm glad to say after the first twenty-one years our movement voted to bring its policy into conformity with its practice. Since that time women have been given opportunity to pursue license, ordination, degrees, hold offices in executive leadership, and teach in our universities. A woman can be a university president, a district superintendent, even the highest elected national office which is the general superintendent.

Denominations and non-denoms alike struggle on both sides of the issue. There are nuances and intricacies with the role of women in the Church. On the one hand, some do not allow women to hold positions of leadership over men. This is not motivated by bias or discrimination in any respect. Brilliant minds with heartfelt convictions have arrived prayerfully at a decision that needs to be respected and honored. These are individuals who value the integrity of Scripture very highly. And, many millions of women want the church world to know they believe this way, not from coercion but cohesion. These are deeply held views based upon theological understanding from a context that demands such an interpretation in order to be accurate. On the other hand, some believe in order to be true to Scripture we must mine timeless principles out of their other-worldly context to bring them into a current modality of ministry that respects the emergence of culture. There are also millions who want the church world to know the Bible has the highest place in their hearts, and they do not adhere to a liberal feminism, but at the same time they deeply believe women should lead in the twenty-first century. They have arrived at this decision with a careful exegesis and hermeneutic.

As I say, there are sticking points and I don't think the discussion is going away any time soon, at least not from my estimation. Regardless, who are the women in your life who have helped shape you? Brought you to this point? Are there ladies who have been influential in your life? There was probably a lady who taught Sunday School, or one who ushered in the small church, or filled the pulpit when needed, or led the prayer meeting, or counted the offering, or organized the potluck, maybe a housewife gone covert. There's probably a lot of them. Pause. Pray for their wellbeing. Offer thanks for their persuasion. All around you are mighty, godly women able to slay the enemy general.

Deflected Accolades

Judges 8:23

"No," Gideon replied, "I won't be your king, and my son won't be king either. Only the LORD is your ruler."

History is filled with special people who deflected accolades and chose the right thing over the wrong. Gideon states an important principle during the era of the Judges. The Lord is supposed to be your king. I will not ascend any throne. Gideon was not perfect, not by any stretch. Even in this instance he collected all the gold from his conquest and fashioned it into an idol that became a stumbling block to Israel. But at least he had the good sense not to accept the offer of kingship because he understood that was a title that belonged to God alone.

It was never God's plan for Israel to have a king. He only acquiesced to their continual begging. The history of the nations after the conquest of the Promised Land moved from the era of Judges to Prophets and then to Kings. This story of Gideon takes place in the era of Judges. Later, the narrative reiterates the same fact in the era of the Prophets as they are transitioning to Kings. "The Lord answered: Samuel, do everything they want you to do. I am really the one they have rejected as king" (1 Sam 8:7). Gideon and Samuel understood clearly that Israel was never to have a king. God himself would govern them.

Luke said of Jesus, "He will rule the people of Israel forever, and his kingdom will never end" (Luke 1:33). The inbreaking of the kingdom of God looked very different from the expected norm when it actually appeared with Christ. Healings not holdings. Deliverances not duties. Feedings not feudalism. Truth not twist. Direction not diplomacy. The inbreaking of the kingdom resembled rule but in some ways seemed upside down. So much was this the case that when Jesus was questioned by the prefect, Pilate asked him if he was a king. Jesus toyed with him. "Are you asking for yourself?" In other words, *"Want to join the cause?"* And when Pilate pressed him for a straight answer Jesus replied, "My kingdom doesn't belong to this world" (John 18:36).

It is certain when we speak of the kingdom of God we are entering discussion of mystery beyond us. Life will sometimes throw honors your way. Be gracious. Be quick to deflect praise to other people and give glory to God that is rightfully his.

He Intervenes

> *Judges 9:15*
>
> *The thornbush replied, "If you really want me to be your king, then come into my shade and I will protect you. But if you're deceiving me, I'll start a fire that will spread out and destroy the cedars of Lebanon."*

What an amazing allegory is given by Jotham about the evil way his half-brother Abimelech tried to forcibly assume the kingdom of Shechem. Remember Shechem? Years earlier Shechem was the young man who raped Dinah, sister to the twelve sons of Jacob. He was the best of the town. They named the town after him. Simeon and Levi took matters into their own hands and got revenge. They lured the town into a covenant of circumcision. And then while the men were still sore three days later, Simeon and Levi routed the city and killed them all. It was a bloodbath. Father Jacob packed the camp quickly and they made their escape en route to Egypt. By now hundreds of years have passed. The town has been rebuilt. Seventy sons of Jacob went to Egypt, now, centuries later, seventy sons of Gideon are in involved in pure bedlam at Shechem.

The proposition for the kingship went out to the prominent trees of the forest. Olive Tree said, "I'm too busy making oil to wave my branches higher than yours." Fig Tree said, "I can't quit making fruit just to rule." Grape Vine said, "I'm not going to stop making wine simply for the fanfare." But Thorn Bush was happy to be the king.

Then Jotham said if Abimelech was honorable he wished him well; but his evil motives had already shown through in the senseless slaughter of his 68 brothers. Jotham predicted evil would spread like a brush fire through thorn bushes. And it happened just as he prophesied. Ironically, Abimelech's father, Gideon, had been asked to be king and he turned it down. Why? God himself was Israel's king. Yeah, the same Gideon who said his son would not be king. Gideon even named one of his sons Abimelech. Abi – "my father"; melech – "king". My father is king. How ironic that this was the very son, out of the 70, who massacred his brothers and attempted to ascend the throne. Jotham alone escaped by the skin of his teeth, relocated and lived in isolation for safety the rest of his life.

Unspeakable tragedy, horrible carnage, but God will bring beauty from the ashes. Abimelech wasn't from the right tribe anyway. His father Gideon traced his lineage from Joseph. The kingship would come from Judah. In time, the Lion of the Tribe of Judah, who is Jesus, will ascend his throne that will never cease, his unshakeable kingdom. He intervenes in the suffering humanity.

The Punch Lineage

> *Ruth 4:13-22*
>
> *Boaz married Ruth, and the LORD blessed her with a son. After his birth, the women said to Naomi:*
>
> *Praise the LORD! Today he has given you a grandson to take care of you. We pray that the boy will grow up to be famous everywhere in Israel. He will make you happy and take care of you in your old age, because he is the son of your daughter-in-law. And she loves you more than seven sons of your own would love you.*

> Naomi loved the boy and took good care of him. The neighborhood women named him Obed, but they called him "Naomi's Boy."
>
> When Obed grew up he had a son named Jesse, who later became the father of King David. Here is a list of the ancestors of David: Jesse, Obed, Boaz, Salmon, Nahshon, Amminadab, Ram, Hezron, and Perez.

This is a beautiful short story of the life of Ruth, a young widow, and her mother-in-law, Naomi. It shows loyalty and devotion. It's a remarkable example of the caring intermingling and camaraderie of the Jewish heritage. Family takes care of one another. Boaz has a heart that is pure. He's a man of integrity. In keeping with Judeo Law he marries the widow of his dead relative, takes on the property rights of Naomi, and fathers a child so that the name Elimelech can be carried forward. Boaz does things right. He does it by the book. He is a righteous man. He walks in careful obedience.

Two things stand out from the story. First, there is beautiful symbolism in the preservation of the name Elimelech. The name means "My God is King." In a stretch where Israel has played with the idea of having a king like other nations, e.g. - Gideon who turned it down, and Abimelech, his son, who tried to force himself into kingship - comes the subtle recognition on the part of Boaz of how important it is to preserve the name declaring God is the King.

Secondly, here at the end of the short story we are struck with the punch line. It has been hidden until now. The writer has tucked it away masterfully. To now we just think it's a wonderful story of one of the families of Israel; but then we read the punch line. It is actually a punch lineage. Boaz was the great-grandfather of David who Samuel chose as king to replace ungodly Saul. David is the king of record in the score keeping of Israel. His line will last forever. Matthew captures it acutely for us in his first verse, "Jesus Christ, the son of David, the son of Abraham" (Matt 1:1).

Old Testament Theophany

> 1 Samuel 10:3
>
> You'll meet three men on their way to worship God. One of them will be leading three young goats, and another one will be carrying three round loaves of bread, and the last one will be carrying a clay jar of wine.

Though we are told these are men on their way to worship, there are clues that something more is going on here. The Greek word theophany means an appearance of God. These men are on their way up to Bethel - the house of God. I believe this is truly a remarkable appearance of the holy Trinity in human-like form. It calls to mind the holy visitors of Genesis chapter 18 before the destruction of Sodom and Gomorrah. Here in 1 Samuel 10:3 the three men are carrying items that represent their persons. The man carrying three goats evokes thoughts of the sacrificial system of the Old Testament covenant. Typically, this is thought of as the era of God the Father. The man carrying three loaves of bread seems to anticipate the Messiah, Jesus Christ, who names himself the Bread of Life. In the same way a frequent type of the Holy Spirit, in the Old Testament, is wine which is being carried by the third man. There are numerous passages that equate new wine with blessings. In the New Testament (Ephesians 5:18) we are instructed to be filled with the Spirit instead of wine.

Of course, all of this is anachronistic, but the reader of the completed New Testament finds it difficult not to see the allusion when it emerges in the story line. It would be unorthodox exegesis to read these indicators back into the text. However, on a purely devotional thought, it is encouraging to see earmarks of the holy Trinity embedded in the narratives of the old covenant. This is as one would expect it to be if the church fathers who met in Nicaea were correct in articulating the holy Trinity.

What is important to note is the Trinity does not appear aloof and austere but relational. If this is a representation of the holy three, we have them interacting, relating, sharing, and journeying. They are not static. In one real sense, we are separated from the kind of interaction God desires such as walks in the cool of the evening, *"Adam, Eve, where are you?"* In the timelessness of eternity our respect for the Almighty will swell infinitely with reverence at the same time as our friendship grows and grows.

The Blessing of Integrity

1 Samuel 12:3

Let me ask this. Have I ever taken anyone's ox or donkey or forced you to give me anything? Have I ever hurt anyone or taken a bribe to give an unfair decision? Answer me so the Lord

> *and his chosen king can hear you. And if I have done any of these things, I will give it all back.*

Samuel was able to close out fabulously. He finished strong. The prophet was trustworthy and reliable. *"Let me just ask. Have I taken anything that doesn't belong to me?"* What a remarkable example of integrity!

My Dad, James E. Howard, was a wonderful example of integrity to me. He was a pastor for 42 years. Twenty-five of those years he served at the same church. After a quarter of a century of faithful ministry to one congregation they honored him and Mom with a special reception. Story after story poured forth of their integrity. Dad was a community pastor before that was a popular moniker. It seemed as though he knew everyone in the county. We would go to the hospital and he would pop in and out of rooms at the request of people as he passed by. He would introduce himself to some, and before I knew it, he was praying with the individuals. Once, in the last year of Dad's life, following a very serious surgery, as he paced through the hospital on his walker, prematurely at that, he happened by the front counter of the main entrance. He met two new workers that didn't know him yet. I heard him say, "My name is Pastor James Howard, from First Assembly of God. If I can ever be of assistance to you in any way please call. Please know we love you and we are here to be a blessing to you." Here he was in his hospital gown doing visitation with the workers in their environment. He was so comfortable. Unforgettable!

In the last months of his life, as he endured multiple hospital stays, he ministered from the bed. There was Art, a registered nurse, who kept coming to check on Dad even though his shift was completely on the other side of the hospital. Dad told us how he ministered to him when he found Art had been estranged from his father for eleven years. One day Art came in and pointed to his shirt pocket. "Do you know what that is, Pastor? That's my boarding pass. I'm going to see my Dad." There was Freddy, the custodian. In the early morning hours my brother was awakened from the recliner to see a gentlemen emptying the trash. He thought Dad was fully asleep; but Dad spoke out, "Is that you Freddy?" In soft, hushed tones, "Yes sir, Pastor, it's me." Again Dad's voice intoned, "I love you Freddy." And after a precious silent moment, "I love you too, Pastor." Before Dad left the hospital his primary care physician walked into the room and told the family that our father had touched every individual person who worked in the hospital. Every doctor, every nurse, every administrator, every member of the janitorial staff, every single one - all of them had compared notes and realized that he had invested in each one of them. It really stood out to them because often when individuals have received a negative report from the doctors they can become pretty testy and somewhat edgy. Dealing with the fallout in emotions is common. How refreshing to have a patient who remained positive, hopeful, and encouraging!

"The righteous man walks in his integrity; his children are blessed after him" (Prov 20:7).

At Dad's viewing the crowds gathered. Individuals commented that they waited outside an hour and fifteen minutes and it was their honor. A family friend, David Shaddick, came up and showed me a business card that was browned by the years and curled around the edges. On it was a picture of a much younger version of my Dad when he was brand new to the church. He said, "Tonight I'm giving this to your Mom. I carried it in my wallet for twenty-five years. From now on I will carry him in my heart." At the funeral, the next day, the sanctuary was packed with standing room only. We had moved it to a larger church to attempt to accommodate the crowd. I will never forget looking back from the family car at the procession of cars as far as the eye could see. Five months later his five sons combined to lead worship at a men's conference with the theme *Legacy*. It was just beginning to dawn on me what a wonderful example of integrity my father was to me. At times when I am tempted to stray or become weary or get embittered or just let up... the integrity of my father makes me want to finish strong.

Remember Wally Pipp

1 Samuel 12:24

You also must obey the LORD—you must worship him with all your heart and remember the great things he has done for you.

Do you know the name Wally Pipp? Probably not. He was the starting first baseman for the New York Yankees. He was the American League Homerun Champ in 1916 and 1917, the first Yankee to be a homerun champion. He had helped recruit a young player from Columbia University, and even taught him everything he knew about playing first base. Wally Pipp took a day off when he had a bad headache one day, though the manager was looking for a chance to shake-up the lineup a little. Coach Miller Huggins thought he would give the young kid a chance. It was the first game of 2,130 straight for Lou Gehrig. Wally Pipp never started for the Yankees again. Don't skip one day in your walk with the Lord. Stay faithful.

You Are Alright

> *1 Samuel 17:18b*
>
> *Find out how your brothers are doing and bring back something that shows they're alright.*

I'd say David brought back something that showed they were alright, alright! We have the gross image of the handsome, ruddy young man holding the head of his victim, the mighty champion, Goliath. I see him grasping the heathen taunter by the hair, dangling the *cabaso* in one hand, with the other clutching his victim's very own sword. The sword would follow David all through his journeys, not only as a trophy, but also as a practical weapon. Later he would say of Goliath's sword, "There's none like it." With the spoils still in his hands he reports to his superior, Saul. It must have been one drippy mess. I wonder if David ever had the conversation with his father, in which Jesse said, "Son, when I said bring back something, I was thinking more of a note, or maybe a used bow string. That would've been fine."

Keep little reminders of your victories. I have a rock on my shelf from a prayer mountain experience more than twenty years ago. I resolved some things that night, and when I look at that rock I remember my commitment. I keep a journal for answered prayers, spiritual development, significant family events, difficult encounters, as well as victorious triumphs. It is encouraging to go back from time to time and read the track record of God's faithfulness. Bring back something that shows you are alright.

A Really Special Friend

> *1 Samuel 20:14*
>
> *Someday the Lord will wipe out all of your enemies. Then if I'm still alive, please be as kind to me as the Lord has been. But if I'm dead, be kind to my family.*

This was a covenant agreement between two great friends, Jonathan and David. As I write we are enjoying coverage of the London Olympics. It reminds me of a friendship story of Olympic proportions.

Jesse Owens seemed sure to win the long jump at the 1936 Games. The year before he had jumped 26 feet, 8 1/4 inches, a record that would stand for 25 years. As he walked to the long-jump pit, however, Owens saw a tall, blue-eyed, blond German taking practice jumps in the 26-foot range. Owens felt nervous. He was acutely aware of the Nazis' desire to prove "Aryan superiority," especially over blacks. At this point, the tall German introduced himself as Luz Long. "You should be able to qualify with your eyes closed!" he said to Owens, referring to his two jumps. For the next few moments the black son of a sharecropper and the white model of Nazi manhood chatted. Then Long made a suggestion. Since the qualifying distance was only 23 feet, 5 1/2 inches, why not make a mark several inches before the takeoff board and jump from there, just to play it safe? Owens did and qualified easily. In the finals Owens set an Olympic record and earned the second of four golds. The first person to congratulate him was Luz Long, in full view of Adolf Hitler. Owens never again saw Long, who was killed in World War II. "You could melt down all the medals and cups I have," Owens later wrote, "and they wouldn't be a platting on the 24-carat friendship I felt for Luz Long."

David kept his promise to Jonathan, inviting his crippled son, Mephibosheth, to sit at his table every day. And he gave him land to boot. Some friendships transcend the grave.

Give Me a Sign

> 1 Samuel 20:37, 38
>
> *When the boy got near the place where the arrow had landed, Jonathon shouted, "Isn't the arrow on past you?" Jonathon shouted again, "Hurry up! Don't stop!"*

This was a sign to David that matters were beyond his control.

When you think about it, there are actually quite a few instances in Scripture when you read of individuals asking for a sign from God. The example that immediately comes to mind is Gideon placing a "fleece" before the Lord. He needs a little bit of assurance that he is hearing direction from God so he asks for something impossible. Let the morning dew only be accumulated on the wool fleece. That would be a sign that God was with him. This happened. But he was still a little nervous about it, so he prayed the following night that God would let the morning dew cover everything except the fleece. And it happened the second time, too, just as he requested.

Jonathan asked God for a sign. If you will deliver us from the enemy let them taunt me and ask me to come up to them, instead of coming down to pursue me and my armor bearer, as would be expected. David asked the Lord if he and his band of men should go battle against Keilah. The

Lord said yes. The men were uncertain. David asked a second time. God answered with a resounding yes, that he would deliver them.

In this instance, when David is being hunted by his best friend's paranoid father, the two had worked out a signal. Jonathon shot the arrows way past the retriever and yelled to the boy, "Aren't the arrows beyond you?" It meant David's suspicions were true and he needed to run for his life.

I remember a popular sentiment that I heard in lots of church circles growing up. "Don't tempt God, have faith. Don't put a fleece before the Lord." I understand that sentiment. We are not to be suspicious, or rely on portents, or live by omens. But I believe our relationships with the Lord to be far more nuanced than that. I don't see God getting angry in Scripture when his well-intending followers ask for confirmation. To be certain, it isn't healthy to need a sign for any and every thing. But on balance, it is nothing short of wise to pray that God use any possible method to bring clarity, to ask God to close all the wrong doors and open the right one. Give me a sign. Give me a revelation.

Common Sense Isn't Common

1 Samuel 25:25

Don't pay any attention to the good-for-nothing Nabal. His name means 'fool,' and it really fits him!

Nabal didn't have any common sense. His very name means senseless, or foolish. Why did his parents name him this? We don't know. Maybe it was along the lines of Foolhardy, or perhaps, Good Times. All we know is Nabal did a good job of living up to his name. It comes from a word that is used in the Psalms often to mean fool, and once in the Proverbs where it says, "The father of a fool has no joy" (Prov 17:21). Ironically, his wife Abigail excelled in common sense. Her name means "My father is joy," or properly understood, "My father is the source of joy." So, catch this irony, Nabal was a fool and brought zero joy to his father. Which father? He was from the clan of Caleb. Was Caleb rolling over in his grave? His heavenly Father? Did his heavenly Father have no joy? Or both Caleb and the heavenly Father? However, his wife, Abigail, knew her source of joy was found in her father. Which father, her earthly father? Perhaps to an extent. But being a good Hebrew daughter, it was definitely her heavenly Father. She knew her Father was her source of joy.

In the last 24 hours that Nabal was conscious, he foolishly snubbed David and his men, and partied hardy all night long. Abigail bailed him out again with her wisdom and tact. But God found no joy in Nabal. So he was judged and died. And the one who knew her Father was the source of joy became the bride of the King.

You and I are given the opportunity to become the bride of Christ. Boatloads of people all around us are behaving crudely, disrespectfully, and arrogantly; but God will not put up with their debased crassness forever. The time of judgment will come, even as they continue to engage in flippant immorality. But you and I will be clothed in white, resembling Abigail, having RSVP'd the embossed invitation to the Marriage Supper of the Lamb. In a world where common sense isn't common, strive for uncommon valor.

Irony of Two Desperate Kings

1 Samuel 30:6

David was desperate. His soldiers were so upset over what had happened to their sons and daughters that they were thinking about stoning David to death. But he felt the Lord give him strength.

David was desperate. He wasn't king in actuality yet, but he was destined to be king and everybody knew it. The reigning king, Saul, had even vocalized it on numerous occasions. It was all academic.

But on this occasion David could care less about ascending the throne. His wives had been abducted, and his children taken captive. Furthermore all the men in his movement were ready to kill him because their wives and children were taken as well. Their home base of Ziklag, temporary headquarters, had been raided, burned to the ground. And as David surveyed the raised ruins, with frustrated soldiers piping mad on the fringe of mutiny, he allowed the pressures of life to drive him to his knees. "Let's ask God what to do" (1 Samuel 30:7).

Meanwhile, to the north about forty miles, King Saul was very desperate too, and he let it drive him insane. So desperate was he that he lowered his standards and consulted a spiritual medium who brought up the spirit of dead Samuel. If the veracity of this strange episode can be trusted, and I see no reason why it should not, the prophet predicted the death of Saul the next day. And it happened in fact, just as Samuel said, Saul and his sons died in battle on Mount Gilboa.

A careful reading of these Scriptures shows that the two events coincided. In fact, it just may be that on the very morning David's weary warriors brought up the sunrise having marched through the night, Saul and his men were just waking from a restless night of tossing and turning because of breaching the spirit realm with a medium. David overtook the Amalekites to take back everything the enemy had stolen. Saul succumbed to suicide fulfilling Samuel's postmortem prophecy.

The irony of two kings, both in crisis, both desperate, both with troops ready for revolt - one conducts a séance, the other consults God Almighty. Saul seals his fate as a failed monarch project, David solidifies his standing as a man after God's own heart and Israel's great king.

We all have pressure. Let the pressures of life drive you to your knees, not drive you insane.

The Storyline of Humanity

2 Samuel 12:11, 12

Someone from your own family will cause you a lot of trouble, and I will take your wives and give them to another man before your very eyes. He will go to bed with them while everyone looks on.

Almost everyone has heard of the major blunder of David's life. He committed adultery with Bathsheba and she became pregnant. Then he attempted to entice her warrior husband, Uriah, to leave the battlefield and sleep with his wife; but Uriah wasn't willing to do so because of his allegiance to the Ark of the Covenant and his commanding officer and men. So, David, still attempting the cover up, gets Uriah drunk, hoping that he will go home to be with his wife; but he still sleeps on a mat on the ground outside David's gate and the king's own guards can verify it. David ends up murdering Uriah and disguising it as a tragedy of war. Then the king takes the grieving widow as his own wife. He gets off Scot free, and comes off looking like a compassionate king to boot. Everything went remarkably smooth, uncontested for about nine months. Tragedy averted. Right? Wrong! God sees everything and reveals it to his prophet, Nathan.

David is truly repentant. His behavior changes. He fasts and prays and weeps. His countenance is downcast for the seven brief days of his son's life. Psalm 51 catalogs his remorse. It is a glaring failure and very embarrassing.

The above verses are the real lasting curse. There are generations of sword-killings. And his own son, Absalom, has relations with David's wives out in the open, on the rooftop when he ousts his father. Is it the very same rooftop where David first saw Bathsheba? Remember Absalom means "my father is peace." In the revolt Absalom dies and David is reinstated. And we are left with the eerie picture of David crying out, "My son, my son, oh Absalom, my son" (2 Sam 18:33).

Yet, embedded in the account is the storyline of humanity.

On one end of the spectrum is a human father crying, "My son, my son." On the other end of the spectrum is a Son, who is God, crying to his Father, "My God, my God" (Ps 22:1). It's one of David's psalms. And there is real beauty housed in David's words after his baby has died, "I will go to him one day, but he cannot return to me" (2 Sam 12:23, NLT). Sin has devastating effects. Human healing is found in Christ alone. His love is stronger than sin and weaves its blessing into the narrative of anthropology.

The Bygones Backfired

2 Samuel 14:14

We must each die and disappear like water poured out on the ground. But God doesn't take our lives. Instead, he figures out ways of bringing us back when we run away.

These were the words spoken by a woman from Tekoa sent to King David. She was the stealthy spot planted by Joab, David's general. She's leading up to a request to bring the king's son, Absalom, back home to Jerusalem. Absalom had murdered his step brother, Amnon, in an act of retributive justice, so he thought. His father, David, did exonerate him, but after bringing him back he did not really work through steps of forgiveness and restoration. In time Absalom headed a conspiracy to usurp his own father's throne. David had let bygones be bygones, but the bygones backfired!

I have a pastor friend who was absolutely wronged by an individual in leadership in his church. This person was able to designate his personal giving away from the pastor's pay because of the existing salary structure. He would pray with individuals at the altar and then turn them against the pastor with his comments. He would persuade individuals for his cause by giving them a "Pentecostal handshake"; you know, he would shake hands and place a $100 bill in their hand and say things like, "The Lord just put you on my heart." All of this was an effort to sway the populace in his trend away from supporting the pastor. The irony is that all of this happened after my friend had gone out of his way to visit the man numerous times when he had gotten out of church. It was my pastor friend who brought him back in the fold. The bygones backfired!

And yet, this is the heart of God. How many times have we trampled upon his grace? We resist his prompts. We grieve his Spirit. We deserve his judgment but we live in an era of grace. We are so blessed with his mercies that are new every morning (Lam 3:23). Thankfully, our bygones are gone bye-bye. Our greatest challenge may be to extend that same grace to others.

I'll Run No Matter What

2 Samuel 18:23

"I'll run no matter what!" Ahimaaz insisted. "Alright, then run!" Joab said. Ahimaaz took the road through the Jordan Valley and outran the Ethiopian.

One soldier was afraid to take the life of the rebel, Absalom, because he overheard the king's command to bring him back unharmed. Joab had to do the deed himself. And then his armor bearers finished him off. But this young man, Ahimaaz, is fearless. He volunteers to bear the bad news of Absalom's death to the king. Joab refuses him because he usually brought good news, and sends another. Ahimaaz persists to the point where General Joab says, *"Oh, what could it hurt, the other runner is already way out front. If you want to run, take off."*

Ahimaaz knew the territory. He took a shortcut. He ran faster than the Ethiopian. He was the official courier of the battle's victory in the records. Ahimaaz means brother of anger. He was the son of Zadok which means righteousness. He may have lived life with a holy indignation, this son of righteousness. In time he became the high priest. "I'll run no matter what!"

I think of heroes and heroines who have run no matter what. In the early 1900s some departing missionaries packed their belongings in coffins instead of cargo trunks because they didn't expect to return. That is no holds barred commitment! "I'll run no matter what!"

I have read of women who were not allowed to hold credentials as licensed ministers, but who were given exhorter's papers and could evangelize. They held "revivals" in towns for as long as four to five years! They could not be called "pastors" but new churches were established and the kingdom grew. "I'll run no matter what!"

I remember being in a district board meeting in which a young man was receiving accolades that he wasn't even aware of. He had taken a tough assignment in a small town notorious for chewing up pastors and spitting them out. But he was anxious for an opportunity. The district officials were preparing to close the little church, but he begged for a chance to take it. What did they have to lose? Now, several years later he was being heralded as an example of faithfulness and determination. It was remarkable how the environment had turned around in the life of the church. "I'll run no matter what!"

You are tempted to slack off. You have run the back hills and no one has recognized. No matter. Run anyway. At times you get tired. You feel like you can't go on. Get your second wind of the Spirit. Run. Run to your king, faithful courier. "I'll run no matter what!"

Dumb, Dumber and Dumbest

> *2 Samuel 24:10*
>
> *After David had everyone counted, he felt guilty and told the LORD, "What I did was stupid and terribly wrong. LORD, please forgive me."*

Ever done anything really stupid? I have. Recently I locked our only car key in the automobile. It's one of those fancy, shmancy keys shaped like a little box that you can't duplicate at the hardware store. No, you have to go to the dealer. And I just despise the thought of spending so much money for a spare key. I didn't realize that if you leave the key in the ignition there is a safety feature that will lock the doors automatically after one minute. So, I pulled the car up to the front of the church parking lot, shut it off, hopped out and ran back in the building to help Stefanie carry things out. And just that quick, *bam,* locked out. Boy, did I feel stupid forking out $50.00 to the locksmith! I vowed silently, "I'll never do that again." Dumb.

One week later I was meeting my son, Zakary, at the school parking lot. He was going to drive the car home while I jumped on the bus with my other son, Nicholas, for the freshmen basketball trip. We didn't quite make the connection point at the same time. I was rushed. He was making his way across the parking lot. I texted him, "I left the key on the driver seat. The driver door is unlocked." Uh huh, you guessed it. He called just as the bus was ready to pull away, "Dad, the car is locked, and I can see the key on the seat!" What makes it worse, same company, same truck, same locksmith, another fifty bucks! Are you kidding me? The first incident was stupid. But the second one? I don't know what to say about that. Fool me once, shame on you. Fool me twice, shame on me. But what about me fooling myself? And twice? It needs a new word creation of Dr. Seuss proportions - *Bongboozledydaggadyshmackeder!* I could have saved money if I would have invested in a spare key. Dumber.

There is dumb. There is dumber. Then there is dumbest. Here we have David saying, *"Lord, that was just stupid on my part! I am so sorry."* And I can relate. His secretive pride crept in unawares. He is seemingly oblivious to counsel, even the word of his trusted advisers. The text says Satan was involved. This counting was grossly immoral. The trickledown effect of poor decisions by leadership is astounding. In this instance thousands of people died because of his error. I deeply regret the dumbest decisions of my life. I hate it when my blunders cause pain in the lives of innocents. The best we can each do is to read the Bible purposefully; pray meaningfully; and try our best to obey carefully. We have to live this way every single day. I want to walk close to him in order to have less moments that are dumb, dumber and dumbest.

Steps of Trepidation

> *1 Kings 13:17-20*
>
> *"The Lord warned me not to eat or drink or to go home the same way I came."*
>
> *The old prophet said, "I'm a prophet too. One of the Lord's angels told me to take you to my house and give you something to eat and drink."*
>
> *The prophet from Judah did not know that the old prophet was lying, so he went home with him and ate and drank. During the meal the Lord gave the old prophet a message for the prophet from Judah: Listen to the Lord's message. You have disobeyed the Lord your God. He told you not to eat or drink anything here, but you came home and ate with me. And so, when you die, your body won't be buried in your family tomb.*

This is just the most bizarre scenario imaginable. The young, unnamed prophet, who is righteous and godly, is lured to the home of the old, lying prophet. During the meal the old prophet suddenly receives a revelation. He tells the young prophet he will be judged with a sentence of death because he didn't obey the Lord. Really? Isn't verse 23 a strange verse? "When the man of God had finished eating and drinking." Are you kidding me? *"Hey, you're going to die! And could you pass the potatoes?"* I'll bet that was one interesting meal. What was the departing greeting like? *"Come again when you can. Say hello to the family, would you? We'll have to do it again."* And the nervous, young prophet replies, *"Oh yeah, definitely. Hey, and next time I'll bring my Green Chili Salsa."* All the while his feet take steps of trepidation towards the door.

There are others who follow in his footsteps. Jeroboam's wife leaves the prophet, Ahijah, pulling off her disguise, his words still ringing in her ears. *"Your child will die when you walk into town."* What does she do? Walk slower, perhaps. No, she must speed up to be with her dying son. *But no, wait, slow up. What am I doing?* How horrible the steps leading to the inevitable.

And Saul walked that path too. Oh those painful steps leaving the Witch of Endor, recalling what Samuel's spirit predicted, *"Tomorrow you will be here with me in the place of the dead."* What did he and his men discuss on the trek back? Sports? Weather? Politics? His feet carried him right out into the battlefield, right up that fateful hill.

There was One who took steps of trepidation that he had never done anything to invite. Jesus, perfect, sinless, shouldered the cross, carried it each painful step down the Via Dolorosa. It's not as if we have any choice. Whether we are facing good news or bad news, our feet will move forward. Sunshine or rainy day, our feet will roll out of the bed and start taking steps in a direction. Either that, or we curl up and die. But what is so amazing about Jesus is he faces and embraces his steps of trepidation. He walks his way of suffering so that you and I may be free.

Singing the Blues

> *1 Kings 19:13*
>
> *And when Elijah heard it, he covered his face with his coat. He went out and stood at the entrance to the cave.*

A voice asked, "Elijah, why are you here?"

How is it possible that Elijah is depressed? He had food delivered by ravens. I wonder if it was free if it didn't get there in thirty minutes. He spoke a multiplication miracle to a poverty stricken widow. He raised a dead boy to life. He confronted four-hundred-fifty false prophets of Baal in front of everyone on Mount Carmel, and God answered his prayer with fire from heaven, for Pete's sake. What's more, the prophet, Obadiah, a writer of holy Scripture, was just afraid of him in the previous chapter! Elijah prayed down rain in a severe drought, and then outran a chariot the length of a marathon. What is this guy doing down in the mulligrubs? Why is he running scared from Jezebel?

I don't know about you, but I appreciate guys like Elijah and Obadiah being real. They are raw and earthy. No fluff. That's what I like. Get real. I really value the authenticity. Even the mighty Elijah sat under the broom tree, strumming his six-string, singing the blues.

There is a hint of surprise by the Lord too. Gentle, not scolding, he speaks, *"What are you doing here, Elijah?"* First an impression, verse 9, and then a voice, verse 13. And both times Elijah responds with the exact same words. In essence, *"I've been faithful and worked hard. They've turned against us prophets. I'm all alone. I'm doomed to die."*

God comforts him with words that reassure him he is, in fact, not alone. *"No, I have plans for a new king named Jehu. And I also want you to anoint your successor, the prophet Elisha. Oh, by the way, there are seven thousand faithful Israelites who have never bowed a knee to Baal."*

Part of authentic, Christian living is to admit when we feel overwhelmed, in over our heads, all alone. We can get so busy with the work of the Lord that we forget the Lord of the work. It is his work. We are in a community of believers. We are also in the company of a great cloud of witnesses who have finished their races (Heb 12:1). Most importantly, we are constantly filled with the Holy Spirit (Eph 5:18), and are co-heirs with Jesus (Rom 8:17). Stay encouraged.

My, Oh My, Micaiah

> *1 Kings 22:19*
>
> *Micaiah replied: Listen to this! I also saw the Lord seated on his throne with every creature in heaven gathered around him.*

Micaiah had been summoned to the king before. Frankly, it hadn't gone very well. He always tried his best to be absolutely honorable as a prophet for the Lord. But no matter how hard he tried to hear God and speak truth, King Ahab always resented his remarks. Sure enough the courier arrived, his instructions falling flat for lack of emotion.

"Look, just tell the king whatever he wants to hear. All the other prophets have gotten him in a good mood for his guests. King Jehoshaphat is even visiting. Don't louse things up. For once, would you just go along with the status quo?"

"Don't you get it?" retorted Micaiah. *"I'm not with those guys. I don't work off of exit polls. I'm not a speech writer, okay. I will say only what God tells me to say, and nothing else."*

"Micaiah, he doesn't really like you. You have no idea how you're tempting fate!"

"Who's tempting who? That's the question."

The clanging of symbols was ringing in the distance. The ecstatic prophets were dancing with twirling timbrels. The thud of drums grew increasingly louder with each step. Utterances, some intelligible, filled the natural amphitheater. The courier escorted Micaiah, winding, negotiating the narrow canyon walls. The sounds of the hundreds of false prophets of Baal now, a cacophony, deafening in the arena. Onlookers ranting. In an instant he was there.

Rams' horns blasting announce a new participant. For a moment Micaiah was blinded by light. There was the prophet, Zedekiah, acting out the goring of the enemy. He had fashioned horns made from iron. Over and over he rammed the mock enemy. Each time he made contact there was an accompanying roar from the crowd. The sea of pagans divided, their crease creating a natural seam for him to access the thrones. Two of them had been erected for the occasion with much pomp and circumstance. Ahab, high above the commoners, surrounded by his entourage. And there, Jehoshaphat, also raised, seated on his throne, dazzling, brilliant. Here, out in the open space the magnificence of the sun banking off the canyon wall behind the two kings pierced downward like a shaft of light. Micaiah moved forward, his eyes adjusting to the sudden sunshine.

A last shout from the courier above the noise of the orators. *"Just give him what he wants, Micaiah."*

"Only what God wants, nothing else."

Now standing at the foot of the dual thrones, Ahab raises his flat palm. The gesture brings a delayed muting of all the chaos. Thumps and jingles rattle less until there is silence.

The courier announces, *"Presenting to his majesty, Micaiah, son of Imlah."*

The regal speaks, *"Seer, have you seen?"*

A slight delay for effect. *"Yes,"* comes the reply. *"You know you can trust my visions, O great King Ahab."*

"And what do you say, Micaiah?"

Catching the smirk of the courier from the corner of his peripheral vision, he blurts out a sarcastic tone. *"Go into battle and succeed. Go forward into victory, O King."*

An eruption of cheers and clapping, music crescendos and jubilation swells to a thunder in an instant. Unity of purpose. One in heart and mind. A joint Israel and Judah. Who will ever stop us now?

But Ahab raises his hand a second time.

It takes longer for the noise to settle. Some were premature in their eager celebration.

"Silence. How many times, Micaiah? How many times do I have to make you swear to me that you will speak the truth?"

"I will tell you what I saw." A new, harsh tone accompanied his words. *"The Israelites scattered all over the hillside, just like sheep without a shepherd. These people don't have a leader."*

"Oh great, here we go," flamed Ahab to his colleague, Jehoshaphat.

Peering up beneath his turban, Micaiah gazes upon the purple robes and lifted high chairs draped in magnificent tapestries, their strong men shouldering the elite. He surveys the ebony poles, with ivory clasps. He notes the pewter dishes. Crowns, glistening in the sunshine, jewel-laden crowns disguising hair that flows long upon garments too bedazzling for words.

"I saw the Lord, Almighty, seated upon his throne. And the entourage of holy beings surrounded him on his right and on his left. God was having a holy conference. God asked, 'Who will trick Ahab to go into battle against Ramath Gilead?' One had one idea; and another had another idea. But finally, a spirit came forward and said, 'I've got it. I'll trick him by being a lying spirit in the mouths of his own prophets.' Then God said, 'That's it. You've got it. Take off.' So you see, king, all of these prophets are lying to you the same way I lied when I said you would win just a moment ago!"

At this declaration, Zedekiah came up and slapped Micaiah on the face. *"O yeah, just when did the spirit stop speaking though me and start speaking through you?"*

"You'll have time to figure it out from your private suite in the prison!" barked Micaiah.

Ahab interrupts the bedlam. *"Seize Micaiah. Throw him in prison. Don't let him have anything but bread and water until I return."*

Micaiah's voice escalates, *"If you ever return, then, I'm not a speaker for God! Mark my words all of you!"*

My, oh my, Micaiah. Speaks truth, doesn't hold anything back. Refuses to couch his words in palatable sermonettes. Watch his words come true. Notice Jehoshaphat being diverted out of harm's way in battle. See the random arrow strike Ahab, he bleeds. His charioteer props him up, and wipes the blood again and again from the floor. Defeat happened precisely as the man of God had said it would. He ignores the deafening shouts of a unanimous rebellion. Truth prevails. God's throne is mightier. My, oh my, Micaiah.

Christian Voodoo?

2 Kings 1:15

The angel from the Lord said to Elijah, "Go with him and don't be afraid." So Elijah got up and went with the officer.

Did I read this verse right? Are you kidding me? Okay, Elijah has just called down fire from heaven to consume two companies of soldiers. He now has a third company begging for their lives. So why does the angel tell Elijah not to be afraid? It's because everything done by Elijah, every fete, is accomplished by the power of the Lord.

I can relate and so can you. There have been times I have felt I was used in a special way by God's Spirit. Then, there are other times when I feel I have been spinning my wheels. How often have I prayed the three-word prayer, "Give me words?" I have been empowered, inspiring, anointed and gifted. I have been places that are amazing. I can tell stories that will raise the hairs on the back of your neck. And yet, I regularly feel stymied, humdrum, mundane, and uninspiring. I leak, emptied I come, a beggar craving a morsel of bread from the king's table.

There are some in Christian circles who will diss my lack of faith. They are the ones for whom faith equals posture. They strike a pose. They are the ones who are overbearing in their answer to the greeting, "How are you?" Out blurts the word, "Blessed." Sometimes it is intended to teach, to instruct. "I'm too blessed to be stressed." It is often voiced with just the air that intones, "If you had faith like me, you would be blessed too." But I don't buy it. I call it superstition. It's Christian voodoo. Speak incantations, get powers. Get real with me. Such faith indicates deep-seated fear. I believe God much rather prefers authenticity. When you're really excited and happy, let those emotions out. When you're really down or afraid, let those emotions out. It seems to me there is an unspoken goal in some faith circles to get everybody happy at the same time. I'm not down on faith. Don't get me wrong. The answer to hyper faith is not lack of faith; but there is a much more biblical approach. "Rejoice with those who rejoice, and mourn with those who mourn" (Rom 12:15).

God doesn't send a messenger to Elijah to rebuke him. *"Oh man, you were so close to the goal. Why did you take a step backward? C'mon."* No, God's angel delivers the message Elijah needs to hear, *"Don't be afraid."*

Doubly Blessed

>*2 Kings 2:9*
>
>*After they had reached the other side, Elijah said, "Elisha, the Lord will soon take me away. What can I do for you before that happens?"*
>
>*Elisha answered, "Please give me twice as much of your power as you give the other prophets, so I can be the one who takes your place as their leader."*

Remember that Elisha had a request when his mentor, Elijah, was departing. "Let me have a double portion of your anointing." He followed Elijah's every move with undying commitment. He wouldn't let him out of his sight to the end, even with other prophets confirming and vying for attention.

It is at least interesting that in his ministry career the Bible records Elisha doing twice as many miracles as his predecessor. The book of the kings records 7 miracles of Elijah, but 14 of Elisha. It also records twice as many oral prophecies. Interestingly, Elijah's career lasted somewhere around 12 to 13 years, and his understudy, Elisha, ministered about 25 years.

Only one obvious miscalculation was still intact when Elisha died. Both he and Elijah had raised one person from the dead. However, even postmortem, God gave Elisha the desire of his heart. A dead man was thrown in his grave quickly because raiders were coming on the scene. And when the corpse touched the dead prophet it came back to life.

Elijah told Elisha his request for a double portion would be granted on one condition: he had to be watching the prophet when he departed. No credentials, no certification or degrees, as important as those things are. No, the criteria was relationship, seeing, being in proximity, staying close. It speaks of our interaction with Almighty. We must be close to him, currently, right now in relationship with him. That's the ticket. And sometimes we are doubly blessed.

Elisha Room

> *2 Kings 4:10*
>
> *Why don't we build him a small room on the flat roof of our house? We can put a bed, a table and chair, and an oil lamp in it. Then whenever he comes, he can stay with us.*

A number of years ago I was asked to be the speaker at a special banquet in honor of newly ordained ministers. I asked my wife, Stefanie, to help me on a project. She is very good with crafts. We went to a craft supply store and purchased the items needed to make a Bible that would fit on the bookshelf in each of their libraries. We painted it to appear just like any other Bible you would have in your collection. The Bible was made of cardboard and was hollow. In it we recreated the Elisha Room of 2 Kings 4:10. There was a little chair, and a tiny table. And a bed with a little end table that had a lantern on it. It was very simple and primitive looking. And on the inside cover, which served as the lid to the room, was etched in calligraphy, "Let's make a small room on the roof and put in it a bed and a table, a chair and a lamp for him. Then he can stay there whenever he comes to us" (2 Kgs 4:10).

The night of the banquet I arrived early and hid the five gifts in the wooden podium. No one knew they were there. I will never forget the reaction in the room as I pulled out the boxes, handed them to each ordainee and said, "Tonight I would like you to open your Bibles, literally, to 2 Kings 4:10."

I spoke of the four crucial components in the life of the ordained minister. The chair - There will be many meetings to chair over the course of your ministry. Lead with integrity, bravery and excellence. The table - Never neglect your study desk. Keep learning, stay sharp, be relevant. Get stretched. Take your people on a journey. The lamp - It symbolizes the infilling of the Holy Spirit. Keep your lamp trimmed and filled with oil. Let your prayer-life be fervent. This will enable your light to shine brilliantly. And the bed - You need rest. You need it regularly and systematically. Find outlets. Take vacations. Have retreats. Don't run on empty for long stretches of the journey because you cannot feed your people out of that place.

In a sense the Elisha Room speaks to us all, not just prophets. Lead with excellence. Study to show yourself approved. Keep the prayer lamp burning. Stay rested and refreshed. Have you visited the Elisha Room lately? Could you stop by today?

No Guarantees

> 2 Kings 23:25, 26
>
> *No other king before or after Josiah tried as hard as he did to obey the Law of Moses. But the Lord was still furious with the people of Judah because Manasseh had done so many things to make him angry.*

This is a tremendous effort from a great king. Josiah adhered to the words of the holy Scriptures that had been recovered during the renovation project for the temple which he instigated. He destroyed all the false idols and their altars. He burned the bones of the dead, false prophets and scattered their ashes over the remains of the altars. This was a way of rendering those altars useless. He brought serious reforms that rivaled that of his great-grandfather, Hezekiah. But even this couldn't restore the nation's favored status with God. Josiah's grandfather Manasseh, and his father, Amon, had crossed the line on immorality and idolatry. The nation had been toggling between the true God and the Baals for centuries now.

Godly Josiah died in a battle he felt he had to fight, even though apparently God was prompting him not to go. He was trying to fend off King Neco from Egypt who had joined forces with Assyria at that time. An arrow pierced Josiah's good heart and though they raced him back to Jerusalem, he still died. Jeremiah, the great prophet, even wrote a funeral dirge in his honor. Though it isn't recorded for us in the book of Jeremiah, a tacit eulogy is written, Jeremiah 22:15. Many people feel one of the lamentations Jeremiah wrote, Lamentations 4:1-22, was originally the funeral dirge he wrote in honor of Josiah. It is a beautiful acrostic using the 22 letters of the Hebrew alphabet.

We tend to think individually, especially Americans. In our estimation a good man should receive good benefits. The evil individual should get what's coming to him. That is not always the case this side of heaven. There are no guarantees. There are countless examples in human history of godly, faithful individuals who sacrificed their lives for the greater good. The Hebrew approach is much more inclusive of community. It takes into account the condition of culture and the collective heart.

As to judgment, you and I will stand before God as individuals. The Bema Seat described in 2 Corinthians 5:10 is a one-on-one commendation before our Christ. Good deeds are rewarded, false motives are shown for what they are and burn away. Later, the Great White Throne Judgment involves all humanity divided into two groups. Sheep move right, goats form a line left.

There are times when an individual's honor is swallowed up by culture's conformity. In the broad, panoramic view of history, God is justified and right, regardless of isolated blips on our radar screens.

What's in a Name?

> 1 Chronicles 3:1-8
>
> *King David ruled from Hebron for seven years and six months, and during that time he had six sons, who were born in the following order: Amnon, Daniel, Absalom, Adonijah, Shephatiah, and Ithream. Ahinoam from Jezreel was the mother of Amnon; Abigail from Carmel was the mother of Daniel; Maacah daughter of King Talmai of Geshur was the mother of Absalom; Haggith was the mother of Adonijah; Abital was the mother of Shephatiah; and Eglah was the mother of Ithream.*
>
> *David then ruled from Jerusalem for thirty-three years, and during that time, he had thirteen more sons. His wife Bathsheba daughter of Ammiel gave birth to Shimea, Shobab, Nathan, and Solomon. David's other sons included Ibhar, Elishua, Eliphelet, Nogah, Nepheg, Japhia, Elishama, Eliada, and Eliphelet.*

What's in a name? The names of David's sons indicate just where the heart of the king is. I suspect every generation plays with the way names roll off the tongue, and the spelling of them, and what is implied. For example, in English I am aware of names like Axel, Cage, and Crew. If you spell a word a different way it becomes a lovely name, Destanie, Trinaty, or Brooklynne. I love my two nephews' names, Jade and Blaze. Animal names are in vogue these days, Tiger, think golf sensation, Bear Gryles, the ultimate survivor. Or Falcon, remember Balloon Boy? How sad that parents would ever venture to name children in a way that slants them toward a curse, but it is happening in our time, Evil, Pagan.

In the first eight verses of 1 Chronicles 3 we have the names of King David's sons detailed. To us foreigners we only see names that are unrecognizable. But the names of the king speak of God's having the highest place in his life. Imagine the banter around the Davidic household as names filled the air that had significance spiritually. Amnon (Faithful); Daniel (God is my Judge); Absalom (My Father is Peace); Adonijah (My Lord is Yah[weh]); Shephatiah (Yah[weh] has Judged); and Ithream (Excellence of People). Don't forget to carry out the trash Shimea (Heard) and Shobab (Take Back). No, Nathan (To Give), it's your turn to set the table; Solomon (To Amend) will help with the dishes. In addition to these David named other sons Ibhar (He Chooses); Elishua (My God Has Heard); Eliphelet (My God is Deliverance); Nogah (Illumines); Nepheg (Spring Forth); Japhia (Shine Out); Elishama (My God Has Heard); Eliada (God Knows); and Eliphelet (My God is Deliverance).

Twice David named his sons the same concept using variations, "My God has heard" and "My God has judged." On one occasion he even named two of his sons the exact same name and same spelling, probably designating them with different pet names or pronunciations, "My God is deliverance." Perhaps the older one died, though we don't know, and the younger was named for his older brother.

If you are a follower of Jesus your name has been written in the Lamb's Book of Life. You are a child of God. He knows you by name. Take comfort today in the fact that you are known by God.

On Another Level

> *1 Chronicles 14:15*
>
> *Wait there until you hear the treetops making the sound of marching troops.*

God is simply on another level, a plane we can't understand, a mystery we can't crack. Whenever the Bible has him interacting with humanity there are traces of his greatness that show through in the language. 1 Chronicles 14:15, "Wait there until you hear the treetops making the sound of marching troops." Just imagine, the feet of God's warriors are shuffling through the tops of the Balsam Trees. That's how high he is. How high is the Most High! He comes down to the top of the mountain to speak with Moses who has ascended to the heights for forty days without eating bread or drinking water. Moses, the most humble man on earth (Numbers 12:3). At our very best we are only scraping the surface on what he is like. Isaiah worded it this way, "Our righteousness is as filthy rags" (Isaiah 64:6); and another place in Isaiah it says, "As high as the heavens are above the earth, so are my ways beyond your figuring out" (Isaiah 55:9). So, God is in an entirely other dimension.

And yet God takes us to another level. Consider the statement, "You are seated with Christ in heavenly realms far above all rule, authority, power and dominion." (Eph 1:21). These descriptors of dark, spiritual hierarchy are all "under his feet" (Eph 1:22). Now think about it. If you are seated with Christ in heavenly places and powers of darkness are under his feet, where is the darkness in relation to you? It is under your feet. How else does one qualify Jesus' statement, "I have given you authority to tread on scorpions and snakes and to overcome all the power of the enemy" (Luke 10:19)? On another occasion Jesus spoke of giving his followers the keys to the kingdom of heaven. "Whatever you bind on earth is bound in heaven. Whatsoever you loose on earth is loosed in heaven." (Matt 18:18). And when Jesus was leaving the earth he made a statement to reiterate this authority. "They will cast out demons in my name" (Mark 16:17).

God is on an entirely other level. He will not lower himself and so jeopardize holiness. He lowered himself when Jesus came as a human, conquering the cross. That will not happen again. However, he invites you and me to come up to his level. Come on up. The view is wonderful from up here.

Be Careful Little Eyes What You See

1 Chronicles 20:6, 7

Another one of the Philistine soldiers who was a descendant of the Rephaim was as big as a giant and had six fingers on each hand and six toes on each foot. During a battle at Gath, he made fun of Israel, so David's nephew Jonathan killed him.

David had killed Goliath when he was a ruddy, young enthusiast for God. We all know that. But what is not as well-known is the defeat of one of Goliath's descendants by one of David's family members.

I have a great memory from my childhood. One day after Sunday School my Uncle Vaughn, who was my teacher, pulled me aside and told me, "Keith, when I'm up there teaching your eyes are locked on me. You could stare a hole right through me." He went onto compliment the way I paid attention in class, and had some really nice things to say. It made an impression on me. I was mesmerized by my cool Uncle Vaughn. He played the guitar and sang like a dream. I just thought he was amazing. In time he would evangelize, pastor churches, sing with wife and sons, and raise two sons to be in full-time ministry. How sad we were when God called him home at the age of forty-six! I can't wait to see him again in eternity. In children's choir we sang a simple song, "Oh be careful little eyes what you see." My eyes saw mentors and models. I am not the product of my own choosing. I am a composite of God's calling, my obedience, and others' influence. Now, little eyes have been watching me.

David took down Goliath; and his nephew Jonathan handled the residue. Who have you watched? Who's watching you?

Oh, the Music!

> 1 Chronicles 25:1
>
> *David and the temple officials chose the descendants of Asaph, Heman, and Jeduthun to be in charge of music. They were to praise the Lord by playing cymbals, harps and other stringed instruments.*

I remember from my childhood the testimony of an elderly lady in our congregation. She stood up to share about the way she was drawn into the Pentecostal Church as a young lady. It happened that she would walk down the sidewalk past the church services on the way to her church which was more traditional and stoic. She commented that the energy was like a magnet and the joyful expressions of the people were contagious. I still remember this phrase, "And the music, oh, the music! It was glorious!" She went on to describe how one day she ventured in just to see what was going on, and never left.

I'm impressed with the remarkable symmetry and balance of King David's symphonic court. Two-hundred-eighty-eight musicians stemming from one family of three brothers. They were neatly divided into twenty-four groups of twelve for rotating gigs available at the bequest of the monarch, all of them skilled musicians. They were the Nashville, studio-quality players of Israel. Can you just imagine what the family reunions were like? After the turkey and dressing, "Hey Cuz, let me show you this piece I've been playing with. I was hoping we could collaborate. It goes a little something like this."

The four sons of Asaph provided music anytime the king requested it, a veritable iPod for David. And David, being a thorough-going musician, arranger and psalmist himself, most likely used many occasions as a cohort for mentoring. The Sons of Asaph became a bona fide school of psaltery. They contributed a dozen of the psalms. The six sons of Jeduthun were assigned music making for the Lord. Apparently they were improvisational artists who created a setting, a mood, a backdrop of music that splashed on people as they approached the tabernacle. They were the parking lot music of today's churches, the sounds hovering in the courtyard. The fourteen sons of Heman were given the specific task of music for the worship gatherings. They were the Planetshakers, the Hillsong, the Gateway Worship, the Integrity Hosanna of their day. Oh, the music!

Music is the one trans-cultural language of earth. All people groups employ it to express joy, sadness, anger, hope, melancholy, brilliance, love, hate, adoration - on and on, you name it. And it is a gift of expression from God. Today, is it possible that you could be enraptured by intentional sounds set to notation? Captivated by the majesty of God's chamber? Oh, the music!

A Tribute to My Friend Jap

> *1 Chronicles 29:13, 14*
>
> *We thank you, our God, and praise you. But why should we be happy that we have given you these gifts? They belong to you, and we have only given back what is already yours.*

This year a wonderful mentor of mine stepped into glory. His name is Jasper Weaver, everyone called him Jap for short. Jap was an amazing pastor, a true community leader. He had a witty, winsome personality, a pocket full of quick comebacks, and a litany of jokes that you begged to hear again and again. It was rumored that he always hid a hundred dollar bill in his boot, though I never asked him.

Now, Jap was a true cowboy. I'm not one at all. I really don't know that much about it. One time I went to the fairgrounds with Jap and he whispered to me, "See that guy over there leaning on the rail. He's a cowboy wannabe." I asked how he could tell. He chimed, "Just look at the crease on his jeans, and notice the dent in his hat." Years ago Jap had a horse that was the National Reserve Grand Champion cutting horse. His name was Smokin' Handlebar. Jap showed me video of the horse. It was amazing to watch that horse work the cows, back and forth, letting them know which way they were supposed to go. Jap was also quite an amazing artist. He drew sketches of western scenes, horses, cowboys, hills, horse shoes, cactus, what not. He has official, registered and numbered prints of some of his pieces. There is a littering of his treasured work all throughout the West Slope of Colorado, much of it on truck-stop napkins which he would doodle on as he talked to individuals about Jesus. Having one of these napkins became a novelty, somewhat of a collector's item.

I remember a story he used to tell. Jap and Velma were pastoring in a community in Utah. When they accepted the church, the landscaping had fallen in disrepair. It was overgrown with tall weeds interspersed with patches of dirt. The artists in them would not allow God's house to look this way. So Jap and Velma set to work transforming the front area of the church. They mowed the weeds, then seeded grass. They brought in flowers and bushes. In time they made a flowing stream that wound through the lush garden, even built a scenic bridge and walkway so people could meander through and enjoy. Every girl in town wanted to have her wedding there. They loved to come and take pictures on site. One day a passerby stood at the front of the church and looked over the Eden-like prayer garden and commented, "Isn't God's handiwork beautiful!" to which Jap quipped, "Yeah, but you should've seen it when he had it to himself!"

Jap's story comes to mind as I read of David handing over the reins to Solomon. In the prayer of inauguration he says, "We have only given back what is already yours." It is a remarkable concept that you and I get to partner with God. He has given us free reign in his earth. It is a veritable canvass for our ideas, a playground for creative genius. It is incredibly important that we steward this gift responsibly. David saved gold, silver, bronze, iron, wood, onyx, turquoise, colored gems, marble and all kinds of precious stones. He also exercised restraint with individuals who deserved death. Joab, Shemei, and Adonijah were given clemency during his lifetime because of timing and appropriateness; but in his dying he left instructions how to handle them to his young heir, Solomon. Yes, the earth is the Lord's. It all belongs to him. But he has given you and me the privilege to draw, to speak, to train, to plant, to grow, to decide, to plan. To laugh, to weep, to encourage, to cherish.

Jasper's grandson, Levi, wrote a moving eulogy about his grandfather. Of his last encounter he writes, "I leaned in to hug him. He shakily handed me a hundred dollar bill (which I felt guilty taking) and whispered something no one else in the room could hear. 'We'll wake up one of these days.' Dementia or no, that was profound." A few days later 800 friends would gather on a cold, Wednesday morning, in the middle of the week, to say goodbye to their friend. They were all pallbearers that day. His son, the pastor, instructed the crowd to move to the middle if they felt close to his Dad, and the casket was handed down the center aisle out the back, a "crowd-surfing" of sorts, to the hearse. Hand after hand honoring the hands that blessed, prayed, and greeted.

There is a beautiful garden in your life. It's disguised as a patch of weeds. Isn't God's handiwork beautiful!

Running Interference

> 2 Chronicles 10:15-19
>
> *When the people realized that Rehoboam would not listen to them, they shouted: "We don't have to be loyal to David's family. We can do what we want. Come on, people of Israel, let's go home! Rehoboam can rule his own people."*
>
> *Adoniram was in charge of the work force, and Rehoboam sent him to talk to the people. But they stoned him to death. Then Rehoboam ran to his chariot and hurried back to Jerusalem.*
>
> *Everyone from Israel's northern tribes went home, leaving Rehoboam to rule only the people from Judah. And since that day, the people of Israel have been opposed to David's descendants in Judah. All of this happened just as Ahijah the Lord's prophet from Shiloh had told Jeroboam.*

Poor Adoniram. All he does is carry out the new king's wishes. Rehoboam has named him Secretary of Labor, as it were. The king sends him to make sure these policies are implemented. But like a scab in a labor strike, Adoniram finds himself in the middle of a riot. They stone him to death. He is a casualty of change. He is collateral damage. All because he was simply running interference for the monarch, trying to carry out his wishes.

Rehoboam seems to come off as impetuous and foolish. And the coming chapters will confirm the suspicions. He is young and untested. We are left with the impression that if he had only followed the advice of his advisers to lighten up the load on his father's work force, he would have been successful. But who is to say? In actuality, to come off as soft would've spelled certain doom. It was a very important decision. Don't forget his rival, Jeroboam, was offering sacrifices of goats to demons. There was just a lot going wrong on both sides of the split kingdom. In the course of time, Rehoboam, King of Judah, determined to attack his sister nation, Israel. But there are key words in verse 24, "Don't go to war against the people from Israel - they are your relatives. Go home! I am the Lord, and I made these things happen." Intertwined in the narrative we keep reading hints that these events are fulfillment of prophecy.

I'll bet at one time or another, possibly even right now, you have been part of a congregation in transition that mirrors that of the exchange of power from Solomon to Rehoboam. Running interference is risky. Stay loyal. Stay supportive. Be wise by not fueling gossip. Encourage the disgruntled to follow the proper chains of command. Pray for discernment. Be determined in your resolve to maintain absolute integrity. Pursue soft tones rather than harsh ones. Sincere smiles, honest words, and when you don't know what to say, say nothing at all. Learn diplomacy Christ ambassador. Trust that God is truly working through the matters at hand.

In a Word

> 2 Chronicles 21:20
>
> *Jehoram was thirty-two years old when he became king, and he ruled eight years from Jerusalem. He died and no one even felt sad. He was buried in Jerusalem, but not in the royal tombs.*

What a somber, disgusting asterisk to the life of King Jehoram! How sad to live a sinful, evil, wicked life and die! And then when you die no one even cares.

Almost two decades ago I penned a poem while reflecting on the sadness of a funeral of a godless man which I attended. Makes you want to make your existence matter.

> *In a Word*
>
> *Cold - the chapel, not fit to say good-bye*
> *Empty - the pews, friends, absent, where are they?*
> *Lifeless - the words, spoken by someone who didn't know him*
> *Sad - the mourners, uncertain of his soul's fate*
> *Broken - the heart of God, at his proposal rejected*
> *Shame - in a word, it is a shame*
>
> *March 12, 1996*

Hezekiah's Hesitation

> 2 Chronicles 31:20, 21
>
> *Everything Hezekiah did while he was king of Judah, including what he did for the temple in Jerusalem, was right and good. He was a successful king, because he obeyed the Lord God with all his heart.*

Nearly every Sunday School student has fallen for the trick at one time or another. *"Turn to the book of Hezekiah."* And the onion skin pages start flipping frantically. After a few moments quizzical eyes look up in bewilderment before finally turning to the table of contents. Then one of them exclaims, *"Wait a minute. There is no book called Hezekiah!"*

Well, Hezekiah didn't have his own book in the Bible; but he accomplished magnificent feats. In a time of moral sliding, he led the nation of Judah in serious reforms. King Hezekiah turned things around very quickly. While many people laughed and mocked his appeal, and many priests smirked, many others bought into his acts of repentance. Over a matter of weeks more and more Levitical priests repented and went through ceremonial cleansing. Even though his daddy was wicked King Ahab, Hezekiah led the Jews to celebrate the Passover on a grand scale such as had not occurred since the time of David and Solomon about 250 years earlier. It was a season of true repentance and renewal. Morale was high. The people's spirits were lifted and encouraged.

Hezekiah had remarkable answers to prayer during his administration. He saw God deliver him by wiping out Sennacharib's army of 185,000 in a night. This happened because he took their threatening letter with him to prayer and laid it out before the Lord in the temple. He received a healing miracle when he was on his deathbed. The prophet Isaiah gave him the privilege of receiving a sign. Hezekiah asked the shadow to move backwards up the staircase. It did, and he received fifteen extra years of life.

The late W.A. Criswell preached about all this in 1962. "In 2 Chronicles 32 and [verse] 31 'The ambassadors of the princes of Babylon, who sent unto him' - Hezekiah - 'to inquire of the wonder that was done in the land.' Listen, everybody was talking about Hezekiah - everybody." The brass from Babylon had come to figure out how he was so successful. Hezekiah should have resisted giving a tour to these arch rivals, the enemy. He must have had an instant when he hesitated. That red flag moment. *Hold on here, what am I doing?* It is George Bailey sitting at the desk of old man Potter! *Don't do it, Hezekiah!* But he did. And he paid dearly, as did the people he led. Criswell says it was the same pride that Lucifer displayed in Isaiah 14 that caused Hezekiah's downfall.

Listen to that little voice inside your head. Have a holy hesitation today.

Testing, Testing, 1, 2, 3

> 2 Chronicles 32:31b
>
> *God let Hezekiah give his own answer to test him and to see if he would remain faithful.*

Testing, testing, 1, 2, 3. Ever heard those words through a microphone? How about these words through the radio? *This is a test. This is only a test.*

I never really liked tests. I only liked the sense of accomplishment when it was over.

This morning as I read Scripture in my devotions I experienced what theologians call the illumination of the Holy Spirit. In layman's terms, the words leapt off the printed page right into my heart. I knew God spoke to me.

The text was written about King Hezekiah. *"God left him to test him and to know everything that was in his heart"* (2 Chr 32:31, NIV). In that moment the Holy Spirit spoke to me in an undeniable way, "*Your test is almost over.*" You see, in my personal walk with God, I have been experiencing 2 Chronicles 32, lived out loud. Sennacherib taunting; soul-searching to rid myself of pride, like Hezekiah did; crying out to God in desperation like Isaiah and Hezekiah did - *Your test is almost over.*

It occurs to me that God's tests are always POP-quizzes. I hate POP-quizzes. I would like him to give advance notice. *Next Thursday, remember, you have a test. You will need a #2 pencil; use a cover sheet; here are some review questions for your upcoming FINAL!* But we don't get that with God. It's always a POP-quiz. Perhaps if we knew the tests were coming we would ditch class on that day.

Not only does the test let God *"know everything that is in my heart."* But, also, the test allows *me* to see what is in my own heart.

Humorous (but serious) points to ponder:

- God, will this count on my final grade?
- Lord, does this go on my permanent record?
- Father, do you grade on the curve, or will I be assessed as an individual?

A Slam on the Worship Wars

Ezra 3:13

Their shouting and crying were so noisy that it all sounded alike and could be heard a long way off.

The foundation has been completed for the rebuilding of the temple, and there is such rejoicing at the unified accomplishment. A flood of memories. Hope of coming victories. Tears of joy intermingling with breathy sighs of relief. A veritable cacophony of exuberant, extemporaneous worship builds to a roar. Old and young alike are included. It is a subtle slam on the current worship wars that break the heart of God. Nothing should divide God's people, not musical styles, or carpet colors, or whipped cream.

Open and Honest Prayer

> Ezra 8:22, 23
>
> *I was ashamed to ask the king to send soldiers and cavalry to protect us against enemies along the way. After all, we had told the king that our God takes care of everyone who truly worships him, but that he gets very angry and punishes anyone who refuses to obey. So we went without food and asked God himself to protect us, and he answered our prayers.*

God's heart is stirred by honest, sincere prayer. He is moved to answer seeking hearts.

Watchman Nee was a strong believer in Communist China in the twentieth century. His mother, having been converted by Methodist missionaries, changed her son's name to "Bell Ringer" or "Watchman" because of the obvious Christian ties. He has been criticized for some unorthodox views on the role of emotions in the preacher, and statements about the Bible becoming authoritative only when one understands "the reality behind it." Some say he had the earmarks of a guru. Though I could be wrong, I think he has been misunderstood largely. I think he meant only to say emotions play a very important part in communicating; and Scripture should be more than just printed ink on paper. However, I will lay that discussion aside. There are over forty volumes from his life that have been translated for brighter minds to sift.

Watchman Nee spent the last twenty years of his life in prison because of his faith in Christ. There is a powerful story from his life.

He tells of meeting a young man who said he was too young to devote his life to the Lord. He wanted more time to party and enjoy sin. He said to Watchman Nee, "The thief on the cross was saved, but he had his fling, and it was high time that he repented. But I - I am young."

Nee responded, "Well, what do you want to do?"

He said, "I want to wait another forty years and have a good time, and then I will repent." To his astonishment Nee said, "Let us pray."

The young man said, "I can't pray." Undeterred, Watchman Nee told him, "Yes you can. You can tell the Lord all you have told me. He is the Friend of unrepentant sinners like you."

He resisted, saying there was no way he could tell those things to God. Watchman Nee persisted, "Why not? Whatever is in your heart, you tell it to him. He will help you."

Finally the young man began to tell the Lord that he didn't want to repent, but he knew he needed a Savior. As he prayed he began to weep. God worked in his foolhardy heart to bring about salvation.

Are you in the habit of being absolutely honest with the Lord? Do you disclose everything? He already knows anyway.

No Easy Undertaking

> *Ezra 10:13, 14*
>
> *But there are so many of us, and we can't just stay out here in this downpour. A lot of us have sinned by marrying foreign women, and the matter can't be settled in only a day or two. Why can't our officials stay on in Jerusalem and take care of this for us? Let everyone who has sinned in this way meet here at a certain time with leaders and judges from their own towns. If we take care of this problem, God will surely stop being so terribly angry with us.*

We can sometimes find ourselves in dilemmas that require tender care. Some problems cannot be fixed in a day or two. There are layers that have to be nuanced and peeled back with the care of kit gloves. You can't un-ring a bell. The rain drops are caroming off the brows of the Israelites. In the midst of the downpour there was a vow effected to make things right. It was not a swift, decisive cut, like that of a medieval pendulum. Rather, over the coming days they tooled-out the tough decisions. It involved divorces. Lives were changed forever. In the wake of this rigid resolve healing came to God's people.

Otto Kilcher had a cow named Waise that was orphaned when her momma died. They bottle-fed her as a young calf. Waise means "orphan" in German. She provided milk for the family for seventeen years. Not only that, she had calved numerous other cows through the years. Otto described in such compassionate tones the relationship between him and his milk cow. He said, she's like "a real family friend. You milk every morning at 7:00 and every evening at 7:00."[iv] Now, in the Alaskan October, he feared she wouldn't make it through another harsh winter. The previous year she almost starved for lack of food, and quite nearly froze to death. There was a hay shortage. They couldn't afford to feed her through the winter. Even if they could, the chances were great that she wouldn't survive. "The right thing to do," explained Otto, "while she's happy, while the grass is green, while she's doing fine;" he searched for words, "is to butcher her and salvage the meat. It's the right thing to do for her; and it's the right thing to do for my family. It isn't gonna' be easy and I'm not looking forward to it." His son Eivin was given the hard task of pulling the trigger. Otto wanted his grown son to "take the reins." He saw it as part of his role as a parent. And, anyway, he didn't have the heart to pull the trigger himself. Eivin said, "In a little bit of a sick way it is an honor. From the time I was young and bottle-fed this cow, to now." His voice trailed off. This was no easy undertaking.

The deed was done. The cow was butchered. They cooked meat that very day. It provided four-hundred pounds of beef for the long winter. Otto divided up the meat and gave away portions to the neighbors and workers. Hear the substance of his words as he spoke of the sacrifice. "There's a depth to it. There's a reverence there, and an understanding that there's a great, big circle. And she's a part of that." Eivin said he would never eat meat that was grown in a slaughter house, but he was "proud" to eat meat that was raised the right way.

Some of life's issues are thorny. When life presents you with a quandary, any decision made will bring about pain, here's what to do: pray for direction, garner rigid resolve, and move forward into the task that is no easy undertaking.

Great Projects in Bite-Sized Chunks

Nehemiah 6:3

I sent messengers to tell them, "My work is too important to stop now and go there. I can't afford to slow down the work just to visit with you."

A journey of a thousand miles begins with just one step. The Abominable Snowman sang to Rudolph, *"Just put one foot in front of the other, and soon you'll be walking 'cross the floor. Just put one foot in front of the other, and soon you'll be walking out the door."* Do you have goals you want accomplish? Just do it. Great projects are accomplished in bite-sized chunks.

Any worthwhile project I have accomplished in life has been finished because of a steady commitment that moved in the rhythm God gave me for that stretch of the journey. Learning to play the piano and the guitar, it has brought me such joy in life; but it would not have happened without the discipline of practice. Keeping a private journal for two decades has brought such insight to my soul, and a track record of God's faithfulness. Yet it takes the self-mastery of putting pen to paper whether I feel like it or not. In fact, some of the most insightful encounters have come on days when I felt dead to creativity. Academic degrees: high school, college, graduate-level; the writing of two full-score musicals; the recording of a jazz album; even the writing of this devotional book - all of these things took consistency. Preaching over 2,300 sermons - are you kidding me? I was the wallflower kid, so shy, timid, and bashful. I could never stand up in front of people and talk. How did that happen? It happened by studying and praying each week. It happened by asking God to give me words.

The difference between successfully completing projects, and sputtering through a series of false starts, is simple. You need determination mixed with a steady pace. It's all about time management. You have been entrusted with a great gift by your creator. He has allotted you a certain number of days.

Nehemiah rebuilt the walls of Jerusalem in 52 days (Neh 6:15). What an accomplishment! He wouldn't be distracted by threats, accolades or diversions. Don't chase rabbit trails today. Stick to the straight and narrow.

A Sudden Flash of Inspiration

Nehemiah 6:12, 13

Suddenly I realized that God had not given Shemaiah this message. But Tobiah and Sanballat had paid him to trick me and to frighten me into doing something wrong, because they wanted to ruin my good name.

Nehemiah had a sudden flash of inspiration. He knew that Shemaiah, his Jewish brother, was lying. He was in cohort with the enemy. How did Nehemiah know this? He knew it because the Holy Spirit showed him. It is similar to the way Elisha would get direction from the Holy Spirit about the enemy's plans (2 Kgs 6:8-12). The king of Aram was absolutely frustrated, thought there was an insider, you know, a nark. No. They explained that the prophet Elisha knew what was spoken in secret and would reveal this to the Israelites.

I will tell of an instant when the Holy Spirit revealed something to me in a flash of inspiration. As a school teacher I became aware of family that was new to the school and had some very real needs for housing. This family with five children reminded me so much of my own family growing up. I sat there at my desk thinking about them. I felt the prompting of the Holy Spirit that I should pray for them. So I did. Imagine my surprise when this family moved in right next door to us. Over the next few years we befriended the family. We invited them to church for Friend Day. They weren't able to come. However, one of the daughters began to attend the Youth Group. My wife, Stefanie, was there for the wife in a special way through a very difficult stretch for their family.

They moved away. We thought we had lost contact with them permanently. One day I was moving items in the backyard closer to the RV gate so that we could load them easily. We would be moving in a matter of days. I looked over the wall at their empty house. No one had lived there for many months. I wondered what had ever happened to them. I felt the same prompting of the Holy Spirit. I paused and prayed over them, wherever they were, that God would remember them and supply everything they needed. The next night, Saturday evening, as I sat putting the finishing touches on some sermon notes, our doorbell rang. It was the mother and one of the daughters. They were considering moving back into the neighborhood. A few minutes later, two of the sisters joined them. They were just coming by to say hi. I told them of the two distinct times I had prayed for them. I have a feeling God is doing something really special in their lives. The story is still in process of being written. Our relationship started in a sudden flash of inspiration.

Such Reverence

Nehemiah 8:12

When the people returned to their homes, they celebrated by eating and drinking and by sharing their food with those in need, because they had understood what had been read to them.

Years earlier, when the foundation of the temple was completed, the people wept for joy. Some of the people had cheered. It was a mixture of praise pleasing to the heart of God. Now, as the great project is nearing completion, Ezra, the scribe, takes his place on a platform erected just for the occasion. There is such reverence for God's holy Word. When he opens the book of the Law, everyone stands. They listened intently. How long did they stand? Hours? Was the entire Law recited? Apparently. There were instructors who followed up on the reading by intermingling with the crowd explaining any thorny issues. The people were glad because they heard the Word and understood! It resulted in celebration in their homes because their hearts were so glad to receive the revelation.

May there be celebration in our hearts today at the hearing and understanding of God's holy Word.

4

Prophets and Poets Believing

GROUP 4: PROPHETS AND POETS BELIEVING

Nashty and Vashti

> *Esther 1:10-12*
>
> *By the seventh day, King Xerxes was feeling happy because of so much wine. And he asked his seven personal servants, Mehuman, Biztha, Harbona, Bigtha, Abagtha, Zethar, and Carkas, to bring Queen Vashti to him. The king wanted her to wear her crown and let his people and his officials see how beautiful she was. The king's servants told Queen Vashti what he had said, but she refused to go to him, and this made him terribly angry.*

Steve Nash is one of our family's all-time favorite NBA stars. He played for the Dallas Mavericks. My wife and I grew up in Texas. He returned to the Phoenix Suns about the same time we moved to the Phoenix area. He has been a staple here for nearly a decade, and the Valley of the Sun is still grieving his loss to the L A Lakers. I'm confident Steve will end up as the all-time NBA assist leader. On occasions he will penetrate-dribble, keep it alive through the lane, come off the baseline, thread a look-off pass between two defenders to a cutter for a wide open lay-up - *yeeoowhh!* I always look at Zak and Nic and say, *"That was just Nashty!"*

Queen Vashti does not get credited with the assist. King Xerxes wants to parade her for his party. Try to imagine, if you can, the degree of luxury, opulence, and waste. You may have heard of the lifestyles of some professional athletes who sign multimillion dollar contracts and cannot control their money. It has been reported that it is nothing to spend fifty thousand dollars on wardrobe. Dez Bryant, of the Dallas Cowboys, spent that much money on one meal at a restaurant. They have "entourages" of upwards of 20, 30, even 40 men, for protection and prestige. There is even a dating service that alerts available women with a text message once an athlete sets foot on the premises of a club. He is a sitting duck to the money-crazed gold diggers. Athletes and rappers frequently "make it rain" at strip clubs, that is, throwing enough money in the air to make confetti of hundred dollar bills.

Take that kind of cash, combine it with unlimited, totalitarian governmental control, and you have the Persian kings. J.M. Cook has written that it was nothing for the king to entertain 1,500 guests for a luncheon.[v] His tent in the middle, and four lines stretched out in the shape of a plus, as far as the eye could see. When the king went to war, all of his comforts were gunny sacked with him in tow. His personal chef would prepare the finest meals for him and his invited guests, even as the foot soldiers did his bidding in battle.

Xerxes has been on a seven-day drinking binge. All of his advisors are just as wasted. Suddenly, in a flash of inspiration, he decides to parade his prized possession, his wife, in front of all his guests to show-off her beauty. Vashti would not play along with such tomfoolery. It cost Vashti her life.

I say, good play, Vashti. You made the right call. This doesn't show up in the stat sheet, but she serves as an important foreshadowing to the miracle of Esther who goes into the king unannounced and is still received. This was after three days of fasting and prayer. It was a key moment in the rescue of the Jewish people from certain annihilation.

Esther's Keen Sense

Esther 4:11-14

"There is a law about going in to see the king, and all his officials and his people know about this law. Anyone who goes in to see the king without being invited by him will be put to death. The only way that anyone can be saved is for the king to hold out the gold scepter to that person. And it's been thirty days since he has asked for me."

When Mordecai was told what Esther had said, he sent back this reply, "Don't think that you will escape being killed with the rest of the Jews, just because you live in the king's palace. If you don't speak up now, we will somehow get help, but you and your family will be killed. It could be that you were made queen for a time like this!"

With Vashti's dire consequences as the backdrop, we now feel the gravity of the situation for Esther, Mordecai and all the Jews. In light of Queen Vashti's sudden demise because of her refusal to appear at the whim of the king, we can see clearly that it is nothing shy of miraculous for the same king to extend his scepter welcoming Esther's unsolicited visit. There is pure hatred on the part of Haman and his family members, directed toward the Jewish people. He is a powerful, influential man, with the ability and persuasion to affect racial genocide.

Queen Esther shows a keen sense of proper timing and protocol. She becomes convinced by her cousin, Mordecai, that the fear is justified. She is the one who initiates the three-day fast to pray for deliverance. As the story unfolds we see her accepted by the king. But even then, she knew that wasn't enough. She doesn't just blurt out a request to him. Instead, she invites him to dinner, along with the evil Haman. And at that point, she still resists the urge to bring accusation. She waits one more night, and invites the two to dinner again the next day. This would prove strategic. For it was in this night that God worked through the king's sleeplessness, and Haman's selfish restlessness, to set the stage for the validation of her request to the king the next day.

What if she had rushed things? What if Esther were too anxious? Is it possible to have the right motives, and the right solution, but the wrong timing and demeanor?

In your present situation, what is God speaking to your heart to do? Would you say you have given ample time to seek, to wait, to listen?

Holy Trinity Inferred

Job 33:1-4

Job, listen to me! Pay close attention. Everything I will say is true and sincere, just as surely as the Spirit of God All-Powerful gave me the breath of life.

Elihu has listened silently to the empty arguments of Job's friends. He is a mysterious, young man whose name means, "He is my God." Elihu speaks words of wisdom that segue seamlessly into a theophany of whirlwind. Elihu is the prelude to the voice of God speaking directly to Job. He makes reference to the Holy Spirit. This is important. Job is thought to be the oldest literature in the Bible. Predating Genesis, it was written approximately 3000 B.C. Here we have the imagery of a young man, the Son; a wind, the Spirit; and the thunderous voice of God, the Father. The holy Trinity is inferred in the earliest narrative of human history.

I Didn't Even Know

Psalm 19:12,13

None of us know our own faults. Forgive me when I sin without knowing it. Don't let me do wrong on purpose, Lord, or let sin have control over my life. Then I will be innocent, and not guilty of some terrible fault.

Here's how hypocrisy works. I find fault with another person for some wrongdoing. But then I become aware of the same pattern of inconsistency in my own life. How is this possible? It is because I'm busy living my life in real time. Since I'm me, I have the inside scoop on what I'm feeling, meaning and intend. I allow myself mistakes in spoken communication, misunderstood actions, and follow-through on commitments. Why? It's because I have a context my life situation is housed in. I instantly understand me, and I don't have to explain. I typically extend grace to myself because I know what I've been through, and I know what I meant. It becomes hypocritical when I don't extend that same grace to those around me. Without all the facts I assume, assess and evaluate. I surmise they could've done better, so I judge.

Now the psalmist comes along and tells me I don't even know my own heart. But I thought I did. No. There are two types of sins. I commit sins on purpose. These are typically glaring failures that haunt my conscience. I want to confess them the moment I become aware of them; put them under the blood of Jesus. Other sins, the ones that are really thorny, are the result of my inbred human nature, embedded deep in my psyche. They sometimes fly under the radar of my conscience. But others notice them. Others must have Doppler. Historically these have been delineated as sins of commission and sins of omission. Sins that I commit - what I do that I shouldn't; versus sins I omit - what I haven't done that I should do.

The secret is to be filled with grace toward others and myself, while at the same time not being soft on myself and my friends. A holy, grace-filled accountability is what's needed. One that allows for mistakes without them being shocking, and at once calls for action steps that insure success. After all, God extended this privilege to you and me. He covered me when I didn't even know.

Confessions of a Techie-Schizo

Psalm 27:7-10

Please listen when I pray! Have pity. Answer my prayer. My heart tells me to pray. I am eager to see your face, so don't hide from me. I am your servant, and you have helped me. Don't turn from me in anger. You alone keep me safe. Don't reject or desert me. Even if my father and mother should desert me, you will take care of me.

The traffic bottle-necked. It was at a complete stand still, perfect time to call home and check in. You must know we have call-forwarding. It becomes important to the story. You should also know I picked up my wife's cell phone accidentally as I headed out the door that morning. They look alike. I had both cell phones with me.

So, here I am, stopped on the highway. I pick up the cell phone and dial home using Stefanie's cell phone. At that moment my cell phone rang. It may seem bizarre to you, but pastors are adept at carrying on two conversations at the same time. I picked up my cell phone and answered, *Hello*. A half second later I heard through her phone (which was set to speaker phone) a deep voice, *Hello*. Who was this man answering the phone at my house? Confused and bedazzled, wondering why there was no response from my phone, I said again, *Yes, hello*. And a half-second later I heard from Stefanie's phone, *Yes, hello*.

You're one step ahead of me, aren't you?

I had called from Stefanie's cell phone to our home. Stefanie was online. The call was forwarded to my cell phone. I was talking to myself. And answering myself. That's the classic definition of a schizophrenic. A techie-schizophrenic; but a schizophrenic none-the-less. It boggles my mind to think of the technology involved that induced my neurosis: a signal ran from Stef's cell phone to a cellular tower, beamed off a satellite in outer space, tracked through the phone line to my house, where somehow it knew the line was busy and routed it through a satellite in outer space, bounced back to my cell phone – all in a fraction of a second.

I wonder how often we are prayer-schizophrenics, talking to ourselves. The mystery of prayer is that it involves dialogue. Monologues are what happen in talk shows, i.e. - David Letterman, or Jay Leno. A monologue is the opening performance to an audience. But prayer is not that; it is dialogue, that is, two-way communication. Also, prayer is dia*logue*, not dia*tribe*. Diatribe is a ranting and raving, carrying on; it's a speech to plead your cause. Prayer is not that; it involves listening, gleaning, seeking, and waiting.

Hints to help prayer today:

- God, am I talking too much? (Pause)
- Lord, do I listen well? (Silence)
- Father, is there anything you've wanted to say to me? (Wait)

Beauty

Psalm 48:1, 2

The Lord God is wonderful! He deserves all praise in the city where he lives. His holy mountain, beautiful and majestic, brings joy to all on earth. Mount Zion, truly sacred, is home for the Great King.

Psalm 48 is a description of beauty. At first brush we think it is talking about his mountain, his city, his throne. But these things just house him. As we read on, we realize he is the beautiful One. It is about him. God is beautiful.

We are drawn to beauty. From our earliest recollections the attractive is magnetic to our eyes. There is beauty in nature, in literature and the arts. And we are especially drawn to human beauty. It is normal to notice complexion, shape, form, and softness of face. There is something about pretty eyes and a beautiful smile. The beautiful ones in the earth have a great advantage in terms of being hired, promoted and elevated. Now, that is a fact. Why? We like to be around beautiful people. And subconsciously, on a purely associative level, it makes us feel more beautiful ourselves.

The temptation of the beautiful human beings is to become consumed with self, as if they themselves have generated quality. It may be that a beautiful person can become confused and take her or his eyes off God and instead, look to self. The greatest of human beauty is a mere sampling of God's infinite beauty. Instead of deflecting credit and praise to him in every area, as we always should do, the very attractive person begins to feed off the attention in an unhealthy way.

On the other hand, there is also an advantage to lack of beauty. I've been blessed with the gift of uniqueness. Physical attributes that I used to think of as devastating, i.e. - ears that stick out, acne, or a boney, skinny frame - I now appreciate. They too are an advantage to me, because they cause me to stand out in a crowd of ordinariness. It took me a long time to realize there are varying degrees of beauty. It may be that we take a lifetime to realize the things that are truly beautiful. My uncle used to say jokingly, "Beauty is only skin deep, but ugly goes all the way to the bone." But the truth is beauty is not skin deep. Beauty is intrinsic. Our bodies age, and yet, can remain beautiful to the grave. In our youth we are drawn to physical attractiveness in such a powerful way that inner beauty can fade to the background. The appreciation for physical beauty never diminishes, yet inner beauty comes to the forefront more and more. At least it should be this way.

Some never leave the rudimentary levels of junior high romance. They are stuck in childish lusts and cravings that dictate them. They ache and yearn, never satisfied. But some, the beautiful ones, are able to go deeper. Kindness, tenderness, joy, peace, compassion – these are the qualities of beautiful love. And they are the by-product of God's Spirit in our lives. These qualities are like 3-D glasses that allow us to see the real beauty in every human we meet. And it is all God's idea.

How fortunate when a human has the complete package, outer attraction that is matched by pure character, motives and desires.

How empty when a human has only the shell of beauty. How fleeting. How careless. How sad!

God is beautiful.

A Hen and a Pig and a Sacrifice

Psalms 50:14

I am God Most High! The only sacrifice I want is for you to be thankful and to keep your word.

A hen and a pig were asked by the barnyard committee to consider making a contribution to the morning breakfast of bacon and eggs. The hen said, "Why, sure, I'll be glad to help." The pig snorted, "Now, wait a minute. Bacon and eggs? For the hen it's a contribution; but for me it's a real sacrifice!"

God knows a thing or two about sacrifice. He gave regulations and prohibitions, restraints and orders. Cereal, grain, first-fruits, breast, thigh, bread-waving, oil libations - He had seen every kind of sacrifice. He saw rams, lambs, goats, calves, birds - you name it. He knew of one small animal shared among two households, or elaborate gifts from one individual - aromas, smoke, fire, and the like. There was nothing he had not witnessed. And yet, after experiencing countless animal sacrifices, and still before the dedication of the temple which would result in ritual sacrifice, God makes an amazing statement through his servant, David. "I am God Most High! The only sacrifice I want is for you to be thankful and to keep your word" (Ps 50:14).

Next time you go to church and feel a sense of overwhelm at the thought of trying to be good enough because you're not measuring up, when you feel insufficient for the task, just stop, climb down off the performance treadmill, and remind yourself of this verse. Be thankful and do what you say you will do. Hmm...I think I can handle that. I am often guilty of making things too complicated.

Simplify. Here it is.

Thank God and be authentic.

The Instant Message God

> *Psalm 70:5*
>
> *I am poor and needy, but you, the Lord God, care about me. You are the one who saves me. Please hurry and help!*

"You are the one who saves me. Please hurry and help!" How many times do we cry out this phrase in the course of one day? Perhaps we don't use the identical words from memory; but the essence of the truth needs to bear fruit deep within our spirits. God is as close as the mention of his name. So call on him frequently. He wants to help. If you wanted audience with a dignitary, you would have to go through a battery of secretaries and need an appointment. But think of this, the Creator of the entire universe grants you instant access anytime you need him. Today you may need him while sitting at a red light, or at the Emergency Room, or while writing a paper, or refereeing job relationships. I-M him often today. He is the Instant Message God.

Oh, I Get It

> *Psalms 73:17*
>
> *Then I went to your temple, and there I understood what will happen to my enemies.*

Put up with a little ridiculous diatribe in order to amplify Psalm 73. It puts eternal priorities in perspective.

Where does that guy get off being so bossy? He doesn't appreciate what he has. Doesn't he know he could lose it all in an instant? He goes around snubbing people, looking down his nose at lesser-thans. The clothes, the job title, the vehicle, the attitude - all of it designed to impress, so unimpressive. Hope he enjoys it while it lasts. But does he have to gloat in it? I think he really feels he's better than the rest of us. Does he have to be teaching lessons all the time? Is he the master mentor of humanity? He doesn't get that all of this is fleeting.

I've seen better integrity in the simple poor of El Salvador. I've witnessed the impoverished in Costa Rica more devoted than him. I've seen people who work the land and the mines in the slopes of Colorado who have demonstrated better wisdom and insight. I've seen the soup-line, street people of Phoenix show more warmth.

Then I read the Bible, I pause to pray, I go to church, I hear about eternity. Oh, I get it. This is the only heaven some will ever know. This is as good as it gets for them. And this is the only hell we will ever know. This is as bad as it gets for some for us.

The Absence of I

> Psalm 80:19
>
> Lord God All-Powerful, Make us strong again! Smile on us and save us.

In Psalm 80 there is a noticeable absence of the word "I." What you do find is the word "us" in each stanza. It is similar to the way Daniel includes himself in the confessional prayer for the sins of his people, Israel.

The only instance of singular reference in Psalm 80 is that there is one vine. A vine out of Egypt, a vine planted by the right hand of God, a vine that is called, "the Son you have raised up for yourself" (Ps 80:15 NIV). This is an anticipation of Jesus. His important statements in John 15 about remaining in the vine draw from this psalm where Asaph demonstrates selflessness. Jesus said his Father prunes, trims and cultivates his vine. If we do not remain grafted as by horticultural technique, we will be removed.

If ever there was a selfless person it was Jesus Christ. He modeled perfectly the absence of I.

The First Mistletoe

> Psalm 85:10
>
> Mercy and truth have met,
> Righteousness and peace have kissed (GWT).

I appreciate God's Word Translation here in Psalm 85. It captures the true essence of the verse. The Hebrew poem is using a literary device called parallelism. The first line makes the statement; while the second line restates it using similar words. This reinforcement is what brings the ambiance, not rhyme. The Jewish mind would understand Mercy and Righteousness to correspond, as well the couplet of Truth with Peace. At first glance we have the primary meaning of the passage, which is King David remembering better days in the past, and also looking forward to brighter days in the future. On balance, though, I don't feel it forces a terse opinion on the passage to simply recognize something in retrospect. We have this exchange between Mercy/Righteousness, which mirrors the qualities of God the Father (Ps 79:8, 9; Lk 16:24), and Truth/Peace, or attributes aligned with the Son (Isa 9:6; John 14:6). In the New Testament, Paul (1 Tim 1:2; 2 Tim 1:2), Peter (1 Pet 1:3), and John (2 John 1:2), each use identical descriptors of God the Father and Jesus Christ.

"Righteousness and peace have kissed." When did this divine kiss take place? My personal view is that the heavenly righteousness of the Father, interfaced the truth residing in infant form on earth. This metaphor of endearment coincides with the precise moment of the Incarnation. Heaven and earth occupy one bundled space. Mercy and truth comingle. Righteousness and peace subsist. Psalm 85 hangs the first mistletoe over the manger.

The Dis-ease of Disease

Psalm 94:19

And when I was burdened with worries you comforted me and made me feel secure.

We all know individuals who stress about every little thing and it just drives us nuts. On the other end of the spectrum, some are so nonchalant that it drives us crazy too. Okay, a little bit of worry is not a bad thing. In a worry-free world no events would start on time. In fact, they would never make it to the calendar in the first place. Flights wouldn't leave on time. Bus stops would be non-existent. Time clocks would never be punched. And churches, oh dear pastors, there would be no published worship service times. Hey, think back to grade school. There is a rationale to marking students tardy at school. It's a wonderful life lesson.

Some worry is a good thing, but there are worriers who endure a completely unrealistic approach to living. Stressed about every teeny complication. Worrying can become an illness. It's called Generalized Anxiety Disorder, and may be connected to a whole host of illnesses including heart disease, cancer, stroke, depression and neurological disorders. Have you ever considered that disease is actually dis-ease.

It does no good to worry. But when we do, God doesn't abandon us. He comforts us and makes us secure. He fills us with peace that doesn't make any sense. Next time you become aware that you are actively engaging in worry - stop! Take a deep breath, and pray Psalm 94:19. "And when I was burdened with worries you comforted me, and made me feel secure."

Fulcrum and Counterweights

Psalm 97:2

Dark clouds surround him, and his throne is supported by justice and fairness.

What a great verse, Psalm 97:2. You picture the fury of a dark, cloud-canopy as the backdrop. It speaks of his power. "His throne is supported by justice and fairness."

Solomon built his temple to the Lord and readily confessed it was not able even to begin to contain God. The heavens could not do that. But that didn't stop Solomon from trying his very best to honor the Lord with a temple made from man's very best materials. Can we even picture the beauty of a perfectly square holy place overlaid with pure gold, even the floor? It took twenty tons of fine gold to cover it. Golden angelic figurines drape the entire back wall with their wings touching in the center. The temple was fitted perfectly with intentional furnishings, each piece immaculate, as well as functional for the duties of the priests in worship and sacrifice.

Interestingly, there were two pillars at the entrance to the temple. These columns served an ascetic purpose, but were not truly meant for support of the structure. The cap on top of each column was approximately eighteen meters high. Solomon gave the pillars names: Jachin and Boaz. The interpretation of their names might be something along the lines of Security and Strength. We don't know who wrote Psalm 97. It comes in Book 4 of the collection of Psalms. One of these Psalms is attributed to Moses, two to David. The other 14 in the group we are unsure of. Who knows? Perhaps Solomon was even the one who wrote Psalm 97. If that were the case, we see some similarities in Psalm 97:2 with Solomon's naming the support columns of the temple. And, again, the columns were not loadbearing. Psalm 97 says God's throne is founded on Justice and Fairness. Solomon, from the Chronicles above, is quoted as naming the pillars Security and Strength, very similar conceptual picture and imagery.

It may be difficult sometimes to conceptualize God as just and fair in our world. Towers fall because of terrorists. Natural disasters like hurricanes, tsunamis, wildfires, and tornadoes devastate lives and change landscapes. Criminal, twisted pedophiles abduct and exploit innocent children. Famine, hunger and poverty decimate entire nations. But the reality is God so values free choice that he allows for humanity's exploration and experimentation. Often injustice is the consequence of our broken, frail, sinful existence. We humans make choices that have negative impact on other lives. And we are just now scratching the surface on the interaction of our choices with nature; though storms that sometimes seem selective leave the greatest theologians scratching the surface of their heads. I am confident to say God remains just and fair. He has a track record of faithfulness. In the end, he will be completely justified, and every knee will bow, and every tongue will confess that he is right.

Theorists speculate the naming of the two columns by Solomon hints at something else. Another interpretation of the names Jachin and Boaz hints at a fulcrum and sand-weighted device. There is a view that at the time of the seizure of the temple hundreds of years later, the high priest gave the signal, the tumblers turned, sand spilled on the counterweight, a trap-door opened, and the priests hid the Ark of the Covenant underneath in a hidden chamber. You know it has never been recovered. It is at least interesting that there are two different measurements for these pillars at two different times in Israel's history. Were they lowered? Just a theory, that's all. Don't freak out. But in a real sense, the presence of God is not recovered right now, it seems hidden. Eternity will prove God's justice and fairness. They will be on display for all to see.

Within

> *Psalm 103:1*
>
> *With all my heart I praise the Lord,*
> *and with all that I am I praise his holy name!*

Following a moving experience in which I was reminded of the need to pray for my family, and realized how important it is to image Christ to them.

Within

Within

Where no one else sees
Where I play to an Audience of One
Where life vibrates to the cadence of my heartbeat

Within

O let me honor You

December 7, 2001

Code Talkers

Psalm 119:105

Your word is a lamp that gives light wherever I walk.

During World War II there was a very special group of marines, 420 Navajo Indians, who served as Marine Corp Radio Operators. They were known as code talkers. They were recruited specifically for this cause. Using their own native language, they developed the secret for code transmission. It proved to be unbreakable and was the only successful code the Allies were able to utilize. The code talkers were so devoted that even after the war ended in 1945, and they came home; they still kept their secret heroism from their own family members. It remained classified for twenty-three years until 1968. They were not recognized publicly for their heroics until the year 2000 when they were honored with the Congressional Gold Medal by the United States Congress. Many of them had already died. Now that's devotion.

Some believe the Bible hides embedded codes. The Bible Code supposedly reveals obscure messages. Letters are numbered and coded. Discerning minds can find historical facts cited and future events indicated. Some pretty fascinating facts have been uncovered. The word "Torah" is found by counting every fifty letters at the beginning of Genesis. It does the same thing in Exodus. It is claimed that names of historical figures such as Yitzhak Rabin and John F. Kennedy can be found by searching the Hebrew text for patterns, as well as words like "spaceship." Countless claims have been made.

I do not doubt that it is possible. It wouldn't surprise me for the Bible to contain all kinds of surprises. This is as it should be. The God of the universe has given his written revelation. Since his fingerprints are on it, one would expect it to drip with the extraordinary and supernatural. But there is no need for exaggerated sensationalism. It is antithetical to God's ways to assume he hides from us and wants us to figure him out like a puzzle. Quite the opposite is true. Christ plainly chooses the path of humanity. He lives the miraculous right out in plain view. He invites followers. He discloses truth. He unveils hope. He reveals mystery. God ordained that the holy Scriptures would reveal the plan of salvation. If the purest simpleton will read the Bible and pray, God will show truth. He delights is giving away wisdom (Jas 1:5).

God is not a code talker. I'm sure there is much of the Bible we are unable to understand. But we have our plates full concentrating on the simple truths. Mark Twain once said, "It ain't those parts of the Bible that I can't understand that bother me, it is the parts that I do understand."[vi]

Eat Mor Chikin

Psalm 127:2

It is useless to get up early and stay up late in order to earn a living. God takes care of his own, even while they sleep.

Psalm 127:2 informs a sound, business ethic. The basic implication is this: don't lose half a night's sleep crunching numbers, and trying to figure out ways to one-up the competition. Almost seems un-American. Work hard each business day, but leave the work behind you when you get home. Offer a good product, be honest, live by your values, and leave the rest to God. This is easier for some lines of work than others, but it is possible in every occupation.

Truett Cathy, founding CEO of Chick-fil-A, had a choice to make. Would he open the doors of his restaurants on Sundays? Others taunted, saying he'd never make it in fast food if he didn't. Wisely, he reasoned that there are many choices for food when people go out to eat. They're not going to eat any one type of food several times a week. He concluded when they hear we are closed on Sundays they'll come on other days of the week, so long as we offer a quality product for a fair price. Truett's son, Dan, has continued the tradition. This position was tested severely when the Olympics came to Atlanta in 1996. There was a public outcry for the restaurant to open its doors. The company stayed true to its values.

Dan Cathy has said, "You can change your position, but you have to have a rational reason for the change and be consistent and communicate that to your customers. Two different brands cannot be visible to the customer. Your authenticity is questioned after that, and your brand loses equity."[vii] There are profound spiritual and practical lessons to be drawn from such integrity. I am fond of that kind of consistency. And I'm not the only one. Apparently a lot of people have decided to *eat mor chikin*. The company grossed 4.1 billion dollars in sales last year.

Unity

> *Psalm 133:1-3*
>
> *It is truly wonderful when relatives live together in peace. It is as beautiful as olive oil poured on Aaron's head and running down his beard and the collar of his robe. It is like the dew from Mount Hermon, falling on Zion's mountains, where the LORD has promised to bless his people with life forevermore.*

The word "where" (CEV) is better understood "there." The Hebrew word *sham* means "there." It is a directional word. David makes a statement to begin the Psalm. *It is just beautiful when people get along together.* Then he gives two examples: 1.) It's like the anointing ceremony of a priest. The flask was broken. Oil poured down from the top of the head into the beard. It continued until it saturated Aaron all the way to the tips of his clothes. It is a picture of all-inclusiveness. From the top down, everyone is included in the blessing. 2.) It is like the dew of Mount Hermon, the larger mountain, dripping down to smaller Mount Zion, all the way down into the foothills. A physical impossibility, as the two are separated by many miles. But notice again, it starts at the top and trickles to all. For "there" the Lord bestows his blessings, even life for evermore. Where? Where Aaron is? No. Where Mount Hermon is? No. Where there is unity, the blessings of the Lord cannot help but reside. Teamwork fosters zest.

Hanging Harps and Hope

> *Psalm 137:1-3*
>
> *Beside the rivers of Babylon we thought about Jerusalem, and we sat down and cried. We hung our small harps on the willow trees. Our enemies had brought us here as their prisoners, and now they wanted us to sing and entertain them. They insulted us and shouted, "Sing about Zion!"*

The Babylonians have added insult to injury. They are pouring salt on the wounds. It is not unlike the heavy-handed slave owner demanding entertainment, or else the whip. But there may be more here than meets the eye. The exiles, now humbled in spirit, are remembering the greatest king of their history, David. Numerous Talmudic sources mention an ancient legend that David would hang his harp on the tree, and then precisely at midnight the wind of the Spirit would blow across the strings, making music, and waking him to study Torah. I'm not saying this is true, only that it is very interesting.

There are recordings online in which you can hear replicas of ancient Israeli harps being played by the wind blowing upon them. It is a music other-worldly.

In the place of their despair the captives remembered Jerusalem. They hung their harps in the Willows. What has often been interpreted as a sign of utter despair, hanging the harp in the willow, may be quite the opposite. It could be they were voicing silent faith through the use of a powerful symbol. The hanging harps mean hope.

Impassioned Pleas

Psalm 144:5

Open the heavens like a curtain and come down, Lord. Touch the mountains and make them send up smoke.

David's prayer is so passionate. It's similar to Isaiah's cry, which sounds so powerful in the language of the king, "Oh that You would rend the heavens! That You would come down! That the mountains might shake at your presence" (Isa 61:1, NKJV). Hear the urgency of his groan – "Ohhh!" The plea – "rend the heavens," tear them apart. Get down here and rattle mountains! Our God does not mind our impassioned pleas.

My Heart's Keeping

Proverbs 3:3

Let love and loyalty always show like a necklace, and write them in your mind.

A poem in reflection upon Proverbs 3:3.

My Heart's Keeping

What makes this heart race
inside me?
It rages

Sometimes it surfaces in
the physical reality
I sense pain
soreness
Like today…

But daily on a subconscious level
An intuitive motor idles
A real me idols

Always that self fears deadlines, ultimatums,
deficiencies, lack, and obscurity

Until I come to You
let my heart keep Your commandments
and, so, rest

February 3, 2009

Bait Christian

Proverbs 11:6

Honesty can keep you safe, but if you can't be trusted, you trap yourself.

The TV show, Bait Car, features a vehicle that is monitored by law enforcement equipped with the latest, most sophisticated technology in surveillance. It is set up as a trap intended to be stolen. The fallacy of the plan collapses around the thief as the police close in for the arrest. Individuals who are up to no good get snookered. The video doesn't lie. These robbers are toast, caught red-handed. The culprits, once caught, say the funniest things. One of them blurted out through his tears, "Oh God, help me. Oh God, why is this happening?"

This is the day of hidden cameras in stores, businesses and even in and around homes. You are being videoed by surveillance in traffic on roadways, bank lobbies, convenience stores, post offices, libraries, stadiums, schools and amusement parks. Add to this the fact that plethora of cell phones capture endless data. In theory, if an individual had the means and resources to do so, a fairly complete documentary could be assimilated to showcase your life built upon a compilation of all the stuff that is out there. But if you're going to be naughty, *busted!* Have you ever thought through the implications of living in the technology age? Really?

Newsflash! What happens in Vegas does not stay in Vegas, nor does it stay in Venice, nor Viet Nam, nor Van Vleck, Texas, for that matter. You can be posed and posted in a heartbeat without your even being aware. We have friends on our profiles. We are linked and we're liked. But our networks are not very social. We "lol" but just not inside.

Here is the point. If it has not happened already, it will. Someone will be watching to see if you're the real deal. Some Christians have been handed too much change by a cashier intentionally just to see if they will do the right thing. I know of a Christian man who took something for his own use that he felt justified in taking, and thought that no one knew. Years later his otherwise flawless reputation still carried that one smudge. When you are alone, do what's right. You just might be enacting an episode of Bait Christian in real time.

An anomaly of our day is the compartmentalization of Christianity. We shove God into one of the file boxes of our lives. Now, you be a good little Jesus and stay in there until I need you. This is just wrong. Christ must be the hub of our existence. When he is at the center we long to do right simply because it's the right thing to do. And then there are no worries, even if the cameras are rolling.

My Friend's Advice

Proverbs 12:15

Fools think they know what is best,
but a sensible person listens to advice.

A poem inspired by words from a friend, Buddy Bishop, that reminded me of something my father-in-law has always said. Another friend, Bill Ross had passed away recently. He would say these words often too.

My Friend's Advice

My dear friend
    Wise in years
        Said to me

"You'd better watch those boys of yours:
You'll turn around twice and they'll be grown"

    He was right
        I turned to see
            So big so fast

I turned to thank my friend for his advice.
But he was gone

    So now I turned
        To pass his wisdom on…

October 7, 2002

Five Mississippi

Proverbs 15:28

Good people think before they answer, but the wicked speak evil without ever thinking.

When we were kids we played tackle football in the backyard. We used the 'ole 5 Mississippi Rule. You know, the defense couldn't rush the quarterback until they had counted one-Mississippi; two-Mississippi; three-Mississippi; four-Mississippi; five-Mississippi. What I remember is that one-Mississippi was pronounced clearly and audibly; but as the play developed, and the routes were executed, the QB's eyes would widen in the pocket, then the rusher would resort to a tactic known neighborhood-wide. He barked a sort of monosyllabic grunt so that the last count came out as *Fighmippey!* This was typically accompanied by crossing the line of scrimmage simultaneously with the first syllable of his blurb, an offense rivaling that of short cutting at the local elementary. The play was followed by shouts of "Off sides!" If it was too obvious you might gain the moniker, "Cheater." A particularly heinous offense might conjure up chants of "Cheater, cheater, pumpkin eater!" Few recovered enough dignity after such disgrace to be able to go on and lead a successful life!

What if all of us Christians mastered the art of the 5 Mississippi Rule before we speak! "Good people think before they answer, but the wicked speak evil without ever thinking" (Prov 15:28). Lil' advice from one who is working on it, pray it before you say it! There is a companion proverb that says, "Even a fool is thought wise if he keeps silent" (Prov 17:28).

Podiaoralitis - in layman's terms, it is foot-in-mouth disease. Open mouth, insert foot. How many times does it happen in the course of one day? Some people speak because they have something to say; others speak because they just have to say something. This sickness is spreading at pandemic proportions in our day. It is off the charts at the Centers for Disease Control. Mom was right. If you don't have something nice to say, don't say anything at all. Paul touched on this topic, "Do nothing out of selfish ambition or vain conceit, but in humility consider others better than yourselves" (Phil 1:3). And again, "Do not let any unwholesome talk come out of your mouths, but only what is helpful for building others up according to their needs, that it may benefit those who listen" (Eph 4:29).

Five Mississippi to collect your thoughts. Pray it before you say it.

Disarming Antagonists

> *Proverbs 16:32*
>
> *Controlling your temper is better than being a hero who captures a city.*

I know of an individual, a real trusted friend, who was approached by a stranger in the parking lot after getting out of his Toyota. "How does it feel to keep Americans out of work?" My friend could have lectured about the scores of American workers who assemble foreign cars at factories right here in the United States. He could have spoken of the amount of prayer and thought that had gone into such an important purchase, how mileage was considered, how craftsmanship was premium, how the Lord had opened the door for the buy. Instead, in that moment my friend smiled, and said, "You know what? You have a good day."

The point is not philosophy of what constitutes national loyalty. The point is we are approached often by well-intending individuals who are out of line. "A soft answer turns away wrath" (Prov 15:1). You have the ability, through the Holy Spirit, to diffuse explosions by disarming antagonists. What conversations can you keep from detonating today?

That's What Friends are For

Proverbs 17:17

A friend is always a friend, and relatives are born to share our troubles.

In Fort Worth, Texas, in the first half of the twentieth century, sandwiched between the Great Depression and World War II, two teenage students attended the same high school. One was a quirky seventeen-year-old named Sam, and he was a devout Christian. Some of the kids thought he was odd, especially John. Sam was always inviting kids to church. He would write Scriptures on the chalkboard at school so that his classmates would see them. Sam had invited John to church a number of times, but John had no frame of reference for church at all.

One night, John was deeply troubled after coming home from a bar at two o'clock in the morning. He walked in the door and saw the family Bible sitting on the coffee table. It wasn't used, it was more for decoration. In desperation he flipped the Bible open to see a picture of Jesus standing at a door. The caption read, "Behold, I stand at the door, and knock: if any man hear my voice, and open the door, I will come in to him, and will sup with him, and he with me (Rev 3:20, KJV)." He felt strangely moved and called his friend Sam who invited him to church. The two of them sat on the back row. The minister invited individuals to come to the front and invite Jesus into their hearts. John was afraid. Sam said he would go down to the front with him. And that's what they did. John Osteen walked down to the front to accept Jesus with Sam Martin at his side.

John became a famous preacher. He was the founding pastor of Lakewood Church in Houston, Texas for forty years. Sam Martin pastored in small places all of his ministry career. In his 70s John got news that his friend was working as a greeter at a local department store. John drove several hours to meet with him. He invited Sam to join his staff in Houston. For the last 8 years of Sam's life he was on staff at one of the largest churches in America. Sam had been there for John when he was in need; now John was there for Sam when he was in need. That's what friends are for.[viii]

Use It or Lose It

Proverbs 19:27

If you stop learning, you will forget what you already know.

Ever wondered how many years you will live? Probably not on a purely cognitive level. We usually don't allow ourselves to think that way. But on some kind of subconscious level I think it's on the back burner continually. At age 46 I would like to think I'm not to the halfway mark yet. Will I make 100? Statistics are against me though; and so is the normalcy rate of Scripture. Psalm 90:10 is poetry, not meant for hard and fast science; but it says we're given 70 or 80 years. How sad are we when those days are cut short! Especially when they are cut short super early. None of us is guaranteed any amount of years. The fact that you are reading this right now proves that you have lived longer than millions and millions of humans throughout history.

I read the obituaries in the newspaper. That's something I never used to do, didn't care. Now, I know how much more important that page is than the sports page or the comics. When I read the obits I feel a little secure if everyone on the page is older than me. I feel a little concerned if some are younger. Sometimes there are just a couple of deceased, sometimes a dozen or more. One time I was shocked that 3 out of the 4 on the page were younger than me.

We don't know how many days we are given; but we do know how to enjoy them. Keep learning. That's the secret.

My in-laws have modeled a zest for life that is mesmerizing. They are in their 70s. They are youthful. Jerry works out religiously. Mamie too, she is the tennis evangelist of Corte Bella. They eat right, they get rest, they have energy that is spellbinding. After starting out as itinerant evangelists for around 6 or 7 years, they pastored churches for 26 years before becoming missionaries to Central America for a decade and a half. Now, retired, they keep an active schedule of fill-in pastoral ministry, conducting missionary services, but most of all - just ask Jerry - his number one job is be at every event possible for his four grandchildren. I respect my in-laws very much. I want to be ever-learning like them.

I've experienced the reality of Proverbs 19:27 personally. When I am actively engaged in learning on a consistent basis, my retention of facts and figures is better. Being engaged intellectually keeps my memory intact better. Conversely, when I have fallen into slothful behavior for any stretch of time, I find it difficult to recall information that I should know. How about you today? Will you use it or lose it?

Coach

Proverbs 20:5

Someone's thoughts may be as deep as the ocean, but if you are smart you will discover them.

My family loves basketball. Both of our boys, Zakary, and Nicholas, have been a huge part of the high school program. And Stefanie and I, well, we just love being supportive parents. Almost every game the boys' grandparents are in the stands too. It is a wonderful season of life. This past year I had a surprise opportunity. I was asked to Coach the freshmen basketball team at the high school. Our church board values creative endeavor so much that they're allowing me to do this. We're finding a way to make it work. I love coaching these kids.

The truth is I've been a coach for a long time. A number of years ago I received training to be what is called a life coach. The main difference between a mentor and a coach is this: a mentor pours into an individual. A coach, on the other hand, draws out of the individual gifts and abilities that he may not even know he has. I'll just bet there are people all around you who would love to have their gifts and abilities released. And you're going to be used to draw them out. Hey, coach those around you to a greater level of serving God. Drop and give me twenty minutes in prayer.

Thirty Second Tune-Up

Proverbs 23:7

For as he thinks in his heart, so is he. (NKJV)

Do you have thirty seconds to retool your day? The secret is to live in appreciation instead of obligation. Stop and think about how much fun you get to have because God allowed you to live in the 21st Century (especially those of us in the United States). There is a release of inexplicable energy in your spirit when you decide to operate in the mode of delight instead of duty. Rather than seeking to trudge through the task list today, i.e. – "I've got to get Brutus to the vet. When will I squeeze in time to buy the groceries? Yikes – I forgot the water bill!" Instead, take this for a test drive – "Isn't it amazing that we have healthcare for our animals! Wow, look at all these choices and selections of quality food! I'm so blessed to live with indoor plumbing!" Almost everything we do is a privilege. Hmmm.....

Ask yourself: What am I celebrating? Who can I encourage? How?

Wordly Wisdom

Proverbs 25:9-11

When you and someone else can't get along, don't gossip about it. Others will find out, and your reputation will then be ruined. The right word at the right time is like precious gold set in silver.

Look at the title carefully. It is not worldly wisdom, but a play on words, word-ly wisdom. Once I preached a sermon for National Women's Ministries Day intended to be titled Wordly Women; but there was a typo in the bulletin so that my sermon title was printed Worldly Women. That was an interesting Sunday.

Almost always it is the case with the proverbs that each verse stands on its own merit. They are a collection of maxims that teach valuable life lessons in compact, concise statements. They are delicious sound bites that instruct. However, this is not always the case. Sometimes sections teach in the proverbs. For instance, there is a strong modeling of father-son relationships in the first seven chapters. There is a group of sayings, thirty in all, that spans chapters 22, 23 and 24. Have you ever considered how perfectly Proverbs 25: 9, 10 and 11 are knit together. Read it carefully for word-ly wisdom.

"When you and someone else can't get along, don't gossip about it. Others will find out, and your reputation will then be ruined. The right word at the right time is like precious gold set in silver" (Prov 25 9-11).

We are not to gossip. If there are ever any words to be spoken as directives they are to be handled through the proper channels of leadership and in the right timing. This safeguards your own reputation, and bolsters others' confidence in your trust level. The right word in the right timing equals pristine clarity, apples of gold in settings of silver.

Right in the Happy Middle

Proverbs 30:7, 8

There are two things, Lord, I want you to do for me before I die: Make me absolutely honest and don't let me be too poor or too rich. Give me just what I need.

Do you realize how counter-cultural this prayer request is. Why this is anti-American! "God, don't give me too much money." Have you prayed it recently? I haven't.

I have a friend who is thoughtful and wise. Once at the beginning of the new year I asked him if he had any goals. He said, "Yes, I would like to live on less and be happier." My professor in seminary always advised, "Be like a British pastor. Drive a little car and have a big library." A wise sage in my life has said, "If you can ever get to the point where money works for you instead of you working for money, then you have done well." The profound nature of those comments has always stuck with me.

Proverbs 30:7-8 encapsulates that sentiment. God, don't let me get the big head, and think, "I've got this!" No, I don't *got this!* Any financial good of our lives is because of God's blessings. So I should save like an ant, budget like a miser, be a spendthrift, do everything I can in my own strength and ingenuity but just know, I am never exempt from difficulty.

On the other hand, I trust for God's provision so that I don't get depressed about finances and spiral downward. If I have food, clothing and shelter I will be grateful. I'll remember there are individuals who are truly poor. I will not allow discouragements to tempt me to steal.

Not so rich that I'm snooty, not so poverty stricken that I'm hopeless, my prayer, God keep me right in the happy middle.

Praise to Whom Praise is Due

Proverbs 31:31

Show her respect—praise her in public for what she has done.

I'll just bet there is a female in your circle of acquaintances who deserves praise. My wife, Stefanie, is just such a one.

She has mastered the bread machine, carrying it to a whole new level. Yes, she's made hundreds of loaves of bread (3 or 4 per week for all of the teenage years of our two boys); but she also uses it to make creative dough that is left out to rise after the kneading. She then cooks it on stoneware for old school pizza. She uses it to make a crust for the most awesome German Cabbage Rolls. Stef has a pasta cutter for cranking out spaghetti and, oh, Butternut Raviolis. Mmm. She makes fresh sorbet. Yeah, I know, I'm not joking. She makes cinnamon rolls and smoothies and fresh soups and stews and hot rolls and a host of other specialties. Stef has a real green thumb. She home-grows tomatoes, blueberries, strawberries, cucumbers and herbs like basil, cilantro, and mint. I confess, at times I have done dishes with ulterior motives. I told her once, if I clean them up, there's a high likelihood she'll dirty them again. Enough about food. I could go on and on.

The thing that is most impressive to me is my wife's love for the Lord. She disciplines herself to be in the Word and prayer each morning, first thing. She is very committed to serving the Lord. She works hard leading the worship band at church, directing, choosing songs, recruiting. She leads Little People's Church, conducting worship service for 3, 4 and 5 year-olds. She always takes healthy snacks for them. She makes sure their ministry room is bright, clean and fun. She serves on the Design Team for the church and has painted and decorated. She is the church's bookkeeper and maintains meticulous records. Honestly, it is mind-boggling to me when I consider the load she carries with such grace. Our lives are filled with activity every moment. The church is the hub of our lives. Somehow, it always works out that we have enough time. Sometimes, just in the nick of time.

I haven't even touched on laundry, (she makes her own detergent with borax and other ingredients); and driving the family car like a taxi; and running appliances at off-peak hours; and home budget management; and piano lessons and making her own bath soap. She knits hats with team logos to sell on EBay. As I write all this it seems incomprehensible; but I promise, it is all true.

We are celebrating Stefanie's being ten years beyond brain surgery. The days preceding it were very difficult. And the recovery was super intense. There was a time when we didn't know what her energy level would look like. Now, she works out every day. She eats right. She stays fit and beautiful. She needs to have a nap each day, and manages headaches; but overall she is doing remarkably well. We praise the Lord for this. She is the closest thing to Jesus I've seen. My life friend. She is truly a Proverbs 31 wife.

What females do you know who you should "praise publicly?" No, this is not a chauvinistic comment that assumes readers are males. Ladies included, what females do you know who you should "praise publicly?"

Fly a Kite

> *Ecclesiastes 3:14*
>
> *Everything God has done will last forever; nothing he does can ever be changed. God has done all this, so that we will worship him.*

Embedded in this moping tirade of the worthlessness of existence you keep reading little blips of hope like this one in verse 14. One has to be careful with Ecclesiastes. As to its literary construction, it is first and foremost poetry. A poetical piece that delivers a powerful punch in the end. The wise Solomon keeps our interest by teasing us along. He knows we're not going to take him serious about the despair. *Everything I leave to my heirs is going to be wasted. Nothing is new under the sun; it's all been done before. It all makes no sense, just a chasing after the wind.* We can't accept these depressive verses as the final word on the book. It would be like reading a coupon from the newspaper and then saying, "The newspaper is reporting that the world will expire the end of the month." We wouldn't do that. In the same way, we need to take all of Ecclesiastes into consideration to detect the true meaning.

We've all felt boredom, hopelessness, fatigue. We've all said, "What's the point?" at one time or another. We can get so frustrated with this temporary struggle. But everything God does is eternal. Catch it. Everything. Everything he does lasts forever. You are one of those things. God created you as an eternal being. You will exist forever. God has set eternity in our hearts.

In the wake of the 9/11 tragedy I felt a real deep-seeded concern for our nation. I was so serious for a couple of days. I remember not smiling or laughing. I was stoic. It really set me in a subtle downward spiral. My son, Zak, came up to me and said, "Dad, can we go out front and play Frisbee?" We did, for an hour or so, just threw the Frisbee back and forth. Chased it, flipped it, boomeranged it. We laughed and chuckled. It is amazing how therapeutic a toy can be!

The point Solomon wants to make is to enjoy life. Take in every moment. Live each day to the fullest. You're just chasing the wind? So what? Go fly a kite. Make the most of it. There will be many ups and downs over the course of life. Fear God. Honor him. Give him first place. Let him have top billing in your life. Despair is temporary. Joy springs forth eternal.

Save Some Kick

Ecclesiastes 9:11, 12

Here is something else I have learned: The fastest runners and the greatest heroes don't always win races and battles. Wisdom, intelligence, and skill don't always make you healthy, rich, or popular. We each have our share of bad luck. None of us know when we might fall victim to a sudden disaster and find ourselves like fish in a net or birds in a trap.

When I was a freshman in high school there was a phenomenal basketball superstar, a graduating senior headed to college on a full-ride scholarship. He played the game as if he had ice water in his veins, so cool under pressure. He was always the go-to guy and he always delivered. However, the summer before he was to leave for school, our small town staggered at the news of his car crash, hit by a train while out drinking and carousing with his buddies. His injuries were severe. He lost it all in a heartbeat, his scholarship, his abilities, and his dream.

Think about the events that capture our undivided attention. What are the episodes that grab the audience of the community? Often they are crises on various levels. How sad when someone who shows real promise doesn't produce! The most likely to succeed often does not. The sheer disappointment of someone with all the ability in the world who crashes and burns! Star quarterback marries head-cheerleader, divorce proceedings, rumors of alcoholism, unfaithfulness gossiped about. The pastor who collapses under an unbearable self-imposed pressure. The painful words, "Hand me your minister's card."

We all stumble. We all fall. There is limitless grace for all. You don't fall from grace. That is a huge lesson to us all.

A companion lesson is to move forward at a steady, realistic pace. Don't be too hard on yourself. We live in an unrealistic world of comparisons. Just think of how many TV shows feature timed competitions. Just notice the unreal, humanly impossible, body-shapes of mannequins in the display windows of malls. How borderline ridiculous are the fakes of hyper media that seem to spout unlimited resources! Underneath the glamorized, airbrushed veneer lurks emotional frenzy.

Neighbor, what's your hurry? Just like good ribs, go low and slow. In a more language-of-the-king type wording, King James Version says, "The race is not to the swift, nor the battle to the strong." Slow and steady wins the race? Perhaps. But maybe it would be more biblical to say, slow and steady finishes the race. Rather than having an impressive start, concentrate on finishing strong. Save some kick for the end. God is looking for finishers. Enjoy your leg of the journey today.

Boring!

> *Song of Solomon 3:11*
>
> *Come out, you daughters of Zion, and look at the King...wearing the crown, the crown with which his mother crowned him on the day of his wedding, the day his heart rejoiced. (NIV)*

There is a restaurant we love to frequent that specializes in serving baked potatoes in a variety of choices. When you order, the front clerk calls out your request to the cook. He will say. *Gimme' a steak-tater all the way!* Or, *one Ranch-covered, sour-cream loaded!* Whenever someone wishes to have a plain potato with only butter he has a special descriptor. Gimme' a BORING! And it echoes down the workers of the serving line. BORING! ... BORING! ... BORING!

Try to imagine church without ladies. BORING! In the early days of our movement it was the ladies who carried the brunt of church work in Assemblies of God churches. It was the ladies who took up offerings, cleaned the buildings, ushered in the services, led the singing, preached if needed. The Assemblies of God has benefited greatly from the ministry of women since its inception. I am proud to be part of a movement that has offered credentials to women from the beginning days. A careful study of Scripture shows this is proper.

A church without women involved? BORING!

Questions to ponder:

- How may I better honor the women in my circle of acquaintances?
- Who will I encourage today? How?

Snow White and the Seven Grieves

> *Isaiah 1:18*
>
> *I, the Lord, invite you to come and talk it over. Your sins are scarlet red, but they will be whiter than snow or wool.*

I once preached an illustrated sermon based upon this very Scripture. It was titled, *Snow White and the Seven Grieves*. In it each grief was portrayed by one of the dwarfs. Catholic tradition has held that there are seven grievances that are particularly heinous in terms of offending the Holy Spirit. They are pride, greed, envy, anger, lust, gluttony and sloth. Obviously it is not an exhaustive sin list; but it is to say, all sins have their root in one of these seven. You will not find a Bible verse that states this; but it may be a biblical concept. At least it stands to reason.

In Isaiah 1 God speaks an oracle through his servant decrying the absolute debauchery and filthiness that his chosen people Israel had become. The description is horrid. You are bruised from head to toe. You are nothing but oozing sores. There is not one place on your entire body where you are healthy. I would say that sounds pretty hopeless. And yet in this setting come the words our souls ache to hear. "Come, let us reason. Though our sins be as scarlet they shall be white as snow."

A number of years ago my friend, Pete Seilhymer, was on a missions excursion in the high mountains of Tibet. They took communion at 18,600 feet. In a concentrated effort to break strongholds, they had communion at seven different locations surrounding the villages below. In an act of homage to the true Almighty God they did something that was very Tibetan. When they were done they poured the juice out on the fresh snow, a sacred libation crystallizing their worship and commitment to Jesus Christ. Pete describes the crimson stain splattering the pure white blanket of snow. Instantly, he thought of Isaiah 1:18; and often, when he receives communion, to this day, he is reminded of that event.

How would God forgive the totality of human sin? His only Son, perfect and pure, would be splattered and spent on a cruel cross. In exchange for our belief, we are made snow white and relieved of all our grievous sins. It is quite an exchange - snow white for the seven grieves.

Greatest Joy

Isaiah 11:3

His greatest joy will be to obey the Lord.

What is your greatest joy? What would you say it is? Perhaps eating at a certain restaurant with dear friends or having family together for a meal during the holidays. Maybe it is having the dream job, driving a fine automobile, living in an extraordinary home. Your greatest joy may be something really admirable, serving the less fortunate, volunteering at the Little League, or cleaning the church. The arts? Writing, singing, playing, dancing, performing? Is it people oriented? Coffee with a confidant, a family member's special occasion, the rapt happiness of a mentee progressing. What would you say is your greatest joy?

Jesus, his greatest joy? Obeying his Father. He took great delight in obeying his Father's will.

I wonder what it would take for me to even begin to orient myself in that direction. I mean, really. Not just mouthing some propositional truth that is empty and lifeless to me; but I mean to really, truly delight in obedience of my heavenly Father's every whim. *"Father, is there anything you would like right now? Can I do anything for you?"* That is not my natural inclination. I am bent an entirely other direction. This is going to take some discipline, some patience, some long obedience in the same direction.

Before the Ice Cream Melts

Isaiah 24:3-6

The earth will be stripped bare and left that way. This is what the Lord has promised. The earth wilts away; its mighty leaders melt to nothing. The earth is polluted because its people disobeyed the laws of God, breaking their agreement that was to last forever. The earth is under a curse; its people are dying out because of their sins.

As I write, we are in San Diego for a few days of vacation. The other night my family was on Mission Beach. Nic was enjoying being with his friends from the basketball team. Stefanie, Zak and I were enjoying ice cream cones in giant waffle cones. Yum! As we approached the beach entrance from the boardwalk, there were guys in green shirts, with unkempt dreadlocks, and broad smiles, holding clipboards. One of them approached us and said, "Wanna help stop global warming before your ice cream melts? You know how we get when our ice cream melts." As I smiled and nodded and passed on by, he couldn't know the flurry of thoughts in my mind in that moment.

Before proceeding, let me say, I'm not convinced global warming has been approached clinically. I don't think there's been enough time to monitor accurately systems of climate that have been in cycles for somewhere around six thousand years. Our recent documentation is only a blip on the screen of human history. I speak as a young earth theorist. If one chooses to believe in an evolution of millions of years this only serves to bolster my point. We just don't have enough information. The only thing that can prove it from a scientific standpoint is time, much more time. It is deeply saddening that the ozone layer has torn in places and people groups suffer physical maladies in those regions. Who is to say it hasn't been that way before?

Having said that, I am concerned that we have not been good stewards of the earth. That was one of the primary responsibilities given to Adam. So, I recycle. I re-purpose. I despise the wasteful littering of our oceans and rivers. I think it is wise to use wind turbines and solar panels. I believe Christians should be good citizens and stand hand in hand with community leaders to do the obvious things we can to help.

Two polar opposites in their opinions are John F. Hought and the team of Tim LaHaye and Jerry B. Jenkins, famous for their popular *Left Behind* series. Their positions and views are stated in books that detail their respective approaches. Hought is a very liberal theologian who has written, *The Promise of Nature: Ecology and Cosmic Purpose*[ix] in which he takes aim at Christians, particularly rapture-believing Protestants, and blames them for the disrepair of the planet. He says that Christians have an escapists mentality. Looking for something better, we are content to trash the planet and wait, bags packed, expecting the new heavens and earth under the Messiah. He would say believers have a scorched-earth approach that shows no regard for the balance of the planet. Hought's hope to care for and tend the planet is admirable; but he offers no hope, no salvation, and no afterlife. To him, the earth is the eternal thing. Humanity is the one invading the territory of Mother Earth.

On the other end of the spectrum LaHaye and Jenkins break from their popular writing to articulate the thoughtful and scholarly *Are We Living in the End Times?*[x] They base their views on a prophetic interpretation of Scripture that posits Israel as a privileged nation, God's chosen people. LaHaye and Jenkins do not envision a scorched earth that has been entirely depleted post-rapture. Though the entire planet is shaken by catastrophe during the Great Tribulation, the physical land of Israel is blessed. While the devastation of the Tribulation wreaks havoc on planet earth, now absented of its raptured believers, the physical land of Israel flourishes. The theme surfaces that honoring God is what brings favor upon the earth. That is to say, it is unfair to say individuals who believe in a physical rapture of the church are uncaring about the earth. Rather, events are on course that track with God's prophetic plan in which God the Father has intervened in the affairs of human history.

What we are experiencing currently is "the whole earth groaning in the pains of child birth" (Rom 8:22). The language of Isaiah 24 sounds remarkably, eerily similar to global warming - the earth wilting under heat, its leaders melting away. It clearly says in verse 6 the earth is under a curse and its people are dying out because of their sin.

I worship Father God not Mother Earth! I intend to eat my ice cream before it melts, dispose properly of the sticky label when I'm done, and do everything possible in good conscience and stewardship to care for the planet, this beautiful, privileged blue jewel in the cosmos, that has been hand-crafted by our Lord.

I Wait

Isaiah 30:31

But those who wait on the Lord shall renew their strength; They shall mount up with wings like eagles, They shall run and not be weary, They shall walk and not faint. (NKJV)

A devotional prayer. Note the word "wait" is translated as "hope" by NIV, and "trust" by CEV. These tie into the motif of faith throughout this devotional.

I Wait

I wait ...
I wait ...
I wait on the LORD

Is there anything You have for me?
Anything you would like to say?

The Joy is in the seeking

I exchange my chaos for Your peace
I exchange my unsettledness for Your security
I exchange my emptiness for Your fullness

April 4, 2005

Migration to Salvation

Isaiah 49:20-23

Jerusalem is a woman whose children were born while she was in deep sorrow over the loss of her husband. Now those children will come and seek room in the crowded city, and Jerusalem will ask, "Am I really their mother? How could I have given birth when I was still mourning in a foreign land? Who raised these children? Where have they come from?"

The Lord God says: "I will soon give a signal for the nations to return your sons and your daughters to the arms of Jerusalem. The kings and queens of those nations where they were raised will come and bow down. They will take care of you just like a slave taking care of a child. Then you will know that I am the Lord. You won't be disappointed if you trust me."

Have you ever heard a Bible teacher say there are biblical passages about the Jews returning to their homeland in fulfillment of prophecy?

The Jewish people were nomads dispersed, wandering as homeless persons without a physical state for much of the past 2,000 years. Following WWII the physical state of Israel was staked by boundaries. Already, they had begun to come home. The Palestinian National Information Center says the first Jewish settlement was established in Palestine in 1837 by the help of the British Jew Montfort. At that time there were only 1,500 Jews there. It shortly swelled to 10,000 by 1840. The stream slowed so that 15,000 Jews were there by 1860; and 22,000 in 1881. By the turn of the century 25,000 were in their homeland.

The state of Israel was proclaimed on May 14, 1948. The "Law of Return" was intended to allow 1,500 per day; but in actuality more than 13,000 Jews were migrating each day. Jews were returning en masse to the land of their heritage. Today about 42% of the world's Jews live in Israel. Scholars use the rough data available to them to estimate there are somewhere between 13.5 to 15.5 million Jews on the planet. They are returning in droves to the land of Israel.

Here in this passage, God moved upon Isaiah to speak to the issue twenty-five centuries in advance. He says, when you see this happen, "Then you will know that I am the Lord, You won't be disappointed if you trust in me." The apostle Paul references all Israel being saved. Obviously, not every Jew to the individual will acknowledge the lordship of Jesus Christ; but mass numbers will be saved once "the complete number of you Gentiles has come in." You can read about it in Romans 11:25-29. The conditions of population and migration are primed for large numbers of Jews to come to saving faith in the Lord Jesus Christ.

Pause to pray for God's chosen people, Israel.

A Flood of Mercy

Isaiah 54:7-10

I rejected you for a while, but with love and tenderness I will embrace you again. For a while, I turned away in furious anger. Now I will have mercy and love you forever! I, your protector and Lord, make this promise. I once promised Noah that I would never again destroy the earth by a flood. Now I have promised that I will never again get angry and punish you. Every mountain and hill may disappear. But I will always be kind and merciful to you; I won't break my agreement to give your nation peace.

Two distinct times in Scripture God promises something of magnanimous proportions. I mean he makes hundreds of promises, no doubt. And they all are great! But these two that I'm talking about, whoa!

God floods the earth because of humanity's wickedness, then afterward he PROMISES he will never flood the earth again. Now fast forward thousands of years later. The earth has been repopulated. Abraham is promised descendants. Moses is promised deliverance. Isaiah, moved upon by the Holy Spirit, PROMISES "I will never be angry with you again." Isaiah connects this great promise to the flood. The same way God promised never to flood the earth again; now he promises to never be angry again. So this time he floods the earth with mercy!

But, wait a minute. Isn't this promise made to Jews in the Old Testament. This promise was made by Isaiah in the middle of a section that details the Messiah, Isaiah 52-54. It translates perfectly to the New Testament grace provided in Jesus Christ. Remember Paul's words, "A man is a Jew if he is one inwardly; and circumcision is circumcision of the heart, by the Spirit, not by the written code. Such a man's praise is not from men, but from God." (Rom 2:29 NIV)

You may think you've seen God's anger. Trust me. You have never seen God angry. Perez-Uzzah, Achan, Nadab, and Abihu, these guys could tell us a thing or two about God's anger. No, these are the days of grace, a flood of mercy. Swim in it.

Interstate Isaiah

> *Isaiah 66:18-21*
>
> *I know everything you do and think! The time has now come to bring together the people of every language and nation and to show them my glory by proving what I can do. I will send the survivors to Tarshish, Pul, Lud, Meshech, Tubal, Javan, and to the distant islands. I will send them to announce my wonderful glory to nations that have never heard about me.*
>
> *They will bring your relatives from the nations as an offering to me, the Lord. They will come to Jerusalem, my holy mountain, on horses, chariots, wagons, mules, and camels. It will be like the people of Israel bringing the right offering to my temple. I promise that some of them will be priests and others will be helpers in my temple. I, the Lord, have spoken.*

One of my favorite witnessing tools is the Roman Road to Salvation. You have probably heard of it. It involves walking an individual through the key, important verses in the book of Romans that lead to faith in Jesus Christ. It is used the world over very successfully.

May I introduce you to Interstate Isaiah. Perhaps not a plan that singles out God's love for the individual as much as it displays a panoramic view of God's grand plan for salvation for all humanity on earth. Of all the prophets Isaiah is hands-down the most messianic. Living some 700 years before Christ, he anticipates him as if he were John the Baptist baptizing in the water and catches a glimpse of Jesus in his peripheral vision, stepping in the river's edge.

Isaiah 7:14 Isaiah states boldly the Incarnation, "But the Lord will give you proof. A virgin is pregnant; she will have a son and name him Immanuel." It means "God with us."

Isaiah 9:6 In continuation of the birth announcement Isaiah writes seven centuries ahead of time, "A child has been born for us. We have been given a son who will be our ruler. His name will be Wonderful Advisor and Mighty God, Eternal Father and Prince of Peace."

Isaiah 11:16 In a passage that speaks of one of David's descendants as a signal to bring the nations together, Isaiah prophecies that all the banished Jews from around the world will come home. Judah and Israel will again reunite so that there is no more division. "Then for his people who survive, there will be a good road from Assyria, just as there was a good road for their ancestors when they left Egypt."

Isaiah 19:23, 24 Continuing the discussion of the Interstate motif, this text speaks of a healing of the nations, so that enemies, together, worship the one true Lord. "At that time a good road will run from Egypt to Assyria. The Egyptians and Assyrians will travel back and forth from Egypt to Assyria, and they will worship together. Israel will join together with these two countries. They will be a blessing to everyone on earth."

Isaiah 33:8 In a verse that catalogs the desperation of the Israelites without God, Isaiah writes, "No one travels anymore; every road is empty. Treaties are broken, and no respect is shown to any who keep promises."

Isaiah 35:8 However, the hope for the redemption of the lost world is promised in language that tracks with Christianity. "A good road will be there and it will be named 'God's Sacred Highway.' It will be for God's people. No one unfit to worship God will walk on that road. And no fools can walk on that highway." Note that NIV uses the phrase "the Way of Holiness" matching identically with the book of Acts in which believers were called followers of "the Way."

Isaiah 40:3 This verse echoes and expands the thought: "Someone is shouting: 'Clear a path in the desert! Make a straight road for the Lord our God.'" And, of course, Mark uses this very verse to begin his gospel of the good news of Jesus Christ.

Isaiah 52:14 In this portion dubbed the suffering servant, Isaiah paints a picture of Jesus' crucifixion. "Many were horrified at what happened to him. But everyone who saw him was even more horrified because he suffered until he no longer looked human."

Isaiah 53:5 And the carnage continues until it accomplishes humanity's ultimate good. "He was wounded and crushed because of our sins; by taking our punishment, he made us completely well."

Isaiah 62:10 So the coronation is set. Ceremony that rivals any ceremony ever conducted occurs. The people of Jerusalem celebrate the completion of the Interstate Isaiah. "People of Jerusalem open your gates! Repair the road to the city and clear it of stones; raise a banner and help the nations find their way."

Isaiah 66:18 In language that is remarkably close to the Great Commission of Matthew 28:18-20 and Mark 16:15-18, Isaiah records a closing statement to his book, "The time has now come to bring together the people of every language and nation and to show them my glory."

Have you taken the on-ramp to enter Interstate Isaiah?

He's an Early Almond

Jeremiah 1:11, 12

The Lord showed me something in a vision. Then he asked, "What do you see, Jeremiah?" I answered, "A branch of almonds that ripen early."

"That's right," the Lord replied, "and I always rise early to keep a promise."

I remember reading that President George W. Bush had the practice of beginning his press conferences precisely one minute early. It was a discipline that kept the press crew and media personnel hopping. This shows there are different manners of being on time. One could lag a few minutes behind the stated time and still be considered on time; but always the ambiguous, elusive late-mark lurks in people's minds. And the line is drawn at a different place in each mind. Another more stoic approach is to be bat on. No one could argue the accuracy. However, there is a way of being on time in the earliest possible way.

Elsewhere I have written in these posts, "God is never late. He misses plenty of opportunities to be early; but he is always right on time." I think that is an accurate statement. I wasn't just trying to be cute. As a matter of fairness and opportunity, God doesn't jump the gun. He allows his invention, time, to run its course. That's right, he made time. Time punches in on the time clock for him. However, I must say, he is the earliest possible "on time."

He has just called the young man, Jeremiah, to prophetic ministry. Jeremiah says, *"Thanks, but, you know, I've never really been good at public speaking."* God gently reaches out and touches his mouth. Is it a gesture as to say, *"Shh"*? Or is the touch to heal stammering and lack of confidence, and provide ability? Or is it both? Then, God tests the alignment and perceptiveness of his new voice. *"Jeremiah, I'm showing you something right now, what is it?"* Like Clarence in It's A Wonderful Life, *"Wow, this is amazing."* Joseph retorts, *"If you ever get your wings you'll be able to see things on your own."* Jeremiah exclaims, "I see an almond (shaqed) branch." God says, "I am watching (shaqad) over my word to fulfill it." Two identical looking words in the Hebrew, almond and watching, only a change in the vowel markings, a real play on words. The almond tree was known for waking up early from the winter. It would blossom in January and February in Israel, months ahead of the other crops. God was demonstrating to his new voice that he fulfills his promises at the earliest possible moment. In the lifetime of Jeremiah he was referring to the promises of blessings and curses dependent upon Israel's obedience, (Leviticus 26, Deuteronomy 28).

He has plans in mind for you. He is watching over his word to perform it. He's an early almond. He can't wait to be on time in your situation.

Job Posting: Prophet

> *Jeremiah 11:18-23*
>
> *Some people plotted to kill me. And like a lamb being led to the butcher, I knew nothing about their plans. But then the Lord told me that they had planned to chop me down like a tree— fruit and all— so that no one would ever remember me again.*
>
> *I prayed, "Lord All-Powerful, you always do what is right, and you know every thought. So I trust you to help me and to take revenge."*
>
> *Then the Lord said: Jeremiah, some men from Anathoth say they will kill you, if you keep on speaking for me. But I will punish them. Their young men will die in battle, and their children will starve to death. And when I am finished, no one from their families will be left alive.*

Once I was speaking at a gathering of multiple churches. I had a frog in my throat and the host pastor brought me a glass of water. I said, "Thanks Pastor, according to the Bible you will receive a prophet's reward." He chimed, "Now, why would you do that to me? I thought you liked me. Most of them ended up beaten and in prison." Try being Jeremiah, for instance.

Job Posting: Needed, One Prophet

Responsibilities: Preach for fifty years without any converts; Prophesy to an obstinate people; Tell them things about judgment they don't want to hear; Be thrown into a cistern; Have your volume of work burned before your eyes and recreate it from memory; Be the target of a conspiracy to take your life from your own hometown and family members; Remain single for life; Do not father children; Do not attend any parties; Regret being born; Do not attend funerals, not even of your own family members; Be a laughing stock and target of mockery; and complain to the Lord about your persecution only to have him tell you it will get worse.

Salary: Nil

Benefits: None

Any takers? Oh-ho no, not this little grey duck! There are individuals who are faithful to God in the midst of seemingly insurmountable difficulties. Their pay is recorded in eternity. Their reward is on high.

The office of the prophet is an important part of the five-fold ministry gift to the Church (Eph 4:11). In this age, it seems to me, there are many self-proclaimed prophets, itching to speak a word, at ease uttering the phrase, "Thus sayeth the Lord." Still, I have known several who walk in very careful obedience, the absolute real deal, whether in forth-telling, edifying presently with Scripture, or bringing a prophetic encouragement. And, yes, sometimes the prophetic urge even requires judgment that is laced with grace. There are ones who do so without putting on airs, reluctant to accept any credit, always pointing to the Lord when they have been used. In true humility, void of any arrogance, these ones have blessed the Church universally. And in heaven they have a prophet's reward.

The Weeping Prophet

Jeremiah 13:17

If you are too proud to listen, I will weep alone. Tears will stream from my eyes when the Lord's people are taken away as prisoners.

I don't know if we can grasp how difficult it was in the days of Jeremiah, just before the Jews were exiled to Babylon. He is crying his eyes out and feels he is crying all alone. Perhaps at times he was. This is what earned him the nickname, "The Weeping Prophet." The drought was so bad, so many months without rain, it was as if the ground was dry-heaving from crying so much (Jer 14:2). This finally got the attention of the people. They began to humble themselves in prayer and fasting, but it was too late. Far more than enough generations had passed to prove God's mercy, and also Israel and Judah's lack of faithfulness. A leopard can't change its spots (Jer 13:23). Even after all of this the prophet Jeremiah throws himself before the mercy of God. He has preached all of his adult life that judgment was coming. They would be deported. And yet, still, in spite of this, and at the risk of his prophetic reputation, he begged God for his prophecies to be wrong so that God would have mercy. But God was tired of showing mercy to an obstinate people (Jer 15:6). Jeremiah then regretted ever being born. It was bad, really bad. So bad, in fact, that Jeremiah feared God would disown him as his prophet. Ironically, he was successful in fulfilling the call of God on his life. The grind, the wrestling, his five-fold lament, every tear was accounted for by God. Eternity will prove the reward for the faithfulness of the weeping prophet.

The Diaspora – Figs Gone Figurative

Jeremiah 24:8-10

The rotten figs stand for King Zedekiah of Judah, his officials, and all the others who were not taken away to Babylonia, whether they stayed here in Judah or went to live in Egypt. I will punish them with a terrible disaster, and everyone on earth will tremble when they hear about it. I will force the people of Judah to go to foreign countries, where they will be cursed and insulted. War and hunger and disease will strike them, until they finally disappear from the land that I gave them and their ancestors.

Scattered.

Jeremiah saw two baskets of figs in his vision. One of them was filled with ripe figs, ready to be eaten. This basket represented the Jewish people who were sent to Babylon for 70 years of exile. They were told to build houses, plant gardens and vineyards, and raise children. They were going to be there for a while. After the 70 years, right on cue, they returned.

"With the Lord a day is a like a thousand years, and a thousand years are like a day" (2 Peter 3:8, NIV). Elsewhere in these posts I have compared the Jews being exiled to Babylon for 70 years with a teenage daughter being sent to her room to think about her actions, at least figuratively. That was what happened to the good figs. What happened to the "naughty figs" (Jer 24:2, KJV)?

Let me give you another allegorical picture. I mean, these are figs gone figurative! The Babylonian captives were like a batch of fresh figs on the Lord's counter that he set aside for a salad to prepare in a little while; but the rest of the Jews, the ones that remained in Jerusalem, were like a bad batch that he tossed off his back porch.

The second basket was filled with spoiled figs. They had gone bad. This represented the remaining Jews who would be scattered to the nations. Scattered, dispersed - the diaspora. The Lord spoke through the prophet Jeremiah that the Jews would be scattered, but then brought back in time. Not only did Jeremiah speak of it in these verses, but he repeated himself for emphasis in Jeremiah 29:16-20. It was an event so tremendous that it would displace the deliverance from Egypt as the most notable event in Israel's history (Jer 23:7, 8).

Interesting thing about the fig. It is dispersed by birds and mammals that scatter its seeds in droppings. It's true. God has a fig tree in his garden. In 1948 Israel was established again as a physical state. God began gathering scattered and dispersed figs from all over his Garden Earth.

His eye is on the sparrow. And, his eye is even on the seed that is in the sparrow's beak. If he has that kind of a watchful eye, don't you think he sees your every need today?

Creative Genius

> *Jeremiah 33:1-3, 20, 25*
>
> *I was still being held prisoner in the courtyard of the palace guards when the Lord told me: I am the Lord, and I created the whole world. Ask me, and I will tell you things that you don't know and can't find out...I, the Lord, have an agreement with day and night, so they always come at the right time. You can't break the agreement I made with them... Jeremiah, I will never break my agreement with the day and the night or let the sky and the earth stop obeying my commands.*

God is masterful in his design. The world and universe did not evolve but was created by the spoken word of God. Many persons today believe in coincidence. The Earth just happens to be the right distance from the Sun. If we were any closer we would burn up, any further away we would freeze. The diameter of our planet is just the right size so that there are 24 hours in one day, three eight-hour segments for work, rest and play. The earth's axis, which is 23.44 degrees, is just the right angle to provide seasons. If we were straight-up perpendicular there would be no change of temperature as our planet performs its annual ellipsoidal pattern around the Sun. This would not only make for a boring planet; but there would no hope of the hot and cold cycles so crucial for sustaining life. Earth is a magnificent, crown jewel suspended in space. This privileged, blue planet just happens to contain all the essentials for the sustenance of life - animal life, vegetative life, sea life, and human life. There are just too many coincidences for me. I believe it was all by design. Someone has said the chances of evolution being true would be equivalent to a tornado blowing through a junk yard and leaving a 747, fully intact, in its wake.

We must care for the planet. Recycle plastics, cardboard and aluminum. Support measures that burn cleaner fuel. Preserve forests. Set aside land for sanctuaries as the population continues to increase. However, we must know that no effort on our part can cause the earth to stop spinning, just as no effort on our part could have started it spinning in the first place. We can no more hold up the planet than a gnat can plug the Hoover Dam. God has made a covenant agreement with Factory Universe. It will sustain life as long as his breath stays in Adam. We work with our hands in his garden. We respect his garden. Still, in the final analysis the best we can do is to enjoy his creative genius.

Optical Omnipotent

Jeremiah 39:5-7

The Babylonian troops caught up with them near Jericho. They arrested Zedekiah and took him to the town of Riblah in the land of Hamath, where Nebuchadnezzar put him on trial, then found him guilty and gave orders for him to be punished. Zedekiah's sons were killed there in front of him, and so were the leaders of Judah's ruling families. His eyes were poked out, and he was put in chains, so he could be dragged off to Babylonia.

This is to me one of the saddest situations imaginable in history. Zedekiah watches his sons killed right before his eyes. Did he groan, gasp? Did he shout, "No"? Then he has his eyes gouged out so that his last memory of sight is their painful death that he was powerless to stop. Now that image is permanently seared on his conscience and recall. Talk about adding insult to injury. It's like pouring salt on an open wound.

Zedekiah had not been courageous enough to surrender to Nebuchadnezzar as Jeremiah instructed. The prophet had told him things would go easy for him if he gave in, but hard if he resisted. There is a cruel evil in the world that conceives of deeds so dark as to maximize their felt pain and inflicted injury. I believe the heart of God hurts for all the Zedekiah's of the world who have endured senseless violence, intentional carnage, and reckless rage.

The man Zedekiah was a poor king, disobedient and fearful. However, his name means "Yahweh is righteous." Could it be that this horrible story mirrors the unimaginable pain our heavenly Father experienced as he watched his own sinless Son killed before his eyes. I do not subscribe to a strict Penal Substitutionary Atonement theory. I don't envision a mean tyrant slamming down a gavel. I picture a weeping Father raining tears upon Calvary's mountain. Our heavenly Father watched his Son being killed. Did he wish to lose his sight in that moment? But his is an all-seeing eye, optical Omnipotent.

The Silence of Madmen

> *Jeremiah 48:2*
>
> *No one honors you, Moab. In Heshbon, enemies make plans to end your life. My sword will leave only silence in your town named "Quiet."*

There is a maddening silence in Moab.

The nation was being judged in Jeremiah's catalog of nations that were being brought to accountability. One of the towns is named Nebo. Apparently it is the name of the pagan god they had worshiped. Another town of Moab is mentioned in the first verse, Kiriathaim. It means "encounter" or "befall" and Jeremiah says judgment will befall it and it will be left in ruins. Verse 2 continues the indictment naming the city of Heshbon, from a word meaning "account" or "to think", but Jeremiah says Moab's enemies are the ones thinking up the plans for her destruction.

And then there is the town in Moab named Madmen. It has an intended play on words, the Hebrew word madmen sounds very close to the word that means silence, so that's why CEV translates it as "Quiet." It also has an unintended inference in English. It bears a striking double entendre that falls on the ears. The town of Madmen has no Soundness at all. Is there any soundness to be found? Or, is it pure madness? The theme continues throughout the chapter. Verse 33 speaks of silencing their shouts at the celebrations. In their place verse 34 points out weeping and cries being heard. The motif is carried forward to the end of the chapter. In point of fact, verse 44 states flatly, "I, the Lord, have spoken." And once his judgment is spoken, the silence is loud. Ultimately, the Lord will silence all mad men. The silence is maddening. The quiet is deafening.

In the presence of the voice that spoke the worlds into creation there is but one response, cupped-hand over mouth, silence.

New Morning, New Mercy

> *Lamentations 3:21-24*
>
> *Then I remember something that fills me with hope. The Lord's kindness never fails! If he had not been merciful, we would have*

> been destroyed. The Lord can always be trusted to show mercy each morning. Deep in my heart I say, "The Lord is all I need; I can depend on him!"

The Jews are receiving their due. After years of negligent disobedience, even with the prophets warning repeatedly, now they have been shipped off to Babylon. Every verse in the laments to this point, every word, has been about judgment, horror and devastation. There is weeping and sadness. Disaster at every turn. Now, here, at the exact halfway point, precisely the middle of the numbered lament poems, comes this ray of hope. The weeping prophet, Jeremiah, is reminded of God's faithfulness. No matter what difficulties we face, and even when we deserve it, he still remains just, fair, and totally justified in every action. Jeremiah is enlightened with the hope that mercy is new every single morning. New morning, new mercy.

Second Addams Family

> Hosea 6:7
>
> At a place named Adam, you betrayed me by breaking our agreement.

The loveable Charles Addams gave life to his loveable characters, misfits, oddballs and eccentrics, who made up the do-good comedic sitcom, The Addams Family. Could it be that we are The Second Addams Family?

The name Adam has to do with rosy cheeks, the redness in the blush of his face. It is the only human name that God gave, at least directly. It hints at the word for blood, dam (pronounced like the a in father). Adam had red, life-giving blood flowing through his veins. The similar sounding word, Edom, is the name of the nation that has a hint of red in its name. Edom came from the individual Esau, a reddish, hairy man who loved red stew (Gen 25:30).

There is an ancient city called Adam. It is the specific location where God dammed the water upstream allowing the Israelites to cross the Jordan on dry ground and enter the Promised Land under Joshua's leadership. It is pure coincidence that our English word dam means to stop the flow.

The Contemporary English Version is different from the others. Instead of taking Hosea 6:7 to mean "like Adam they have broken the covenant - they were unfaithful to me there"; CEV interprets it to read "at a place named Adam you betrayed me by breaking our agreement." Instead of immediately equating the Jewish people's unfaithfulness with the first man, a specific geographic location is cited as the spot where a covenant was broken, the ancient city of Adam. What agreement was broken?

I believe it calls to mind the covenant that Moses led the people to agree upon before he died. In verbal chant, in which the people amen his words, Moses reminds the people about the covenant he and they made with God at Mount Horeb. And now, he renews it with them at Mount Ebal and Mount Gerazim, (Deut 27-29), the choosing of blessings or curses. In between the two mountains there is a natural amphitheater. A speaker's voice can be heard from the two mountainsides. Chants from one mountainside can be heard from the other mountain and vice versa. The place where they crossed the Jordan, Adam, is only about 15 miles from there. You can gaze down from those mountains and see Adam right on the Jordan. You can look up from Adam and see the mountains that remind of the covenant.

The prophet Hosea's main point is to speak about how Israel broke covenant relationship with God, the same way a prostitute was rescued, cleaned up, loved - and yet, betrayed her husband-rescuer and cheated with other lovers in spite of everything that had been done for her. The message is that God's people had been saved dramatically, but chose to cheat on God with other false gods.

Adam and Eve were given a perfect place and rebelled. Israel was given a new Eden, the Promised Land. They crossed into it at a placed called Adam. And in just the same way, like Adam, they rebelled. You and I have crossed into our Eden via the One that the Bible names the Second Adam. We are a mixed lot, this Second Addams Family. We are made up of redeemed misfits, oddballs and eccentrics. God forbid that we ever rebel and turn away.

Insight on Predestination

> *Obadiah 1:1-4*
>
> *The Lord God gave Obadiah a message about Edom, and this is what we heard: "I, the Lord, have sent a messenger with orders for the nations to attack Edom." The Lord said to Edom: I will make you the weakest and most despised nation. You live in a mountain fortress, because your pride makes you feel safe from attack, but you are mistaken. I will still bring you down, even if you fly higher than an eagle or nest among the stars. I, the Lord, have spoken!*

Tucked away toward the ending of the Old Testament, Obadiah is a judgment against the nation of Edom. It is nearly identical in scope to Jeremiah 49:7-22. Both prophets scold the enemy of the Jews. Interestingly, this little book informs the important concept of the free-will's involvement. It has a role to play in salvation.

There is a school of thought in theology that believes God has foreordained those who are going to be saved. Humanity has no role to play in the process. The ones who will be saved are the elect. They are predestined to salvation. This view is called Calvinism. It is named after the wonderful, French theologian, John Calvin, who did most of his work from Geneva, Switzerland. He was very instrumental in the Reformation of the Church, along with the likes of Martin Luther, Martin Bucer and Ulrich Zwingli to name a few. A major component of Calvinism is Romans 9:10-18 with its controversial designation "Jacob I have loved, but Esau I have hated."

If you will read patiently this rather long explanation, I hope to offer you another view on this Scripture, an insight on predestination.

It is a sibling rivalry, but not just of two brothers; rather it is a sibling rivalry of two nations. Esau became the nation of Edom. Jacob became the nation of Israel. The names Esau and Edom are used interchangeably just the same way Jacob and Israel are used interchangeably. The reason Edom was judged was because they celebrated Judah's misfortune. When Judah was being ransacked, Edom threw a party in the streets (Obad 1:12).

I have lived the balance of my life without ever entertaining the idea that I could initiate or effect my own salvation, but I am not Calvinist/Reformed. Calvinists seem to feel this is an affront to God. I have prayed meaningfully for years, as well as read the Bible purposefully, without even the least prompting that I was in error. I believe it is fully compatible with Scripture to believe God initiates salvation and man chooses either to receive it or deny it.

If Calvinism wishes to contend that Romans 9 implies God judged Esau before he was ever born, it must show proof that the Scripture means Esau the individual, and not Esau the nation. The latter is the language of Scripture. What I mean is this: if God truly hated Esau, he did a much better job of hating others in the Bible. Esau, when met by his estranged brother Jacob after a twenty-year hiatus, was offered a sizeable peace offering. Note carefully his words in response, "But Esau said, 'I already have plenty, my brother. Keep what you have for yourself'" (Gen 33:9, NIV). These certainly are not the words of one for whom the earth has opened up and swallowed alive into Sheol. These words are nowhere kin to the pain of one who endured a rain of burning sulfur upon his city. Were Sisera able to remove the tent peg from his temple, and the prophets of Baal their attacking swords from their throats, these might have a few words to speak in rebuttal to those who say Esau was hated by God.

A better way to explain the statement of Paul in Romans 9 is to understand it in light of the precise wording of Scripture. When Rebekah asked, "Why is this happening to me?" she was told, "Two nations are in your womb" (Gen 25:23, NIV). Pre-birth, God foresaw the people groups that Esau and Jacob would become. That Esau is the founder of the nation certainly bodes well with the view that he deserved judgment. Esau's descendants became what he modeled - no doubt. Yet, properly, God's judgment is upon a nation. This expands and widens the scope of the Romans 9 pronouncement considerably. It lends credence to the model proposed by Greg Boyd who sees similarities between the findings of quantum physics with the openness of God. He uses, for an illustration, an ant colony.[xi] Though it may be predicted with great accuracy how a colony of ants will behave, and even what they accomplish, it is impossible to predict the behavior of one single ant. Similarly, God has predicted the behavior of the nation, Edom, and judged it, apart from any judgment on the individual Esau. Though this is not the precise terminology of Scripture, it is the intent. If Calvinist say otherwise, they must show delineation between the clear interchangeability of Esau and Edom in the Bible.

Obadiah, minor in its recording, is major in its impact. The minor prophet speaks postmortem, of both Esau and Jacob, conservatively by six-hundred years. Though Esau has long been dead, Obadiah says, "How Esau [not Edom] will be ransacked" (Ob 1:6, NIV). But Esau is already dead! The reason cited is "because of the violence against your brother, Jacob...You should not look down on your brother" (Ob 1:10, 12, NIV). How can Esau look down on Jacob from the grave? Esau and Jacob wrestled in Rebekah's womb causing great turmoil; but then Jacob wrestled with God. His name-change signifies this. Yet many years after their respective deaths, Esau and Jacob continued to wrestle according to this text. Verse 18 looms ominous, "There will be no survivors from the house of Esau. The Lord has spoken" (Obad 1:18, NIV). History shows that after the nation of Edom was displaced from their high mountain-fortress, in which they placed such pride and security, they fled, ironically, to Jerusalem and blended in among the Jews as refugees. After the attack by Titus of Jerusalem in A. D. 70, the Jews dispersed. Though Israel is returning to their homeland in droves during our lifetimes, (quite miraculous considering no other nation has been subjugated to nomad status for nearly two-thousand years and survived), we know nothing of Edom. The descendants of Esau appear to have disappeared from the planet. It is a literal fulfillment of Amos 1:11, 12. There are speculations by some of who they are today. But it certainly appears, as a concrete people, they disbanded and are no more. Thus, God's so-called hatred of Esau is no more than his judgment of any nation that rebels against him. And, as mentioned above, Jeremiah mirrors the exact same logic in his catalog of judgments against nations. One wonders why Jeremiah includes his passage in the catalog of nations if he is speaking of an individual.

If some contend this is a misinterpretation of Obadiah, I would point out it is, then, equally wrong to find personal attribute, rather than personification, in Paul's use of Esau in Romans 9. It must be noted there is no hatred of Esau mentioned in his lifetime. In fact, he is "loved" by Isaac (Gen 25:28). If Rebekah hated Esau the text does not mention it, only that she "loved" Jacob. The first mention of hatred of Esau is not until the close of the Old Testament. Malachi 1 speaks of God's judgment against Edom the nation. "I have loved you" says the LORD. "But you ask, 'How have you loved us?' Was not Esau Jacob's brother?" the Lord says. "Yet I have loved Jacob, but Esau I have hated, and I have turned his mountains into a wasteland and left his inheritance to the desert jackals" (Mal 1:2, 3, NIV).

Since Obadiah, Jeremiah, and Malachi all speak of Esau postmortem in a personalized manner, naming him, even though they clearly speak of a nation; and since Paul would have had access to this information; and seeing that Paul was an astute student; it is best to regard Paul's "Esau" as the judgment of the nation Edom. This best fits with the intentional sentiment of the texts in consideration. Furthermore, this view helps explain Paul's statement of Romans 10:13, the very next chapter, in which he says, "All who call out to the Lord will be saved."

Resolve Rests

Joel 3:10

Make swords out of plows, And spears out of garden tools. Strengthen every weakling.

It is very interesting to note the reversal of words in two, contrasting Old Testament prophecies. Here, in Joel 3:10, is the sad reality that everyday tools are being transformed into weapons of war. Plows are being re-purposed to craft swords. Garden instruments are being formed into spears. Similar to the way we have, in our nation's history, sacrificed creature comforts to finance wars. Indian motorcycles went out of business in order to provide military and police vehicles for World War II. There were scrap drives, metal drives, and rubber drives. A nation needed to find a way to equip its troops. This was imaged by Rosie the Riveter. Many women set out to work in the factories during the war so their husbands could go overseas to do battle. It is the can-do spirit that says, "We'll do whatever it takes." It evokes pride, but also sadness that life as it was meant to be enjoyed stands risk of being hijacked by mean-spirited tyrants. The simple pleasures can be replaced very quickly. The sharp edges of plow disks are made into swords. The rake and the hoe are sharpened to mimic spears. This mirrors the fall of humanity into sin, not what we were originally designed to be.

Yet there is another prophecy. The nations among humankind will beat their swords into plowshares, and their spears into pruning hooks. (Isaiah 2:4; Micah 4:3). This is the absolute reversal. It is the prophecy of the day when there will be no more wars. The declaration rings out. Let those sharp edges of the swords stop tearing flesh, and instead break up fallow ground for planting. Aha, those old spears would be great for pruning back the fruit trees, and gathering in the harvest. It is the Eschaton, the eternal era when Jesus' dominion is irrevocably actuated. Simplicity settles, resolve rests, enter eternal age.

Bethlehem Bakery

Micah 5:2

Bethlehem Ephrath, you are one of the smallest towns in the nation of Judah, but the Lord will choose one of your people to rule the nation - someone whose family goes back to ancient times.

So many significant events took place in little Bethlehem. It was the tragic burial site for Asahel. What a waste! Israelites fighting against Israelites.

On another occasion, David's three mighty men broke through the enemy line in order to retrieve him a drink from Bethlehem well. David wouldn't drink it, it was holy water. He poured it out on the ground, a sacrificial libation.

Most remarkable of all, Bethlehem means "House of Bread." All of the events throughout its history, triumphant and troubled, stoke the fires of a holy oven. When Jesus reached the apex of his teaching he told his followers that he was the Bread of Life. The House of Bread let rise One loaf that would feed the hungry masses. O Bethlehem Bakery, give us this day our daily bread.

Trust and Timing

> *Nahum 1:7, 8*
>
> *The Lord is good. He protects those who trust him in times of trouble. But like a roaring flood, the Lord chases his enemies into dark places and destroys them.*

God is always right on time. He misses plenty of opportunities to be early; but he is never late. He is always right on time.

We will get to Nahum momentarily. First, however, Jonah lived about 800 years before Christ. He was told to go preach to the ancient city of Nineveh; but he bought a ticket for the first ship out of town and headed to Tarshish, a city in Spain. It was the complete opposite direction of God's will, perhaps a thousand miles away. Some say it would take three years to sail the ancient path by boat. He was planning to be gone a long time!

You know the story of Jonah and the big fish (Jonah 1:17). We can envision this young prophet, perhaps 20 years old, unwrapping himself from seaweed and going reluctantly to Nineveh to preach. They repented. He sulked.

Nineveh was a very evil, ancient city in modern Iraq. They practiced black magic, sorcery and witchcraft. They were bent on destruction and took great pride in their prowess. They were even a threat to Jonah's people, and here he had evangelized them. The jailhouse conversion of Nineveh was short lived. In a matter of a few years, perhaps three years after Jonah left, their nation, Assyria, did attack Israel. In 770 BC the Assyrians invaded Israel, and came back to finish the job in 721 BC. Assyria wreaked great devastation on the Northern Kingdom.

However, fast forward a little bit. At some stage during this low point God raised up a prophet named Nahum. His message to Nineveh was very different from that of his predecessor, Jonah, who had lived perhaps a hundred years earlier. The word from the Lord is basically, *"That's it, Nineveh, I've had it. You're judged."*

Do you think Jonah is watching from his vantage point in eternity and saying, *"See, God, I told you so."* No. He now has the opportunity to sample God's wisdom directly without a strainer. I am certain Jonah, seeing Nahum's ministry, understood the beautiful balance found in

God's mercy and his judgment. God's mercy and judgment are like two palms coming together to form the praying hands, perfectly symmetrical and appropriate.

It could be that there are important components in your life that are coming into place. Timing is very important to God. "The Lord is good. He protects those who trust him in times of trouble. But like a roaring flood God chases his enemies into dark places and destroys them."

He Welcomes Our Wrestling

Habakkuk 2:4

I, the Lord, refuse to accept anyone who is proud. Only those who live by faith are acceptable to me.

There are a good number of scholars who hold that Habakkuk was a temple prophet. See 1 Chronicles 25:1 where David and the temple officials hand-selected them. This would mean he used a lyre, harp and cymbals as he prophesied. This puts him in company with Elisha who called for the harpist so he could prophesy (2 Kgs 3:15); and David who played for Saul to drive the evil spirit away (1 Sam 16:23). The same speculators see Habakkuk 3:19 as an indicator that he was a Levite and Temple singer.

More important than what he does is who he is. Habakkuk lives up to his name. It means to wrestle, or to embrace. So, in this respect, he is like Israel. Remember that Jacob was renamed "he wrestles with God." What has surfaced as a theme throughout these posts is the motif of faith that fights for all its worth. I write as one who exercises believing faith in prayer for healing of the sick. My approach is to administer healing in Jesus' name, not to ask and beg for it. So, it may sound strange to hear a Pentecostal say this. A more impressive faith to me, than the flashy, impressive charisma that often accompanies legitimate God-experiences, is the faith that hones in on courage, hope that grapples, the time-tested Resilients left standing in the fray of incomprehensible foes. Isn't this what faith looks like?

So what is Habakkuk wrestling with? The age old question. Why does evil go unchecked? When will justice be served? He allows himself, in acceptable Hebrew acumen, to question what God is doing. This is the crux of chapter 1. And this is not viewed as a lack of faith. It is quite the opposite: it is most faith building. Habakkuk braces himself for God's reply. Will he be angry? Will he put him in his place? It could mean instant judgment. Chapter 2 reveals God's response. In essence, "Don't worry. I'm watching. Pride hasn't escaped my attention." Then he makes the statement that the apostle Paul postulates as his springboard of discussion for his most important work, Romans. "Only those who live by faith are acceptable to me." God knows our motives, our thoughts, our hearts. He knows us entirely. We may be real with him. He welcomes our wrestling.

Up on the Camelback

Habakkuk 3:19

The Lord gives me strength. He makes my feet as sure as those of a deer, and he helps me stand on the mountains.

For my son Zakary's 18th birthday, he and I packed a lunch, left early in the morning, drove across town and hiked Camelback Mountain. The sheer red, sandstone cliffs make the hump of earth a telltale landmark in Phoenix. At 2,700 feet above sea level it is not that high. I have lived in the west slope of Colorado surrounded by fourteeners. The peaks there reach to the heavens. However, the Echo Canyon Trail at Camelback is a strenuous workout, especially for a partially-active quadragenarian living in denial of sedentary tendencies. It ascends a full quarter mile up in only 1.2 miles of trail. You negotiate loose rocks, large boulders, and, at times, even use handrails to ascend the course.

I really slowed Zakary down. I had to stop often, gulp water, and breathe hard. For Zak it was nothing. He just scooted right up the hill, standing erect, not even breathing hard, hardly even drinking water when I would stop to rest. We were only about 2/10ths of a mile from the top when I really hit a wall. Zak said, "Dad, we don't have to finish." I told him that it was really important to me to finish. And after a brief pause, we started again. I instantly remembered the above Scripture, "You make my feet like hinds feet." Even though the very end of the trail is some of the steepest, I found a second wind. Energized by the prospects of finishing we went quickly, up, around a bend, over a natural land hurdle, a little jaunt and then, we were there. Up on the Camelback.

You can see the entire city from up there. It's a full view 360 degrees. Zak and I sat and talked about life, responsibility, character, integrity, finishing what you start. I gave him a little gift to remember the occasion. It was a truly special day. I'm so glad I didn't stop short.

Many times life is like that. You can feel so discouraged and tired. You can think about quitting. Those are the moments when you need to cry out to God in prayer. He will give you a second wind so you can keep climbing. And when you and I arrive to our destination someday, when we peak, we will realize in an instant it was worth all the struggle. Keep wrestling.

Our Crooning Crown

Zephaniah 3:17

The Lord your God wins victory after victory and is always with you. He celebrates and sings because of you, and he will refresh your life with his love.

After all the judgment, I mean Zephaniah swims with it, comes this refreshing, sweet refrain. What a welcome prose! God sings over us because he is so glad about our redemption. It reminds me of the uncomposed Jesus of Luke 10:18-20, for a moment undignified, celebrating with his disciples who have authority over Satan. Then he gathers himself and offers instruction on what to really be happy about - that our names are written in heaven.

The minor prophets all follow a template of stern judgment that culminates in restoration and tender love. God isn't bent on devastating, destructive punishment. He disciplines with a purpose. In this way his kindness can lead us to repentance. The word of the Lord, through Zephaniah, ripped into all the nations, including his own Jewish people. Now, with the punishment ended, the heavenly Father has a precious moment with his chosen ones, like a parent of a tearful, remorseful child, he gathers her up in his arms. He is so moved by the moment that he spills forth in song. The serenading Savior, our crooning Crown.

The Desired of All Nations

Haggai 2:3-9

Does anyone remember how glorious this temple used to be? Now it looks like nothing. But cheer up! Because I, the Lord All-Powerful, will be here to help you with the work, just as I promised your ancestors when I brought them out of Egypt. Don't worry. My Spirit is right here with you.

Soon I will again shake the heavens and the earth, the sea and the dry land. I will shake the nations, and their treasures will be brought here. Then the brightness of my glory will fill this temple. All silver and gold belong to me, and I promise that this new

> *temple will be more glorious than the first one. I will also bless this city with peace.*

There is so much going on here in such short space. We have a choice to make when interpreting the Hebrew word *chemdaw*. The CEV has chosen to track with a "treasure." A study of the word shows that many translations choose the word "desire" when translating this word. I believe there are good reasons to choose the word "desire."

According to the NAS Exhaustive Concordance *chemdaw* can mean "beautiful, desire, desirable, choice, pleasant, precious, valuable, or wealth." Strong's Concordance defines it as "desire, delight." Brown Driver Briggs also hones in on the "desire/desirable" emphasis of the word. You can see how it would be easy to say a treasure is desired, and how desire is synonymous with valuable treasure. This still doesn't resolve things. Which is intended here? A valuable treasure or a priceless person?

The word is typically associated with a person. For instance, when Samuel anointed Saul the king of Israel he told him, "And who does all Israel *desire* but you and your father's family" (1 Sam 9:20, HOL)? In a negative connotation it is used to describe the atrocities of the Antichrist. "He will show no regard for the gods of his fathers, or the one *desired* by women, nor will he regard any god, but will exalt himself above them all" (Daniel 11:37, NIV).

Even still, some argue both of these instances could speak of a treasure and not a person. In other words, *Saul's family now has all the treasure*. And, *the Antichrist is not impressed by treasures of others*. As I mentioned above, the CEV follows this pattern; but still teaches the idea of referencing an individual. For instance, see Luke 11:29-32, which clearly speaks of Jesus, but has been translated "Here is *something* [not someone] far greater than Solomon...Jonah." I think one main reason people shy away from the term "desire" is the discomfort associated with Jesus being prophesied of as "the desired of women." Just what does that mean? There are uncertain connotations.

I recall a sermon I heard a long time ago. I was on staff with Al Roever. It was always a delight to hear his messages. Al studied romantic languages at Rice University and graduated with a 4.0 GPA. He has a brilliant mind. His messages are deep, and thought-provoking. His years of study in Hebrew culture, and in particular the works Alfred Edersheim, inform his views. He spoke that day of the Jewish idea behind these verses. Every young Hebrew woman hoped that she would be the privileged one who would carry this child, "the Desired of all Nations."

Haggai is set in a context of rebuilding the temple. Things had stalled for a period of 18 years because of an edict by King Artaxerxes from Persia. Jerusalem's neighbors prodded him to do that. The Spirit of God pours through the prophet Haggai. *It is not a time for you to live in nice homes and let the temple be neglected. The foundation is finished, but you must complete the job.* One of the things the Lord tells Haggai is, "Don't worry, my Spirit is right here with you." The precise wording has, "I am" is right here with you. So closely knit is the Trinity. God is the essence of being, he is very Spirit.

At the beginning and the chapter's end Haggai connects a person with this deliverance, not a physical object. He mentions Zerubbabel, the governor. He is already involved in the rebuilding project. His name means "begotten out of Babylon." In time there would be another, "the only begotten Son"(John 3:16, NKJV). Paul points out that Jesus made good the delivery of a new kind of temple. "Or don't you not know that your body is a temple of the Holy Spirit who is in you?" (1 Cor 6:19)?

These thoughts prompted me to include Haggai 2:6 in my Christmas musical, *A Child Is Born to Us*. Jesus is the Desired of All Nations. He will bless the city with peace.

Again, What's in a Name?

> *Zechariah 1:1*
>
> *I am the prophet Zechariah, the son of Berechiah and the grandson of Iddo.*

Zechariah is an important prophetic book. It prompts the Jews who have returned from exile in Babylon to finish what they started, to rebuild the temple. And it informs end-time events. The book begins with this simple declarative introduction, "I am the prophet Zechariah, the son of Berechiah, and the grandson of Iddo." Many people believe this phrase becomes the template for understanding the book. The names are important. Zechariah means, "God remembers." Berechiah means "God blesses." And the name Iddo has to do with timing. Iddo was Zachariah's grandfather. He was the priest of his family line. In time Zechariah would take his place.

Seems we have done this before in these posts. Tell me again, what's in a name? Here we have three generations of godly individuals. Their three names taken together mean, "God remembers, and he will bless in the proper time." This is really the theme of the book of Zechariah in a nutshell.

Perhaps you need to know today, "God remembers, and he will bless in the proper time."

Last Joshua

> Zechariah 3:8
>
> *Listen carefully, High Priest Joshua and all of you other priests. You are a sign of things to come, because I am going to bring back my servant, the Chosen King.*

The priest here, Joshua, is not to be confused with the earlier, General Joshua, mighty deliverer who marched Israel into the Promised Land. This Joshua, along with Zerubabbel, Ezra, Nehemiah and others, was instrumental in the reestablishment of Jerusalem after the return from Babylon. There are thousands of other Joshuas in history. You probably have a few in your circle of acquaintances. Priest Joshua was told that he was a sign of things to come, "my servant, the Chosen King." The original Hebrew text does not say king, but branch or sprout. This was a term understood to indicate royalty.

Jesus was born in Bethlehem. The Geek name Jesus is the Hebrew name Yeshua, or Joshua. The name Jesus is precious to you and me, but it was a common name in his culture. There were probably a couple of Joshuas on his block already. But this Joshua fulfilled the meaning of the name. Similar to the way that the first Adam was righted by the Last Adam, the Last Joshua will be the fulfillment of all who came before him and hoped for him. God is salvation. God is deliverance.

Riders on the Storm

> Zechariah 9:9, 10
>
> *Everyone in Jerusalem, celebrate and shout! Your king has won a victory, and he is coming to you. He is humble and rides on a donkey; he comes on the colt of a donkey. I, the LORD, will take away war chariots and horses from Israel and Jerusalem. Bows that were made for battle will be broken. I will bring peace to nations, and your king will rule from sea to sea. His kingdom will reach from the Euphrates River across the earth.*

Zakary and Nicholas, our two sons, have been an important part of Youngker High School Basketball. Zak graduated last year as the all-time leading scorer, a 3-point sharp shooter. Nic will be playing varsity ball as a sophomore this coming season. He was the leading scorer in

Freshmen ball last season. It has been so fun for our family being part of a great team with super coaches, outstanding team players, and tremendous family support. When the Youngker Rough Riders take the floor for home games the song by the Doors, *Riders on the Storm*, blasts through the sound system, eerily letting the opponents know they are in for a battle.

Jim Morrison, the voice behind the song, was a strange character. It is said he would often hitchhike the dusty, blacktop, Florida highway, from Tallahassee to Clearwater, 280 miles away, to see his girlfriend, Mary Werbelow. According to Stephen Davis, we can picture him "with his thumb up and his imagination on fire with lust and poetry and Nietsche and God knows what else."[xii] He began to scrawl images of a lonely hitchhiker in his notebook, "an existential traveler, faceless and dangerous, a drifting stranger with violent fantasies, a mystery tramp, the killer on the road." It's the image from a screenplay he wrote in which a hitchhiker goes on a murdering spree. *Riders on the Storm* was the last song Jim Morrison recorded. He went to France and died shortly afterward, allegedly from a heroin overdose.

There are times when the Scriptures impose necessary time gaps. For instance consider that there are at least two thousand years between the first part of Isaiah 9:6, and the second half of the verse. "A child has been born for us..." That part has been fulfilled. "We have been given a Son who will be our ruler." That part has not been fulfilled. He has not ruled. To borrow more traditional language from this verse, there has never been a time when the "government has rested on his shoulders."

It is similar with Zechariah 9:9, 10. "Everyone in Jerusalem, celebrate and shout! Your king has won a victory, and he is coming to you. He is humble and rides on a donkey." That's verse 9 and it has been fulfilled. It is the perfect description of Jesus' Triumphal Entry. And there are New Testament writers who confirm this. However, the very next verse has not been fulfilled. "I, the Lord, will take away war chariots and horses from Israel and Jerusalem. Bows that were made for battle will be broken. I will bring peace to nations, and your king will rule from sea to sea. His kingdom will reach from the Euphrates River across the earth."

In ancient times, for a ruler to ride into town on a donkey was an indication of coming in peace. It was a sure declaration of war for him to arrive racing on a horse. The first time Jesus came gently to Jerusalem, riding on a donkey. When he comes the second time he will be mounted on a white horse. A "rider [who] is called Faithful and True, with justice he judges and makes war." And we will be "riding on white horses" with him (Rev 19:11-14, NIV). He rides on "the wings of the wind" (2 Sam

22:11; Ps 18:10; 104:3; LEB). The earth will witness the true Riders on the Storm.

Jesus and Jimmy the Greek

> *Zechariah 12:10*
>
> *And I will pour out on the house of David and the inhabitants of Jerusalem a spirit of grace and supplication. They will look on me, the one they have pierced, and they will mourn for him as one mourns for an only child, and grieve bitterly for him as one grieves for a firstborn son.*

Jimmy the Greek was the infamous prognosticator of all things sports, and co-host at CBS in the 70s with Brent Musberger, Phyllis George and Irv Cross. He fell instantly from the height of sports television fame. After years of missteps with gambling, and tense moments with coworkers, there was one final mistake. Jimmy made comments that were decidedly racist. He was fired in the fallout. It is almost certain he was not racist, but simply garbled some statements in one of worst recorded gaffs of all times. He spent the rest of his life apologizing. His life spiraled downward. He died a very broken man. One of the co-hosts, the famous former NFL player-star, Irv Cross said, "I'm no doctor, but he probably died of a broken heart."

In Zechariah 12:10 we have a pinpoint of Jesus' death. This verse, combined with Psalm 34:20, "He protects all his bones, not one of them will be broken," makes for a very specific prophecy that was fulfilled at Jesus' death. The day that Jesus hung on the cross they came to him, planning to break his legs like the thieves next to him. The reason they would break the legs of criminals on the cross was so that they would not be able to lift up and gasp for a breath. Death on a cross was slow torture because it involved raising up to receive a breath, but dropping again under the strain. One couldn't stay down because of the caving in of the chest. It would cause suffocation. With the legs broken it would speed death. However, Jesus had already died so they jabbed a spear in his side instead. Years earlier at Baby Jesus' dedication, Simeon had told his mother, Mary, that when her son was pierced, a sword would pierce her own soul too (Luke 2:35). Now, at Skull Hill, she felt the cold steel penetrate her inner person simultaneous with her son's demise. Blood and water poured out of his side. Medical science has shown this is the sign of a torn heart. Quite literally, Jesus died of a broken heart. "He was pierced for our transgressions" (Isa 53:5). His heart was broken so that our broken hearts could be repaired.

5

A New Living Hope

GROUP 5: A NEW LIVING HOPE

Bethlehem Remembered

> *Matthew 2:1*
>
> *After Jesus was born in Bethlehem in the territory of Judea during the rule of King Herod, magi came from the east to Jerusalem.*

A song to honor the birthplace of Jesus.

Bethlehem Remembered

In the hillsides of Judah nestled away
Is a township that time has passed by
And though David was born there she still holds no sway
Just an off of the path village site

Many wise men have searched through the Scriptures to tell
The location that Christ should appear
There is Nazareth mentioned and Egypt as well
But his birthplace is perfectly clear

You Bethlehem will not be forgotten
Though you are small in size
For out of you will come One who's mighty
Opening up our eyes

Wouldn't Boaz be prideful and Ruth moved to tears
That their town is the place of a king?
Poor Naomi was bitter but now she can cheer
And her spirit can well up and sing

You Bethlehem will not be forgotten
Though Rachel died near you
For from her line life comes to many
Birthing a Savior true

He will be Mighty, Transformer, Ancient of Days
Maker of all that is alive
He will be Holy, and Righteous, Perfect in Ways
End of the fear and the strife

Open up our eyes

You are Mighty, You are Holy
Coming this hour, raised up in power
Hope for the world's demise

You are Mighty, Transformer, Ancient of Days
Maker of all that is alive
You are Holy, and Righteous, Perfect in Ways
End of the fear and the strife

Coming from you Bethlehem

The Trellis of Your Faith

> Matthew 6:3
>
> *When you give to the poor, don't let anyone know about it. Then your gift will be given in secret. Your Father knows what is done in secret, and he will reward you.*

Listen to the New American Standard Bible translation of the same verse. "But when you give to the poor, do not let your left hand know what your right hand is doing." How could NASB and CEV be so drastically different? One school of interpretation is called "formal equivalence" which can tend sometimes to be a little wooden sounding. The translators attempt to stay as close to the original language as possible. The words are transliterated and used when possible. The other school is called "dynamic equivalence." This method attempts to bring any idioms through into the new language and puts them in everyday language so we can get the jest of it.

In this particular case the CEV did a good job a capturing the jest of the verse, but failed to grasp a significant underpinning. There is an embedded truth in the original idiomatic phrase, "Don't let your left hand know what your right hand is doing."

Dallas Willard writes about "indirect preparedness" in his book, *The Spirit of the Disciplines*. It is his term for describing the way we become so accomplished at something that we don't even have to think about it. "Certainly this is not something that can be consciously enacted, for the effort to hide our right hand from our left hand would have precisely the effect of calling attention to what our right hand is doing. Only the right hand's habit of doing good can indirectly prepare it to act unconsciously."[xiii]

When something is really easy to us, so simple that we can perform it as if by second nature, then we have reached "indirect preparedness." How do we get to that level? I mean, in anything? How do we perform tasks without even thinking of it? Driving a car, playing the piano, or speaking Japanese – any skill you are good at, whether it came easily or not, required consistency. You had to discipline yourself to get better. It will be the same in the practice of good deeds. You have to practice it so often that it becomes second nature, to the point that you don't even realize, on a conscious level, that you are performing a task. That is when you know love has taken hold. When someone points out that you are kind, and you honestly did not try to be, it indicates that the fruit of the Spirit is being intertwined upon the trellis of your faith.

Stunning Beauty of Nature

Matthew 6:30

God gives such beauty to everything that grows in the fields. Even though it is here today and thrown into a fire tomorrow. He will surely do even more for you! Why do you have such little faith?

There is such stunning beauty in nature. I've had the privilege of seeing breath-taking vignettes. I recall stepping into a collection basin at the bottom of a natural double water fall in the northern part of El Salvador. The rains came in a downpour. It seemed like it was louder than a jet airplane passing. The massive sounds of millions of gallons of water falling to earth is spectacular. Then, afterward, the jungle came alive with sounds of its own, a magnificent counterpoint.

I've stood atop Imogene Pass in the West Slope of Colorado, with its dazzling views at 14,000 feet. One is very aware of the concept of forever from that place. It is cold and windy there even in July. I try to envision the Colorado National Guard in 1903 staying through the winter in the quaint, little Fort Peabody (which is still preserved historically) in order to stave off the two opposing parties, miners and mine management, from the two sides of the mountains. The shell formations contrast with rocks the size of buildings. Natural minerals fill the mountains: iron, zinc, ore, magnesium, coal, silver, and even some gold. Beautiful flowers dot the hillsides. There are Columbines, Castillejas, Geranium, and many other wildflowers. My friend, the late Charlie Steinberg, used to always say on Jeep rides, "Respect the mountain and the mountain will respect you."

I've been in the rain forests of Costa Rica. I recall being astounded at the sound produced in nature, a cacophony of natural rhythms and pitches. Shade so dense and thick, the light of the sun can barely penetrate the floor. Insects, animals, myriad of plant life, life forms I had never considered. Nature is absolutely beautiful.

Do these few I've mentioned outweigh the majesty of standing on the shore at the coastline looking into the depths of the endless ocean? Is there any wonder primitive thinkers believed the world was flat? How massive is the earth! Yet how small in comparison to other planets in our own solar system. Our sun, 93,000 million miles away, dwarfs our privileged planet but is dwarfed itself by stars so huge they would make our sun entirely unnoticed. And that is only our little cul de sac of the cosmos.

But if you move in the other direction, getting smaller, considering the discoveries of nanotechnology, there are ordered worlds existing in microscopic dimensions unknown to our senses, but which have huge impact on our very existence. Move smaller from a coffee bean to a sesame seed onto a grain of salt. Go a million times smaller to an amoeba and a paramecium and a human egg. Go smaller still to the skin cell, the red blood cell, the sperm. Just keep getting smaller and smaller, mitochondria, lysosome, E coli bacterium. You're not even close to the end, keep going until you are now measuring in nanometers, a billionth of a meter, and you will find the measles virus, HIV, influenza, hepatitis, ribosomes, hemoglobin, tRNA, and antibody. But you are not there yet. You must get smaller. Keep going until you are measuring in picometers, one trillionth of a meter. Now you will be able to see glucose, adenine, and water molecules, and finally, at 340 picometers, the carbon atom. And if you could open the carbon atom and look inside you know what you would find? A nucleus of protons and neutrons, opposites that are attracting each other, surrounded by swirling electrons that orbit just like the planets do around the sun, a universe within a universe.

How fantastic is nature! And if that is how God takes care of his cosmos, how much more will he take care of you! O you of little faith. Flowers of the field and birds of the air find meaningful existence in him. Do not worry. You are more valuable.

A-S-K

Matthew 7:7

Ask, and you will receive. Search, and you will find. Knock, and the door will be opened for you.

This hallmark verse from Jesus' own lips offers us a natural, little acronym to help us remember the promise. A-Ask. S-Search. K-Knock. A-S-K. We should always ask for help and never stop hoping that God will give us the desires of our hearts.

A very close friend relayed this story to me. I know specific details, but I will speak in a very general way. That way I can encourage you without belying a friend's privacy.

He was very discouraged because he was just coming out of a dating relationship that went wrong. He was really focusing on his relationship with the Lord. He was feeling as if he wanted to ask a certain young lady on a date. He prayed and asked the Lord for a sign. His prayer was very specific and candid. "Lord, I know that she is going to the Christian concert at the arena. If you want me to ask her out, allow me to see her at the concert. I know there are going to be eighteen thousand people there that night. But if I even see her there I will take it as a sign from you that I should invite her out on a date."

The night of the concert came. He sat in his seat, ground level, center section, close to the stage. As he was wondering if he would even catch a glimpse of her in the massive crowd, to his amazement, he saw her a great distance away. She was meandering down the steps, headed from mezzanine to the lower level. Speechless, he watched her traipse across the stage front, up the side aisle, to his same row. She worked her way over the seated concert-goers, to her seat, the empty one, right next to his.

The two dated a few times. They mutually decided to be friends only. They encouraged one another in an important time. Later my friend married very happily, and has, not only a wonderful wife, but also, two beautiful children. I have often wondered what would've happened if he had never asked the Lord.

Is there anything you would like to ask the Lord today?

Scariest Verse in the Bible

Matthew 7:21-23

Not everyone who calls me their Lord will get into the kingdom of heaven. Only the ones who obey my Father in heaven will get in. On the day of judgment many will call me their Lord. They will say, "We preached in your name, and in your name we forced out demons and worked many miracles." But I will tell them, "I will have nothing to do with you! Get out of my sight, you evil people!"

Matthew 7 speaks of individuals that do not make heaven. They complain, "But Lord, we even cast demons out in your name." But Jesus responds, "Depart from me. I never knew you."

How is it possible that someone could cast demons out of an individual by the authority of Christ and still be a virtual unknown to him? The same way an individual could be the producer of a powerful, study Bible that would bless hundreds of thousands, and yet be caught attempting to cross the state line with a sixteen-year-old girl in the car. The same way that a powerful evangelist could preach to auditoriums, jammed with thousands of guests, and yet die from sclerosis of the liver, an alcoholic.

How? Because it's not what you do that counts, but who you are. Your identity must be completely grounded in relationship with Christ.

The disciples rejoiced that the demons were subject to them in his name. Jesus hooped it up with them momentarily. "I know, I know. I saw Satan being hurled from the sky like lightning." But immediately he refocused the conversation. "Nonetheless, do not rejoice in this; rather, rejoice that your name is written in the Lamb's Book of Life."

This is the scariest verse in the Bible. Today, remember to spend time with Jesus. Do your best. But keep in mind, what you do is not nearly as important as who you are. Be legit.

Healed Emphatically

Matthew 8:17

So God's promise came true, just as the prophet Isaiah had said, "He healed our diseases and made us well."

Matthew, Mark and Luke each reference this quote of Isaiah embedded in a series of miraculous events. Matthew's account of it has Peter's mother-in-law raised from a bed-ridden fever; numerous exorcisms

Dr. Rawlings, a devout atheist, "considered all religion 'hocus-pocus' and death nothing more than a painless extinction." But something happened in 1977 that brought a dramatic change in the life of Dr. Rawlings. He was resuscitating a man, terrified and screaming.

"Each time he regained heartbeat and respiration, the patient screamed, 'I am in hell!' He was terrified and pleaded with me to help him. I was scared to death. . . Then I noticed a genuinely alarmed look on his face. He had a terrified look worse than the expression seen in death! This patient had a grotesque grimace expressing sheer horror! His pupils were dilated, and he was perspiring and trembling — he looked as if his hair was on end."

"Then still another strange thing happened. He said, 'Don't you understand? I am in hell... Don't let me go back to hell!' ...the man was serious, and it finally occurred to me that he was indeed in trouble. He was in a panic like I had never seen before." Dr. Rawlings believed no one, who could have heard his screams and saw the look of terror on his face, could doubt for a single minute that he was actually in a place called hell!

Take a minute to read these sobering lyrics by Nicole Nordeman from her song entitled, *What If*.

What if you're right?
And he was just another nice guy
What if you're right?
What if it's true?
They say the cross will only make a fool of you
And what if it's true?

What if he takes his place in history
With all the prophets and the kings
Who taught us love and came in peace
But then the story ends
What then?

But what if you're wrong?
What if there's more?
What if there's hope you never dreamed of hoping for?
What if you jump?
And just close your eyes?
What if the arms that catch you, catch you by surprise?
What if He's more than enough?
What if it's love?

To consider:

- This is the only heaven some will ever know. This is as good as it gets.
- This is the only hell some will ever know. This is as bad as it gets.

The True You of You

Matthew 16:24-26

The Then Jesus said to his disciples: If any of you want to be my followers, you must forget about yourself. You must take up your cross and follow me. If you want to save your life, you will destroy it. But if you give up your life for me, you will find it. What will you gain, if you own the whole world but destroy yourself? What would you give to get back your soul?

The late British pastor and evangelist, Alan Redpath, told the story of his two daughters running into his study one night. The older daughter hugged him tightly and said to her sister, "I have all of Daddy. You can't have any." The younger daughter who happened to be very witty quipped, "You may have all of Daddy, but Daddy has all of me."

The famed exegete, F.B. Meyer, wrote, "We must exchange the self-life for the Christ-life."[xiv] But that exchange may not come as easily as one might think. As Redpath has said, "Trust not in the shelter of home and family ties. They will not last, no matter how precious they are. Live sacramentally like broken bread and poured-out wine."[xv] Some way, we must suppress our own selfishness, and allow Christ to take up the highest priority of our existence. There is a true self in each one of us, the "true you" of you, the spirit man, made in the likeness of God. Being the true self means being completely selfless and entirely other oriented. It means being focused on God, and focused on others. The apostle Paul echoed the same sentiment when he told the church in Corinth, "I die every day - I mean that, brothers - just as surely as I glory over you in Christ Jesus our Lord" (1 Cor 15:31). He could say this to reiterate a statement he had made to them earlier, "Count yourselves dead to sin but alive to God in Christ Jesus" (1 Cor 1:30). We don't have anything. If we do happen to have something of substance inside us it is because he has more of us. All of the strength is in him. We have all of our heavenly Daddy, and our heavenly Daddy has all of us.

And He Healed Them All

Matthew 15:29-31

From there Jesus went along Lake Galilee. Then he climbed a hill and sat down. Large crowds came and brought many people who were paralyzed or blind or lame or unable to talk. They placed them, and many others, in front of Jesus, and he healed them all. Everyone was amazed at what they saw and heard. People who had never spoken could now speak. The lame were healed, the paralyzed could walk, and the blind were able to see. Everyone was praising the God of Israel.

Can you just imagine a paralyzed person being carried up a hillside by concerned friends. Picture them negotiating crags and outcroppings. *"No, not there. We're about to drop him. There, take that path."* They brought blind persons. Really? Recently, I saw a blind, young man tap his way skillfully across a gymnasium to the exit. I had the impression he had never been in the room before, or maybe he had, but it required great awareness on his part. A hillside is unlike a smooth gym floor. The lame. Did they hobble? Were they carried? The mute. Did they groan? Were they entirely silent? The masses, stumbling on foot, and stammering of tongue, escorted, brought, entouraged to Jesus. The return trip down the hill was much easier for all of them. Jumping, skipping, shouting, carrying mats. Walking sticks are now pole vaults. They leap over the ditches that had been unrealistic obstacles only moments before. Mats are now cargo. *"Hey, can I carry something for you?" "No, no. I've got it. I mean, hey, you carried me on the way up. The least I can do is carry my own mat back down!"*

A pastor friend, Dary Northrup, recently challenged us in the listening audience with the theology intoned by the story of the men who tore through the roof to bring their lame friend to Jesus. The wording of the text says, "When Jesus saw their faith [the carriers'] he said, 'Friend, your sins [the lame man's] are forgiven'" (Luke 5:20). It is definitely a moment for pause. Did I read that right? Wait. He saw *their* faith, and he forgave and healed *him*. Hmm.

"And he healed them all." We tend to think of the paralyzed, blind, lame and mute here. He healed all of them. True. I suggest, there was healing on a deeper level though, for all of them, the sick ones and the caregivers. Beneath visible surface pain, something was pulsating in the psyche of the community. Eyes were opened and emotions were encouraged. Lips were loosed and loyalties were leveled. The mangled were unbent, but wrong thinking was untwisted too. "And he healed them all."

The Amazing Mind Reader

Matthew 16:23

Jesus turned to Peter and said, "Satan get away from me! You're in my way because you think like everyone else and not like God."

Wow! What would it be like to think like God?

The Bible speaks plainly about Jesus' ability to know the thoughts of others. There was a statement made by Jesus when a paralytic had been lowered through the roof to him for healing. The religious leaders were bothered by his equating himself with God. "Immediately Jesus knew in his spirit that this was what they were thinking in their hearts" (Mark 2:8; Luke 5:22). On another occasion, a man with a shriveled hand was healed in a way that went against protocol for Sabbath observance. This really ticked off the teachers of the Law, "but Jesus knew what they were thinking" (Luke 6:8). One time the entourage of disciples was traveling and didn't bring proper provisions, post-miraculous feedings I might add. They were blaming one another for not bringing enough bread. The Lord tried to use the situation as an object lesson. He told them to watch out for the "leaven" of the Pharisees. The disciples, like us often, didn't get it. They thought he was implying something about the fact they had forgotten bread. "Jesus knew what they were thinking and said: You surely don't have much faith! Why are you talking about not having bread?" (Matt 16:8).

Come one, come all! See the amazing mind reader! He will know your thoughts and yet, not embarrass you in front of your friends!

How does Jesus do this? Well, he's God. It comes with the territory. He knows everything without it bothering him. Apparently, it's a family trait. His Father reads minds too. "You have looked deep into my heart, Lord, and you know all about me. Before I even speak a word you know what I will say" (Ps 139:1, 4). The heavenly Father made an amazing statement through his prophet in Isaiah 29:13. Matthew and Mark both quoted Jesus saying it. It must have been very important. "These people honor me with their lips but their hearts are far from me" (Matt 15:8; Mark 7:6). I have done that. I will be honest. There have been times my mouth went through the motions about something while my heart said something different. How horrible! How absolutely hypocritical and embarrassing to even write! But true.

There is a view screen playing continually in your mind. Some things have been placed in cue. That is, they are on the back burner so to speak. But some things keep getting lots of attention on the screen. These are the things that you default to. Oh, for a few moments your mind can be distracted by work assignments, obligations to others, even by worship. But when you are alone, on pause, these items pop up on the view screen. These items define you. "As a man thinks in his heart so is he" (Prov 4:27 KJV).

He is the amazing mind reader. He can read your mind just as easily as the card reader at your local store reads the information off your plastic. He doesn't even need to swipe a magnetic strip. Ask yourself, "Who am I?" Ask God, "Lord, who am I?"

Catch and Release

Matthew 17:24b, 25

"Does your teacher pay the temple tax?" "Yes, he does," Peter answered.

Here's how I think this went down. Peter feels challenged on the spot. Kind of like when a neighborhood kid says, "My dad's bigger than your dad." Pete says, *"Whadya' mean, Jesus, pay taxes? Why, of course Jesus pays taxes!"* Then as they start the walk back to the house, *"Hey Matthew, does Jesus pay taxes? Hey, uh Andrew. Jesus pays taxes, doesn't he?"*

Yeah, I have nothing to base this on except for Peter's reputation of being quick to speak, e.g. - suggesting three tabernacles at the transfiguration on the mountain; the rebuke of Jesus' profession of his impending death; or the infamous *"I'll never deny you"* at the Last Supper. Yes, Peter suffered from foot-in-mouth disease. I see him muttering to himself on the way home, *"Does Jesus pay taxes? I sure hope Jesus pays taxes."*

Notice Jesus speaks up before Peter ever says a thing. Basically, Jesus says the king's children are exempt from paying taxes. In other words, *"I'm the Son of God who made everything that exists. I don't get taxed on anything. I own everything."* But Jesus was also concerned about the situation of his disciples, their reputation not just his own, their bills. By extension, we as joint heirs, get the benefit of diplomatic immunity. But he knows that we are trapped in the now and the not yet, so he tells Peter to go do something that he enjoyed and was good at. Peter was a fisherman. God used Peter's interest and abilities to meet the need.

When you have a really important decision to make, go through the paces of good spiritual stewardship. You know, pray, read the Bible, ask advice of trusted spiritual leaders, attempt to discern direction from the

Lord. But don't forget to ask yourself, *"What would I like to do? What am I good at? What comes naturally? What am I gifted to do?"*

Jesus has used the episode to bait his learning disciple along. And Peter will get to see his own strength through the test of the line. Jesus needed no sonar depth finder. You talk about catch and release. Whew, what a relief it was to Peter to get this provision.

Small Huddles

> *Matthew 18:20*
>
> *Whenever two or three of you come together in my name, I am there with you.*

Jesus operates out of centrifugal force that models delegation to us. He is all-powerful God, never tiring or waning in strength. And yet, he is not all things to all people at all times. He often pulls away from the crowds to be alone in prayer (Mark 1:35; Lk 9:19). Like a quarterback going through the paces, he reads the multitude and calls an audible (Mark 6:39, 40). "Okay, guys, new game plan. Let's divide them into groups of fifties and hundreds." He's attracted to small huddles. I'm intrigued most by his system of three, twelve, and seventy. He sent out seventy in groups of two. He had twelve disciples that camped out with him for three and a half years. However, the most close-knit unit was his inner three.

Jesus had Peter, James and John with him for some really important moments of his earthly ministry. They joined him on the Mount of Transfiguration (Matt 17:1-9). They accompanied him into the inner room when a dead girl was raised to life (Mark 5:37-42). He also invited them to the back recesses of Gethsemane, the prayer garden (Mk 13:42-46).

Here, in this verse, Jesus gives us a hint of his logic. There is power and accountability in three. Neil Cole has written, "I believe two or three is the ideal size for effective church fellowship and ministry that will penetrate the rest of the church and ultimately the Kingdom."[xvi] He then details seven areas that are strengthened because of it – community; accountability; confidentiality; flexibility; communication; direction and leadership. Who are the closest three individuals in your life?

Keep Fiddling Away

Matthew 20:25-28

Jesus called the disciples together and said, "You know that foreign rulers like to order their people around. And their great leaders have full power over everyone they rule. But don't act like them. If you want to be great, you must be the servant of all the others. And if you want to be first, you must be the slave of the rest. The Son of Man did not come to be a slave master, but a slave who will give his life to rescue many people."

Many years ago, the great violinist, Niccolo Paganini, was performing before a packed house one evening, surrounded by a full orchestra. As he began the final piece one of the strings on his violin snapped. In his genius, Paganini was able to continue playing the piece on the remaining three strings. A moment later, a second string snapped.

Still, Paganini continued, playing the concerto on the remaining two strings. And then, a third string snapped, but still Paganini continued to play. He finished the piece, note for note, with one string on his violin. When the performance was over, the crowd rose in thunderous applause.

Paganini, ever the humble musician, raised his violin in the air and proclaimed to the audience, "Paganini, and one string!" He cued the conductor, the orchestra began playing, and he performed his encore, note for note, with one string on his violin.

If you've made a mess of your life with sin, you may be tempted to say, *"I have lost so much. I have so little left. I've wasted everything."* But the fact is, even if you're down to one string, God can still make music with your life. He can do more with a little than we can do with a lot. The measure of greatness in your life will be how you have handled difficulty.

Catcalling and Raucous Bellowing

Matthew 20:29, 30

Jesus was followed by a large crowd as he and his disciples were leaving Jericho. Two blind men were sitting beside the road. And when they heard that Jesus was coming their way, they shouted, "Lord, and son of David, have pity on us!"

In Jesus' teaching he was fond of the phrase, "He who has ears to hear let him hear." These two blind men had ears to hear. They were unable to see. But they heard that Jesus was passing by, and so they began to make a scene. It must have been embarrassing to the onlookers because they asked them repeatedly to be quiet. But the blind men kept calling out to Jesus with praise until he noticed them and granted their request.

Personally, I've experienced that it's difficult not to notice a blind person. My own experience is certainly not clinical and empirical; but I find myself magnetically drawn to blind persons. Their heads are typically raised because they feel the proper posture of their necks and do not see the horrible posture of the downcast society all around them. Often a smile is the default facial expression because they haven't seen the stoicism that is cultural. There is a walking stick, a seeing-eye dog, a person in the lead - something that gives them away.

I wonder if Jesus would've seen these blind men anyway, without their catcalling and raucous bellowing. Would he have passed them by? Remember that on one occasion Jesus walked on the water. He came to the place on the lake where his disciples were. The Scripture says he would've passed them by, but they thought he was a ghost and called out. Were there other blind men in the parade that day that Jesus passed? These men couldn't see; but they could hear and they could speak. They used the senses available to them to get the attention of Jesus. What resources are available to you to get Jesus' attention?

A Very Taxing Burden

Matthew 22:17-21

"Tell us what you think! Should we pay taxes to the Emperor or not?" Jesus knew their evil thoughts and said, "Why are you trying to test me? You show-offs! Let me see one of the coins used for paying taxes." They brought him a silver coin, and he asked, "Whose picture and name are on it?" "The Emperor's," they answered. Then Jesus told them, "Give the emperor what belongs to him and give God what belongs to God."

This is now the second time in a short period that Jesus is hounded about taxes. First the two-drama tax, so he sends Peter fishing. *"The first fish you catch, open its mouth, and take out a coin and pay the tax."* Now the Emperor's tax, so he becomes an art connoisseur. *"Show me the picture."*

These Pharisees are absolutely relentless. They will not stop. They are like gnats swarming, pestering, annoying. You just want to swat them. *"What is the deal? Don't you guys get it? I'm exempt, alright. I'm the Son.*

But I'll go ahead and humor you. Show me the coin. Whose image is this on the coin?" You just get the feeling this is a taxing burden to Jesus. I'd be willing to bet you have a taxing burden too. Something that makes you think, *"Are you kidding me? Will this never end?"*

Ironically, Jesus didn't need to see the coin. He knew, and so did everyone else, whose picture was on the coin. Maybe he was pointing out that the Pharisees had a coin and he didn't. *"Let me see one of the coins."* Perhaps, as the false accusers held the flimsy excuse in their shaky fingers, holy conviction settled on them. Sometimes the answer is the most obvious thing, right under your nose? To coin a phrase, heads you win. As easily as flipping a coin, Jesus can turn the tables on your situation.

A Literal Underground Church

> Matthew 24:8-11
>
> But this is just the beginning of troubles.
>
> You will be arrested, punished, and even killed. Because of me, you will be hated by people of all nations. Many will give up and will betray and hate each other. Many false prophets will come and fool a lot of people.

Richard Wurmbrand's faith in Christ came at a great price. When the Jewish, young man from Bucharest embraced the Jesus shared with him by a carpenter, he could not have known what atrocities awaited him. He spent stints in seven different prisons strictly because of his being a Christian. Wurmbrand was a leader in the underground church. His denunciation of Communism led to sentences of 8 ½ years, and eventually 25 years. Thankfully, his last sentence was ended after five years when he was granted amnesty.

Wurmbrand was kept in solitary confinement in a crude cell twelve feet beneath the surface that had no lights or windows. No sounds were ever heard down that far. The guards even placed felt on the soles of their shoes. The silence was deafening. There, deep beneath the surface in the Jilava, Romania prison, he began his mind-saving measure, a pattern of sleeping during the day and staying awake at night. He would work his brain through the night crafting a sermon that he would then preach to an imaginary audience. It was a literal underground church. Later, he was able to recall 350 of the sermons, so disciplined and active was his memory. He tapped on the walls and pipes developing a simple system of the alphabet, and later, Morse Code, in order to communicate with others imprisoned in the cavern. He called it being "sunlight" to his fellow inmates. He was tortured. The bottoms of his feet were beaten so badly that he could find no words to describe the pain. Then the next day the same beating was repeated until it revealed bone. His wife, who spent time in prison as well, was told by secret police, maliciously, that they had attended her husband's funeral.

Richard Wurmbrand appeared before a Senate Judicial subcommittee. In his testimony he raised his shirt and revealed 18 tortuous flesh wounds. They used knives, red-hot irons, drugs, deprivation and other brainwashing techniques. They would broadcast phrases denouncing Christianity and praising Communism. "Communism is good. Communism is good. Communism is good." "Christianity is dead. Christianity is dead. Christianity is dead." On one occasion they crucified a cat in front of the prisoners. The prisoners were told if they would give damaging information against their family members the cat would be freed. Under this duress the inmates would give the guards the untrue information they wanted. Then their family members would be brought in and tortured just like the cat.

As horrifying as the story of Richard Wurmbrand is, he is only one of many bishops, priests, monks, and Catholic nuns to have been tortured in Romania. And they represent only a drop in the bucket compared to the history of those slaughtered worldwide for their faith in Christ. The findings of an Italian journalist named Antonio Socci are alarming. Approximately 70 million Christians have been martyred for their faith in the 2,000 year history of the Church. What's striking is 65% of those killings happened in the twentieth century!

Pause. Pray for the persecuted church.

Do Well by God

> *Matthew 25:15, 25, 28*
>
> *The man knew what each servant could do. So he handed 5,000 coins to the first servant, 2,000 to the second, and 1,000 to the third. Then he left the country...I was frightened and went and hid your money in the ground...Then the master said, "Now your money will be taken away and given to the servant with 10,000 coins!"*

I'm wondering what part obedience has to play in it all. The one with only one talent, the traditional language, hid his one talent and was judged. And the one with five? He not only doubles his gift but receives the one talent of the sloppy servant too. Doesn't he accelerate and exponentially expand his talents even beyond the other faithful servant with two talents?

The Contemporary English Version has picked up on a nuance cleverly. The talent represented a weight. It may well be that the intention of the passage is that each servant was weighed out so many coins. This kind of changes the perception of the passage. First, the emphasis is definitely on money, not abilities. And furthermore, none of them has only one coin, but varying amounts of coins. This diffuses the idea that says some people only have one ability. Most have multiple abilities that are experimented with and developed.

The great challenge for many is to resist the temptation to do many things poorly. Sometimes I think it would be wonderful to do one thing and do it well. Some are blessed with that lot. However, to be a jack of all trades requires a listening ear that obeys carefully, a renaissance kind of discernment that is in the right place at the right time. The obvious intention of this passage is to do something, don't just nest egg your abilities. And hopefully you have moved out of that space. The subtle intention, though, is to excel and rise above. How? Whether 1, 2, 5, 10 or how every many talents, develop that listening ear and follow through with careful obedience. Do well by God's evaluation today. Do very well.

Table Fellowship

> Matthew 26:26
>
> *During the meal Jesus took some bread in his hands. He blessed the bread and broke it. Then he gave it to his disciples and said, "Take this and eat it. This is my body."*

As was customary for the Passover Feast, Jesus took in his hands the unleavened, flat bread. Jesus held the bread and blessed it, and then broke it, and next gave it to his disciples. Something may have clicked for them. No doubt they had shared hundreds of meals together in the course of the three to three-and-a-half years camping with Jesus in his itinerant ministry. Did they take turns praying over the meals? Did Jesus always bless the food? Who knows? But this was the Passover, a very special occasion. Jesus broke protocol for the routine of the Seder meal, and did something that must have been eerily familiar to the disciples. They recorded it precisely the same way as the feeding of the five thousand.

While enjoying table fellowship he takes the bread in his hands and blesses it. Then he breaks it. Next he hands it to his disciples. If they are keen, their minds race back to the hillside dotted with well over five thousand followers and only five loaves and two small fish. Jesus was moved with compassion and told the disciples to organize the crowd into groups of 50 and 100. He lifted the bread toward heaven and said a blessing. He broke the bread. Then he gave it to the disciples who distributed it to the masses. They picked up twelve baskets full of leftovers that day. Each disciple had a full basket after the crowd was fed. Sitting at the Lord's Supper the disciples realize he has made the claim, "I am the 'Bread of Life.'"

Incidentally, our lives follow the same prescription. We are very blessed. And yes, we go through times of extreme brokenness. But it is all for the sake of disbursing Jesus to the needy.

Remember, he was born in Bethlehem, the House of Bread. Jesus is still feeding the multitudes today. Will you be a faithful disciple and distribute the bread?

Jesus Barabbas or Jesus Christ?

> Matthew 27:17
>
> *So when the crowd came together, Pilate asked them, "Which prisoner do you want me to set free? Do you want Jesus Barabbas or Jesus who is called the Messiah?"*

What? Did I read that right? Jesus Barabbas or Jesus who is called Messiah? What's going on?

There is a fresh discussion among scholars as to whether the name Jesus was also part of Barabbas's name. It involves digging into literary criticism. The Bible versions we read today are the product of copies (manuscripts) of the originals (autographs). We have none of the originals, but a vast reservoir of wealth in copies that dwarfs any of the classical Greek writers such as Herodotus, Thucydides, Plato, Aristotle and so forth. More than 5,300 of them! If this discussion is new to you, don't let it be alarming. The Bible we have is miraculously preserved. There are a good number of discrepancies (variant readings), most of which are spelling errors. You can imagine the difficulties of distributing Scriptures without the use of a standardized dictionary, no word processing software with spell check. This was in the days before the printing press. And no copiers, at least not automated, human only. The holy Scriptures evolved organically as an accumulation. The word bible means library. So, as the centuries passed, different geographic regions had slightly differing hand-written copies that were then copied again by hand and perpetually advanced along. This is as it should be, exactly what one would expect to find under the close scrutiny of the science of textual criticism.

Pardon the verbose explanation; but this is something I think is very important. I've devoted my life to studying this out. I've found my faith stronger having been stretched.

The Contemporary English Version has decided to follow the pattern of one variant that does appear in numerous manuscripts, but does not appear in many others. The CEV joins with Good News Translation in calling the criminal Jesus Barabbas. Eugene Peterson has also worded it this way in his hugely popular, *The Message*. Interestingly, New International Version chose not to include Jesus Barabbas in its 1984 text, but made the change for its updated 2011 version. And the New American Bible Revised Edition has [Jesus] Barabbas with the brackets indicating the perplexity.

Jesus, is the Hellenized version of a common Hebrew name, Yeshua, that is Joshua. It's a great name. It means God is salvation. Yesous, Greek, is the Hellenized form. Apparently, one of the early church fathers, Origen, tried to do the church-world a favor and left Jesus off the name Barabbas. In the third century he wrote, "In the whole range of the Scriptures we know that no one who is a sinner [is called] Jesus." Origen had great intentions, but the reality is Jesus was a very common name. God wanted it that way. He was fully human and could relate to every struggle in every way. There were probably two other kids named Yeshua on his block alone.

At the time Jesus was arrested for sedition the Romans had a man in custody who was a notorious terrorist. His name was Barabbas. Here's where it gets interesting. Barabbas (or Bar Abbas) is the Hellenistic form of the Aramaic name Bar Abba which means, "son of the father." Perhaps Pilate was unaware entirely of the decision he was making that day. His question to the crowd really came off this way... "Do you want Jesus Barabbas or do you want Jesus Christ?" Strange things happen when we mix languages into one sentence. Imagine, if you can, a novel which has a character named Goodbye. As a play on words the writer has a line, "Goodbye said so long with a *Sayonara!*" This verse mixes Hebrew, Aramaic and Greek. But the idea and sentiment comes through this way: "Do you want me to release to you Yeshua son of the father? Or do you want me to release to you Yeshua Son of the Father who is called Messiah?"

What's your pleasure? Do you want the Jesus, son of the father, who is a known murderer and insurrectionist, the axis and epitome of everything human and wrong and sinful? Or do you want the Jesus, Son of the Father, who is called Christ, the good and pure, undefiled and perfect, ascent and climax of everything godly and right and holy?

In God's master plan the crowd chose to crucify him. Which Jesus do you side with today?

A Downpour in the Desert

> *Mark 1:2-4*
>
> *It began just as God had said in the book written by Isaiah the prophet, "I am sending my messenger to get the way ready for you. In the desert someone is shouting, 'Get the road ready for the Lord! Make a straight path for him.'" So John the Baptist showed up in the desert and told everyone, "Turn back to God and be baptized! Then your sins will be forgiven."*

As I write we are experiencing a tremendous thunderstorm here in Buckeye, Arizona. For the last 15 minutes we have been dumped on. It has rained so hard it is nearly unbelievable. The temperature topped out at 115 degrees today, not a cloud in sight. Tonight, we were sitting on the couch watching television. The emergency broadcasting system beeped in to say there was a thunderstorm warning. At the time of the warning there was no sound of a storm at all – near silence. Within minutes the wind was roaring and rain was pouring. I looked out in the backyard in disbelief at the size of the puddles, nay, small lakes, resulting from the rain. The newscast called it "one of the worst storms in years." The monsoon season is phenomenal.

Isaiah, in Messianic tempo, speaks prophetically of "streams in the desert" (Isa 32:2; 35:6; 43:19, 20). In the New Testament, Mark must have grasped Isaiah's sentiment when he writes of John coming, the forerunner of Jesus, baptizing in the desert region. He is the *living water* bringing the forgiveness of sins.

The liberating truth of Christ is a stream in the desert. The joys of forgiveness; purpose; significance; and worth; once realized by the repentant sinner, comprise a flash flood of peace swelling over the desert of gloom. Just as suddenly as a storm can arise, so the comfort of Christ's hope can come on the scene.

"And in the last days I will pour my Spirit on all people" (Joel 2:28).

Tips for the Thirsty Soul:
- Long for God like the watchman for the dawn, like the hunted deer longing for water
- Expect him to give you the desire of your heart
- Only water quenches true thirst. Just like soda, or coffee, does not satisfy the physical thirst, only the Living Water will satisfy the spiritual thirst.

A Really Clever Impostor?

Mark 2:1-8

Jesus went back to Capernaum, and a few days later people heard that he was at home. Then so many of them came to the house that there wasn't even standing room left in front of the door. Jesus was still teaching when four people came up, carrying a man on a mat because he could not walk. But because of the crowd, they could not get him to Jesus. So they made a hole in the roof above him and let the man down in front of everyone.

When Jesus saw how much faith they had, he said to the man, "My friend, your sins are forgiven." Some of the teachers of the Law of Moses were sitting there. They started wondering, "Why would he say such a thing? He must think he is God! Only God can forgive sins." At once, Jesus knew what they were thinking, and he said, "Why are you thinking such things?"

Is Jesus Christ God? Or was he just a really clever impostor? A number of years ago in his premier work, *Mere Christianity*, C.S. Lewis wrote words that are immortalized in Christian history. "A man who was merely a man and said the sort of things Jesus said would not be a great moral teacher. He would either be a lunatic - on a level with the man who says he is a poached egg - or else he would be the Devil of Hell. You must make your choice. Either this man was, and is, the Son of God: or else a madman or something worse. You can shut Him up for a fool, you can spit at Him and kill Him as a demon; or you can fall at His feet and call Him Lord and God. But let us not come with any patronising nonsense about His being a great human teacher. He has not left that open to us."[xvii]

There are many instances in the Scripture where Jesus behaves deistic. There are the obvious miracles of healing. It is very God-like to give sight, hearing, or the ability to walk. Equally impressive is his command of very nature. Waves and wind beckon at his command. Certainly spirit realm bleeds over into natural often in the life of Jesus Christ. He exorcises evil spirits. They beg for him to be merciful. This is as it should be. One would expect that from any one laying claim to the office of holy God. There are no express verses in which Jesus says, "I am God." What you find are obvious intonations to the effect that he is God. One instance that is very obvious is the language of John, chapters 6 through 8, where the contradiction becomes very sharp between Jesus and the religious leaders. The main issue? That he claimed to be the Son of God. This made him very God.

The Patristic Fathers penned it this way in the fourth century at Nicaea, "We believe in one Lord, Jesus Christ, the only Son of God, eternally begotten of the Father, God from God, Light from Light, true God from true God, begotten, not made, of one Being with the Father."

This text is an example of one of the times Jesus made his detractors so angry because he didn't come right out and claim deity, but it was so obvious as to be undeniable. When presented with such a bold display of faith, a clever impostor might illicit self-praise. Converts tore through the layers of a roof to get their lame friend to him. A fake might possibly try to conjure up something mystifying by using black magic. But what does Jesus say, "Your sins are forgiven." Can't you just hear the naysayers? *"Why only God can forgive sins! Just who does he think he is?"* That's what we would expect from God, the unexpected. It is totally opposite of where the carnal mind goes on a first reading. The element of surprise. We expect the unexpected from God. But it is so natural and normal to Jesus, totally lacking any pretense. His sincere response to their genuine act of faith is to reward the seeker with what he longs for most of all, forgiveness.

Next, he knows what they're thinking. Look carefully at the text to notice it. There has been no exchange of words. Jesus knew their thoughts. This is not mental telepathy, it is Omniscience. Isn't that what you would expect from your Messiah? And to top it off, he heals the lame man in an absolute miracle that silences the inaudible skeptics. No fanfare, no choreography, he just heals him with a question to the doubters, "Which is easier? Forgiving or healing?:" As if to say, "They're really the same thing. Aren't they?"

How would God behave? How would a clever impostor behave? One would expect God to be unexpected; to forgive; to know all; to read minds. It is just as it should be. Logically, Jesus is God.

Incompatible Capacities

> Mark 9:1-13
>
> *I can assure you that some of the people standing here will not die before they see God's kingdom come with power.*
>
> *Six days later Jesus took Peter, James, and John with him. They went up on a high mountain, where they could be alone. There in front of the disciples, Jesus was completely changed. And his clothes became much whiter than any bleach on earth could make them.*
>
> *Then Elijah and Moses appeared and were talking with Jesus. Peter said to Jesus, "Teacher, it is good for us to be here! Let us make three shelters, one for you, one for Moses, and one for Elijah."*
>
> *But Peter and the others were terribly frightened, and he did not know what he was talking about. The shadow of a cloud passed over and covered them. From the cloud a voice said, "This is my Son, and I love him. Listen to what he says!"*
>
> *At once the disciples looked around, but they saw only Jesus. As Jesus and his disciples were coming down the mountain, he told them not to say a word about what they had seen, until the Son of Man had been raised from death.*
>
> *So they kept it to themselves. But they wondered what he meant by the words "raised from death."*
>
> *The disciples asked Jesus, "Don't the teachers of the Law of Moses say that Elijah must come before the Messiah does?"*
>
> *Jesus answered: Elijah certainly will come to get everything ready. But don't the Scriptures also say that the Son of Man must suffer terribly and be rejected? I can assure you that Elijah has already come. And people treated him just as they wanted to, as the Scriptures say they would.*

Ever not understood something and just kept quiet?

A friend told me recently, "Often, I don't hear him. I just nod and pretend like I do." Who knows the things he has agreed to or allowed without truly realizing it!

There is an ancient Chinese proverb that is really apropos to classrooms. It says, "He who asks a question is a fool for five minutes. He who doesn't ask the question is a fool for a lifetime." Hmm. That's really good.

A lot of times we don't ask for clarification. It could be for numerous reasons. Perhaps we can't hear and are embarrassed. Or, the individual has a habit of mumbling and it becomes laborsome to keep asking. Maybe we don't want to look dumb. It could be that we've had several chances to learn the concept but we still don't get it. This was the case for the disciples.

The rag tag group that Jesus surrounded himself with was continually asking questions. Sometimes Jesus became frustrated. "Do you still not see or understand?" (Mark 8:17). "Are you still so dull?" (Matt 15:16). They were intelligent. Granted, they may not have been the upper echelon of society. Certainly there were more scholarly minds in the rabbinical schools. The disciples were "unschooled, ordinary men" (Acts 4:13). But the group that comprised the disciples was made up of men who ran fishing businesses; one was a tax code specialist; and at least one belonged to a religious organization, the Zealots, which rivaled modern fraternal clubs or secret societies. They are world wise, road weary grads of the school of hard knocks.

Our human capacities are sometimes not compatible with downloading divine concepts. And this is true for anyone. Sometimes God-shapes can't fit in these peanut brains.

Observe the lack of clarification in these verses. First, Peter exclaims, "Lord, it is good for us to be here" (verse 5). The very fact that he mentions it lets us know he is questioning if it's good for them to be there. Jesus is draped in a pure white robe. Two dead people who are among the most influential people from another time and place of Jewish history are flanking him. *"Are we really supposed to be seeing this, Lord?"* Secondly, so, Peter suggests something. But the Scripture says, "He didn't know what he was talking about" (verse 6). I love the quip by Mark Rutland, "And not knowing what to speak, he spoke..." And then he adds, "Some people speak because they have something to say. And some people speak because they just have to say something." Thirdly, honoring Jesus' gag order, they don't say anything more about it until after he has risen from the dead. Not a word. Even on the trip down the mountain, "they wondered what he meant by the words 'raised from death.'"

Fourthly, as a diversionary tactic, a roundabout way of getting to their point they asked, "Don't the teachers of the Law of Moses say that Elijah must come before Messiah does?" In other words, *"Why are we leaving? Isn't that Elijah back there with Moses. Hello? Moses, the one who talked about Elijah coming as a pointer to Messiah? Jesus, I think it could be advantageous to play the Elijah card next time the Pharisees start taunting."* But Jesus' last comment stumps the roast, Elijah already came and they didn't recognize him. *"Oh, it's over!"* Though it is not here in Mark's account, Matthew adds one last color commentary, "Then the disciples understood that Jesus was talking to them about John the Baptist" (Matt 17:13). The disciples understood. They got it. They figured something out.

Okay, Moses and Elijah, we really saw them. And we're still alive to talk about it. And Jesus was bright white, all the sudden, glorious. We can't tell anybody about it right now. And the Elijah text is really an allusion to John the Baptist. We got that one. And something about rising from death. What do you think he meant about that? The Son of Man rising from death. What could that be about?

Thread-Breadth Window

Mark 10:25-27

In fact, it's easier for a camel to go through the eye of a needle than for a rich person to get into God's kingdom. Jesus' disciples were even more amazed. They asked each other, "How can anyone ever be saved?" Jesus looked at them and said, "There are some things that people cannot do, but God can do anything."

It is a long-standing belief that the gate spoken of here was a smaller gate within the larger gate, perhaps a small door that would open to allow one individual through, without having to open up the larger gate. It would be used at night, for instance, as a safety control measure. Or it could be used in the daytime simply to monitor the entrances and exits better, a sort of ancient surveillance system if you will. The picture, on this view, is that a camel could narrowly squeeze through such a gate, but it would require kneeling, and being relieved of all its burdens, cargo and baggage. This is the only way a camel could fit through. It's a great thought. Unfortunately there is not one ounce of truth to it. The "eye of the needle" gate as it has been called, is a fabrication, an invention of medieval times. There was no such gate in ancient times.

If this bursts your bubble, be encouraged by the "true" truth of this passage. And that is, you see, nothing is impossible with God.

Don't let this thought escape you. The disciples obviously knew of no "eye of the needle" gate. If they had they wouldn't have responded the way they did when Jesus made his statement. "How can anyone ever be saved?" They knew what Jesus was describing. The reality is he imaged the preposterous for us. He's describing something that is absolutely unreasonable. Try to imagine a massive animal that can weigh as much as 2,200 pounds, compressing itself through a thread-breadth opening. I remember Tim Allen's character in the original *Santa Clause* funneling through the rooftop piping. If you are able to picture this in your mind's eye, try to make that scene much more microscopic. How much bigger is that camel than Saint Nick! How much smaller is the pin hole than the roof pipe! This is hyperbole on steroids. He might as well say, "Snake a submarine through a fiber optic cable." Jesus wants to evoke a feeling of utter hopelessness that it could ever happen, complete and total dismissal that anything like it could ever occur. Having dashed all hopes that a rich man could ever have even a sliver of hope of salvation, he now presents the point. "But God can do anything."

There is nothing God can't do. Nothing! Absolutely nothing! What impossibility do you face right now? Can you find it somewhere deep inside yourself to simply have faith? Believe that God will work a miracle for you. If you have a thread-breadth window there is plenty of room for God to work.

To Coin a Phrase

> *Mark 12:13-17, 43, 44*
>
> *The Pharisees got together with Herod's followers. Then they sent some men to trick Jesus into saying something wrong. They went to him and said, "Teacher, we know that you are honest. You treat everyone with the same respect, no matter who they are. And you teach the truth about what God wants people to do. Tell us, should we pay taxes to the Emperor or not?"*
>
> *Jesus knew what they were up to, and he said, "Why are you trying to test me? Show me a coin!" They brought him a silver coin, and he asked, "Whose picture and name are on it?" "The Emperor's," they answered.*
>
> *Then Jesus told them, "Give the Emperor what belongs to him and give God what belongs to God." The men were amazed at Jesus.*
>
> *…Jesus told his disciples to gather around him. Then he said: I tell you that this poor widow has put in more than all the others. Everyone else gave what they didn't need. But she is very poor and gave everything she had. Now she doesn't have a cent to live on.*

Jesus has just been asked what to do about paying taxes. The religious leaders are setting a trap for him. They are sure he will say, "Of course you should pay taxes." Then they would say, "Aha, see, he isn't supportive of the cause of his own Jewish people. He doesn't understand what it's like to be oppressed. I knew it. He's been bought out by the government." But if Jesus answers, "No, don't pay taxes," they have plan B. "Oh, I see Jesus. So, you're a rebel who resists authority! What kind of holy man rebels? Can you say, 'Tax evasion'?"

They did not count on plan C, for Christ. Undeterred, he responds in paraphrase, "Flash the cash. Show me the coin. Isn't someone's picture on it? Whose is it? Well then, give Caesar what's his and God what is his." In deflecting any self-honor, Jesus squelched the opportunity to have his own picture and inscription on a coin. That's what his disciples really wanted. "Are you at this time going to restore the kingdom of Israel?" "Can we sit on your right and left when your kingdom comes?" It is clear they are poised to take on Rome. But Jesus wasn't aiming for such a small prize.

At the close of this chapter, fresh on the heels of the coin ordeal, Jesus recognizes true greatness. It involves a coin, but Caesar is nowhere to be found. This widow is influential, a real mover and shaker. She doesn't impress the brass of her day. She will not be ringing the bell for the stock exchange. But she has persuaded the stockholders of heaven. She gave more than all the wealthy combined.

We humans are prone to be impressed by the influential, persuasive and powerful. It is interesting to consider what impresses God. In his economy, first is last, last is first, and greatest is servant of all. He is opposite of everything that earth's inhabitants value. To coin a phrase, this is no small change.

Mary Mother

Luke 1:28

The angel greeted Mary and said, "You are truly blessed! The Lord is with you."

Here is Mary Mother receiving Emmanuel in holy conception. It is, quite literally, the fleshing out of the Incarnation. Jesus is "God with us," and so she is told, "The Lord is with you." He was with Mary unlike any other. He was within her. No human can recall being inside mother; though I'm sure compassionate warmth is conveyed by the carrier. But for the mom there are unforgettable connections, seared impressions upon the psyche, emotional love forged by the experience of internalized life. She undergoes tremendous change of physique, and tremendous change of emotions.

In addition, Mary underwent tremendous change spiritually. I'm very impressed with Mary. She recognized her need for a Savior. She carried him so he could carry the cross. In the now infamous words of Mark Lowry, "The child that you've delivered, will soon deliver you. Mary did you know?" I believe she knew. Perhaps in time. Perhaps when the sword pierced her own soul (Lk 2:35) that day he was hanging on a cross, suspended between heaven and earth.

Isaiah spoke seven centuries in advance, about the birth of Jesus. "Therefore the Lord himself will give you a sign: Behold, a virgin will be with child and bear a son, and she will call his name Immanuel" (Isa 7:14, NASB). Isaiah said that he would be called *emanu el*. It means God is with us. It may not be entirely accurate to treat *emanu* as an adjective, but a distinction of our God is that he is the *with-us* God. Through messianic reverberations Isaiah proclaims, "For a child will be born to us, a son will be given to us; And the government will rest on his shoulders; And his name will be Wonderful Counselor, Mighty God, Eternal Father, Prince of Peace" (Isa 9:6, NASB). What kind of counselor is he? He is Wonderful Counselor. What kind of God? He is Mighty God. What kind of father? He is Eternal Father. What kind of prince is he? He is Peace Prince. Mary cradled the embodiment of Isaiah 9:6 within her person. God within her is God with us.

He Has Staked His Claim

Luke 3:38

The family of Jesus went all the way back to Adam and then to God.

Luke presents a genealogy different from the one Matthew wrote. Each had a reason for writing the way he did. There is every indication that Matthew wrote as a Jew to Jewish people in order to convince them that Jesus was the fulfillment of their anticipated Messiah. Matthew quotes Jesus in five distinct teaching blocks representing Torah. He quotes Isaiah, the messianic prophet, more often than the others. He presents the perfect God who has become a man.

Luke's approach is different. Apparently he targets a Greek audience, so he presents Jesus as the perfect man who is God. "The family of Jesus went all the way back to Adam, and then to God," Luke says. Paul distinguished between the First Adam and the Last Adam (1 Cor 15:45). The perfect Adam undoes all the wrong of the sinful Adam and his descendants.

Genealogies are important because of connectedness, not for pedigree. Jesus is not the last in some great line of super mortals. His family line has a few horse thieves. But notice that he connects directly to David's monarchy; to Abraham's bloodline; and to Adam's race. His perfect, sinless life validates the salvation he offers. He has staked his claim on all humanity. Any who confess sin and believe in him are saved.

71 Mustang Fastback

Luke 4:9

Finally, the devil took Jesus to Jerusalem and had him stand on top of the temple. The devil said, "If you are God's Son, jump off."

Uncle Vaughn had a 71 Mustang Fastback, army green that thing, whew - it would fly. I remember him saying once, "You don't floor it when the light turns green, but just knowing you could is..." His voice trailed off and he didn't finish the sentence. We knew what he meant, raw power, unbridled inertia, torque, horses and turbines.

Jesus didn't push the pedal to the floor. This last temptation is poignant and capsulizes the sentiment of all three. *Just jump! Jump off, if you're really the Son of God you won't get hurt.* Each of the three temptations is geared in some way towards a selfish display. *C'mon, show me you can do it.* That same sinister taunt followed him all the way to the cross, "If you're really the Son of God come down off that cross. Then we'll believe" (Matt 27:42). When Eugene Peterson coins the phrase Anarchist in place of what is typically translated Antichrist, I understand that. It seems to make perfect sense. "Before that day comes a couple of things have to happen. First, the apostasy. Second, the debut of the Anarchist, a real dog of Satan" (2 Thes 2:3). The anarchy that is fast becoming the norm of our culture is itself a Petri Dish for the culture of the end times.

Satan's schemes against Jesus are the same ones he uses against us. Flex your muscles, show your power. Typically it is in the most unsuspecting way - when we are right and we know it; when we are totally justified; or when are perceived to be in authority over someone else. These are the times we are tempted to be forceful, brutal, terse, or curt. I've found there are times these attributes are needed, but not often.

It seems to me, the more authority I've been granted in life, the more I must work to be under gentle control.

The time will come when Jesus will floor it. When he "punches it" he will crush the serpent's head with his heel (Gen 3:15). Then we will see who will jump!

What Does It Mean to Pray?

> *Luke 5:16*
>
> *But Jesus would often go to some place where he could be alone and pray.*

Jesus prayed often. His practice was to pray in a disciplined way, a set quiet time, if you will, making prayer time his most important appointment of each day. All the gospel writers showed Jesus in prayer, but especially Luke. He showed Jesus often in prayer (Lk 6:12; 9:18; 11:1; 22:39). There is every indication that Jesus conducted a structured, daily time with his Father.

It raises the question, why did he even need to pray? He was God, very God. There is the sense in which everything he accomplished in his earthly life was done in the power of the Holy Spirit. What a model he is to you and me. In his last meeting with his disciples he even told them, "I tell you for certain that if you have faith in me, you will do the same things I am doing. You will do even greater things, now that I am going back to the Father" (John 14:12). Perhaps he did not speak this in terms of greater miracles, in and of themselves. I mean, after all, even if you raise someone from the dead, they will not be any more alive than the dead ones he raised. No, I think he is speaking of the exponential growth of the Church because he himself is interceding to the Father, and the Spirit has been poured out. Christians are sprinkled like salt in the earth. Effectiveness is not confined to his one human body any longer.

Jesus' prayer communion with his Father was the most meaningful relationship in his life. When asked about prayer by his disciples, Jesus didn't emphasize allotment of time, a certain method, or even consistency. When he was asked how to pray by his disciples, he seized the moment to drive home the most important aspects. Worship vertically to your "Father who is in heaven." Love horizontally to "those who have trespassed against us." This is the heart of meaningful prayer.

Fruitful Consequences

Luke 6:43

A good tree cannot produce bad fruit, and a bad tree cannot produce good fruit.

You don't plant tomato seeds if you hope to grow watermelons. No one sows carrots and reaps grapefruit. Whatever you plant grows. Whatever you water flourishes. You don't expect to harvest apples from a lemon tree. It would be ridiculous to expect peanuts from a grapevine. Whatever you nourish thrives. Give careful attention to your prayer garden. Let pesky weeds garner your attention. Train the vines and leaves. Till the best possible soil so the good seed can take root. Then others will note the blessed, fruitful consequences.

Listen to How You Listen

Luke 8:18

Pay attention to how you listen! Everyone who has something will be given more, but people who have nothing will lose what little they think they have.

"Pay attention to how you listen." A number of years ago a book was written under the title, *How to Read a Book*.[xviii] In it Mortimer J. Adler and Charles Van Doren describe the proper way to affirm or deny the content of a work. It's not enough to just say I like a book, or I don't like it. When one learns to read critically, perhaps she will reject it on the basis that the author did not include pertinent information. Or possibly she will find agreement with the book because it is well documented.

The same logic is at work here in Jesus' statement. It's not enough to simply let sound waves funnel down your ear canal when you here a message. It is not enough to simply track printed ink with your cornea from the onion-skin pages of your Bible. Listen to how you listen. Take note of how you take note. Be particular and exclusive. Demand of yourself the very best commitment to discernment.

Afterlife

Luke 12:4

My friends, don't be afraid of people. They can kill you, but after that, there is nothing else they can do.

I can't think of anything more horrific than murder, can you? The unsettling of spirit that jolts the victim's family members is unspeakable. Truly, entire neighborhoods are stunned, like a collective punch in the communal gut. And yet, newscast after newscast reports regularly and consistently that life has been snubbed out, taken, cheated, halted, stopped prematurely.

Notice there is an assumption of eternity from which Jesus speaks. A key word in this verse is "after". Christ says, "They can kill you, but after that, there is nothing else they can do." There is an afterlife. Afterlife - that word is such a funny human invention. Afterlife is the main life, that's "real" living, the premier existence. Just as being alive in mother's womb seems to us, safe, but very primitive; the vantage point of those who have already arrived in afterlife must make our current estate seem so antiquated. From the standpoint of eternal Deity, self-existent Omnipotence, the very best that this life can offer is but preliminary to what awaits us in eternity. So the term afterlife falls flat. And yet, the taking of this life still concerns him greatly. God commands that it not be done (Exod 20:13). He abhors the stealing and destroying of life. Jesus addresses this very issue when he contrasts himself with Satan, giving a veritable job description. "The thief's purpose is to steal and kill and destroy. My purpose is to give them a rich and satisfying life" (John 10:10, NLT). After this life is completed, a life awaits that betrays all description with puny earthly words.

The Glory of Humility

> Luke 14:10
>
> *When you are invited to be a guest, go and sit in the worst place. Then the one who invited you may come and say, "My friend, take a better seat!" You will then be honored in front of all the other guests.*

Elsewhere in this devotional I have written about the last days of my Dad's life, James E. Howard. He was truly a remarkable man, more newsworthy than any book could ever describe. He captured the struggle of ultimate reward. He lived his faith, pounding it out through remarkable testimony, endless acts of kindness, and love in the face of unspeakable suffering. My Dad emulated Jacob, wrestling with God, not letting go until he was blessed. Remember that the name Israel means, "He wrestles with God."

The apostle Paul pondered life and death. "For to me to live is Christ and to die is gain. If I am to go on living in the body, this will mean fruitful labor for me. Yet what shall I choose? I do not know! I am *torn* between the two: I desire to depart and be with Christ, which is better by far; but it is more necessary for you that I remain in the body" (Phil 1:21-24). Based upon this passage I wrote an instrumental, guitar ballad in Dad's honor titled, *Torn*.

There were lighthearted moments of banter and laughter, even in the midst of a horrible disease. When Dad got shaved in the hospital, after not having shaved for a few days, the razor tugged and pulled, and he exclaimed, "Holy mackerel!" If you only knew my Dad. He just never used that phrase. One time he asked a staff member in a jovial tone, "Are you the chef or the chauffeur?" Another time, he needed to get to the restroom, but Mom was determined to help him. Clouded by morphine, and yet always the consummate gentlemen, in that moment he said to her, "Sir, if you'll kindly step aside." Such serious matters, and yet, appropriate moments of brevity lightened the family burden.

God gave Dad times when heaven bled through into earth's sphere. Once he sat up in the hospital bed and said, "Why Momma!" Grandmother Howard had been with the Lord for many years. I wrote a note to myself that once he woke once and said, "I've seen some visions. I just can't remember, (pause) - beautiful streets." Just a few days before he died he mustered the strength to call his sons to himself to bless us, pray over us, and prophesy over us. It is a priceless memory.

When Dad started his last week on this earth, in a semi-coherent state, he spoke words that resonated in our spirits in a profound, deep way. "This is the day I enter into my perpetual glory." It was a holy, reverent moment. Now, Dad was a very humble man. He never wanted anything for himself. His entire life was at all times, always about other people. So, this was something very out of character for him. The sacredness of the moment was weighty.

About three months after Dad was gone I was studying Luke 14. I understood the "glory" Dad entered into perpetually. It is the glory of humility. "When you are invited to be a guest, go and sit in the worst place. Then the one who invited you may come and say, 'My friend, take a better seat!' You will then be *honored* in front of all the other guests." The word "honored" is the Greek word, "doxa", or glory. It is the word from which we derive doxology. This verse really drives home the point: the one who truly humbles himself before his Lord, is blessed immensely with the reward of God in eternity. All glory belongs to God, only, rightly. Yet, he is happy to splash blessings on his loved ones.

To the Day

Luke 19:41, 42

When Jesus came closer and could see Jerusalem, he cried and said: It is too bad that today your people don't know what will bring them peace! Now it is hidden from them.

Jack Van Impe has made interesting observations on this verse, Luke 19:42, in conjunction with the prophecy from Daniel 9:24-27, which says there will be 70 "sevens" in order to finish transgression. This "seven", referred to in Daniel, is typically thought to be a seven-year period. One of the "sevens" is separate from the rest, tacked on the end. It corresponds with the tribulation in the book of the Revelation. Particularly interesting is verses 26 and 27. After 7 "sevens" have passed, and 62 more "sevens", the "prince will be cut off." The two designations combine for 69 "sevens" (69 X 7) which equals 483 years. A Jewish calculation of a year would be 360 days. And 483 X 360 = 173,880 days. Van Impe has postulated that from the command to rebuild the temple on March 14, 445 B.C., to the time when Jesus rode into Jerusalem on a donkey, April 6, 32 A.D. is precisely 173,880 days.

Many are quick to jump on the band wagon of criticism. Some relegate this kind of speculation to sloppy exegesis and adventurous manipulation. I always want to point out, I am not surprised that the Bible is a miracle book. It is as one would expect. There are amazing "so-called" coincidences.

It just may be that the Author of Life rode into Jerusalem with a crowd cheering wildly, but he was weeping. Hear the disciples inquire, "What's wrong, Lord? Don't cry. They're cheering for you. This is it. This is the big break we've been waiting for!" But he cries and says, "It is too bad that today, this very day, your people don't recognize just what it is that will bring them peace." From there it was just a short distance to the cross.

Living Logos

John 1:1

In the beginning was the one who is called the Word. The Word was with God and was truly God.

Since ancient times philosophers have tried to bring definition to the tripartite being that is the quintessential human. Ethos, pathos and logos. Paul seems to agree with what thinking minds wrote in his day, or at least gives it a mental nod. "I pray that God, who gives peace, will make you completely holy. And may your *spirit, soul, and body* be kept healthy and faultless until our Lord Jesus Christ returns" (1 Thess 5:23). The soul typically is defined as the seat of our emotions, intellect and will. Note that in Paul's preference the spirit is listed first, the physical body is last.

Ethos has to do with what is right in a matter. Think of our word ethical. Pathos is about feelings and emotions. You can see it embedded in our words empathy and sympathy. The irony of the word logos is that it translates "word." It represents reason. Words and ideas are really powerful things. Yet we are not three persons. We are each one holistic being. There is blending, bleeding and spill over in all areas of our being - spirit, soul, and body. Blaise Pascal spoke poetically, "The heart has reasons, which the reason cannot understand."

Jesus is the abiding embodiment of the rationale of God. He is the expression of God's will to us, the carrying out of God's purposes, our holy go-between, our high priest, the God-man, our living logos.

Eternal Wind

> *John 3:8*
>
> *Only God's Spirit gives new life. The Spirit is like the wind that blows wherever it wants to. You can hear the wind, but you don't know where it comes from or where it is going.*

A poem based on Janice Miller's reflection upon the wind's song.[xix] *Pronounced *ha-ha-gee-us puh-new-muh*, the Greek wording of the Holy Spirit. There is a subtle play on words by Jesus, in that, in the Greek language, there is one word for spirit, wind, and breath.

Eternal Wind

O Holy Spirit
   Break over me in splendid praise
      Ambient and polyphonic

Ὁ ἅγιος πνευύμα*
   Express unvoiced thanks
      Break silence with delight

O Sacred Wind
   Sure Embrasure melodious sphere
      Fortissimo surrounding

O Gentle Breath
Still my small voice
Pianissimo internal

July 2, 2009

Seeker Sensitive Worshiper

John 4:23, 24

But a time is coming, and it is already here! Even now the true worshipers are being led by the Spirit to worship the Father according to the truth. These are the ones the Father is seeking to worship him. God is Spirit, and those who worship God must be led by the Spirit to worship him according to the truth.

I like the way Contemporary English version captures it in a blend, "The true worshipers are being led by the Spirit to worship the Father in truth."

You can't help but see an allusion to the holy Trinity in these verses. First, the Holy Spirit, next, the heavenly Father, and the triad is completed with the reference to the Truth. There are a little over 100 times the writers of the four Gospels mention truth. Almost every one of the verses is a quote of Jesus saying the words, "I tell you the truth." In fact, the reason Jesus went to the cross was because he was speaking the truth (John 8:40). Jesus divulged to his disciples only moments before going to the Garden of Gethsemane, "I am the way, the truth and the life" (John 14:3).

Jesus described to the woman at the well two modes of worshiping the Father, spirit and truth. On a purely analytical approach, Spirit leans more towards feelings, sensations, emotions, warmth, and other felt descriptors that play upon the senses. It can be spiritual to be in a contemporary worship service and sense the weight of the glory of God. It would've been spiritual to have been a peasant in medieval times, working throughout the week to grow turnips and potatoes, and then to walk inside one of the magnificent European Cathedrals. It was formally described as transcendence. Spirituality involves being aware of the One greater than yourself. Spirit is a perfectly valid worship experience.

Truth, on the other hand, indicates learned, thoughtful, reflective, applied knowledge. It is embraced more than encountered. Its channels are revelation not sensation. The ecstasy of truth is discovery. With truth one envisions the diligent student dusting off the books from the library shelf and digging to discern. To differentiate truth from spirit, think of discipline versus experience; or epiphany versus exposure. Truth is when a light goes off in your head. Spirit is enjoying the glow and warmth of the light. Truth is a perfectly valid worship experience.

Both spirit and truth are needed for the authentic worshiper. This is the kind of worshiper the Father seeks. A popular buzz word in church-speak is "seeker sensitive." I am very much in favor of having an environment that welcomes newcomers in a non-threatening way. I think this is crucial in order to interface in a relevant way with culture. I believe it pleases the heart of God when individuals who have not really met him are exposed to his presence. There is one qualifier though. The One seeker we must be most sensitive to is the Father and his desires. "He seeks those who will worship him in Spirit and truth." Be very sensitive to the Seeker today.

Aching, Yearning, Longing

John 4:32; 6:55

But Jesus told them, "I have food you don't know anything about."

My flesh is the true food, and my blood is the true drink.

In John 4 Jesus gives foreshadowing of one of his most important teaching concepts. John does too, crafty inspired author that he is, he caught on. The disciples return with food to see Jesus in full discussion with the Samaritan woman at the well. They offer Jesus a bite to eat. Jesus responds, *"Oh, I have food to eat alright. You guys don't know a thing about it."* While the other disciples are arguing over whether someone made a McDonald's run, or if Jesus has a private stash, imagine if you will, John, off to the side, scratching his head, taking all of this in. Just what could it mean?

By John 6, which appears to happen fairly quickly chronologically, Jesus uses perhaps his greatest miracle to drive home an important point. It is an object lesson of magnanimous proportion. He feeds five thousand plus with only a few loaves and fish. First, notice the pattern. He blesses the food, breaks the food, and distributes the food. And the multitude is nourished. It is the inescapable pattern of ministry - blessed; broken; distributed.

Jesus was very blessed. His life on earth was spectacular - miracles, deliverance, and hope. He lived a very blessed life. At Calvary he was severely broken, so much so that Isaiah prophesied, he hardly looked human (Isa 52:14). He was crushed. However, his resurrection stumped

Satanic strategies. He arose and ascended and is distributed to feed salvation to the multitudes of the world.

We are blessed immeasurably, the promise of salvation; the hope of eternity; rescue here and now from the evil vices of life. Yet we are also broken. Sometimes it comes in cycles. Very broken, beat up by the very patrons we wish to help, or weighed down by devastating loss. Like Gideon's torches, often the only way the light of the world can escape us to shine in dark places is by the painful process of brokenness. And yet, irony of ironies, when we are squeezed, like Jesus was in the Garden of Gethsemane, olives *as it were* in the press, our brokenness is spread around to touch the masses. The multitude is fed again.

I have claimed this verse in times of prayer and fasting. Give me the food that I don't know about.

Jesus' brilliance is on full display. He connects intimacy with the Father analogously with food. Think of what food is. Food is our lifeline. It is sustenance. Food often represents table fellowship. Food is joy. Some time when you are in a crowded restaurant you should just look around and see what everyone is doing - talking, taking and chewing, smiling, swallowing and enjoying, laughing. Only God could come up with the idea of food.

So first, Jesus makes a statement. In John 4, there's this food that I have and you guys don't know anything about it. Then in John 6 he feeds a multitude of hungry people. The crowd thinks they have hit the jackpot. *The mother lode. Let's follow this guy. Free lunch, yeah, sign me up.* They do not know it's been an elaborate set-up. Jesus wants to talk to them about the other food. But the Scripture says that many of them turned away from him at this point.

Now, it's not as if Jesus doesn't want to meet their physical needs. No, not at all. He is very concerned for them. He is moved with compassion for them. Relief ministry does not have to be void of gospel message. Nor does evangelism need to be exclusive from felt needs. It is not either/or. It is very much both/and.

Still, Jesus uses this occasion to talk about real lifeline, real nourishment, real sustenance. Just as everyone's meal has worn off and they're ready for round two at the buffet, he clarifies the statement of John 4, the one that had dawned on John. "My flesh is the true food, and my blood is the true drink" (John 6:55). This statement alone has led to countless volumes that line library shelves regarding transubstantiation versus consubstantiation, and memorial versus real presence. Jesus is not asking us to be cannibals. He uses hyperbole to make a point. On some level he wants us to know we must internalize him. We must be so close to him that it is as if we're in him and he is in us. All hunger, craving, lusting, longing and yearning of the physical world will be stilled; true life-giving sustenance comes from a living, breathing relationship with Almighty. It is an itch you can't scratch, the God-shaped hole. It goes under the banner of aching, yearning, longing, hurting, desiring.

He has spread the table for fellowship today. Do we acknowledge his extended scepter? Or will we turn away from him?

A Little Dirt Don't Hurt

> *John 9:5-7*
>
> *"While I am in the world, I am the light for the world." After Jesus said this, he spit on the ground. He made some mud and smeared it on the man's eyes. Then he said, "Go wash off the mud in Siloam Pool." The man went and washed in Siloam, which means "One Who Is Sent." When he had washed off the mud, he could see.*

Jesus did something "for the first time in history" (9:32) by doing the same thing he had already done prehistory. Let me explain. No one born blind had ever been given sight before - true. Never been done. And Jesus did it. His new follower is mind-blown, and so is the crowd. But just how did Jesus do it?

I imagine him conjecturing with his disciples as they happen upon the blind man. The disciples ask who had sinned, the young man or his parents? It was a Sabbath and Jesus decided, *"Um, yeah, I can use this."* He reaches down and grabs a little dirt and spits in it. Not very couth. *"Hold steady, this won't hurt a bit. Let's see, uh, oh yes, I believe this is how we did it. Mmm-hmm, it goes a little something like this."* Emerile would say *"Bam!"* right here. *"Go wash now."*

In the Genesis creation-account God took muddy soil and fashioned the first man. He breathed life into him (Gen 2:6, 7). According to Colossians 1:15 Christ was present with the Father before creation as the preeminent One.

It is an amazing miracle; but it's not even the main point of the story. Jesus could have healed the blind man on another day; but he chose the Sabbath. He knew it would evoke a response from the religious elite. And boy did it!

The Pharisees are performing interrogation. *What happened? Who did this? How did he do it? How dare he!* The parents disown their son. They're balking because they don't want to lose their country club privileges. *He's old enough. Ask him yourself.*

And Jesus? Well, he's proving his point. The blind man is seeing, in more than one way. It is clear he is now a Christ-follower. And the sighted Pharisees? Oh, they can't see their noses on their own faces. They have sight but they are groping spiritually. Jesus said on one occasion they were blind leading the blind into the ditch (Luke 6:39). Just another day, another encounter, another instance of his being light in a dark world (John 9:5), to prove a little dirt don't hurt. His was a soiled Incarnation.

What would you say your lumen rating is?

Doubting Thomas, I Doubt It

John 11:14-16

Then Jesus told them plainly, "Lazarus is dead! I am glad I wasn't there, because now you will have a chance to put your faith in me. Let's go to him." Thomas, whose nickname was "Twin," said to the other disciples, "Come on. Let's go, so we can die with him."

This is it, Thomas's big moment. All of the other disciples were afraid to go with Jesus back to Judea. Last time they were there things didn't go so well. The crowd rioted and wanted to stone Jesus. The reciprocal effect of being a disciple is that the crowd didn't hit their target. And rocks hurt. But Thomas stands for what's right. *"Come on. Let's go, so we can die with him."*

'Believing Thomas,' you probably don't know him by that name. Generations have dubbed him 'Doubting Thomas,' because of his antics post-resurrection; but then, all the disciples were acting strange during that stretch. Are you kidding me? A dead man raised to life? Who does that? And so, Thomas follows stated principles of deductive logic and is labeled "doubter" to infinity.

I'm a little like Thomas and so are you. I have the capacity to be unfaithful at any stretch along the journey, around any bend, at any turn. I must continually curb doubt and discipline myself along this trellis of faith.

Dietrich Bonhoeffer wrote, "The knowledge of Jesus Christ, metamorphosis, renewal, love, or whatever other name we may give it, is something living, and not something which is given, fixed and possessed once and for all. For this reason there arises every day anew the question how here, today and in my present situation I am to remain and to be preserved in this new life with God, with Jesus Christ."[xx]

Tradition holds that Thomas may have been the only apostle to go outside of the Roman Empire preaching the gospel. He most likely traveled as far as India, a true missionary, where after converting countless thousands, he was martyred because of his faith in Christ. Thomas, a doubter, I doubt it!

Lazarus, a Mob Hit

> *John 12:9-11*
>
> *A lot of people came when they heard that Jesus was there. They also wanted to see Lazarus, because Jesus had raised him from death. So the chief priests made plans to kill Lazarus. He was the reason that many of the people were turning from them and putting their faith in Jesus.*

John described both a great falling away from Jesus, and an influx of believers.

Many turned away from Jesus when he began teaching that they must eat his body and drink his blood. They had enjoyed the bread and fish, but this was not the kind of meal they envisioned. If they would have taken the time simply to ask enough questions and pay attention carefully, they would have realized his point was to embrace a very serious commitment. The truth is many had enjoyed the benefits of following Jesus, but didn't want any responsibilities too demanding.

What was it, then, that caused a great increase of believers? Lazarus was raised from the dead. This is the longing nestled inside the hearts of all humanity. Fear of death looms large. Consistently polls show death is the second greatest fear that people have. Public speaking is number one. Comedian Jerry Seinfeld has cleverly said, "This means at a funeral, most people would rather be the guy in the casket than the one giving the eulogy." We fear death. If we could conquer death, oh, now that would be real food. That would be nourishment. That would be sustenance.

It is mind-boggling the depths to which the religious elite were willing to go to protect their positions. They were conspiring to kill Lazarus. Just think of this. They wanted to kill him. Why? Because people were finding hope in Jesus. This is nothing short of a mob hit. This is the Jewish mafia. "Lazarus died. Jesus raised him back to life. People are following Jesus. Easy, let's just make Lazarus go away." You see, they thought they could stop the life-giver by being death-givers. How many would they have been willing to kill? If Jesus kept raising dead persons to life, would they have just kept killing them?

Ultimately, of course, they "killed the author of life" (Acts 3:15). They were certain the problem had been dealt with successfully. What they did not count on was Jesus being able to control matters from both sides of the grave.

Come to Jesus today. I mean really come to him. Be more than a freeloader. Really, truly ingest his teachings. You will find life beginning to emerge inwardly.

Judas, Dine In or Carry Out?

> John 13:21-30
>
> After Jesus had said these things, he was deeply troubled and told his disciples, "I tell you for certain that one of you will betray me." They were confused about what he meant. And they just stared at each other.
>
> Jesus' favorite disciple was sitting next to him at the meal, and Simon motioned for that disciple to find out which one Jesus meant. So the disciple leaned toward Jesus and asked, "Lord, which one of us are you talking about?"
>
> Jesus answered, "I will dip this piece of bread in the sauce and give it to the one I was talking about." Then Jesus dipped the bread and gave it to Judas, the son of Simon Iscariot. Right then Satan took control of Judas.
>
> Jesus said, "Judas, go quickly and do what you have to do." No one at the meal understood what Jesus meant. But because Judas was in charge of the money, some of them thought that Jesus had told him to buy something they needed for the festival. Others thought that Jesus had told him to give some money to the poor. Judas took the piece of bread and went out. It was already night.

Here, we are invited to peek inside holy territory. Jesus chooses the sacred institution of the Passover meal for something very important.

The Lamb of God is revealing true love. It is a love that recovers lost identity by dying on a cross. He washes his servants' feet. Judas was there for this, by the way. Apparently, he got his soiled feet moistened and dried by the Master. But then Judas turned the holy meal into a late night run through the drive-through. As he's leaving, bread in hand, does he eat it? Perhaps. Or he may have tossed the provisions on the ground as soon as he left. Though he may have eaten physically, he did not partake spiritually. He couldn't eat a bite because he was so full. He rejected the Bread of Life that was offered to him and instead savored satanic morsels. The devil had completely filled him. The irony is that Jesus identified his betrayer, specifically, pointed him out in front of all the disciples; but it was cloaked in mystery. *"Wait a minute. Did that just happen? Did Jesus say Judas would betray him, hand him bread, and then Judas left? No. No way. He's just taking care of financial matters."* Judas's *doing* camouflaged his *being*. So we have the rest of the disciples taking in this first, important communion - dining, wrestling, ingesting truth. But Judas tosses the Bread of Life in a doggie bag. Such flippant disregard for the holy!

Dietrich Bonhoeffer was a brilliant mind. He wrote his dissertation about true communion at only twenty-one years of age. It was titled *Sanctorum Communio* (Communion of Saints). He died April 9, 1945 in the courtyard of the Flossënburg Concentration Camp, hanged by direct order of Adolf Hitler. It was just days before the Allies took the city and freed the camp. He writes extensively about our disunion with God. He refers to Adam and Eve's knowledge of good and evil as "stolen likeness."[xxi] This disunion can allow for a Pharisee to perform all kinds of actions but have a heart that is judgmental. This disunion can allow a despot to massacre six million Jews under the brand of a distorted Christianity that advocates Aryan Supremacy. Bonhoeffer once led the prisoners at Tegel in Holy Communion with their meager provisions, no wine, just water, no bread, just crumbs. I'll bet he would have gladly picked up Judas's scraps off the ground to have been able to participate.

In Bonhoeffer's unfinished chapter on the love of God and the decay of the world, he speaks of how connection with God fosters true "proving" and "doing." And these are ultimately undergirded by "love." It is a love that God initiates and to which we respond. I can't help but wonder if Bonhoeffer's unfinished chapter would have led to the statement of Jesus about loving one another. Jesus says this is how everyone will know that we are his disciples. We have received genuine love from him. The connection is restored if we will only accept it. And now, the proving, the doing of this connection, is to pass on the love to one another.

The disciples are confused and disoriented by the events of the meal; but at least they stayed, wrestled, hoped, and adhered. They went through it together. Not Judas though, they dined in while he carried out. They ordered in; he ordered out. They were orderly in; he was ordered out!

Purely Incarnational

John 16:18-22

"What is this 'little while' that he is talking about? We don't know what he means." Jesus knew that they had some questions, so he said: You are wondering what I meant when I said that for a little while you won't see me, but after a while you will see me. I tell you for certain that you will cry and be sad, but the world will be happy. You will be sad, but later you will be happy.

When a woman is about to give birth, she is in great pain. But after it is all over, she forgets the pain and is happy, because she has brought a child into the world. You are now very sad. But later I will see you, and you will be so happy that no one will be able to change the way you feel.

When Adam and Eve sinned judgment came in the form of toilsome work for the man and painful childbirth for the woman. Of course, the curse and sin has fingers. It has spider-webbed into a gigantic schema in our day with countless bunny trails of endless tracing. Times and cultures change. Many women work by the sweat of their brows, and many men are commonly in the delivery room as coaches and supporters. By the way, I readily admit women are far more pain tolerant than men. I'm not volunteering to experience labor pains, even if it were possible. Do not sign me up. I was there for the birth of both of our boys and I can only say, *Aye, yi, yi!*

When Jesus wanted to describe the gap in between his leaving this earth and the outpouring of the Holy Spirit on the Day of Pentecost he used imagery of a woman experiencing the pain of child birth, and the exquisite joy that follows the birth of her child. It is just interesting that the One who was there at creation and lived through the sin-entrance in real time, saw his Father pronounce childbirth-pain in judgment, this One compares his leaving the earth and the Holy Spirit's coming with the pain of childbirth. And he says it is so worth it! Just a like a mother cradling her newborn. Great, profound joy. It was worth it.

When Jesus died there was a period of great turmoil and uncertainty. The disciples all cowered in fear. They hunkered down and hid out. Even after the others declared he was alive, Thomas refused to be conned. He would have to see Jesus and touch his hands and wounded side. Apparently Peter quit for a season, went back to the fishing business. Eventually, after multiple Christ-sightings they rallied and came together for prayer in the upper room. They may have been pushed to it by the pains of separation and uncertainty. They prayed for ten days, and apparently the numbers swelled. There were 120 there when the contractions began. Acts 2:1-4 records an outpouring of the Holy Spirit so profound - the "Birthday of the Church" it is often called.

Paul picks up on this analogy. "We know that all creation is still groaning and is in pain, like a woman about to give birth" (Rom 8:22). The earth bends under its current burden; but one day, in the glorious Day, in the Eschaton, decay will be defeated, ruin will be renovated. Behold, all things are new! "The one sitting on the throne said, 'I am making everything new'" (Rev 21:5). Jesus, purely Incarnational, entirely other-worldly, comes into our sphere and redeems our loss.

The High Priestly Prayer

> *John 17:11-20*
>
> *Holy Father, I am no longer in the world. I am coming to you, but my followers are still in the world. So keep them safe by the power of the name that you have given me. Then they will be one with each other, just as you and I are one. While I was with them, I kept them safe by the power you have given me. I guarded them, and not one of them was lost, except the one who had to be lost. This happened so that what the Scriptures say would come true.*
>
> *I am on my way to you. But I say these things while I am still in the world, so that my followers will have the same complete joy that I do. I have told them your message. But the people of this world hate them, because they don't belong to this world, just as I don't.*
>
> *Father, I don't ask you to take my followers out of the world, but keep them safe from the evil one. They don't belong to this world, and neither do I. Your word is the truth. So let this truth make them completely yours. I am sending them into the world, just as you sent me. I have given myself completely for their sake, so that they may belong completely to the truth.*

> *I am not praying just for these followers. I am also praying for everyone else who will have faith because of what my followers will say about me.*

Why do we get saved and stay here on this earth? Why not just get zapped right to heaven the moment we profess faith in Christ? Can you just see it! The repentant sinner kneels at the altar and... Wham! They're gone. In heaven. But then, who would be there to pray with them? How would anyone get saved? Who would administer that? How would there be any church services? Our entire reason for remaining in this world is to carry out the desires of the compassionate heart of God for global evangelization.

This entire life is a test. Our existence on this earth is like a car slaloming through orange cones on wet pavement. It is a test. It is enjoyable and filled with happiness. There are great outbursts of laughter and high times of joy. It is a test. There is sadness immeasurable, grief the depths of which cannot be tracked on sonar. There is pain indiscretionary, and selective taunting. It is a test. When we get to heaven, that will be real living. When we get there, oh, that will be unspeakable joy. The above text gave rise to the popular saying, "We are in the world but not of it."

Jesus knew you would be in a rough and tumble world. His high priestly prayer of John 17, moments before going to the cross, included you. He specifically included all who would believe in him. He believes in you. You can make it. Nail this portion of the test today.

Taser versus Transformer

> *John 18:3-6*
>
> *Judas had promised to betray Jesus. So he went to the garden with some Roman soldiers and temple police, who had been sent by the chief priests and the Pharisees. They carried torches, lanterns, and weapons. Jesus already knew everything that was going to happen, but he asked, "Who are you looking for?"*
>
> *They answered, "We are looking for Jesus from Nazareth!"*
>
> *Jesus told them, "I am Jesus!" At once they all backed away and fell to the ground.*

On one level, the arrest of Jesus and his subsequent crucifixion are a matter of course. To the onlooker, it is another common criminal being led to his death. But embedded in the narrative are clues, pointers that show us his divinity. The brilliance of deity cannot be diminished by anemic dusk.

The soldiers backed up and fell to the ground. It was like a taser trying to overpower a Transformer when the soldiers took Jesus.

Pilate asked Jesus if he was a king, and heard Jesus say his kingdom is not of this world. He was terrified when the crowd told him that Jesus claimed to be the Son of God. Upon further inquiry Jesus told Pilate he would have no power unless it was given to him by God. It was like a 7th Grade Vice President quizzing a Prime Minister as Pilate interrogated him.

The soldiers doubled up their fists and struck his face. They spit on him. They struck him with clubs. At the end of it all, I wonder if they will experience recall as they watch Jesus leading his mighty army riding on a white horse. It was like a green, toy soldier commandeering a five-star general.

Our Lord said he was thirsty. They dipped the sponge, moistened his lips. Here we have the Living Water parched. It was like the owner of Aquafina sipping from a Dixie cup, a massive reservoir filling from a rain puddle.

There can be no doubt Jesus was in full control of his arrest and crucifixion. His life was not taken from him, he laid it down freely. "No greater love has a man than this, that he lay down his life for his friends" (John 15:13, NIV).

Thank you, dear Friend.

The Symbol of the Cross

> *John 19:16-18*
>
> *Then Pilate handed Jesus over to be nailed to a cross. Jesus was taken away, and he carried his cross to a place known as "The Skull." In Aramaic this place is called "Golgotha." There Jesus was nailed to the cross, and on each side of him a man was also nailed to a cross.*

It is at least interesting to note the signs God gives us in his creation that speak of his death and resurrection.

The Pine Tree crosses of springtime are a remarkable testimony to God's masterful plan of salvation. The Pine Trees know when Easter is coming. They start their new growth in the weeks before Easter each year. First, they start to give off yellow shoots. Then, as Easter gets closer, the top shoot branches off to form a cross. By Easter each year, most of the Pine Trees are covered with little golden crosses.

And then there is the Donkey's Cross. Almost all miniature donkeys have the distinctive mark of the cross on their backs. Of course, Jesus rode into Jerusalem on the back of a donkey (Zech 9:9). The legend goes that the little animal loved our Lord so much that when Jesus was sentenced to be crucified, it wanted to help him bear the burden of the cross. The donkey was driven away but returned to pay its respects when everyone else had gone. As it turned away sadly, the shadow of the cross fell over its shoulders. The mark has remained there ever since as a permanent tribute to the donkey's love and loyalty. And that's why he displays his cross on his back. Of the glorious age of the Eschaton, Hosea writes, "In that day I will make a covenant for them with the beasts of the field and the birds of the air and the creatures that move along the ground" (Hos 2:18, NIV).

Okay, is it proof positive that Jesus has marked his cross upon nature? I'd say no. I'm cautious against such unsubstantiated claims. But one is hard-pressed to deny God when there are unique indicators of his existence all around. It would be okay to respond, silently in your heart, "Isn't that something?" These are legends. They are not intended to be taken as literal truths. Yet, when you see these kinds of samplings in God's handiwork it seems to be undeniable that God is leaving clues of Himself.

"For since the creation of the world God's invisible qualities – his eternal power and divine nature-have been clearly seen, being understood from what has been made, so that men are without excuse" (Rom 1:20).

Personal Reflection:

- If there were no God would I expect to see coincidences in nature that seem to authenticate Him?
- Why does God seem to hide himself in some ways? What can I learn from this?
- Which takes more of a leap of faith: to believe in God? Or not to believe in God?

The Breath of God
    John 20:22

Then he breathed on them and said, "Receive the Holy Spirit."

Here we have a microcosm of the creation. "And the Spirit of God was hovering over the waters" (Gen 1:2, NIV). Like a hen brooding over its young, the Spirit stayed. "God's Spirit brooded like a bird above the watery abyss" (Gen 1:2, MES)

God knows what his weary disciples need, post-resurrection, in their frightful state. His gentle breath models the mighty wind that would rush over them in just a few days at Pentecost.

Let it breath on me, let it breath on me

Let the breath of God now breathe on me

Let it breath on me, let it breath on me

Let the breath of God now breathe on me

Upwardly Mobile

John 21:18, 19

"I tell you for certain that when you were a young man, you dressed yourself and went wherever you wanted to go. But when you are old, you will hold out your hands. Then others will wrap your belt around you and lead you where you don't want to go." Jesus said this to tell how Peter would die and bring honor to God. Then he said to Peter, "Follow me!"

I have a brother, Tim, who is a pastor and also a career radio-personality. He jokes whenever he is involved with a live, remote broadcast. Tim has a certain way of pronouncing a long "I" sound in a whimsical tone, "We're going *MOBĪLE*!"

Movement is the essence of life. If we are not moving we are not living. One of the biggest struggles of aging is loss of mobility. If one loses the ability to drive this is such a huge loss. If one loses the ability to walk upright, pain free, it can be so debilitating. There will be no walkers or wheelchairs in heaven, as wonderful as these inventions are. By the way, I will be out of a job. There is no need for preaching in heaven. And I'm told there will be no sound engineers either. But I digress.

Jesus has just reinstated Peter in the most deliberate manner. Three times he asked him if he loved his Lord, once for each denial during the long night of Jesus' trial and crucifixion. The first time Jesus asked Peter if he loved him it was appreciated and affirmative. The second time it was a little annoying. "Lord, did you forget that you just asked me that?"

But I think by the third time, smiles cracked on faces around the morning breakfast fire. Spontaneous nudges prompted around the circle. Peter and the whole gang figured out what was happening. It was total, complete reversal and undoing of any wrong. It is expunged entirely from Peter's permanent record.

Now, Jesus moves to another matter of business. *"When you were young, Pete, you could just run and play and go anywhere you wanted. But as you age, you won't be so mobile. And, as a matter of fact, you'll have to be led. You don't want to go where they're going to lead you. But just trust me on this one."* That's an apt paraphrase of the jest. And then the words that must have rung out like a bell sounding, "Follow me." Those words had been the very first invitation from Jesus. Before there was ever a thrice denial; before there was even one miracle or demon driven out; before walking on water or standing in a cloud of Transfiguration; before any of those things - follow me. Jesus had made it through crucifixion. Now he extended the invitation to his right-hand man. Tradition says Peter did follow the Lord. He was crucified upside down because he didn't consider himself worthy to be hung on a cross as Jesus had been.[xxii]

"All who are wise follow a road that leads upward to life and away from death" (Prov 15:24). We are not being led down a primrose path; rather we are upwardly mobile.

Pneumatic Uplift

> *Acts 2:4*
>
> *All of them were filled with the Holy Spirit and began to speak in other tongues as the Spirit enabled them (NIV).*

This poem is thoughtful prayer. Following its inscription I lifted my hands and spoke in unknown tongues. Mysterious uplifting happened. Pronounced **ta puh-new-ma-ton*, Greek words for *the Spirit*, and °*tain sarka*, Greek words for *the body*, in this sense, fleshliness or carnal nature.

> *Pneumatic Uplift*
>
> *Father,*
>
> *If I allow it to, the sense of*
> *Overwhelm is so great that it*
> *Washes me away till I am left*

*A petrified skeleton of the man I
Could be*

But

*If I allow Him to, the sense of
Breath is so great that it
Surges upon me in waves of
Renewal leaving in its wake
Wholly, holy uplift*

Grant Spirit

I choose τὸ πνεύματον*

I refuse τὴν σάρκα°

July 11, 2008

Heavenly Languages

> Acts 2:38, 39
>
> Peter said to them, "Turn to God and be baptized, every one of you, in the name of Jesus Christ for the forgiveness of your sins, and you will receive the gift of the Holy Spirit. This promise is for you and your children. It is for everyone our Lord God will choose, no matter where they live."

Let's do a little thoughtful work on this chapter, together, you and me. It is an important chapter. The first verses begin with the dramatics of the Day of Pentecost. The chapter leads up to a powerful statement by Peter in verses 38 and 39. This powerful, dramatic experience is available to all believers. I want to walk through a sequential progression, moving through some key points logically.

There is resistance to the Pentecostal belief of being filled with the Holy Spirit, which teaches the physical evidence is speaking in tongues initially. Two primary contentions are voiced typically.

1. The word "tongues" is the same word for "languages". In other words, some wish to strain out the strangeness of the event by making it more sanguine. The followers of Jesus didn't speak unknown tongues that day. Since "tongues" may also be translated "languages," the contention

is that they spoke known, existing languages they had never learned. It's referred to as *xenolalia*. This is miraculous still, because they talked in another language, but not goofy jibberish. *I can avoid my friends feeling there is anything bizarre in the Bible, or in my practice of the Bible.* But if that's the contention let's carry it forward fully. This also means they saw "languages" in the form of fire descending upon each one (Acts 2:3). You see, it's the same word. What does that look like? This kind of logic leads into circular thinking unresolved. The belief that the word "tongues" should be understood only to mean "languages" leads to another misunderstanding.

2. They didn't speak in "unknown" languages, but in "known" languages. It is true that a list of other nationalities was given in Acts 2. It doesn't appear to be an exhaustive list, more of a categorical sampling. However, there is no proof only known languages were spoken that day. In case of point, the facts seem to indicate precisely the opposite. Fifteen languages are named as examples. But there were at least a hundred and twenty who received the Spirit in the upper room, and then spilled out into the streets. So what "languages" were the rest speaking? A major point is many thought they were drunk (Acts 2:13). Either they were speaking "unknown" tongues, or their speech was slurred. Perhaps it was a combination of the two, meaning they spoke in unknown tongues and also appeared intoxicated. Supporting this thought is the command of Paul to the church in Ephesus, "Don't be drunk with wine, because that will ruin your life. Instead, be filled with the Holy Spirit" (Eph 5:18, NLT). There was a mixture of known languages and unknown languages in this cacophony of praise heavenward. This is the opinion I side with; and it is only an opinion, but I believe it is an informed one. To borrow from the verbiage of the apostle Paul, there were unknown, heavenly languages as well as known, earthly languages on the Day of Pentecost.

I would point out that *glossolalia* has been experienced the world over by Christians since the Day of Pentecost. There has never been a time when the earth was without a Pentecostal witness from then until now. Scripture supports a Pentecostal expression of worship. And both reason and experience line up, as one would expect, in reinforcement of Scripture.

Have you received the gift of the Holy Spirit yet?

The Holy Spirit's Prompting
Acts 3:3, 4

> *The man saw Peter and John entering the temple, and he asked them for money. But they looked straight at him and said, "Look up at us!"*

This is seemingly spontaneous. Peter and John are engaging in active listening, both to their environment and to the Holy Spirit.

Once I was driving down the main street. In an instant, out of the blue, I thought of an individual who had visited our church only one time. I saw his guest registration card in my mind. I don't mean I saw a vision; but then again, perhaps I did. It just felt like I was using my imagination. There was a momentary flash of inspiration. I felt that I could remember his street address. I felt great clarity. Months had passed since he came to church. I had never been to his house. It felt as though the Holy Spirit was giving me voice prompts. *Take a right. Continue straight. Left here. See, there on the corner.* I stopped in front of what looked like an abandoned house. I sat there for a moment and argued with the Holy Spirit. *Lord, this place is empty.* I felt a strong prompt to get out and knock on the front door. I sheepishly stepped onto the front porch, a little embarrassed. I knocked on the door. I looked through the curtain-less windows into a deserted living room. After a customary pause, I turned to walk away. *I knew it. I didn't hear from you.* As I made my way back to the car I heard a voice coming from around the corner of the house. "Pastor Keith. Is that you? What are you doing here?" I was shocked. "Mike, hey, how are you?" I told him that I was just thinking of him. The Holy Spirit had placed him on my heart. He retorted, "I was out back, in the alley. The truck is completely loaded. If you would've come two minutes later you would have missed me." I don't know if it was as encouraging to him as it was to me. We were able to pray together. It gave a nice touch point on his way out of town. What a blessing, and all at the orchestration of the Holy Spirit's prompting!

Way

> *Acts 9:1, 2*
>
> *Saul kept on threatening to kill the Lord's followers. He even went to the high priest and asked for letters to the Jewish leaders in Damascus. He did this because he wanted to arrest and take to Jerusalem any man or woman who had accepted the Lord's Way.*

Way. Now, pronounce it correctly. It must be spoken with that notorious surfer dude or valley girl air. I realize this word is so 15 minutes ago.

Way! It is so 3G! Nonetheless, at risk of time-stamping myself, in the first part of this century, there was a popular way of saying *WAY!*

For a number of years I read one chapter from Proverbs each day. I read the corresponding chapter for the calendar day. For instance on the 2nd of the month I read chapter 2. I asked God to give me what I would call my "wisdom verse" for the day. That is, *let one verse resonate inside my spirit today in such a way that it brings to bear your attributes in my life.* How, then, has such obvious repetition in Proverbs 2 escaped my watchful eye? Truly God's word is living and active. I like to say the Bible is living and *interactive*. See if these words from Proverbs 2 do not strike you as intended to drive home a point.

"...*Walk* is blameless..." (7) "...*course* of the just..." (8) "...*way* of his faithful ones ... (8) "...*ways* of wicked men ..." (12) "...*way*ward wife with her seductive words ..." (16) "...*paths* to the spirits of the dead..." (18) "...*paths* of life ..." (19) "...*walk* in the *ways* of good men..." (20) "...*paths* of the righteous ..." (20). NIV

Choices, choices, choices! It's like the signpost leading out of the Old West town. As the wagon train pulled out, the driver was admonished, *"Choose your rut carefully. You'll be in it the next 53 miles."*

Personal Reflection:

- What consequences in my life today are the direct results of decisions I've made?
- What decisions am I making, right now, that will take me to the land of new consequences?

The Right Stuff

> *Acts 17:31-34*
>
> *"He has set a day when he will judge the world's people with fairness. And he has chosen the man Jesus to do the judging for him. God has given proof of this to all of us by raising Jesus from death."*
>
> *As soon as the people heard Paul say a man had been raised from death, some of them started laughing. Others said, "We will hear you talk about this some other time." When Paul left the council meeting, some of the men put their faith in the Lord and went with Paul. One of them was a council member named*

> *Dionysius. A woman named Damaris and several others also put their faith in the Lord.*

How does one conquer death? I recently became aware of something I do without even thinking about it, on a subconscious level. When I read the obituaries I go through a mental checklist. "Ah, yeah, I'm younger than all the names on this page. I'm okay." Or, "Ooh, there's one who's younger than me, and she's already dead. Whoa." The biggest funerals are for teenagers. There seems to be a general feeling of injustice. I remember attending the funeral of Gerald, my friend, the son of another minister in town. It was the first time I was a pallbearer. He fell off the top of a hay stack on the back of a truck and broke his neck. He was only sixteen years old. It happened the Friday afternoon when school was released for the Christmas break. I remember Coach Schilling telling all of us that afternoon in Driver's Education Class to be very careful over the break because statistics said that one of us wouldn't return. It seemed everybody in town was at the funeral. Death stuns us all. In one moment a person lives, in the next the body is lifeless. What's more, none of us are experts at it. We've only lived.

The first modern chemist, Antoine Lavoisier, purported the law of conservation of mass. In the 1700s he compared and contrasted physical reactions and chemical reactions. Chemical reactions may change the substance of an object but not the chemical makeup. You can fold a newspaper to change its shape; that's a physical reaction. But obviously, it is still made up of the same chemicals. However, when you burn a newspaper it turns to a pile of ashes, a chemical reaction. Yet, the pile is still made up of the same exact chemicals; even though they have now taken on a different shape and essence. So he proved that nothing is lost or created in chemical reactions. In other words, it's all the same stuff. Our entire world is a child's sandbox of chemicals. We are allowed to reshape them, rearrange them, reconfigure them, but it's all the same stuff. Just think of the implications when we play with food, art, medical science, and practical, every day inventions. But is that all there is? Shuffling around atoms, moving dirt back and forth?

What about the difference between life and death? Is there a qualitative difference between dead cells and living cells? Are we nothing more than a chance coincidence, random gathering of the right kind of cells and chemicals? The right stuff? Interestingly, in the early 1900s Dr. Duncan McDougall conducted experiments on his dying patients and concluded that there was a measurable difference in weight of approximately 21 grams. The person who had just died was slightly lighter than a moment before when they were alive. McDougall believed this was the soul departing. This was admittedly inconclusive and didn't follow established principles of clinical studies. However, many believe there is a difference between living weight and dead weight, a non-chemical, non-material, yet measurable component. Is it true? Don't know. Not making a theological statement, but here is a theological statement - there is One who conquered death. Jesus Christ rose from the dead. What the greatest minds are unable to explain because they can't get handles on it, Jesus has handled. Your Lord is greater than death. It was the clear message of the early church. Jesus Christ has risen from the dead. The response to the gospel has always produced mixed reviews that are identical to Acts 17.

There are three responses:

- You're crazy. Dead people don't rise.
- I want to hear more and think this over.
- I believe he did it. He conquered death.

As for me, I believe. He is risen. He is risen indeed.

Shepherd Savior

Acts 20:28

Look after yourselves and everyone the Holy Spirit has placed in your care. Be like shepherds to God's church. It is the flock he bought with the blood of his own Son.

God really knew the condition of the flock he tended. He told Aaron not to offer any animal that had defects. It could not be lame, or have an eye gouged out. It couldn't be diseased or weak. He also told the ancient priestly tribe not to use any animals that were bought from foreigners because they were just as poor of quality. He knew the condition of the flocks of Israel literally; and he also knew the condition of the figurative flock. He knew who was inappropriate and unworthy to offer sacrifices at the altar. He knew the ones who were impure sexually. He knew the ones who had physical maladies or disease. He knew the ones who disrespected his altar and offered without the correct procedure. All of these were prohibited. He was a mighty deliverer from Egypt, but a shepherd Savior in the wilderness. He's a demanding shepherd; but it's because they are in the wilderness and he is a rescuing, delivering shepherd. He delivered the Israelites from the land of Egypt so he's not allowing them to be soft on themselves. God pushes for excellence like a coach demanding the very best but somehow knowing when too much is too much.

In the New Testament Jesus again picks up this mantle, he is a gentle Shepherd, knowing, caring, guiding, instructing. Upon his departure his apostles take up the charge, shepherding the flock. This is the very language Paul used here in these verses, "Be like shepherds to God's church"; as well as Peter, "Be shepherds of God's flock" (1 Peter 5:2). They were emulating our master.

Jesus says, "My sheep listen to my voice, I know them and they follow me" (John 10:27). I am told that, even to this day, in the Bedouin culture that is the Middle East, shepherds will gather multiple flocks at the watering hole. When it's time to leave, the shepherd will simply give his distinct call. His sheep know his voice. The flocks, which have mixed, automatically separate and trail their leader. Listen for your shepherd Savior to lead you into green pastures today.

This Was All a Misunderstanding

Acts 25:8

Then Paul spoke in his own defense, "I have not broken the Law of my people. And I have not done anything against either the temple or the Emperor."

Paul is defending himself against charges that he is entirely innocent of. It all started when he was honoring the wishes of his superiors in Jerusalem, fellow apostles who advised him to perform a rite of worship at the temple showing that he did not oppose his own Jewish people. But angry people will perceive what they want to perceive. They would not hear him out. Even though he was doing everything properly, by the book, they wouldn't relent. They were convinced he was a troublemaker. This was all a misunderstanding.

The rebel rousers became so obstinate they took a vow to kill him. Paul finds himself entouraged to Caesarea. Over the next few weeks he stands trial before notable dignitaries. First, it's Felix, then Festus, who wants to send him back to Jerusalem, which would've meant certain ambush by the Jews. King Agrippa and Bernice are intrigued and impressed by him, but not interested in changing the situation. It is all preparatory to his trip to see the emperor in Rome. Through it all Paul maintains remarkable integrity and witnesses faithfully for his Lord.

It is entirely possible to be in right standing with the Lord, serving him faithfully, being right in the center of his will, and yet, face unimaginable opposition the whole way. In fact, before his arrest, Paul was warned in a prophecy that he shouldn't travel to Jerusalem because he would be arrested. With his friends weeping and urging him not to go, he reminded them that he was not only willing to be arrested, but to die for the Lord. He was so confident with his sense of God's direction that he went onto Jerusalem undeterred. And the prophecy happened just as he had been told.

Consider this. There is ridicule, mistreatment, appearances before various courts, and so forth, and Paul will never be a free man again, at least not in this life. But in spite of the great difficulty Paul will write some pretty important New Testament documents from the prison cell over the coming years. Where would the Church be today without his having obeyed the leading of the Lord?

It just may be that, mixed in with your enjoyable service to the King, you will also encounter some challenges along the way. What kingdom advances may come from your struggle?

Shake the Snake

> *Acts 28:3*
>
> *After Paul had gathered some wood and had put it on the fire, the heat caused a snake to crawl out, and it bit him on the hand.*

This is just so typical of the devil. Here is the apostle Paul right on the heels of a great victory in his life. Then comes this unsuspecting attack. He has endured fourteen days on the open sea in a devastating storm. When all 276 people on board had given up hope entirely, Paul was the one who got the mind of the Lord on the situation and coaxed them to safety, the Holy Spirit guiding his directives via the captain with whom he had gained favor. Wet from the brisk swim and cold rain, which must have felt like a winning coach's Gatorade bath, and trying to warm himself at the fire on the shore's safety, in an instant, out comes a snake that latches on his hand.

It will be the same for you. When you are riding high from the sweet taste of a moral victory, beware, the enemy will set snares for you. He will try to capture you. Know it's coming. "We are not ignorant of the devil's devices" (2 Cor 2:11). We are most vulnerable when we have just experienced a great success. Lulls will creep in unsuspectingly, like a deep snow settling on the cold ground overnight as you sleep. After the high of a great team effort in ministry, expect an explosion from a surprising source. *Didn't see that one coming*! It can depress you into a real low. For instance, I know of countless pastors who have experienced turmoil after the new building program is completed. We must do as Paul did.

Steady as she goes. Shake the venom right back into the fire. Shake the snake. Remember it's not about you. It's not about you when sneak attacks come, dodge them. It's not about you when unmerited praises come, deflect them. Christian, remember, you have a Captain of your ship. Carry on.

6

Letters That Show Loyalty

GROUP 6: LETTERS THAT SHOW LOYALTY

Luther's Gate

> Romans 1:16, 17
>
> *I am proud of the good news! It is God's powerful way of saving all people who have faith, whether they are Jews or Gentiles. The good news tells how God accepts everyone who has faith, but only those who have faith. It is just as the Scriptures say, "The people God accepts because of their faith will live."*

Martin Luther kept a rigid system of good works but was immensely frustrated with his sinful state. He was a friar with the Mendicant Order of Augustinian Monks. He was far beyond frustration, working so hard with all of his strength, attempting to be good enough for salvation. His schedule would begin with the midnight *Readings,* followed by the *Lauds* at 3:00 a.m. that would often last until daylight. If they were finished in time they would get some sleep until 6:00 a.m. at which time they would wash and then attend *Prime*. Next came *Chapters* where they received assignments and judicial duties for the day. They would read and study until 9:00 a.m. when *Terse* was said, followed by high mass. The office of *Sext* occurred at noon followed by the meal and communal recreation. They could do anything they wanted up until 3:00 p.m. when the *None* service began. Farming and housekeeping filled the afternoon until twilight when the *Vespers* prayer service began. *Compline* was the last prayer service of the day, and it began at 9:00 p.m. At that point they were free to go off to bed before beginning it all again in a couple of hours.

If your image of a monastery is docile and restful you might reconsider. I'm exhausted just reading about it. Luther's efforts involved fasting, flagellation and confession. Often monks and friars would flagellate themselves to the point of drawing blood. Imagine the discomfort of the monk's garb on a bruised back.

It was not until Luther came across Romans 1:16, 17 in his studies that he recognized it is by faith that we are saved through grace, not by our good works. It is commonly referred to as Luther's Gate. Oh the grace that flooded his soul. Luther recorded about that occasion, "And now, in the same degree as I had formerly hated the word 'righteousness of God,' even so did I begin to love and extol it as the sweetest word of all. Thus was this place in St. Paul to me the very gate of paradise."[xxiii] Have you entered through the gate into God's garden?

The Christian Hokey Pokey

Romans 4:16

Everything depends on having faith in God, so that God's promise is assured by his gift of undeserved grace. This promise isn't only for Abraham's descendants who have the Law. It is for all who are Abraham's descendants because they have faith, just as he did. Abraham is the ancestor of us all.

I don't believe I have ever met a Christian that has not, at one time or another, willingly or by provocation, participated in the kid-song, *Father Abraham had Many Sons*. It is our Christian version of the Hokey Pokey.

Do you remember when the religious leaders got in an argument with Jesus? They claimed special credentials because they were from the lineage of Abraham. I can just hear the dripping arrogance as they retort, "Abraham is our father." Jesus said in essence, *"I know you're from the line of Abraham, but if you were really his children you would recognize me and love me."* It was then he leveled the most severe indictment. "Your father is the devil." (John 8:41-46).

Yikes! Here they are, very religious individuals, trained classically in Judaism, observers of Torah and reciters of the prophets, wearing wide phylacteries, touted as Rabbis, respected and looked up to - and Jesus has the nerve to say to them, *"Your daddy is the devil."* So we learn that Jesus has something more in mind than just being from Abraham's bloodline. You must have faith.

It could be that the apostle Paul had this exchange in mind as he penned his Magna Carta, the letter to the Romans. In chapter 4, after having proved that all have sinned (Rom 3:23) with scathing remarks of the poor condition of humanity, he proceeds to dismantle any hope that we can somehow be good enough to earn salvation. In fact, our paycheck for our sinful actions is death (Rom 6:23). Paul has words of help in chapter four. "God becomes angry when his law is broken. But where there isn't a law, it cannot be broken. Everything depends on having faith in God, so that God's promise is assured by his gift of undeserved grace. The promise isn't only for Abraham's descendants who have the law, it is for all who are Abraham's descendants because they have faith, just as he did. Abraham is the ancestor of us all" (Rom 4:15, 16).

So this is what faith looks like. Not being goody-two-shoes. Not performing flawlessly on the balance beam. Not being squeaky clean. Not churning out ridiculous results on the treadmill. Rather, we are free to believe and hope and trust.

Everything depends on faith. I am one of them. And so are you. So let's just praise the Lord!

The Golf Clap of Heaven

Romans 5:1-5

By faith we have been made acceptable to God. And now, because of our Lord Jesus Christ, we live at peace with God. Christ has also introduced us to God's undeserved kindness on which we take our stand. So we are happy, as we look forward to sharing in the glory of God. But that's not all! We gladly suffer, because we know that suffering helps us to endure. And endurance builds character, which gives us a hope that will never disappoint us. All of this happens because God has given us the Holy Spirit, who fills our hearts with his love.

A poem from personal devotions in a particularly difficult stretch.

The Golf Clap of Heaven

> O God, dear Lord
>   Grant me strength
>   To crucify injustices
>   To take the high road of humility
>   To silence the noisy crowd
>   To hear the golf clap of heaven
>   Amen

October 22, 2004

I've Stepped in the Sticker Patch

Romans 7:17

So I am not the one doing these evil things. The sin that lives in me is what does them.

One time when I was a kid I stepped on a sliver of glass. Mom and Dad worked for what seemed like hours to dislodge it. I'm sure it was minutes in reality. Oh the pain! It was horrible, the prodding, poking, digging; but it did not belong in me and it had to come out.

Bible teacher, Pres Gillham, illustrates Romans 7:17 this way. Suppose I were walking along barefooted and there was a stick pin that had fallen on the floor and was pointing up. I step on the pin unwittingly, and all of the sudden it lodges deep into my heel. At this point the stick pin causes me pain, it is unpleasant to onlookers, and if it is not dealt with will get infected. Eventually, gangrene will set in. The pin is inside me, but it is not part of me. It does not belong in me. It is identical with sin. Every individual on the planet is born with a nature bent on adversity. We must admit it, detest it, and by God's grace, remove it.

If I may take the illustration a step further, believers have pulled the stick pin out; but even Christians step on stickers. These have to be pulled out. And in time you learn to watch out for the sticker patches. Each believer must curb his or her sinful appetite each day. This is accomplished by disciplined, Spirit-filled living. It is important that there has been ongoing relationship with the Lord in the past, and tenure matters. Still, the most important thing is current, life-giving sustenance. "Live by the Spirit and you will not gratify the desires of the flesh" (Gal 5:16). How often have I thought I would like that verse to say, "Live by the Spirit and the desires of the flesh will go away!" That is not what it says. The desires linger, but the Spirit enables to resist, and in fact, changes perspective about desires. I've stepped in the sticker patch, but my heavenly Father masterfully lifts me to a safe place and lovingly pulls them out.

Devotion Stew

> *Romans 8:5*
>
> *People who are ruled by their desires think only of themselves. Everyone who is ruled by the Holy Spirit thinks about spiritual things.*

Romans 8 is such a prolific passage of Scripture. It pegs us all. We each have desires that must be brought under the lordship of Jesus Christ. Our control must be relinquished over to God's governance. I think I have some insight on how this works in my life and I'd like to share from my experience.

I have attempted to live by three life-guiding principles for a good amount of time. The three principles surfaced from the disciplines of praying and Bible reading, journal keeping and reflective thought over the past twenty years. The three didn't come at once; but evolved from within the context of life's journey, a veritable Devotion Stew. I read on purpose, mean to pray and obey the careful way.

Let me tool these out a little more.

1. Read the Bible Purposefully. When I am reading Scripture I try my best to lock in. Don't let my mind drift. It's okay to wonder but not to wander. If I become aware that my eyes have followed the ink but my mind has not followed the thought, I go back, pick up at the place where I last remember paying attention. I am amazed at the richness of the experience when I read on purpose. In time that method has translated to all my reading, whether academic, recreational, or popular. Why bother read if I'm not going to pay attention? Especially to God's Word.

2. Pray meaningfully. If I am not careful I can fall into the habit of reciting a list, or following a set routine. I'm not down on repetition; sometimes that is very important. But I try to watch myself. Am I saying the same words? Have I no creativity in my approach? Are my emotions on board? God knows what is in my heart, of course. But there is something mysterious that happens as I take the time to rattle thoughts together into cohesiveness. God uses this discipline to bring clarity of laser focus. If I'm going to pray I should mean to do it. Don't just check off a list.

3. Obey carefully. I'm the world's worst at giving mental ascent to my actions. Okay, there, I did what you wanted. But obedience is nuanced. There are layers to it. The unfolding of events has a way of revealing character and intent. If I will obey carefully, often I find character flaws in me that must be dealt with.

Notice the three principles do not require specified time or amount. Sometimes the period of time is more extended. Other times it is brief. The most important thing is consistency. Long obedience in the same direction. It has helped me and I hope it will help you.

Rockabilly Red Boots

> *Romans 9:33*
>
> *God says in the Scriptures, "Look! I am placing in Zion a stone to make people stumble and fall. But those who have faith in that one will never be disappointed."*

An event from my teenage years is permanently etched in my memory. The youth group made our way to the event center for a Christian concert. There I was introduced to a style of music I had never experienced before. Leon Patillo came onto the stage. His appearance was trendy. He wore stylish clothes accented with glossy, dark red boots. His electric keyboard was in the shape of a miniature grand. I didn't know him. I only knew that he used to be in the rock band, Santana, and now he was a Christian. I fell in love. I emulated his style and would later sing one of his songs in front of my high school at the talent show. In time, other influences would morph my musical identity, Michael W. Smith and Russ Taff, to name a couple. Leon's rockabilly Fender Rhodes, fusing with all kinds of synth savvy, produced a unique sound that was magnetic. That day the keyboard literally shook as his sustain foot pulsated and the off foot pounded. Who would've thought that hundreds of kids could be so captivated by ancient prose dating back 2,700 years! "I lay in Zion for a foundation a stone. A tried stone, a precious cornerstone, he that believeth shall - shall not make haste."

About 700 years after those words were originally written by Isaiah, the apostle Paul quoted them in Romans 9. There is enough in Romans 9 to keep thinking minds occupied *ad nauseum*. On the one hand, this is the crux of Reformed theology. That is to say, the argument for predestination sure seems strong in Romans 9. "Jacob I have loved, Esau I have hated." Poor 'ole Esau, his fate was decided before he was ever born and he had nothing to say about it. However, free-will thinkers, like myself, see other broad-sweeping statements embedded in the two nations that Jacob and Esau would become. But we all digress. That is not even the point of Romans 9. The real point of Romans 9 is found toward the end of the chapter. Verse 30 begins with the words, "What does all of this mean?" In other words Paul is asking, "What is the main point in my bringing this up?" The main point is that Gentiles have done everything wrong, but if they will just have faith they are saved. And Jews have done everything right, so to speak, but if they do not have faith they will be lost. The above verse is Paul's quote of Isaiah 28:16. It speaks of this "stone" as a foundation. "A tried stone, a precious cornerstone, a sure foundation." Faith is foundational to everything we are as Christians. Belief and trust in Christ make up the very cornerstone of our existence.

A dear friend of mine is a retired pastor named Anthony Poree. He told me once, "Everyone is predestined, predestined to choose. We must choose either heaven or hell." If this is true, this predestination of our own choosing, what would be the criteria? How would we make our selection? What finalizes our choice of either heaven or hell? God has determined that belief in his Son Jesus Christ will be the sole determining factor in one's eternal destiny. Faith for forgiveness alone, nothing else. Paul might say that's what all of this means.

Your faith foundation is sure and steady, as steady as the 4/4 mashed against a minor mode, pounded out that day by Rockabilly Red Boots.

One Form of Identification

Romans 10:8-10

All who are acceptable because of their faith simply say, "The message is as near as your mouth or your heart." And this is the same message we preach about faith. So you will be saved, if you honestly say, "Jesus is Lord," and if you believe with all your heart that God raised him from death. God will accept you and save you, if you truly believe this and tell it to others.

There is a real danger in fantasy. There is a movement unprecedented in history to move toward virtual instead of real. It is an identity of fantasy that promises anonymity. It is the goal of the gaming industry; home recording devices; cable and satellite providers; and the more recent, on-demand video access companies.

The Internet, especially, promises absolute anonymity in multiple layers. This is the aim of browsers, to let you roll seamlessly through the plethora of pages, then simply erase your history. Word to the wise, there is always a history in a server somewhere. In court cases it has been tracked down and proven. Also, consider the false sense of security provided in the alter-ego approach of characters. Some even call them "avatars" connecting an identity with Hinduism, either accidentally or intentionally. You can choose your online and/or gaming look and style. Next time you ask a question online notice some of the cartoon characters in the response boxes. The nation is trending toward individuals having both a professional identity and a separate online identity. Moreover, as wonderful and convenient as the dating sites are, they often foster false representation in the virtual that disappoints in reality. Hey, I love technology, obviously I'm using it right now. However, advances in automation do contribute to an exaggerated and often false identity.

John 10:10 says the thief, Satan, comes to steal, kill and destroy, but Jesus comes to give life. Thieves are looking for identities. Identity theft costs the world's banks $221 billion dollars annually. The devil wants you to look elsewhere for your identity and it comes at a great cost, both fiscally and spiritually. But the secret is to identify with Christ. Your identity is in him. In Deuteronomy 30, Moses hits on the solution. The answer is not out of reach, not up in the sky, not across the sea. "No, the word is very near you; it is in your mouth and it is in your heart so that you may obey it" (Deut 30:14). In other words, it's not hard. This is not rocket science. It is right inside your heart. Paul picks up on this important concept understanding that it is crucial for the natural plan of God's salvation. "If you confess with your mouth, 'Jesus is Lord,' and believe in your heart that God raised him from the dead, you will be saved. For it is with your heart you believe and are justified, and it is with your mouth you confess and are saved" (Romans 10:9, 10). You can't purchase salvation. You will only need one form of identification.

Real. Comforter. Genes.

> *Romans 13:14*
>
> *Let the Lord Jesus Christ be as near to you as the clothes you wear. Then you won't try to satisfy your selfish desires.*

Recently, there has been a sad trend in South Beach. Individuals have been experimenting with a drug called the new LSD, or bath salts. Law enforcement and medical professionals each confirm one adverse side effect is that the person strips their clothes. In a drug-induced altered state they become so disillusioned that they have the desire to go naked. One man even became animal-like and was killed by the police because in his deranged state he stripped not only himself, but a homeless man too, and began devouring his face like a beast. The Causeway Cannibal is a startling reality jolt to all of us, a grim reminder of the horrors in the deterioration of society right before our eyes. Pure barbarianism.

"Let the Lord Jesus Christ be as close to you as the clothes you wear" (Rom 13:14). It is no stretch to state if this individual had been close to Jesus he would have kept his clothes on. He would've been able to exhibit self-control.

We are to keep Jesus so close that it is as if we're wearing him. Don't go naked. Do you have your latest designer Jesus wear on? Wear Jesus well. Make him proud. He is real. He is substance. He is depth. Let everyone around you see your growth. Wearing Jesus is always fashionable. The Holy Spirit adds all the right accessories. He is our comforter. Get him down inside your genes.

Remember Israel means, "wrestles with God." This faith walk requires discipline. Continually have Jesus close to keep the fleshly cravings at bay. Want it. Own it. Wear it. Live it.

Wrestler. Real. Comforter. Genes.

Money and Love Growing Like Trees

Romans 13:8

Let love be your only debt! If you love others, you have done all that the law demands.

Money doesn't grow on trees. How many times have you heard that? Ah, but it does grow like a tree. You know, there are many nations which have either approved, or are discussing, stimulus packages: Greece, Ireland, Denmark, Spain, and Italy. And, of course, the United States; we've had our own bail out, or call it a stimulus, or whatever you will. What do we do with this problem of debt? You know, on a national level it's a real problem. On a personal level, I'm not debt free. I would love to be. I know many friends who are striving to be debt free. Even as a church family, our church is not debt free. Our church has a small amount of debt. We feel good about our equity situation, and the way we're managing it. But we would love to be debt free.

The verse above says, "Let love be your only debt! If you love others, you have done all that the law demands." I've already told you, on the first part of the verse, I haven't gotten it right. I do have debt. But what about the last part of the verse? I remember a song my Dad, James Howard, used to love to sing. *He paid a debt he did not owe. I owed the debt I could not pay. I needed someone to wash my sins away. And now I sing a brand new song, amazing grace. My Jesus paid a debt that I could never play.*

Well, you know what? He's paid all of our debts. And we are forgiven of our sins. How about investing in him today? Invest in eternal things. Invest your money in things that are going to last. Let it grow like a tree that is planted and grows by nourishment over time. And invest your heart in eternal matters. Put your love toward someone else's life today. Money does grow like a tree, love grows like one too. Let love be you only debt.

Beauty in Diversity

Romans 14:1

Welcome all the Lord's followers, even those whose faith is weak. Don't criticize them for having beliefs that are different from yours.

Possibly no other chapter in the entire Bible demonstrates a value for diversity as does Romans 14. "Welcome all the Lord's followers, even those whose faith is weak. Don't criticize them for having beliefs that are different from yours" (Rom 14:1).

With so much heresy in our day, it is important to keep these words in context. There is an acceptance and even push toward syncretism now unlike anything ever seen in history. As a case in point, consider the dastardly implications of *Chrislam*, which combines Christianity with Islam, quoting from the Bible and the Koran, allowing its members to praise God or Allah out loud in the worship service. This is a disgrace to orthodox Christianity and is counterproductive to legitimate ministries that attempt to share the love of God sincerely with Muslim people who are searching for truth. Nor does diversity have to be a watchword for loose sexual orientation or tolerance of amorality. That is not the kind of liberal diversity Paul endorses.

There is one faith, one Lord, one Savior of all. Jesus is his name. We are saved by faith in Jesus Christ alone. And this is because of God's grace.

Paul is writing to "all the Lord's followers." He is speaking of the beautiful diversity within the body of Christ. Having just completed three chapters, 9, 10, and 11, in which he laments the lack of saving faith on the part of his own Jewish people, Israel (who are destined to come to faith in mass numbers), Paul now sets out to offer practical principles to Christians in chapters 12, 13 and 14. In chapter 14, in particular, he instructs Christians how to honor each other's differences. Some saw certain days as important while others observed a strict diet. Paul instructed them not to judge other Christians, but simply to concentrate on exercising their own faith and live by their own convictions. The goal is to live by your beliefs without blasting other believers with them. Mentor without menacing. Empower without encroaching. Inspire without imposing. It's a fine line, a true balancing act. This is what faith looks like, a grace-filled life in a community that allows others to flourish.

No Air Boxing

> *1 Corinthians 9:26, 27*
>
> *I don't box by beating my fists in the air. I keep my body under control and make it my slave, so I won't lose out after telling the good news to others.*

I've taken verbal abuse through the years from my family simply because of my proficiency in playing the dashboard and steering wheel. Sometimes rhythms that I could not possibly pull off were I to sit down at a trap set with a set of sticks, find their way to the console of the car, vibrating into an improvisational mix for my private listening audience in the vehicle. Please, no pirated recordings. I also confess to playing a pretty mean air guitar. Grinding riffs and squealing lead licks. Hands on the wheel, please. No worries, the drums will kick it. And the brassy, slide mouthbone will fill in lulls at each cadence.

Okay, I play air guitar, but Paul did not play air boxing. "I don't box by beating my fists in the air" (1 Cor 9:27). In these four verses, 24-27, the apostle draws upon the picture of the athlete. He images the discipline of conditioning to show us what it's like to be a faithful Christian. But this is not just conditioning; rather, it is conditioning for the purpose of competing. The long distance runner is coming back into the stadium for the final lap, blasting through the home stretch, reaching for the tape. He's finishing with a kick. The athlete he referred to was in the ancient Olympic Games and won only a wreath for a crown. We are competing for a golden crown. And boxing? C'mon, this isn't roadwork. You're not just trailing the coach's pace car, practicing the motion jabs in the air. Realize you're in a battle for your life. Body jabs, jaw blows, head butts and cheap shots - this is a brawl for survival. Condition your spirit man in order to compete and win.

Carlo Carretto wrote poignant words. "However compassionate we may be with others, we dare not be soft or indulgent with ourselves. Excellence comes at a price, and one of the major prices is that of self-control."[xxiv] There is a subtle irony in sacred history. Traditionally things like prayer, Scripture meditation, silence, and so forth have been referred to as the "disciplines." No air boxing. Condition your spirit man to compete. Compete to win.

Discernment

> *1 Corinthians 12:10b*
>
> *Some of us recognize when God's Spirit is present.*

It's the first week of March here in Arizona. And I'm not bragging, to all of my friends who live in other states, I'm really not rubbing it in. The high will be 80 degrees and it is the perfect day for being outdoors. To my friends up north, I get it. Summer is coming. I know, I know. One thing I like to do each year, and something I would encourage you to do, is to go on a discernment walk. Go on a walk through your neighborhood. Instead of the iPod just blasting away with music as you walk, I would encourage you to take in the sounds around you. Listen as your walking down the street. Here birds chirping, listen to dogs barking. Listen to conversations of neighbors standing in their driveways. And just be amazed that we are blessed with the ability to take in sound and to speak out sound. God's has created a universe around us that is filled with sound.

The gift of listening is something that is really lacking in culture today. People truly desire to be heard. Develop that discerning ear to hear them. You were given two ears and one mouth. You should do twice as much listening as you do speaking. The Bible lists, as one of the gifts of the Spirit, "recognizing when God's Spirit is present." And it is a gift; but there is also a sense in which it must be developed. So become a more discerning person this week. Listen to the sounds around you. You will be amazed at what you hear with the aid of the Holy Spirit.

Unclean, Unclean!

2 Corinthians 7:1

So we should stay away from everything that keeps our bodies and spirits from being clean. We should honor God and try to be completely like him.

In an Easter play that my family has participated in annually for a number of years, one character emerges out of the street crowd with matted, unkempt hair, and soiled clothes yelling, "Unclean, unclean!" The leper finds a quick, easy path to Jesus as people part like the Red Sea to avoid contamination. In the drama the character who plays Jesus twirls the filthy wraps off her and tosses them aside. She caresses her own arms, now smooth and pristine.

A never ending challenge of living is the task to remain clean. A prayer of mine has often been voiced in the shower, "Lord, I can wash the outside. I must have you clean the inside."

The secret of proper hygiene is you have a system for regular cleansing that includes a routine. Next time you bathe notice how you begin the same way each time. You lather up, perhaps using a particular exfoliating wash cloth or a mesh sponge. Are you a body wash person or a bar of soap person? You dab shampoo into your hands and work it through your scalp. You scrub, or soak, or rubba dub dub. You have done it the same way for years. And you do it effortlessly. It's your routine. We call it *getting ready*. And when your routine is finished you announce to your family, "I'm ready." Ready for what? Could you not have gone out in public dirty if you wished? Of course you could. Could you not have faced a new challenge of the day unclean? Sure, you could have chosen to. Ready for what, then? Ready in the sense of preparedness. It's our way of saying we are prepared to face the decisions of the day. We are prepared to present ourselves to the obstacles of the day.

No amount of combing, brushing, exfoliating, wiping, lathering, and rinsing can dislodge the dirt of the soul. This must be done through regular, systematic soaking in the Holy Spirit. The most important daily routine is the discipline of prayer. Wash your eyes with tears. They are the windows to your soul. Rinse your spirit with living water. And like your physical baths, sometimes you will have to do it quickly, having allotted just enough time to get ready. Other times you will be able to soak in a luxury tub. The most important thing is consistency. You do not want to stand before God one day and hear him say, "Unclean, unclean!"

Loyalty

2 Corinthians 11:1-6

Please put up with a little of my foolishness. I am as concerned about you as God is. You were like a virgin bride I had chosen only for Christ. But now I fear that you will be tricked, just as Eve was tricked by that lying snake. I am afraid that you might stop thinking about Christ in an honest and sincere way. We told you about Jesus, and you received the Holy Spirit and accepted our message. But you let some people tell you about another Jesus. Now you are ready to receive another spirit and accept a different message. I think I am as good as any of those super apostles. I may not speak as well as they do, but I know as much. And this has already been made perfectly clear to you.

Our church family has decided loyalty is one of our core values. The apostle Paul is talking about loyalty in this text. John MacArthur has recognized the structure Paul had in mind in 2 Corinthians 11:1-6, calling it "an expositor's dream." In the original language you have the word "for" introducing layers of loyalty. They show up like four bullet points outlining the message, twice in verse 2, and at the beginning of verses 4 and 5. MacArthur says it is "loyalty in four ways...loyalty to God, loyalty to Christ, loyalty to the gospel, and loyalty to truth." Because of the way the inferences to the godhead are embedded in the text I am also drawn to a subtle inference to the Trinity. One might see something in Paul's admonition along the lines of, *"Be loyal to God the Father, loyal to God the Son, loyal to God the Holy Spirit – yes be loyal to what you know!"*

Veritable Law Couriers

Galatians 3:18-20

If we have to obey the Law in order to receive God's blessings, those blessings don't really come to us because of God's promise. But God was kind to Abraham and made him a promise. What is the use of the Law? It was given later to show that we sin. But it was only supposed to last until the coming of that descendant who was given the promise. In fact, angels gave the Law to Moses, and he gave it to the people. There is only one God, and the Law did not come directly from him.

In Galatians 3:18-20 the apostle Paul mentions angels being involved in the delivery of the Law. This is something we don't read in the Old Testament, even though it may be alluded to in some versions. It was a long-standing tradition among Jewish teachers that the Law came into existence with the assistance of angels and the mediator Moses. Where does this idea come from?

If you read the traditional Hebrew text of the Old Testament, the Masoretic text, in verses commonly held to speak of the delivery of the Law they do not use the customary word for angels, *mal'akim*. Some individuals use this as a basis for criticizing the New Testament writers for not adhering to the Old Testament but simply following tradition. Passages such as Acts 7:52, 53; Hebrews 1:2, and these verses from Galatians, are ridiculed as being uninformed, when they misquote the Old Testament.

The Greek version of the Old Testament is called the Septuagint. It was translated from Hebrew into Greek in the Third Century BC. The Septuagint does refer to "angels" being involved in the delivery of the Law in Deuteronomy 33:2 and Psalm 68:17. And this is a plausible nuanced translation of the original Hebrew. The New Testament writers, who were writing in Greek, were simply consulting the Greek version of the Old Testament. Makes sense.

So the Bible is proven right again, just as it is every time naysayers try to oppose it. It is incapable of error, truly a beautiful book of God's interaction with humanity. It has been miraculously delivered and preserved.

Angels are not to be worshiped. Hebrews says they are spirits sent to aid the ones who will inherit salvation. There are some goofy ideas in the body of Christ about angels. You will hear some of the strangest theology about them, usually at funerals when well-meaning people will comment about the departed one as their "angel". But angels are very real spiritual beings involved in behind-the-scenes ministry, and delivery of God's messages. They are primarily messengers, it seems. It makes sense that they would be involved in the reception of the Law, a happy, ecstatic reception of God's directives, veritable Law couriers.

Watch how you treat strangers today. You never know, you just might be unaware that they are angels (Hebrews 13:2).

That's Just Wrong

Galatians 6:3

If you think you are better than others, when you really aren't, you are wrong.

I had a conversation one time with someone that required me to say the words, "You're wrong!" It wasn't taken well because the individual immediately began a discourse on the reasons he was correct in his assessment of the situation and individual. I hadn't meant to say, "You were incorrect in your assessment." What I meant to say was, "It was wrong of you to go behind his back." It got even more confusing and it wouldn't be heard.

There are two ways to be wrong. You can make a poor choice. And as a result, you're incorrect. The other way has to do with crossing a line of appropriate, acceptable behavior and demeanor in the unspoken rules of engagement. It is simply wrong to go behind someone's back. That's just wrong.

Paul is straight up. "If you think you're better than others when you really aren't, you're wrong." That's just wrong.

Okay, so, spend some painstaking, possibly painful, time reflecting. Take a prayerful pause. Is being right so important to me that I would be wrong?

Duped by the Mundane

Galatians 6:9

Don't get tired of helping others. You will be rewarded when the time is right, if you don't give up.

I want to tell you something really important. Your contribution matters. Sometimes you can feel swallowed by monotony. You can start to think you don't make a difference. Boredom will creep in and cause poor choices. Don't be duped by the mundane. Don't let yourself feel like a cog in a wheel doing the same thing day after day after day. Please know it matters where you are and what you do.

There is such indifference in the world. A cold lethargy has settled upon society. The environment in which you participate each day is structured for you by God's design. The urgency of the individual is camouflaged by callousness and sarcasm. Don't get caught up in condescending patronization. Don't lower yourself to kicking, screaming, pushing and shoving. Don't even devolve that way inwardly. You're better than that. Rise above. You may deal with an adolescent who is trapped with no vision of rescue for four or five years and it seems like eternity. The only tools he has are anger and resentment, so he lashes out. Though a few adults are blatant, the majority has learned the art of disguising their pain with either a dull apathy, or passive aggressiveness. There is a silent disregard that condescends. There are also vocalized, hurtful outbursts. Both are equal indicators of being stuck, hopeless. Some are in the muddy clay and they have not one glimmer that it will ever be better. Be that glimmer. Be a ray of hope. And at the end of the taxing day, refill your courage in the reservoir. Your identity is in Christ.

The God-Filled Life

> *Ephesians 3:19*
>
> *I want you to know all about Christ's love, although it is too wonderful to be measured. Then your lives will be filled with all that God is.*

Can you imagine if you or I were filled with all that God is? Unfathomable!

Some people think Christianity is for the weak. That's just not true. It's for the strong. If it's so weak, I dare you, take your Bible in your hand and walk right down a main street. I just dare you. Stefanie and I are very proud of our two sons. Zakary and Nicholas did the Forty Day Challenge. They began this school year by carrying their Bibles with them everywhere they went for 40 days. Now that takes guts! And yet there are scores of people who say Christianity is for the weak, it's a crutch. It's for the brainless. It's boring and such a waste of a good life.

How sad that many have never stepped into the adventure! The gateway of Christ's love is the starting point of real living. His love carries us on a journey that is spellbinding with twists and turns. Ooh-hoo, this is too good! The God-filled life brims with expectancy.

Listen carefully to your Tour Guide today.

The Man in the Moon

> Ephesians 3:20, 21
>
> *I pray that Christ Jesus and the church will forever bring praise to God. His power at work in us can do far more than we dare ask or imagine. Amen.*

Little Jimmy had been playing after dinner on the moonlit night. As will sometimes happen, the family members were each taken up with their activities so that time got away from them that night. Mom looked at the clock and told Jimmy it was time to get ready for bed. He should go ahead and she would be up to check on him in a little while. When the time came she checked on him and found him quietly transfixed, staring out his upstairs window into the sky. As she tucked him in, the little boy said, "Mommy, you know one day I'm going to walk on the moon."

That little boy named Jimmy grew. He survived a near fatal, motorcycle crash, which broke nearly every bone in his body. Years later, James Irwin stepped on the surface of the moon. He is one of only twelve humans to do so.

Some three thousand years earlier, Abram stared into the same stars as Jimmy. God put dreams in his heart too. "Afterward the Lord spoke to Abram in a vision and said to him, 'Do not be afraid, Abram, for I will protect you, and your reward will be great'" (Gen 15:1, NLT). His reward was great indeed! Abraham, the father of nations.

What do you dream about? He can do far more than we dare ask or imagine.

Good Stock

> Ephesians 6:1-4
>
> *Children, you belong to the Lord, and you do the right thing when you obey your parents. The first commandment with a promise says, "Obey your father and your mother, and you will have a long and happy life."*
>
> *Parents, don't be hard on your children. Raise them properly. Teach them and instruct them about the Lord.*

Dad is with the Lord now. He was the most gentle of souls. He presented a very calm demeanor. His conversation was flavored with agreeable gestures, um hmms, and soft yeses. I only remember on very rare occasions him ever raising his voice in anger. Having five boys would do that to anyone! He was supportive, steady, and consistent. A very practical man, truthful and honest, good-spirited. Mom is insightful, deep of thought, and imaginative. She is generous to a fault. She is infectious with a stubborn affection, playful and prank-ful. She likes to speculate about meanings of spiritual things, a little bit of a closet theologian. And the two of them together, Mom and Dad, oh my! What a tandem they were. Perfect match made in heaven. It was so easy and natural for me to honor them. Obeying them didn't cost me anything. I am blessed with good stock.

What of the ones who are not so blessed? Some fathers have been anything but honorable, done mean things, cruel, disrespectful, even criminal in some instances. There are mothers who abandon, turn on their own, unthinkable in their tragedy, not natural, unholy. *How am I supposed to give any honor to someone like that?* Well, in the first place, no one has perfect parents. I didn't. I know my boys don't! But one can always honor the office of parenting as a high and holy calling. You may not always vote for each president, or support the decisions of ones you have voted into the position, but you should always respect the office. In the same manner, dignify the office of the parent regardless of personal experiences you have had. Determine to be a better parent to your children. There is no better or more important mentor, teacher, or personal evangelist than that of the parent. How often have I thought, "Lord, help me be an effective pastor to my most important congregation, my family of three."

Honor and obey your parents to the best of your ability. It carries with it a nice reward, the promise of long life.

Our Dream

> *Ephesians 5:25*
>
> *A husband should love his wife as much as Christ loved the church and gave his life for it.*

A song to my bride, Stefanie.

Our Dream

She is lovely as a rose
She is passion in a pose
And everybody knows that I love her

She's a prized and precious thing
Yes and she's my beauty queen
Hear the earth and heavens sing that I love her

Our future spreads out before us
The outcome of the things not yet tried
It's going to be such a wonderful life
With God in front and you by my side

Oh Stefanie, my love
You're everything this man can dream of
And now, somehow, God's given you to me in trust
That I will have, and hold
And cherish you with all of my soul
And from this moment on and on and on
Love you and live out our dream

When two hearts are joined as one
When it's blessed by God above
There is reason then enough to come together

In a fusion, in a trust
In a bond that's true and just
And with faith in LORD Jesus

They come together just like a dream

July 1, 1988

Emptied Excellence

Philippians 2:5-7

Think the same way that Christ Jesus thought: Christ was truly God. But he did not try to remain equal with God. Instead he gave up everything and became a slave, when he became like one of us.

A topic of intrigue among Bible scholars is the theory of kenosis. The Greek word, *kenosis,* is emptiness, and is found here in Philippians 2:7. At issue is just what Christ emptied, what remained, how did this occur?

It is interesting to note how the various translations handle Philippians 2:6. The familiar wording of New King James Version has the phrase, "who, being in the form of God, did not consider it robbery to be equal to God." But just what does that mean exactly? Are we to interpret it to mean Jesus didn't think of it as stealing to be God's equal? The Greek word, *harpagmos,* can mean "robbery", which tends to have a negative connotation, and would imply, not an act of robbery, but the object being robbed. However, it can also mean "catch" or "grasp." This is the thought process behind many other translations. The New International Version says, "who did not consider equality with God something to be grasped." The New American Standard, New Century Version and English Standard Version have very similar renderings.

Blaine Charette teaches one of the most insightful approaches in his work on the kingdom of God. The key to unlocking understanding of the entire concept centers on the fact that Jesus modeled perfect humility. He did not cling to, accumulate, grasp, and hold on to things. His approach was not grasping, stock piling, groping, grabbing and collecting. In the purest example of his upside-down style of rule, or shall we say right-side-up, he empties himself of every selfish desire in order to be completely absolved of any impure human persuasion.

There are translations that capture this intent. New Living Translation mentions it this way, "He did not think of equality with God as something to cling to." And Contemporary English Version says, "He did not think that being equal with God was something to be used for his own benefit." Eugene Peterson's, *The Message*, also captures the sentiment well when it reads that he "didn't think so much of himself that he had to cling to the advantages of that status no matter what."

Consider the irony. The One who is co-Creator, owner of all that is and ever was, in the most pressing moments of his earthly life, relinquished any special privileges, and did not lay claim to his rights. You and I would be so wise to follow the example of his emptied excellence.

Further Up, Further In

>*Philippians 3:20, 21*
>
>*But we are citizens of heaven and are eagerly waiting for our Savior to come from there. Our Lord Jesus Christ has power*

> over everything, and he will make these poor bodies of ours like his own glorious body.

In C. S. Lewis's *Chronicles of Narnia* series, the concluding novel is titled, The Last Battle. At the end of the end he takes up the repeated phrase, "further up, further in."[xxv] It is Lewis's way of describing the beauty of New Narnia, his type for heaven. Peter, Susan, Edmund, and Lucy have now escaped the frigid Hundred Years Winter and are warmed by endless, indescribable spring.

They swim in icy waters but cannot be cold, only refreshed. Having crossed the river they begin to climb further up, and further in.

Running as fast as horses, they cross the plains. They cannot tire. Further up and further in.

They begin to race up the giant waterfall. Lewis pictures the dogs barking while simultaneously lapping water. They gag but don't choke, and their traveling companions laugh. Up, up, up. They can't feel pain. Can you imagine not being able to hurt? Further up, and further in.

They reach the pearly gates, and the jasper wall, they arrived at the golden street. No exhaustion, no tiring. Further up, and further in.

They turn to see old Narnia below. A vast distance is between them now. All of their concerns are so far beneath them. They turn back again and fix their gaze upon the towering mountains up the landscape. They stretch infinitely upward, soaring to heights that seem limitless, further up, and further in. And they have only just begun to journey into infinity.

"O death where is your sting? O hades, where is your victory?" (1 Cor 15:55, NKJV)

Feature Presentation

> Philippians 4:8
>
> *Finally, my friends, keep your minds on whatever is true, pure, right, holy, friendly and proper. Don't ever stop thinking about what is truly worthwhile and worthy of praise.*

At any given time there is something playing on the view screen of your mind. You have your own private theater room equipped with surround sound and high definition. As it turns out there is only one custom recliner, yours. It is the very seat of your emotions, your intellect, and your will. Philosophers have described it historically as the soul of you - ethos, pathos, and logos.

Typically, we humans have a running fare system. When we're on duty we concentrate very hard on the task before us. Completion of the task gives us a sense of accomplishment. However, when the work is done we go off the meter. This is when right thinking is most crucial.

If we were allowed to sneak a peek in the private theaters of minds all around us we would find a huge assortment of enticements: sexual encounters; lust; rape; pornography; assaults; murders; muggings; cheating; scheming; fighting; anger; gossip; thrills (the bad kind); rushes (the bad kind); risks; sarcastic laughter; fearfulness; hatred and worry. But we would also find love; purity; innocence; joyfulness; planning; thrills (the good kind); rushes (the good kind); deep intellectual wrestling; honesty; wholesome laughter; longing for what's right; justice; integrity; and loyalty. Obviously, this is just a sampling of the list.

Paul told the Philippians the secret to success. Right thinking is what leads to the acknowledgement of being able to do all things through Christ (Phil 4:13). When you go off the clock and revert back to default thinking, run everything through the filter screen. "Finally brothers, whatever is true, whatever is noble, whatever is right, whatever is pure, whatever is lovely, whatever is admirable - if anything is excellent or praiseworthy - think about such things" (Phil 4:8, NIV). Condition your mind this way. Just notice the inner peace swelling. What is your feature presentation? What is it rated?

Love Struck

Philippians 4:11-13

I am not complaining about having too little. I have learned to be satisfied with whatever I have. I know what it is to be poor or to have plenty, and I have lived under all kinds of conditions. I know what it means to be full or to be hungry, to have too much or too little. Christ gives me the strength to face anything.

A poem from a stretch with little money or spare time. A tribute to Stefanie's faithfulness and loyalty, her tremendous stick-to-it-iveness.

Love Struck

My love
In the early days
We would say
No money? Oh well…
We'll live on love

*My love
It was never my intent
To make no cents
We have struggled
And we have wrestled
But not with one another*

*My love
You have hit me with the sweetest blows
I am left powerless in your wake
I am love struck*

*My love
I dream for trips and clothes
And fancy shows*

*My love
And dining delights too
I want things for you*

*My love
And recognition
Of your Proverbs wisdom*

*My love
And once in a while
To parade you in style*

*It makes no sense
We have struggled
And we have wrestled
But not with one another*

*We have lived on love
And we have lived well*

*You have hit me with the sweetest blows
Left me powerless in your wake
I am love struck*

February 14, 2007

A Really Happy Life

> *Colossians 1:9-11*
>
> *We have not stopped praying for you since the first day we heard about you. In fact, we always pray that God will show you everything he wants you to do and that you may have all the wisdom and understanding his Spirit gives.*
>
> *Then you will live a life that honors the Lord, and you will always please him by doing good deeds. You will come to know God even better. His glorious power will make you patient and strong enough to endure everything, and you will be truly happy.*

Sometimes non-Christians voice their fear that following the Lord in a disciplined Christian life would be boring and not fulfilling; but this is uninformed. The Christian life, lived out the right way, is life as it was meant to be. Jesus says he came in order that "they may have life, and have it to the full" (John 10:10). Life to the max. Exactly and identically opposite from what the thief offers. This is living by design.

If I honor the Lord and my family honors him with me, my home is filled with peace, prosperity, hope, joy, laughter, freedom, creativity, experimentation, exploration and expectation. To be servant of all is to release an understanding of purpose and meaning that otherwise remains unearthed. To live an existence completely devoted to God is to live a really happy life. I mean, man, if this is boring, just let me get my nerd on.

If Only

> *Colossians 3:2*
>
> *Think about what is up there, not about what is here on earth.*

A longing, poetic prayer that is a confession of distractedness.

If Only

*Oh, if only I could focus entirely upon You
Instead of seven other things that have to be done*

*Clamoring expectations of others
Duties I mishandled
Projects taken on and dropped
Obligations I am powerless to fulfill
Deadlines initiated by yours truly
Echoes of what people will think
Pleasures pending*

*Marty-me, there is only one thing that's needed
I am truly Yours*

Oh, if only I could focus entirely upon You

September 22, 2012

Good Use of the Time

Colossians 4:5, 6

When you are with unbelievers always make good use of the time. Be pleasant and hold their interest when you speak the message. Choose your words carefully and be ready to give answers to anyone who asks questions.

Bill Hybels, in his book, *Becoming a Contagious Christian*, encapsulates the trending sentiment of most of us well-meaning believers. "Far too many Christians have been anesthetized into thinking if they simply live out their faith in an open and consistent fashion, the people around them will see, want it, and somehow figure out how to get it for themselves. Or they reason that maybe these people will come and ask them what makes their life so special and, when they do, they'll seize the opportunity and explain it to them. But let's be honest: that almost never happens."[xxvi]

You will have to be proactive in sharing your faith if you desire effectiveness.

Paul instructs the believers in Colossae to "always make good use of the time." He is very practical in his approach. Develop a pleasant disposition. Work to be an interesting conversationalist. Anticipate questions, have an answer waiting and ready. Be creative in response to the Holy Spirit's lead.

As you have time, over the long haul, learn tips from individuals who have had success. Study Rick Richardson's *Circles of Belonging*. Use Bill Hybel's idea of *Do versus Done*. There is a great tool elaborated upon by both Campus Crusade for Christ and Navigators that shows Christ's cross bridging the gap across a great chasm between the two cliffs of sinful humanity and a holy God. There are occasions when the direct-confrontational techniques of *Way of the Master* by Kirk Cameron and Ray Comfort are very effective. You should commit the tested and tried method called the *Roman Road* to memory. Learn the approach of the gospel track, *The Four Spiritual Laws*. And there are many other wonderful tools. This may sound like work, but take it at your pace. Find a method that works with your personality, style and gifts. Don't be passive about this, it's too important. Determine to make good use of the time.

Military Fatigues

> *1 Thessalonians 1:2, 3*
>
> *We thank God for you and always mention you in our prayers. Each time we pray, we tell God our Father about your faith and loving work and about your firm hope in our Lord Jesus Christ.*

The triad of faith, hope and love is a popular theme of the apostle Paul. He mentions it here in the letter of 1 Thessalonians twice; in Colossians 1:3-5; in Hebrews 6:9-12 (if Paul wrote Hebrews); and of course, in the famous declaration of the love chapter, 1 Corinthians 13:13, "And now these three remain: faith, hope, and love. But the greatest of these is love."

It is really interesting the way he utilizes the theme here in 1 Thessalonians. He opens the letter with the comment above. In the original language there are two separate words, one to modify faith and the other to modify love. It would come off sort of this way, "the task of faith and the fatigue of love." Many translations choose to word it, "your work of faith and labor of love." And then these two thoughts are grouped with the steadfastness of hope.

In essence, Paul is describing the weight of Christian ministry. The task is fatiguing and requires steadfastness.

That's how he opened the book; however, he closes it with another mention of the importance of faith, hope and love. "But we belong to the day. So we must stay sober and let our faith and love be like a suit of armor. Our firm hope that we will be saved is our helmet" (1 Thess 5:8).

In chapter 1 faith and love are connected with the similar ideas of task and fatigue. In chapter 5 they are associated with a protective suit of armor. While we work and labor, faith and love provide us with an Inspector Gadget suit. Is it any wonder we refer to our soldiers' clothing as military fatigues? The actual word Paul chooses is breastplate, meant to guard the heart. And hope, which in chapter 1 was connected with endurance, get this, the ability to keep on working and laboring, endurance, in chapter 5 becomes our helmet of salvation. Hope is guarding our minds.

It calls to mind another popular verse from Paul. "And the peace of God which transcends all understanding will guard your hearts and minds in Christ Jesus" (Phil 4:8).

Okay, Christian soldier. You are headed into warfare today. It doesn't matter if you are a private or a general. Make sure you have your helmet and breastplate secure. "Each time we pray, we tell God our Father about your faith and loving work and about your firm hope in the Lord Jesus Christ."

It's All about You

> 1 Thessalonians 3:1, 2
>
> *Finally, we couldn't stand it any longer. We decided to stay in Athens by ourselves and send our friend Timothy to you.*

See if you also pick up on some of the subtleties used by the apostle Paul that let us know how much he cares about the Thessalonians. He starts off chapter 3 with words of pain in the first verse about their separation, "Finally, we could stand it no longer." Again, in verse 5 he echoes the thought, this time more personally, "At last, when I could stand it no longer I sent Timothy." One verse later you can almost hear the relief in his voice, "You want to see us as much as we want to see you" (1 Thess 3:6). And he speaks of "all the happiness you have brought us" (1 Thess 3:9). He genuinely hopes to be reunited with them. "We pray that God our Father will let us visit you" (1 Thess 3:11).

Paul wants to highlight two things for these people he cares so much about: their faith and their love.

Faith.

"We wanted to make you strong in your faith" (1 Thess 3:2). "Your faith makes us feel better about you" (1 Thess 3:7). "We sincerely pray that we will see you again and help you to have an even greater faith" (1 Thess 3:10). "Your strong faith is like a breath of new life" (1 Thess 3:8).

Love.

"Timothy has now come back from his visit with you and has told us about your faith and love" (1 Thess 3:6). "May the Lord make your love for each other and for everyone else grow by leaps and bounds. This is how our love has grown for you" (1 Thess 3:12).

If you're careful you notice the emphasis on them, not himself. "Your faith...your love...makes us feel better about you." It's all about you. Some people walk into a room and with their actions seem to say, "Here I am." Others have their focus right. When they walk into a room they say, "There you are."

Celestial Super-Band

> 1 Timothy 3:16
>
> Here is the great mystery of our religion:
> Christ came as a human,
> The Spirit proved that he pleased God,
> And he was seen by angels.
> Christ was preached to the nations,
> People in this world put their faith in him,
> And he was taken up to glory.

I have heard individuals comment in various settings that there is shallowness to chorus writing in our contemporary era. I tend to disagree, feeling that it is imperative for each generation to capture the arts in its own expression. I'm captivated by this early Easter hymn recorded by Paul the apostle in 1 Timothy 3:16. I believe these songs have continued unabated down through the ages of the church.

In previous centuries writers succeeded in composing for the resurrection theme. The sixteenth century saw Beethoven and Wordsworth combine to create a masterpiece. "Alleluia, alleluia, hearts to heaven and voices raised, sing to God a hymn of gladness, sing to God a hymn of praise. Christ has conquered and we conquer by his mighty enterprise. We with him to life eternal by his resurrection rise."

In the eighteenth century Charles Wesley penned his time-enduring jewel. "Christ the Lord is risen today, Alleluia. Earth and heaven in chorus say, Alleluia. Raise your joys and triumphs high, Alleluia. Sing ye earth and heaven reply, Alleluia."

Last century Alfred Ackley wrote the standard Easter hymn, "He lives, he lives, Christ Jesus lives today. He walks with me and talks with me along life's narrow way. He lives, he lives, salvation to impart. You ask me how I know he lives, he lives within my heart."

In more recent decades Martha Butler has composed a wonderful Vineyard chorus, "Alleluia, He is Coming." It has an element of surprise and play on the words that brings an epiphany moment on its first hearing. And you look forward to it each time you hear it. One of Hillsong's breakout songs was "Alleluia, Jesus is Alive." Rick Founds's "Lord I Lift Your Name on High" smartly traces the gospel message in one stanza culminating in the phrase "from the grave to the sky." Casting Crowns's "Glorious Day" tells the story in a similar way. "One day the grave could conceal him no longer, one day the stone rolled away from the door. Then he arose, over death he had conquered, now he's ascended, my Lord evermore. Death could not hold him. The grave could not keep him from rising again." And just consider the opening lines of Tim Hughes's "Happy Day," a really powerful tune. "The greatest day in history, death is beaten, you have rescued me. Sing it out, Jesus is alive." There are at least a dozen other new or recent resurrection-themed songs.

There is such beauty and unity in the early hymn that Paul quotes as he writes young, Pastor Timothy. "Here is the great mystery of our religion: Christ came as a human. The Spirit proved that he pleased God, and he was seen by angels. Christ was preached to the nations. People in this world put their faith in him, and he was taken up to glory."

Some day when we get to heaven I want to request a celestial super-band version of this ancient hymn. Let's have Mac Powell smoothing vocals with Russ Taff, Tim Minor and Nikki Leonti roughing in back tones. I want Bach on the harpsichord and Dino on the grand piano. Would you throw a bone to Robey Duke on keys! Some wowing by Stevie Wonder's harmonica, and some percussive kicks by Alex Acuna. We'll have Hadley Hockensmith on guitar, please. And Abe Laboriel on all six strings of the bass. And just for kicks, Mr. Briscoe Darling on the jug. If I get to have this wish in glory, that, my friend will be resurrection!

Recipe for Zero Joy

> *1 Timothy 5:1*
>
> *Don't correct an older man. Encourage him as you would your own father. Treat younger men even as you would your own brother.*

Over the twenty-five years of my ministry there have always been, in each church assignment, at least two older, mature ministers who have provided a safeguard for me. Now, looking back, I see the hand of God in this. There is tremendous power in mentoring. As much as I believe in the concept of Gen X and GenNext churches, this is at least a challenge that must be considered. Who will pour into the life of the leader? And there are lead pastors who accomplish this by life boundaries and personal accountability.

In my youth I didn't know how to fully appreciate older, wiser input. I thought I did. I was, at least, aware of their presence and would absorb things through conversation. In time I learned to seek them out. At this moment, in our congregation there are two retired pastors. They bring me such comfort. They are kind, compassionate and genuine. I love the way a shy smile creeps into the corner of the mouth when they hear me call them my mentor, or my colleague. I am grateful for their tested wisdom. From time to time I will bounce things off them. I'll paint a possible scenario with the words, "What if?" I value them and honor them. And this is as it should be.

Two of the most painful memories I have in ministry involved privately rebuking men who were clearly older than me. It had to be done. I was correct. It was the right thing to do and it was needed. But it is unnatural. It is not as it should be. It brought me no satisfaction. I can tell you that is a recipe for zero joy, speaking harshly to an elder.

What elder do you know in your circles who is worthy of honor today?

A Nameless Verse

> *Titus 1:1*
>
> *I encourage God's own people to have more faith.*

A nameless verse that comes to me in light of my study of Paul's letter to Titus.

A Nameless Verse

Such masterful love that dwarfs my sin!

Unfounded, gross, it shirks repose
Blatant, fool-full, frailty it shows
Cognizant to the dread it knows

Shatters regret epiphanies within!

March 12, 2005

100% Pure

Titus 1:15, 16

Everything is pure for someone whose heart is pure. But nothing is pure for an unbeliever with a dirty mind. That person's mind and conscience are destroyed. Such people claim to know God, but their actions prove that they really don't. They are disgusting. They won't obey God, and they are too worthless to do anything good.

My wife, Stefanie, regularly picks up a jar of honey from Beckner's Farm. It's a happy, easy-paced location. Sometimes the store is unmanned. You walk in, grab your jar of honey, and leave the six dollars in the cigar box. It's on the honor system. The honey is 100% pure. No additives, no preservatives, it is natural. Each time I open the cupboard to see the hand-glued label fixed on the Ball jar I am struck with the simplicity and quality of this organic product.

What kind of label do I wear? How authentic am I? If others were to brand me what kind of impurities would have to be disclosed in the ingredients?

In my prayer time this morning I found myself singing the song by Brian Doerksen, "Refiner's Fire." I encourage you to read the lyrics slowly. If you know it, sing it thoughtfully, reflectively, not in a rush. Ask the Holy Spirit to be Sifter of your existence, filtering out every impurity in your quest to be 100% pure.

*Purify my heart
Let me be as gold
And precious silver
Purify my heart
Let me be as gold
Pure gold*

*Refiner's fire
My heart's one desire
Is to be holy
Set apart for You, Lord
I choose to be holy
Set apart for You, my Master
Ready to do Your will*

*Purify my heart
Cleanse me from within
And make holy
Purify my heart
Cleanse me from my sin
Deep within*

A Model on Mentoring

Titus 2:2-7

Tell the older men to have self-control and to be serious and sensible. Their faith, love, and patience must never fail. Tell the older women to behave as those who love the Lord should. They must not gossip about others or be slaves of wine. They must teach what is proper, so the younger women will be loving wives and mothers. Each of the younger women must be sensible and kind, as well as a good homemaker, who puts her own husband first. Then no one can say insulting things about God's message. Tell the young men to have self-control in everything. Always set a good example for others. Be sincere and serious when you teach.

A popular television series features various forms of communal living in America. Weekly episodes feature the Hutterites, the Amish, and other peripheral movements. Granted, there are dysfunctional displays, after all, it is drama. The tension makes for good TV. And I notice misapplication of Bible beliefs and intentions, as well as improper understanding of Church practice. But as one embedded in American norms, I am struck with the simplicity of their lifestyles. Each movement is absolutely committed to the concept of community. Older trains younger, men lead boys, women teach girls. I believe there is something the broader society can learn from these isolated pockets.

There are popular guidance buzzwords in current culture, coaching, accountability and mentoring to name a few. Each is so important. Coaching has to do with drawing out of the other individual and can be imaged by Proverbs 20:5; "The purposes of a man's heart are deep waters, but a man of understanding can draw them out." An accountability partner provides a safety net for experiencing life. This is someone to come alongside and make observations. Think of Proverbs 27:17, "As iron sharpens iron so one man sharpens another." However, mentoring, rather than drawing out or evaluating, pours into the other person. Titus 2 is the perfect model on mentoring. It instructs the older men to be "serious and sensible." Self-control is paramount. Don't let faith, love and patience fail. This is crucial. Women should guard behavior, never fuel gossip. They "must teach what is proper." Now, that's what the Bible says. Men and women, we have a high responsibility.

The way the Bible pictures it, men will invest in their successors. Men teach boys how to carry themselves, how to treat women, how to act in public. Women will teach girls how to interface the world in healthy ways. Model4Jesus and Modest is Hottest, and others, are helping Christian girls be trendy and fashionable. More and more the important moments of my life are the times spent with my sons, basketball tournaments; making music; turning wrenches on the car; holding hands at the end of the day to pray. I love the trending practice in which Dad takes his daughter on a date and demonstrates to her the way a guy should treat her. That's awesome!

Our world desperately needs individuals to stand out. Don't get sucked in by the vortex. Be contradistinct. Platform this model on mentoring.

Investigative Journalism

Titus 3:5

He saved us because of his mercy, and not because of any good things we have done. God washed us by the power of the Holy Spirit. He gave us new birth and a fresh beginning.

Perhaps the apostle Paul would have done well as an investigative journalist in our media frenzied world. He covers Reporting 101. Paul gives Titus the 5 W's - who, what, where, why and when. And he even throws in the "how" for good measure.

Who? "He." Jesus.

What? "Saved us."

Where? Inside. "God washed us by the power of the Holy Spirit."

Why? "Because of his mercy, and not because of any good things that we have done."

When? The moment we believe. "A fresh beginning."

How? "He gave us a new beginning."

Now that's the scoop. Paul always double checks his sources. He got this straight from the top. Don't let the pressures of life keep you from going to press on this. Read it and weep. God loves you.

Used and Amused

Philemon 17-19

If you consider me a friend because of Christ, then welcome Onesimus as you would welcome me. If he has cheated you or owes you anything, charge it to my account. With my own hand I write: I, PAUL, WILL PAY YOU BACK. But don't forget you owe me your life.

Paul's short letter to Philemon comes off as a reference letter. It is much more than that. It is an exoneration by executive order. Imagine what it would've been like to have been Philemon receiving the letter, being a faithful Christian, wanting to please the apostle, and wanting to please the people he led. Perhaps the letter was read out loud as was customary.

"Hey everyone, gather around. We have a new letter from Paul. Quiet, now, in the back. Let's settle down. Let's hear this." And then when it is read, it becomes apparent that Paul is bringing a gentle correction. Receive Onesimus, the runaway slave, as you would your own brother. He is my own son. Philemon had done nothing wrong. In his culture slavery was accepted. Remember, it was another time and place. However, it would've been rare if he would've considered exoneration without Paul's suggestion. This was quite a shift in thought.

The most amazing play on words happens in Philemon. Onesimus's name means useful, but he had not lived up to his namesake for his master, Philemon. Verse 11 captures the sentiment, "Formerly he was useless to you, but now he has become useful both to you and to me." Hats off to Philemon, a slave owner who had the courage to look at Onesimus differently than he had before. The shift was pretty dramatic; but from now on the one who was previously thought to be useless would be very instrumental in the life of their church. Onesimus had to just sit back and laugh when he realized the way the Lord worked it all out. He was used and amused.

Which character are you in the drama? Onesimus? Do you count the situation pretty useless? It is not hopeless. You are valuable. Or Philemon? Does someone around you need your uplift? Bolster someone's confidence.

New Digs

> Hebrews 1:10-12
>
> *The Scriptures also say, "In the beginning, Lord, you were the one who laid the foundation of the earth and created the heavens. They will all disappear and wear out like clothes, but you will last forever. You will roll them up like a robe and change them like a garment. But you are always the same, and you will live forever."*

There are places in Scripture where the wording of the new heavens and new earth seems to track with renewal. The old heaven and earth get an extreme makeover. Proponents of this view cite verses like 2 Corinthians 5:17, "Therefore, if anyone is in Christ he is a new creation, the old is gone, the new has come." If this is the way God redeems humanity, why would he not do the same with nature? When a person is saved, in an instant the old filth is washed away, the individual is justified, forgiven. In fact, even in eternity, it is not a new body that we are given, rather a resurrected one. God is always in the business of redeeming. However, this verse in Hebrews, along with passages from the Revelation, seems to indicate an instantaneous, broad sweeping culmination where something old is destroyed, obliterated. And in its place is something pristine and new. The sky is rolled up like a scroll. Sounds cataclysmic, almost nuclear. What God created in the beginning, he undoes. The new heaven and new earth are really brand new. He outdoes himself. It's better than Eden. It surpasses all expectations. So a city built on square comes down out of the heavens, 1500 miles built on a square. As high as it is wide and long. It would encompass most of the middle contingent United States, by comparison. Does God go square instead of round in a completely new design? Everything else in his universe that we have ever found has been round. Or, does the square city plop right down on the round, renewed planet?

Is heaven really up, up and away? Will we come and go as we please toying with the universal playground, jetting around at the speed of light? Or is heaven conceived on a spiritual dimension that coexists alongside our physical dimension? There is much left un-addressed by the Bible. It is busy getting us saved in the here and now; it doesn't concern itself too much with descriptions of the then and there. We get little peaks at vignettes, glimpses as it were, through frosted windows. We know of streets that use gold for asphalt, and gates comprised of beautifully cultured pearls. Only the most exquisite gems are mortared together as composite stones for the perimeter walls. And the most magnificent fete of horticulture, a grand tree of life lives at the center flanked by streams of pure, life-giving water, crystal clear, smooth as glass. No power plants or solar plants, no windmill farms necessary in this place, the Lamb is light. The radiance and royalty of plethora of holy creatures is described in the Bible. There is so much we don't know about our heavenly, eternal home. But prepare to be blown away! Stress-less, sinless living, unbroken communion with our Maker. Life the way it was meant to be lived! When God gets his new wardrobe. Like changing clothes. You're gonna' love his new digs.

From His Vantage Point

Hebrews 2:18

And now that Jesus has suffered and was tempted, he can help anyone else who is tempted.

Jesus came to earth as a man so that he could experience life from our point of view.

This paragraph, Hebrews 2:14-18, clearly teaches that Jesus had two motivations in assuming the characteristics of humanity: 1.) To defeat the devil who had previously controlled death; and 2.) To rescue all of us who were in constant fear of dying. That is "why Jesus became one of us" (Heb 2:14).

Among the members of the Trinity there is great love for humanity. The Father says, *"I made humans. I love them so much I gave my only Son."* The Holy Spirit says, *"I've lived in humans."* Jesus says, *"Ah, but I've been one of them."*

Can we even imagine the depth of love that would propel Jesus to descend to our existence. He knows our pains, our aches, our yearnings and longings. He who is without sin opened the way for the Spirit to long intensely inside of us (Jas 4:5).

We are stained with sin; but Jesus views us through rose-colored glasses. From his vantage point we are pristine, brilliantly clean. Ode to Incarnate Joy.

Pistachios, Profiles and Peace

Hebrews 5:6

You are a priest forever, just like Melchizedek.

I have a friend named Elias Malki. He is virtually the Pat Robertson of Arabic television, and airs Christian broadcasting in more than 180 nations daily. Elias is in his 70s; he has a very winsome personality and is humorous in his presentation. Once I picked him up at the airport when he had come to speak as a guest at our church. When I took him to check into the hotel he was asked by the clerk if he wanted an upstairs room or a downstairs room. He replied, "The only footsteps I want above me are angels." He loves pistachios. I know personally he went through a pound in a weekend. Sometimes when he is speaking he will turn and show his distinct facial profile and exclaim, "I love myself. I just love my nose. Isn't it beautiful!" Elias not only has a distinct profile, he also has a distinct name - Malki. Melech is the Hebrew word for king. Malki would be "my king."

Genesis 14 introduces a mysterious figure named Melchizedek. He appears like a bolt of the blue, no record of genealogy. We know nothing of him. The name Melchizedek combines two Hebrew words. *Melek* (king) and *Tsedek* (righteousness). It would mean "my king is right." Or, probably more accurately, "king of righteousness." He was the king of Salem (*Shalem* - peaceful), which calls to mind shalom, peace. Hebrews says of Jesus that he is a king forever in the order of Melchizedek. (Heb 5:6, 10; 6:20; 7:1, 10, 11, 15, 17). This theme is only an amplification of what the Psalms had declared earlier (Ps 110:4). He is associated with Melchizedek, not Aaron. The Levitical priests traced their lineage to Aaron, but Jesus was from the tribe of Judah. He aligns his priesthood with a king who models righteousness from the territory of peace. How fitting that the Prince of Peace would relate to him. Our High Priest predates a sacrificial system. Abraham, the father of all faith, pays tithes to Melchizedek. How remarkable!

Let your righteous King establish his peace in the territory of your heart today.

Solid Food

Hebrews 5:11-14

> *Much more could be said about this subject. But it is hard to explain, and all of you are slow to understand. By now you should have been teachers, but once again you need to be taught the simplest things about what God has said. You need milk instead of solid food. People who live on milk are like babies who don't really know what is right. Solid food is for mature people who have been trained to know right from wrong.*

I grew up in a household that reveled in the delivery of a strong sermon. Its substance might be measured by depth and substance. Or it could be equally appraised upon its call to great commitment. I recall my parents discussing preaching with friends who were comrades in ministry and voicing their appreciation for the backbone of the message. "It wasn't milk toast," they would say.

Most of us would be aghast at the thought of opening a jar of baby food and spooning out a big bite for ourselves. Something about the thought of that little jar gives me the willies. The grit of diet becomes more demanding with maturity. We develop a taste and craving for the real stuff. Solid food is for those who are mature and well. We may stomach a liquid diet for a short time when we are sick; but the sign of healing is longing for solid food. Our spiritual regimen should track proportionately with our growth. A disciplined spirituality requires an intake of substantive, challenging matter.

It is a sad indictment upon the Church of Jesus Christ that some have been saved for 30 years but are stunted in their growth. Instead of becoming seasoned they have repeated a one-year experience 30 times. Babies are cute and adorable unless they stay that way. Pacifiers are not permanent and diapers are not durable. We all must leave the kid table with its milk toast. Table fellowship with our Lord insists upon a menu of solid food, the disciplines that bring sweet communion.

New and Improved

Hebrews 8:12, 13

"I will treat them with kindness, even though they are wicked. I will forget their sins." When the Lord talks about a new agreement, he means that the first one is out of date. And anything that is old and useless will soon disappear.

We love it when a product is expanded, advanced, updated, and somehow made better. There is just something about those words "new and improved" that grab our attention.

The writer of Hebrews describes how much better and superior is our high priest, Jesus Christ, compared to the system of the Old Testament. Under the new covenant we are granted access to the very throne room of God. We are told we may enter boldly. How so? It is because Jesus has purchased our redemption by his sacrificial death. The outdated sacrificial system is done away with. There is no longer need for ongoing morning and evening sacrifices. There is not an annual atonement that reminds us of our inadequacies. Jesus accomplished right-standing with God once and for all. The New Testament is not new and improved, it is just, well, NEW!

How awesome is it to have our sins forgotten! "Therefore if anyone is in Christ he is a new creation; the old has gone, the new has come" (2 Cor 5:17).

This Can't Be Faith

Hebrews 10:37-39

As the Scriptures say, "God is coming soon! It won't be very long. The people God accepts will live because of their faith. But he isn't pleased with anyone who turns back." We are not like those people who turn back and get destroyed. We will keep on having faith until we are saved.

This can't be what faith looks like. Struggling, scrapping, getting by. I thought faith meant the image of the never-tiring, evangelistic, faith-healer who runs on limitless energy and charisma. But this *is* what faith looks like. This is the fiber of faith, faith stripped of any glamour, real and rugged. Faith that pleases God keeps believing and persevering and will not relent. God isn't pleased with anyone who turns back, shirks responsibility, or runs from every challenge. Oh, but when he sees one who shoulders burdens with a good outlook, carries difficulties with dignity, and turns to face a headwind of trials - that trust, that faith, garners his attention.

This can't be faith! But, oh, it is great faith.

Substantive Faith

> *Hebrews 11:1*
>
> *Faith makes us sure of what we hope for and gives us proof of what we cannot see. It was their faith that made our ancestors pleasing to God.*

This is one of those bigger-than-life sound bites from my childhood. I learned this verse in the King James. "Now faith is the substance of things hoped for, the evidence of things not seen." I like the words associated with Hebrews 11:1, sure, substance, proof, evidence. Other versions choose words like confidence, certainty, assurance, conviction, sure and knowing. This topic is the heart of this entire book in a nutshell. Substance, I want something substantive. Proof, I need evidence. That's what my natural capacities long for.

However, what is the substance of the things I hope for? It is faith. What is substantive about it? Hmm. *Evidence, okay, good. Give me some proof. Your honor, I would like to enter into evidence things not seen. Just what does faith look like?*

Do you see what I'm getting at? You will be hard pressed to nail down any indicators of the Spirit. Jesus says the Spirit is like the wind. We don't know where it comes from or where it goes. It blows where it wants to (John 3:8). Give up trying to analyze God and reduce him to a formula. He will not be figured out.

If you can believe "In the beginning God" (Gen. 1:1), you can believe anything that follows. In this unquantifiable constant, life will have substance.

Faith that Lives

> *James 2:14-17*
>
> *My friends, what good is it to say you have faith, when you don't do anything to show that you really do have faith? Can that kind of faith save you? If you know someone who doesn't have any clothes or food, you shouldn't just say, "I hope all goes well for you. I hope you will be warm and have plenty to eat." What good*

> is it to say this, unless you do something to help? Faith that doesn't lead us to do good deeds is all alone and dead!

Faith must demonstrate itself. Has to, or it isn't a living faith. Think of exercising. Use it or you lose it. Not immediately. Not if you miss one day. Someone may commend you for taking care of yourself; but perhaps you know it's been weeks since you've worked out. Eventually, though, motion and movement mark life. Faith that lives is not static. Flex your faith today. We're not going after Hulk here, just steady, consistent demonstrations of what's on the inside.

Jesus said faith is like a mustard-seed sized, gigantic enormity. What! Now, he's not saying you have to be Bif at Gold's Gym of Faith. Remember, he's trying to use temporary, physical examples to describe eternal, spiritual values. God is outside the scope of time and space. Yet, for our sake, Jesus uses time and space to demonstrate faith - a small, tiny seed becoming a massive tree that provides shade and shelter over time. So what is the take? The take is this. Your steady, consistent obedience coupled with unshakable trust makes brute and brawn that will not bend.

James's comment at the end of this chapter lifts into the air and rings, just sort of hangs there in the atmosphere. "Anyone who doesn't breathe is dead, and faith that doesn't do anything is just as dead" (Jas 2:20).

The Courage to Encourage

> *1 Thessalonians 5:14, 15*
>
> *My friends, we beg you to warn anyone who isn't living right. Encourage anyone who feels left out, help all who are weak, and be patient with everyone.*
>
> *Don't be hateful to people, just because they are hateful to you. Rather, be good to each other and to everyone else.*

Willie Mays began his major league baseball career with only one hit in his first 26 at-bats. Though he went on to hit 660 home runs, third on the all-time list, and steal more than 300 bases, his debut was so unimpressive it seemed unlikely he would last more than a few weeks as a big-leaguer, let alone become one of the greatest to play the game.

The turning point for Mays occurred when his manager, Leo Durocher, found him crying in the dugout after yet another miserable performance at the plate.

The coach put his arm around Mays and said, "What's the matter, son?" Mays said, "I can't hit up here. I belong in the minor leagues."

Durocher said this to Willie Mays: "As long as I'm manager of the Giants, you'll be my center fielder."

You know how the story ends. It wasn't long before Mays began hitting the ball, and he was on his way to becoming a legend of the game.

If Willie Mays had been left alone in the dugout that day, his career might have ended before it started. Fortunately for him, and for baseball, someone believed in him even when he didn't believe in himself.

Television sitcoms have changed the landscape of American family life. Treating one another with respect and decency is out. Doing whatever it takes to get a laugh is in, even if the laugh is at the expense of another individual, even if the laugh is at the expense of appropriateness.

So, I hope you have the courage to go against the tide. I hope you have the courage to encourage.

Encourage someone today:

- Do a good deed for someone who cannot possibly return your act of kindness!
- Find an individual who is lacking self-confidence. Say something that will make his or her day.

Wavy Wishfulness

James 1:5-8

If any of you need wisdom, you should ask God, and it will be given to you. God is generous and won't correct you for asking. But when you ask for something, you must have faith and not doubt. Anyone who doubts is like an ocean wave tossed around in a storm. If you are that kind of person, you can't make up your mind, and you surely can't be trusted. So don't expect the Lord to give you anything at all.

Today my family is spending time at the seashore, taking in the cool air, watching the seagulls, and admiring the tide as it rolls in. The water crashes into the rocks again and again. It is just no match for the granite. As beautiful as the picturesque scene is, still it serves as a tremendous object lesson on the wishy-washy nature of doubt. I've never been in the middle of the ocean to see the mighty waves swell and crash into one another. It must be magnificent to watch the waves that seem to be so strong simply dissipate, having burst upon one another in a swirl.

This is the picture James has in mind for the double-minded doubter, rising, swelling, outward show of strength, but nothing of substance to stand when tested. True belief in God is no wavy wishfulness. We are instructed to trust God with great faith. When we ask him for wisdom on a matter, it is imperative that we do not second guess, recoil, rise up, and sink down. Faith is trusting that we have his guidance through the Scripture we read and interpret in context; through the conversations we have with Christian friends, counselors, and mentors; through the *Sitz im Leben* (life situation); through the prayer times in which we voice our need and then wait - if any of you need wisdom, you should ask God, and it will be given to you. God is generous and won't correct you for asking.

Nearness

> *James 4:7, 8*
>
> *Surrender to God! Resist the devil, and he will run from you. Come near to God, and he will come near to you. Clean up your lives, you sinners. Purify your hearts, you people who can't make up your mind.*

Resist the devil and he will flee from you. Draw near to God and he will draw near to you. I'll bet you're a lot like me. I find it very easy to go along with the ways of the flesh; but I find it difficult to discipline myself to simply keep reaching out to get closer him, to draw near to him. I've served God a long time, but I still find that every day I have to discipline myself to take a step to get close to him. But if you can live your life by this life-guiding principle it will really help you. Draw near to God and he will draw near to you. Take a step towards God and he will take a step towards you. Keep reaching out to him and just know that, every time you reach out to him, he will reach out to you.

How Valuable is Faith!

> *1 Peter 1:7*
>
> *Your faith will be like gold that has been tested in a fire. And these trials will prove that your faith is worth much more than gold that can be destroyed. They will show that you will be given praise and honor and glory when Jesus Christ returns.*

How valuable is faith! It is more valuable than gold. Gold is the purest of metals. It's nineteen times heavier than water. Gold is tested with fire and it still lasts. But twice in this chapter Peter says gold will not last. Your faith is more valuable than gold.

Open Heavens

> *1 Peter 3:1-2, 7*
>
> *If you are a wife, you must put your husband first. Even if he opposes our message, you will win him over by what you do. No one else will have to say anything to him, because he will see how you honor God and live a pure life… If you are a husband, you should be thoughtful of your wife. Treat her with honor, because she isn't as strong as you are, and she shares with you in the gift of life. Then nothing will stand in the way of your prayers.*

Though this post targets the married ones, there are principles here for every single servant of Jesus.

Open heavens, unblocked prayers. When a husband and wife honor and respect each other, nothing stands in their way.

Does it feel like your prayers are not heard? Are you spinning your wheels? Examine your inner most treatment of your spouse. Don't go easy on yourself. Be brutal with every motive. It could be you have stymied yourself.

Oh, but you don't know my spouse. You don't know the history.

No. I don't.

And of course it takes two to tango. A successful union requires two walking in careful obedience. So you can't guarantee your own success; but I promise you, you can guarantee your own failure. Don't sabotage yourself and your mate. Remove every barrier to success. Take away every blockage to prayer. Demonstrate your love for the Lord by the way you love your spouse today.

Steady as She Goes

> *1 Peter 5:2, 3*
>
> *Just as shepherds watch over their sheep, you must watch over everyone God has placed in your care. Do it willingly in order to*

> *please God, and not simply because you think you must. Let it be something you want to do, instead of something you do merely to make money. Don't be bossy to those people who are in your care, but set an example for them.*

The voice of the Baltimore Ravens suffers two misfortunes. For one he is involved with football. For the other, he is named Gerry Sandusky. Before you experience shrills down your spine read on. He is not the assistant coach, Jerry Sandusky, affiliated with Penn State University who committed unspeakable sex-crimes against young men. He just happens to have the same name, spelled with a "G" instead of "J". His family has endured countless episodes of taunting of unending misunderstanding ever since. He was asked why he doesn't just change his name. He refuses to because his father, John, was a football coach in the NFL. His Dad's name is on the Super Bowl Championship ring from 1970. He refuses to let his father down. In an ESPN interview with Nick Riley, Gerry said, "If the Penn State situation has taught America anything it is that doing the easy thing in the short term is almost never the right thing to do in the long term."

The best a Christian can hope for in this life is to find a happy pace, and settle in for the long haul in relationship with Jesus. Loving the Lord and loving one another – it's a pretty good life. This is especially so for those in leadership. I've discovered when I enjoy people, really love people, become enthralled with people, in return they are such a joy to me. When I was a young pastor I was given a piece of advice by a pastor mentor. "Don't take too much blame when things wrong; and, don't take too much credit when things go well." This steady-as-she-goes approach has been the bubble-window in my spiritual level. It is invaluable. We don't serve God in a flash but in a flow. We don't run with Jesus in a sprint, we walk with him on a long journey.

Eugene Peterson, the brilliant mind behind The Message Bible, wrote a book titled, *A Long Obedience in the Same Direction*. He writes, "All the water in the oceans cannot sink a ship unless it gets inside. Nor can all the trouble in the world do us harm unless it gets within us."[xxvii] Keep relationships honest and real. If you drift from the Lord, bring corrective measures the moment you become aware of it. Be quick to confess sin. Read the Bible on purpose. Pray in meaningful ways. Obey carefully. And with your brothers and sisters in Christ, keep short accounts. Don't carry heavy grudges. Travel light. Allow no entrance of pride, arrogance, jealousy, or resentment. Steady as she goes, mate, steady as she goes.

A Lamp Shining in a Dark Place

2 Peter 1:18-21

We were there with Jesus on the holy mountain and heard this voice speak from heaven. All of this makes us even more certain that what the prophets said is true. So you should pay close attention to their message, as you would to a lamp shining in some dark place. You must keep on paying attention until daylight comes and the morning star rises in your hearts. But you need to realize that no one alone can understand any of the prophecies in the Scriptures. The prophets did not think these things up on their own, but they were guided by the Spirit of God.

"The prophets did not think these things up on their own, but they were guided by the Spirit of God." Peter is saying, basically, *"You couldn't make this stuff up!"*

Individuals who thoughtlessly chime in on the doubt campaign have not thought through all the implications. Scripture is miraculous, and the Bible is a remarkable book, truly. The Bible, the word means library, is a remarkable collection of books. It was in process of writing for a period of over 1,600 years. There are over 40 authors from all walks of life. One is a king; one is a tax collector. One is a doctor; while another is a fisherman. And there are various styles and genres: poetical; historical; narrative; epistle; apocryphal; prophetic. It would be impossible to fabricate a unified work, such as the holy Bible, that withstands the close scrutiny of textual criticism. Careful exegesis shows no glaring contradictions, none.

The Bible houses brilliance. By way of demonstration, consider the decisions made by the early leaders of the Church. Acts 15 has the elders called together in Jerusalem to discuss the dilemma of Gentiles embracing faith in Christ and how to mesh with Jewish law. The apostles' decision to keep it simple is brilliant, directed by God's Spirit, miraculous in scope.

Paul and Peter are both directors of the burgeoning Church, Paul to the Gentiles, Peter to the Jews. They both have lists that include "self-control" and "love." And Paul and Peter both validate Scripture. The apostle Paul says, "All Scripture is God-breathed." The apostle Peter speaks of Scripture as if it were a lamp shining in a dark place. He says give it the attention it deserves and it will be like the day dawning and arising in your heart. I wonder if Paul and Peter knew they were composing Scripture. What do you think?

Suppose you wanted to pull a hoax on the world. You know, compile a bunch of phony literature, brainwash gullible minds, and lead innocent simpletons down a primrose path. In the first place, what would be your motive? I mean, what could you possibly gain from it? But anyway, let's go with that. How would you control a time span of sixteen centuries? You can't live that long. You can't control what happens before or after you live.

If you were going to pull the wool over the eyes of the world, would you use the rag-tag band of disciples Jesus chose? They're bumbling, fearful, uneducated, rough around the edges. Would your primary strategy be to say your leader was killed and rose from the dead? You can't make this stuff up.

There is a band wagon of skeptics dead-set on devaluing the authenticity of holy Scripture. However, the legitimacy of the biblical texts cannot be denied. There is an embarrassing plethora of manuscripts available in comparison to the Greek classics. For instance, there are only 7 extant manuscripts of Plato; 8 of Thucydides and Suetonius each; and 10 from Caesar. There are a whopping 20 manuscripts available of Tacitus. However, did you know that there are over 2,400 extant manuscripts of the New Testament?

You can trust the Bible. Let faith arise in your heart. Keep paying attention to the lamp shining in a dark place.

Is Salvation a Fixed Invitation List?

> *2 Peter 3:8, 9, 15*
>
> *Dear friends, don't forget that for the Lord one day is the same as a thousand years, and a thousand years is the same as one day. The Lord isn't slow about keeping his promises, as some people think he is. In fact, God is patient, because he wants everyone to turn from sin and no one to be lost...Don't forget that the Lord is patient because he wants people to be saved. This is also what our dear friend Paul said when he wrote you with the wisdom that God had given him.*

"God is patient." Why? "[It's] because he wants everyone to turn from sin and no one to be lost." This statement has implications upon theology. Is salvation a matter of predestination, that is to say, predetermined, fixed by our Maker? Or, does the free will enter into the matter? Does each living individual choose whether they will accept salvation or not?

It is best to let the text speak for itself from a contextual standpoint. The writer is never intending to embed code. He wants his reader to grasp what is said. And here, it could not be any more clear. God wants everyone to be saved. He doesn't want one person to be lost. Not one! By implication when someone is lost, that is outside of the will of God.

God is patient. Patience is incompatible with predestination. What possible purpose could the discipline of patience serve upon a fixed invitation list? The text has told us in verse 8, that God is outside the scope of time. A thousand years or a day; a day or a thousand years, it matters not to him. So, this patience Peter speaks of is not solely about waiting long enough. It's also about great patience morally. God, in his mercy, gives us ample opportunity.

If more time can translate to more salvations, this is incompatible with a fixed invitation list. Reformed theology necessarily requires a wrap-up to any time table. Why? It is because at the time when the last designated, predetermined salvation occurs, no more human history would be necessary. This is simply a given. When the last person is saved, human history is no longer necessary beyond that point. God is sending every person to hell beyond that point. There is no way around this. Every single day beyond this point that God allows the globe to keep spinning, and babies to be born, he is populating hell more and more. This is not compatible with a beneficent God. The very fact that God is willing to allow more time, so that more may be saved, shows the futility of the concept of predestination. If God's time table can be floating, or adjusted, as Peter is suggesting, it shows that God allows humanity to choose salvation. That is to say, his patience is specifically "because he wants everyone to turn from sin and no one to be lost." Verse 15 says, "The Lord is patient because he wants people to be saved." And then Peter concludes by claiming an endorsement by the apostle Paul. He and Paul believed the same way. That's what he is saying. This has remarkable implications upon Romans 9:13, "Jacob I loved; but Esau I hated."

Disappearing Trick

> 1 John 2:17
>
> *The world and the desires it causes are disappearing. But if we obey God, we will live forever.*

How often have I wished that the wrong desires of this life would simply disappear! They do not: they stay. However, "Live by the Spirit and you will not gratify the desires of the sinful nature" (Gal 5:16). There will come a time when our desires will not be a by-product of the sinful world we live in. All temptations will do a disappearing trick. How wonderful will eternity be! It must be amazing to only want what's right, for the first impulse to be purity, for there to be no inclination toward evil, for there to be no cravings to curb - that will be heaven.

God's Kids and the Devil's Kids

> 1 John 3:10
>
> *You can tell God's children from the devil's children, because those who belong to the devil refuse to do right or to love each other.*

There are definitive characteristics of children to their parents. My two boys each have a tiny, little distinguishing pointed bump on their right ears, just like their Dad, and just like their grandfather did.

Two telltale signs mark the children of God and the children of Satan. God's kids do what is right and love one another. Remember Jesus' words to his disciples? "If you love each other, everyone will know that you are my disciples" (John 13:35).

Bear in mind, the devil's kids refuse to do what is right, and refuse to love one another.

Jesus warns, "The thief comes only to steal and kill and destroy; but I have come that they may have life, and have it to the full" (John 10:10).

In this world there are God's kids and the devil's kids. Either way, you bear a striking resemblance to your Daddy.

A Loving Father and a Willing Son

> 1 John 4:10
>
> *Real love isn't our love for God, but his love for us. God sent his Son to be the sacrifice by which our sins are forgiven.*

We avoid discussion of the heavenly Father's involvement in Jesus' death on the cross. It feels as though we are entering discussion on the violation of some trust. It's okay in our minds to think of Jesus initiating the sacrifice because it was his life to give. But what kind of a father allows, what's more, conceives of the death of his own son? That lurking thought might rattle around and clink inside the depths of our minds; but we wouldn't verbalize it. In fact, you are nervous that I even bring up. I mean we are okay with "For God so loved the world"; but "that he gave his only Son?" (John 3:16) Do we really allow our minds to go there?

One thing is certain, there is such profound purity to divine love that we cannot even begin to ascertain its splendor. God, and God alone, can know the mastery of the plan. Human intellect dumbs down. The members of the godhead - Father, Son, and Holy Spirit had council that we are not privy to. We may not ever know.

This doesn't keep us from trying to figure it out though. There is, in theology, a study on the atonement, which is the means by which God makes us acceptable. We are consecrated by the cross of Jesus. The death of Jesus on the cross coincided with the Day of Atonement, an annual event in which the Jewish high priest would offer sacrifices for the forgiveness of sins of the people of Israel. Atonement has a fortunate deflection in English, we may think of what Jesus did as at-one-ment because he has redeemed us.

There are several prominent theories on how this happened. They have been promulgated by thinking minds through the centuries. They are known as Atonement Theories. The Ransom Theory (sometimes called Bargain Theory or Classical Theory) was the belief of the Church for the first thousand years of her history. It was based on Mark 10:45, "For the Son of Man did not come to be served, but to serve, and to give his life as a ransom for many." One of the early church fathers, Origen, gave a written explanation. Adam and Eve's disobedience caused God to abandon humanity. The devil exerted control over them at this point. God had to do something so he agreed upon a payment with Satan. The ransom was paid when Jesus died on the cross. Even though the devil kept his end of the deal, in the end God tricked the devil because Jesus rose from the dead. Satan had it coming to him because of all his conniving and lying. But this theory makes God the Father seem very deceptive. The Satisfaction Theory (or Debt Theory) was put forth by Saint Anselm in the eleventh century. Humankind owes a debt to God. God has too much pride to simply forgive the debt, and there is a need for universal justice. So Jesus volunteers to pay it by suffering on the cross. The imagery often associated with this theory is the sacrificial lamb slain from the creation of the world (Rev 13:8, NIV). But a major drawback of this theory is that it resembles pagan religions in their attempt to appease an angry god by offering human sacrifice. That doesn't seem to capture the love of the Father very well. In medieval times Peter Abelard devised the Moral Exemplar Theory (aka Moral Influence Theory). Jesus gave the perfect example for us of how to live a moral life. We're supposed to follow his demonstration. Only one problem. He's been gone two thousand years and we still haven't figured out how to be moral. And if his example of morality was all that was needed, why did he have to die?

Another model is the <u>Penal Substitution Theory</u>. The idea is that Jesus absorbed all the punishment that we deserved. God wasn't willing to simply forgive outright, so he accepted a substitute. Jesus was the scapegoat of Old Testament law, punished for the sins of others. This theory is ardently upheld by 5-point Calvinist, and most protestants post reformation. The reformers of the 1500s saw hints of substitution embedded in the writings of Paul. However, taken to an extreme, God the Father comes off looking like a penitentiary warden. *I'm ticked and heads are gonna' roll.* The <u>Governmental Theory</u> is similar in that God is demanding punishment be carried out. Since he is the governor of all life he spares humanity and punishes his Son instead. A weakness of this theory is that the cross of Christ is merely a demonstration of what God could have done to us. He would've been completely justified in doing so. However, many people have lived on earth without ever hearing the name Jesus. This would mean they didn't know of the demonstration and couldn't alter behavior. The youngest proposal is the <u>Christus Victor Theory</u>, named after the book of that name in 1931 by Gustaf Aulen. Christus Victor simply means Christ the Victor. Jesus initiated the defeat of the enemy himself. Instead of God the Father paying a ransom Jesus takes on the enemy directly in a no-holds-barred, battle-royal. Jesus defeats the devil and the grave. He is the victor. Aulen claimed the earliest Church believed this way and most Eastern Orthodox Christians adhere to this theory to this day.

So which one is right? Um, yes. Okay, I lean strongly toward a substitution theory. However, I hasten to say, God the Father loves his Son, and God the Father loves humanity. In many respects each of the theories has an element of truth. Jesus' life is a remarkable *example*; and his death on the cross is a perfect *demonstration* of what we deserve. Jesus is the absolute *substitution* that *satisfies* righteousness. A great *ransom* was paid by Christ who is the *victor*! Some of the ways of God must be relegated to mystery. At base it is a loving Father and a willing Son. The cross broke the Savior and at the same time broke the heart of a loving Father because you and I were *meant* to be *at one* with him.

Gnostic Know-It-Alls

2 John 1:7

Many liars have gone out into the world. These deceitful liars are saying that Jesus Christ did not have a truly human body. But they are liars and the enemies of Christ.

One of the most serious threats to the early Church was a loosely connected, but seriously committed contingent of misguided souls that went under the banner of Gnosticism. They were not contracted, card-carrying members as such. It might be hard to nail them down on one agreed upon statement of beliefs. And there is difference of opinion about when they began and when their influence faded. Most feel they emerged about 150 years before the time of Christ. They were certainly a strong influence at the end of the first century of Christianity.

John spent much of his written ministry confronting Gnosticism. "In the beginning was the one who is called the Word. The Word was with God and was truly God...The Word became a human being and lived here with us. We saw his true glory, the glory of the only Son of the Father." (John 1:1, 14) "The Word that gives life was from the beginning, and this is the one our message is about. Our ears have heard, our own eyes have seen, and our hands touched this Word." (1 John 1:1) What John wants to emphasize is that it is crucial for us to understand Jesus had a real, physical body that could be touched, and could feel, and suffered death for our sins. He experienced life from our point of view.

Here's what we know. Gnosticism, from which we get our word knowledge, claimed a superior level of learning and understanding. John used the word "knowledge" 13 times in 1 John. They taught that Christ did not have a physical body. All matter is evil. Only spirit can be holy. Therefore they would say Christ is mind not matter. The fallacy is that Jesus didn't have a real body, which led to the teaching that he didn't die, and he didn't rise from the dead. Some of these false teachers, the elite, felt they were able to ascend above the ordinary. The Gnostic Know-It-Alls! Salvation was attained by being brilliant not by being repentant and faithful. You can see how dangerous it was. This is an absolute mockery of everything holy. There are elements of New Age doctrine interlaced in ancient Gnosticism. There is nothing new about New Age.

There are intellectuals in our day who will say Christ didn't rise from the dead, only swooned and then recovered. Or, the disciples were part of a conspiracy to hide his body in another tomb and only pretend he rose from the dead. They are part and parcel with an enemy who wants nothing more than to destroy the Church. The apostle Paul was adamant if Christ didn't rise from the dead we are all wasting our time (1 Cor 15:2). Jesus' resurrection is the crux of our faith.

Don't stand for clever deception, John calls it a lie. Avoid those who detract from the holy Scriptures, however subtle the attempt. John names them enemies.

One of the names for Jesus is Immanuel. It means "God with us." Jesus was born as a baby, a real baby. He *did* experience life from our point of view. He felt the whips, rods, nails and thorns. He died, really died. He rose, really rose from the dead. Jesus is Lord of all.

Exercise Inside and Out

> 3 John 1:2
>
> *Dear friend, and I pray that all goes well for you. I hope that you are as strong in body, as I know you are in spirit.*

The verse is often used to promote the idea of prosperity. The more popular rendering has it this way: "Beloved, I pray that you may prosper in all things and be in good health, just as your soul prospers" (NKJV). However, a sampling sweep of interpretations shows most translations place more emphasis on the physical well-being aspect. This verse couples well with 1 Timothy 4:8 which says, "While physical training has some value, training in holy living is useful for everything. It has promise for this life now and the life to come." It is often used to bolster spirituality. I've heard individuals say, "See, spiritual training is so much more important than physical training." Well, of course I agree. But I'm drawn to the holistic blend of physicality with spirituality. 3 John 2 and 1 Timothy 4:8 work in conjunction with each other. Both demonstrate the high priority of taking care of ourselves inside and out.

Jester in the Holy Court

> Jude 17, 18
>
> *My dear friends, remember the warning you were given by the apostles of our Lord Jesus Christ. They told you that near the end of time, selfish and godless people would start making fun of God.*

Sam Kinison was the son of Pentecostal preachers. He was himself a Pentecostal evangelist. After a failed marriage he left the ministry and walked away from his Christian walk entirely. He became an overnight sensation as a comedian precisely because of his irreverent mocking of Christians. He even went so far as to make fun of Jesus hanging on the cross in a bit laced with profanity. His premature death caused speculation from many individuals who suggested judgment from God.

In Washington DC, March of this year, at the Reason Rally, comedian Eddie Izzard, exclaimed, "God, if you're there, we're here in Washington, come down now. If you're there this is a pretty good time to show up. I'm sure folks here would love it." Izzard, an atheist, then blurted out, "He never comes down." In his hour on stage he mocked God, the Bible, and religion. It was all gags and grins for the crowd of 8 to 10 thousand people who stood on the National Mall in a driving rain applauding the rant.

Bill Maher, an atheist talk show host and comic, tweeted a very sacrilegious message after the Denver Broncos lost in the playoffs this last season. Tim Tebow's magical run finally came to an end. In the tweet Jesus was ridiculed and Satan was said to be Tebowing. Maher chose the filthiest verbiage available to describe how Jesus had mistreated Tebow. He said Jesus had chosen, Christmas Eve of all things, to - insert euphemism - Tebow. The only reason Maher would attack quarterback Tim Tebow is because of his outspoken faith in Christ. There is no other reason. In this regard Maher is not very innovative. Maher's 2008 comedic documentary called *Religulous*, combining the words religion and ridiculous, mocks organized religion. Agnostics from his own viewpoint have ridiculed his dishonest and hateful techniques of film splicing out of context, and not disclosing his purposes to his interviewees. Amanda Lorber, an agnostic said, "You would have to be in love with Bill Maher not to despise him by the end of the film."[xxviii]

Not all funny people have lowered themselves. Comics such as Don Tersigni and Jim Labrioli should be commended for their wholesome approach to humor. They are persons of faith. They follow in the tradition of Bill Cosby who refused to resort to trash humor or shock humor just for a laugh. This just shows lack of effort and creativity. But the trend in schtick to spout obscenity toward Christ and his people is alarming. According to the words of the apostles it is indicative of the climate that will be prevalent at the end of time. I would not want to be a jester in his holy court.

The Scriptures speak of the fear of Isaac. It is a statement of the respect due Almighty God. Isaac's name means "he laughs." His parents Abraham and Sarah laughed when they heard he would be born. Sarah tried to hide her unbelieving laugh, but it wasn't hidden from God. Abraham, however, had nothing to hide. It's just crazy to have a baby when you're that old. Thomas R. Yoder Neufeld ends his theology, *Recovering Jesus*, with the words, "God finally has the last laugh over injustice and oppression, over sin, and even over death."[xxix] In the end God laughs loudest and longest. "The one enthroned in heaven laughs" (Ps 2:4).

Attitude

Jude 1:20

Dear friends, keep building on the foundation of your most holy faith, as the Holy Spirit helps you to pray.

On the TV Sitcom, Full House, the youngest character was a little girl named Michele. She would always say, "You got a bad attitude, *Mistur!*"

Ralph Williams was a pioneer missionary who took the gospel to El Salvador. He would hike up and down the mountains and thought nothing of hiking 15, 20 or even 25 miles. He had amazing miracles take place in his ministry. He was very candid and talked about a time when he had a bad attitude. He had preached a series of meetings all week long and no one got saved. He was pretty upset about that. And so, Sunday night he just moped around and sulked. He was just so down. Monday morning he was supposed to leave on a truck to go back home. But the truck didn't show up. They said it would be there around noontime. But by noon it still wasn't there. He should come back at 6:00 p.m. When he came back there was still no truck. It was broken down and he would have to come back the next day to catch a different one. The people of the little, small village said, "Say, since you're here anyway, why don't we have church one more night?" Ralph told the local pastor he didn't want to go. The pastor coaxed him with food and hot coffee and said, "C'mon, you don't even have to preach. Please just come. Just sit on the platform behind me." He decided he would go. In the service the pastor said, "Could you read a Scripture for us?" Well, how could he turn him down? So, he stood up to read a Scripture. As he began to read, powerful anointing came upon him. He began to preach. And that night, five people got saved! He went home and repented of his bad attitude.

Don't have a bad attitude *Mistur!*

7

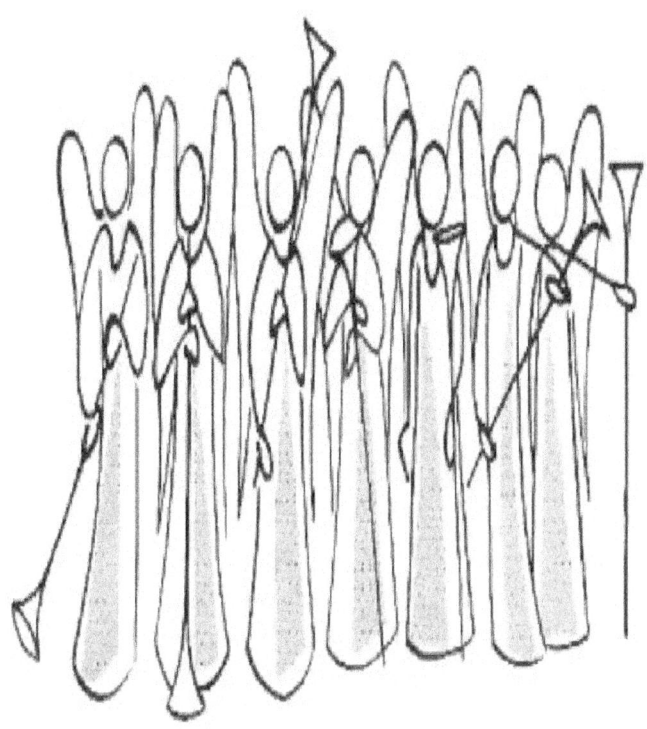

Apocalyptic Assurance

GROUP 7: APOCALYPTIC ASSURANCE

Finiteness Hits a Wall

Ezekiel 1:15-17

I then noticed that on the ground beside each of the four living creatures was a wheel, shining like chrysolite. Each wheel was exactly the same and had a second wheel that cut through the middle of it, so that they could move in any direction without turning.

Eric Altschuler, neuroscientist from the University of California at San Diego, has made some spectacular claims about Bible characters. In 2001 he stated that Samson was a sufferer of antisocial personality disorder. Well, I guess so. I mean, foxes running through the neighbor's field with tails tied together and set on fire; city gates pulled out of their moorings so that the whole community is vulnerable; the temple where the entire city gathered to worship, torn down - yeah, I would say Samson was a little awkward socially. Pardon my drippy sarcasm. And then in 2006, Altschuler revealed his belief that Ezekiel experienced temporal lobe epilepsy. Why? Because he had fainting spells, was super religious, wrote compulsively and had times of not being able to speak. So his visions may have been the dreamy state or aura of a partial seizure. As one whose family has dealt with the challenges of epilepsy may I say in the most sensitive tone possible, "Give me a break!"

Some say Ezekiel was seeing a UFO. Theologians such as Frank E. Carlisle, John Milton, and Dr. Geza Bermes have written of their belief that Ezekiel was encountering some type of manned spacecraft. For each of these individuals, including Altschuler, I doubt their accuracy; though I don't doubt their sincerity. And they are welcomed to doubt me in kind.

What is Ezekiel seeing? Is this a design on God himself? But they are called "creatures" which marks them as created by him. What are these creatures and wheels? A wheel within a wheel. We can't grasp that. Really can't wrap our minds around it. The Contemporary English Version makes a point of mentioning the wheels are identical in dimension. In fact, it delineates it this way, "Each wheel was exactly the same size and had a second wheel cut through the center of it." Even if we try to envision something along the lines of the epic cycles in the movie *Tron*, for instance, we can animate it; but we can't engineer it. Whether this is God's very presence, or his holy beings who carry out his assignments, or if it actually is a description of his heavenly chariot, one thing is certain - this is God's superior intelligence and strength on full display. So let's play with the possibilities a bit.

Two critical criteria for existence are motion and perception. The wheels speak of his movement. He moves in any direction. There is no place he can't move. There is no place he can't maneuver. There is no place he can get stuck. The circular design gives him unlimited direction. Straight, diagonal, or any whim he wills to go. Is there ever a whim with God? However, the movement is not only in a sense of flat direction, that is but one dimension. Keep going. Up, down, frontwards, backwards, just imagine the endless combinations of movements. And here's another point, is it correct to assume there is a reverse gear for God? I mean, eyes all around. Frontward is backward, up is down, right is left, and so forth. We are given the description of the four faces. Since one of them is a human face we assume this to be the front; but in John's companion description in the Revelation, the human face is listed third (Rev 7:11). The emphasis is not on hierarchy or superiority, but rather upon perfect unity and clarity of purpose. This seems to indicate limitless motion and limitless perception. God told Moses he would hide him in a crag, a rock cutout, so that he could pass by. Moses was allowed to see his back as he was leaving. Both Moses and Ezekiel understand there is no sneaking up on God. Perception? He sees in every direction all at the same time. Nothing escapes his attention. Ever! Try to imagine it.

By the descriptors we might think "gory" initially, covered with eyes, multiple faces; but Ezekiel is astounded by the beauty. It is not gory, it is "glory." We balk because we can only think in human terms. This imagery describes God's infinite splendor. Our finite intelligence doesn't allow it to process. Wheels encircling wheels, covered all over with eyes? We hit a wall. But quite literally, Jesus did not hit a wall post-resurrection. He walked right through the wall (John 20:26). Our transformed bodies in eternity will necessarily be a marriage of physical and spiritual. We know that we will recognize one another. But we will also be fluid, spatial but somehow not dense. Only God could dream it up. Heaven will be wonderful beyond words.

Generational Goodness

> *Ezekiel 18:20*
>
> *Only those who sin will be put to death. Children won't suffer for the sins of their parents, and parents won't suffer for the sins of*

> *their children. Good people will be rewarded for what they do, and evil people will be punished for what they do.*

There is a popular teaching that the sins of the fathers are handed down to the next generation, and continue unabated unless someone breaks the chain. I do not believe in generational curses, as such. It is informative that, here, we have a verse under the Old Testament covenant, housed in the immediate context of three generations of one family. God says if Grandpa is faithful he will be rewarded. If Dad is evil he will be judged. But if Son is faithful he will be rewarded. He says emphatically, each one will stand on their own merit. Jesus may have had this passage in mind when, in the New Testament, he rebutted the popular notion that sins are handed down. This is in the setting of a popular proverb, Ezekiel 18:2, "Sour grapes eaten by parents leave a sour taste in the mouths of the children." If not chapter 18, Jesus may have been thinking of a similar, companion verse, Ezekiel 16:44. He mocked the concept of generational curses as out of touch with truth.

Here is what I believe about the matter. I think the devil is a real enemy who wants nothing more than to destroy the servants of God, and keep the lost ones oppressed. He would be foolish not to tempt the children with the same things that worked on the parents. If grandfather was an alcoholic, and mother was an alcoholic, why not try to lure son with booze? If grandmother was passive-aggressive, and father was passive-aggressive, just try to see if daughter could become manipulative. What does he have to lose? I have known of situations where struggles and strangleholds stretched out over multiple generations in the same family. And to be certain, there have been instances involving demonic activity. There is a trend to name spirits by the way they behave - e.g., a spirit of lust, a spirit of suicide, or a Jezebel spirit. I don't believe this is accurate. It is important for us to understand, an evil spirit will behave in any way it needs to accomplish its objective which is to draw persons away from Christ.

However, it is also important, supremely important, for us to understand. Any individual may be free, no matter what their cultural background, regardless of pedigree, race or creed. We can rely on his generational goodness. "All who call out to the Lord will be saved" (Rom 10:13).

Pause to pray for someone you have written off as an impossibility. "With man this is impossible, but not with God; all things are possible with God" (Mark 10:27, NIV).

It's God's Fault

Ezekiel 33:18

The LORD said: Ezekiel, son of man, the people of Israel are complaining that the punishment for their sins is more than they can stand. They have lost all hope for survival, and they blame me.

Ezekiel, in a role reversal, is the consoler, as God bends his ear. "My people complain about their punishment. They don't have any hope, and they're pointing their fingers at me!"

Why does God always get blamed? The utter ridiculousness of it all! God has patiently reached out to his chosen ones. He has called out through his prophets over and over again. Hundreds of years they resisted and drifted. They have fallen into blatant idolatry. And now that judgment comes, how do they respond, "Why has God forsaken us? It's more than we can bear!"

I did a funeral once for a twenty-one year old, young man. He crashed his car killing himself and his girlfriend, after the two of them had been boozing it up all night at a party. This had been so typical of their lifestyle choices. They left behind an infant son. I will never forget the family standing at the casket, weeping hysterically, deep guttural sobs, and profound emotional outcries. One, his sister, raised her tearful face upward and declared, "Why? Why God? Why did you do this?"

But God didn't choose alcohol that night. And God certainly didn't choose for him to get behind the wheel. I was deeply saddened by the loss, as were they. But I was torn. I have dear friends whose son was killed by a drunk driver. I know their pain. I was sad that this young man and his girlfriend died tragically, and much too early. But I was thankful they didn't cause the death of an innocent victim that night.

It is the tendency of humanity to say it's God's fault when things don't go well. We often forget to connect consequences directly to actions. You live today in the land of consequences for decisions you have made in the past.

The book of the Revelation is replete with examples showing that the more difficult the end-time events become, the more angry will be the response of humanity in its bitter resentment toward God.

Don't make God the fall guy. Cry out to him in confession, not in accusation.

Dem Dry Bones

> *Ezekiel 37:3-6*
>
> *He said, "Ezekiel, son of man, can these bones come back to life?" I replied, "LORD God, only you can answer that." He then told me to say: Dry bones, listen to what the LORD is saying to you, "I, the LORD God, will put breath in you, and once again you will live. I will wrap you with muscles and skin and breathe life into you. Then you will know that I am the LORD."*

"Ezekiel, son of man, can these bones come back to life?" Ezekiel's response? "Lord God, only you can answer that." Dead bones rattle together, sinews form, muscles wrap around, skin comes on, breath enters - only God can do this.

I will leave the implications of Ezekiel 37 to the prophecy prognosticators. For a moment leave the prediction booth, and simply appreciate God's holistic love of life.

It is a resurrection that mimics the very creation. Breath enters lifeless beings. The only difference? In the creation account God breathes into dirt. In this re-creation account, God does not choose to start all over again with more dust. He re-purposes broken humanity, specifically, his broken, chosen people, Israel. God takes the scrap pieces and crafts a new, resurrected, warring army. The purpose and timing of this army is open to speculation. God is the preeminent power over all matter. He will do the same with all the honorable dead who are in Christ. His followers have faced innumerable cultural practices as they have gone the way of all the earth historically. Some have been placed six feet under the ground. Others have been entombed. Some have been burned at the stake, drowned in the ocean, stacked in mass graves outside of concentration camps, or burned in fires that were honorable as well as dishonorable. It matters not that decay has set in, that is inevitable. When God's trumpet-voice speaks, breath will enter his loved ones cross generationally and simultaneously - the same breath that hovered at creation; the same breath that Jesus breathed upon his disciples in the upper room; the same breath that filled believers as a violent wind on the Day of Pentecost; the same breath that will whistle through the canyon into a valley of dry bones. God does not show affinity to a culture of death. He values and loves life.

Dem bones, dem bones, dem dry bones, oh hear the word of the Lord.

Gog Me with a Span

Ezekiel 38:17, 18

The Lord said to Gog: Long ago, I had my prophets warn the people of Israel that someday I would send an enemy to attack them. You, Gog, are that enemy, and that day is coming. When you invade Israel, I will become furious.

"You, Gog, are that enemy, and that day is coming." *Gog, you're it. It's just a matter of time.*

God will use his time tested ancient war strategy to lure Gog in. He even compares them to a fish on a hook. They can't resist his bait. Like sharks that have smelled blood, they will be ready for a feeding frenzy.

Let's see, where have we read this before, Israel luring its enemy in? Oh, yes, when the Israelites defeated the city of Ai they used this kind of diversionary tactic to so set an ambush. Joshua 8:3-22 records the brilliance of the war general, Joshua, and how they tricked the enemy into defeat. They took the city, set it on fire, and won the second of many victories in the Promised Land.

Later in Israel's history the same method was used. When the tribe of Benjamin had swelled and rebelled, it became a threat to the welfare of the other eleven tribes. Their immorality and brutality was so arrogant. It had to be dealt with. How did they defeat Benjamin? The Israelites allowed them to think they were weak. They lured them away from their city. However, a contingent of Israelites swept in behind the fighting and set the city on fire. When the smoke arose it was a signal to the rest of the Israelites to turn and attack. It was a terrific ambush. Read about it in Judges 20:29-46.

It is popular to identify the cities of Ezekiel 38 and 39 with modern Russia. However, any serious study should consider the linguistics involved. Though vowels might change, consonants typically stay the same through the years. And the order of letters in the names almost always stays the same. It is wrong to read modern city names into a biblical context, forcing them anachronistically. In 1985 Fred G. Zaspel wrote an excellent paper[xxx] on the topic that is still valuable in the wake of Russia's demotion and the emergence of the Commonwealth of Independent States. Whether Gog and Magog represents Russia remains to be seen. One things is certain. God will have his say. His word will be fulfilled. All it takes is a span of time. God says, "Gog me with a span." Okay, that was a horrible pun, really bad.

Israel is fond of using diversionary tactics. If world powers were astute they would read the Bible. They could know this stuff. Even if they refused to believe it they would be informed. But let's face it. People don't read the Bible. I mean, really read it. The fact that you've made it this far in this devotional puts you in rare air. People give credence to the Bible. They patronize the Bible. But to read it, I mean to read it purposefully, it just doesn't happen that often, particularly among the busy world leaders. So, ironically, God is able to embed his end-time strategy, right in plain sight.

The Dead Sea Lives

Ezekiel 47:8, 9

The man said: This water flows eastward to the Jordan River valley and empties into the Dead Sea, where it turns the salt water into fresh water. Wherever this water flows, there will be all kinds of animals and fish, because it will bring life and fresh water to the Dead Sea.

The Dead Sea Lives. Can you just envision the newspaper headline! Wait, will there be any newspapers left? Can you just envision the Blog headline! The Dead Sea lives. This has never happened historically. Those who wish to relegate Ezekiel's writing to strictly a Second Temple era must explain this. For the above verse is part and parcel of chapter 48. The two run as fluidly together as does the water of this temple stream being spoken of. And those who wish to relegate Ezekiel 48, my next post, to allegory must explain the specificity of the geography.

The Dead Sea is not a sea at all, but a saltwater lake. Since it has 33% salt, buoyancy is automatic, you float. There are healing properties in the Dead Sea salt. It has been used to treat acne, psoriasis, hives, cellulite, dry skin, dandruff, stress and muscle aches. Egyptians used mud from the Dead Sea in mummification. Its shores are the lowest point of elevation on planet earth. Water flows into it, but does not flow out. So, animal life and plant life do not survive there. But in Ezekiel's vision of the glorious age, the Dead Sea will be a sanctuary for all kinds of animal life, fish life, and plant life.

The most important archaeological discovery, ever, in the history of biblical studies, was found at the caves of the Dead Sea. The Dead Sea Scrolls are an important confirmation of the accuracy and authenticity of the holy Scriptures. At the wrap-up of time as we know it, the Dead Sea will be a central component of the topography. This stream is not just flowing, but it seems to me it is exponential and teeming. In other words, if one million gallons flowed from one point to another, it would still be a million gallons. However, this living water is not just pooling up, it is bubbling with expansive life-giving power. Where the river flows everything lives and is green, and fruitful and vegetative. Animal life and fish life, alike, inhabit the region now. Quite literally, the Living Water will bring nourishment and nutrients to everyone and everything in the region, proving that Christ not only resurrects humans, but redeems all of nature as well.

Divided Land, Unified Hearts

Ezekiel 48:29

That's how the land of Israel will be divided among the twelve tribes. I, the LORD God, have spoken.

In the first portion of Ezekiel 48, there is an allotment of land parcels for the twelve tribes of Israel. The land is now redistributed into parallel areas with each tribe having shoreline along the Mediterranean Sea. The tribes stack one another from north to south. However, in the last half of the chapter, another tribe list is given for the names of the city gates of New Jerusalem.

A careful reading shows something very interesting about the two tribe lists. In the latter list, Joseph has replaced Manasseh and Ephraim; whereas, in the former list, Levi is not listed as one of the tribes, properly, because they are the priestly tribe occupying the special land around the temple in the center area. But Levi *is* listed as a tribe in the second list. Now, there are various compilations of tribe lists for Israel in the Bible. It is commonly understood that the lists are fluid, more representative, than specific; so that it isn't as important to have the same twelve names consistently. Some see twenty different lists of the tribes in the Bible. But there is a contingent of scholarship that believes the specific selection of the tribes is intentional in each instance. So, both lists in Ezekiel 48 name twelve tribes, but they have different names for the tribes. Why? They are in the same passage, so obviously it's on purpose.

There are a lot of different theories, but the best one I have read is by Harold Brodsky. He is a Bible scholar and also an Associate Professor of Geography at the University of Maryland. He has written extensively about the Utopian Map in Israel. His view may be summed up this way. Ephraim and Manasseh are the two sons of Joseph. Usually we read of them as separate tribes, with Manasseh being divided in half. He says that according to 19th century biblical exegete, R. Meir Leibush, Ephraim and Manasseh are always called tribes for political purposes, and Levi is not. But when it comes to matters of temple worship, Levi is reckoned as a tribe. In that case Ephraim and Manasseh are paired under the bracket of Joseph. In this way, there are always twelve tribes.

Seen this way, Ezekiel 48 gives a perfect symmetry of policy and spirituality. There are six tribes above the temple, and six beneath. They are balanced perfectly with the tribes descended from Rachel and Leah being closest to the temple, and the tribes descended from Bilhah and Zilpah being furthest out. However, in terms of political implications, Levi switches roles to priests, Joseph morphs to two tribes of Manasseh and Ephraim, and now you have seven tribes north of the city with five beneath. Divided land, unified hearts.

In America we have a balanced government that embodies Isaiah 33:22, "The Lord is our judge, and our ruler; The Lord is our king, and he will keep us safe." This is mimicked by the judicial branch, the legislative branch, and the executive branch. It is comforting to know the New Jerusalem has a balanced system of checks and balances too. He will keep us safe.

Watch Out for the Freshman Fifteen

> *Daniel 1:14-17*
>
> *The guard agreed to do what Daniel had asked. Ten days later, Daniel and his friends looked healthier and better than the young men who had been served food from the royal palace. After this, the guard let them eat vegetables instead of the rich food and wine. God made the four young men smart and wise. They read a lot of books and became well educated. Daniel could also tell the meaning of dreams and visions.*

Our son Zakary began college this year. One of the last things his brother, Nic, told him was a piece of advice, "Remember the Freshman Fifteen." A couple of days ago we were Skyping with Zak and he mentioned a subtle change in his diet since he's been away from home. "They have Blue Bell ice cream in the cafeteria. I eat it every night." Nic laughed and exclaimed, "I told you, Zak. Watch out for the Freshman Fifteen." The truth is Zak is blessed in his frame. Fifteen pounds wouldn't hurt him at all.

The four young, stellar Hebrews were banished with the other Jews to Babylon. They were selected to go into elite training to serve in the royal court. No doubt, one of the sublime tranquilizers intent on reprogramming their psyches was their diet. This, along with a sophisticated education, and plush living quarters in the palace, was intentional. It was a method of making them forget their misery, and had a way of forging their commitment and loyalty. The Babylonians had mastered the art of persuasion. It would be easy for Daniel to do as the others and numb his pain with comfort food. But to do so would mean violating a sacred trust. He had never eaten non-kosher foods. And he would not start now. He and the other three were not vegetarians. They enjoyed the wonderful lamb of the Passover meal. But for a season they endured a training within the training. God blessed their loyal faith and promoted them to levels of leadership they had not envisioned. These staid youths were the rescuers of the redemption strategy.

In the novel *Uncle Tom's Cabin* there was a slave named Adolph. He had been duped into believing he was a free man because he borrowed his master's vest, and lived the life of refinement in the manicured properties of Augustine St. Clare. But Tom would rather be a free man and poor than a wealthy slave. "But you, keep your head in all situations, endure hardship, do the work of an evangelist, discharge all the duties of your ministry" (2 Tim 4:5).

A Word on Hostile Environments

Daniel 2:10, 11

His advisors explained, "Your Majesty, you are demanding the impossible! No king, not even the most famous and powerful, has ever ordered his advisors, magicians, or wise men to do such a thing. It can't be done, except by the gods, and they don't live here on earth."

Daniel was in an environment that was increasingly hostile, a king that is troubled, and a cabinet that was frustrated and threatened. Nerves are frayed, and future success is uncertain. They've got a lot at stake. They have sunk everything into this identity. And now they feel stuck.

A steady, stable spirit will be able to speak volumes into a loud, chaotic climate. Strength of character, forged over time, grounded in principle, finds a ready, listening ear in times of consternation. Many people stammer in that moment, not finishing complete sentences, rattled by uncertainty, they forget how to connect the most basic subjects to verbs. It is true, singular nouns get linked with plural modifiers, and vice versa, and the voice trails off for lack of punch and phrases dangle uncompleted.

You are up to the task of bringing a sense of calm. Take a breath while you breathe a prayer. Finish the sentence in your mind. Speak calmly, slowly, and firmly. When you are certain you have resolution on a subject in your mind, be confident, don't waver. "If anyone speaks he should do it as one speaking the very words of God" (1 Pet 4:11, NIV). Lead on, great leader. You got this!

Determinant Resolve

Daniel 3:17, 18

The God we worship can save us from you and your flaming furnace. But even if he doesn't, we still won't worship your gods and the gold statue you have set up.

It is really a beautiful thing to see faithful people display determinant resolve. When the heart is fixed, and the mind is resolute, it is remarkable the capacity for resilience the human can show. The three young men were the very best the Hebrews had to offer. They are not unlike the Missionaries we send around the world. I have often been amazed to see the very best, most intellectual, overly gifted and anointed ones, called to abandon their homeland, take up stakes, and lead the charge into lands with unfamiliar foods, unfamiliar traditions, unfamiliar language, and unfamiliar culture. It reminds me of a great story of resolve.

E.P. Scott was a missionary to India. He had in his heart to reach heathen people in the interior subcontinent. In spite of his friends' warnings he ventured into very dangerous territory. After a journey of a few days he encountered a group of warriors. In an instant he found himself surrounded by savages who had their spears drawn, with several pointed right at his heart. It may have been purely reflexive, but he reached for his violin, vibrated out the tune "All Hail the Power of Jesus' Name," as he also sang with eyes closed. When he got to the part of the song that has the words, "Let every kindred, every tribe," he opened his eyes to find every spear lowered, and tears upon the cheeks of several warriors. This led to his evangelizing them for the next two years.[xxxi] Now that is determinant resolve.

Daniel's Deliverance

> *Daniel 6:10*
>
> *Daniel heard about the law, but when he returned home, he went upstairs and prayed in front of the window that faced Jerusalem. In the same way that he had always done, he knelt down in prayer three times a day, giving thanks to God.*

Daniel is hurled into a den of lions. It is the equivalent of a member of death row escorted to the electric chair. These are not purring, pussy cats. They are ferocious, hungry beasts ready to devour. Artists typically depict three lions lying at Daniel's feet; but there may have been as many as 150 mauling lions in this pit.

Before the incident with the lions ever happened, Daniel's resolve defined who he was. He showed great humility and respect. He was resolved to do what was right. He had a track record of faithfulness already. He was not a Johnny-come-lately. And verse 23 provides the explanation point. Daniel's faith rescued him.

We may draw end-time connotations from this apocalyptic book; although this portion is narrative and very practical. Truthfully, the devil roams about like a roaring lion, seeking for individuals to devour. "Discipline yourselves; keep alert. Like a roaring lion your adversary, the devil, prowls around looking for someone to devour" (1 Pet 5:8, NRSV). Peter is telling us to be vigilant and resolved, just like faithful Daniel of old.

Literal Lions and Reverie Rams

> *Daniel 9:3-5*
>
> *Then, to show my sorrow, I went without eating and dressed in sackcloth and sat in ashes. I confessed my sins and earnestly prayed to the LORD my God:*
>
> *Our Lord, you are a great and fearsome God, and you faithfully keep your agreement with those who love and obey you. But we have sinned terribly by rebelling against you and rejecting your laws and teachings.*

This is the giant of the faith, Daniel, we're talking about here. Ezekiel included him in his top three, along with Job and Noah (Ezek 14:14, 20). He is knowledgeable, intuitive, has been promoted and carries clout. An ancient Billy Graham of sorts, Daniel served as advisor to high-ranking government officials across multiple administrations. He saw visions and interpreted them. He was privy to God's panoramic view of the end. In every respect Daniel is exemplary, both in the eyes of his own Jewish people, and in the eyes of the nationals to whose nation he has been deported.

Let's learn from this humble dignitary. He read the Bible and interpreted it literally, when possible. This led him to the conclusion that the seventy years Jeremiah had prophesied about were coming to an end. He took Jeremiah at face value. Daniel understood the curses Moses pronounced for disobedience had happened. Moses' words were not metaphoric. He humbles himself with his people, including himself as a part of the problem. In confession he begins to pour out requests to God for their deliverance. Daniel moves beyond head knowledge to act upon his belief. He had literal lions and reverie rams, but these are everyday expectancies.

Much of Scripture is not to be taken literally. To be certain, there are dangers here. Poetry must be interpreted through a lens of hyperbole. Even narrative must be contextualized according to culture. Is there a dictum of Scripture you can take at face value today? Something you can act upon? For instance, "love one another," or "bear one another's burdens?" Would it violate anyone's exegetical stance to operate in forgiveness? Practice kindness today. Just notice who is shocked by it. Perhaps like Daniel, take time to make confession to God.

Crossing the Delaware

Daniel 10:18, 19

The angel touched me a second time, and said, "Don't be frightened! God thinks highly of you, and he intends this for your good. So be brave and strong." At this I regained my strength and replied, "Please speak, you have already made me feel much better."

It was Christmas Day 1776, and the American troops had endured several painful losses in battles. They were cold, sick, and tired. Words were spoken that made them feel much better. Before heading into battle that night, General George Washington had the troops sit on the banks of the Delaware River, and listen to someone read the works of a fellow soldier, Thomas Paine. "These are the times that try men's souls. The summer soldier and the sunshine patriot will, in this crisis, shrink from the service of their country; but he that stands it now, deserves the love and thanks of man and woman." This encouraged them to march into uncertainty. You see, Washington led his troops, that Christmas night, in a surprise attack against the Hessians. These were German soldiers the British had hired to fight for them.

The Hessians didn't have much respect for the American soldiers. They thought of the colonists as novices, untrained and predictable, not bold or daring. Washington's brilliance lay in the element of surprise. He knew the Hessians wouldn't expect an attack during the night, and especially at Christmas time. His men would cross the icy Delaware in the night and attack the unsuspecting enemy which had been holed-up in Trenton. The trickiest part involved maneuvering 18 cannons weighing 2,000 pounds each, onto and off a slippery ferry. Downstream Washington's two commanders, General James Ewing and Colonel John Cadwalader, could not break through the icy river. But Washington was able to break through. This was unnerving because it was already 4:00 a.m. by the time the army was across and ready for the nine mile march to Trenton. It would be daylight before they arrived. But with the heavy artillery now across the river, there was no turning back. They must march onward.

Washington told his troops, "Remember now what you are about to fight for." One of Washington's brave, young warriors was an eighteen-year-old Lieutenant named James Monroe who charged the Hessians' cannons and was badly wounded; but survived to become the fifth president of the United States. Within two hours of the battle's beginning, the Germans surrendered. It was a key turning point in the Revolutionary War.[xxxii]

Words can spur us toward excellence. Today, God's inspired Word might be illuminated to you. Words of knowledge may be sent your direction from other believers through the vocal gifts. He might just as easily allow your attentive ear to eavesdrop on encouraging radio broadcasts, or public conversations in hallways. Be open. Lord, "please speak, you have already made me feel much better."

Apocalyptic Endurance

> *Revelation 1:20*
>
> *I will explain the mystery of the seven stars that you saw at my right side and the seven gold lampstands. The seven stars are the angels of the seven churches, and the lampstands are the seven churches.*

I have a friend who says the church may not look like much when it gets there, but it will arrive safely to the other shore. Many people are fearful that the church is in jeopardy of becoming watered down in a postmodern culture. But notice that the seven churches in the Revelation are lampstands and will continue to support the spread of light. The church is resilient no matter the setting, because Jesus is building his church and "the gates of hell will not prevail against it" (Matt 16:18). There may be challenges for the contemporary church but the work will remain strong. "The Chinese character for signifying the idea of 'crisis' combines two other characters, the one for 'danger' and the other for 'opportunity.'"[xxxiii] There is risk involved in any worthwhile undertaking. Each of the seven churches in the Revelation is in modern-day Turkey. I can't imagine any more difficult field of ministry currently. In the first century they were strongholds of faith, but have become the breeding grounds for apocalyptic endurance.

Glorious Age

Revelation 2:7

If you have ears, listen to what the Spirit says to the churches. I will let everyone who wins the victory eat from the life-giving tree in God's wonderful garden.

This is the complete reversal of Adam's aching appetite. Now, we may eat freely from the Life Tree. Before, it had been guarded by cherubim with flaming swords to keep us safe from an eternal state of separation. Now we are invited to take of its fruit and sample. Eternal day, glorious age, time's end, climax of history. Great day of our liberation into the Eschaton!

Hocus Pocus, Help Us Focus

Revelation 3:17, 18

You claim to be rich and successful and to have everything you need. But you don't know how bad off you are. You are pitiful, poor, blind, and naked. Buy your gold from me. It has been refined in a fire, and it will make you rich. Buy white clothes from me. Wear them and you can cover up your shameful nakedness. Buy medicine for your eyes, so that you will be able to see.

The biblical city Laodicea is infamous for being neither hot nor cold, but lukewarm. Countless writers have commented on the implications. However, there is another powerful innuendo tucked in these verses.

Laodicea was known to have a school of medicine. One of their "medical" endeavors appears to have been a little sleight of hand, shyster, kind of *hocus pocus* called "Phrygian Powder." Yeah, they followed the teachings of Herophilos and combined all kinds of powders and compounds. Grant Osborne has written that they claimed to heal eye diseases.

Jesus says they are "blind." He instructs them to buy salve from him so they "will be able to see." In essence, *"C'mon, you think you can toss some magic powder in the air, Lebron-esk, and lay claim to eye-healing. Hey, you don't even realize you yourselves can't see."* Later with *hocus pocus*, if you want to be able see you need to adjust your focus.

"I always look to you, because you rescue me from every trap" (Ps 25:15).

A Hopeful Horn

> Revelation 4:1
>
> *After this, I looked and saw a door that opened into heaven. Then the voice that had spoken to me at first and that sounded like a trumpet said, "Come up here! I will show you what must happen next."*

This verse is one of the important speaking points on the rapture of the Church, especially within Pentecostal theology. There are differing opinions on the rapture of the Church. You will not read the word rapture in Scripture. The Latin word *raptus* is where it comes from. It means "caught up" or "snatched away." The event itself is described in 1 Thessalonians 4:16-18. The dead who have accepted Christ as Lord are resurrected first, and then the believers who are currently living are "caught up" with them to meet the Lord in the air. We will never be separated from the Lord again.

Those of us who take it to be speaking of a literal, physical rapture fall into mainly three categories of opinion as to when it will happen. There is pre-tribulation; mid-trib; or post-trib. My own belief in a pre-trib rapture speaks of it as an event that occurs *before* the horrors of the tribulation described in the Bible, the seven-year period in which all the fury of God breaks loose against sin and rebellion on planet earth. There are a number of reasons I believe Christians will be in heaven during the time of the wrath of the tribulation. The Bible describes an event called the Marriage Supper of the Lamb, a veritable wedding banquet that celebrates the bride of Christ united with the Lord. We will have to be there for this event. I believe it coincides with the tribulation on earth. If the alternate view is held, that it *follows* the tribulation, it would be the equivalent of God beating the bride to a bloody pulp, and then having her walk down the aisle. This is not consistent with godly character. God does not condone spousal abuse, nor does Christ image his bride in a bloody, stained gown (Eph 5:27). No, the Church will escape Jacob's wrath. The Jews will be on earth during the tribulation. They will be remarkably preserved in the physical land of Israel. Many Jews, scores and scores of them, will acknowledge *Yeshuah Ha-Mashiach*, Jesus Christ, as the anointed One, the living Lord.

The language of Revelation 4:1 mirrors the phrasing of 1 Thessalonians 4:16. In Thessalonians a trumpet blast triggers the event. In the Revelation John says a voice sounds like a trumpet blast. The voice trumps, "Come up here!" It is remarkably close to "caught up" language. It is interesting to note that in the Revelation, chapters 4 through 19 happen in heaven. Though events are described about earth, the locale is heaven. The throne room of God, where praise is incessant, serves as command central for all end-time events. God Almighty runs Air Traffic Control for the apocalypse. He oversees all war stratagems and tactical maneuvers. At the climactic moment in the final conquest, toward the end of chapter 19, Christ will mount his white horse and lead the armies of heaven to earth. This is the first time he touches the earth physically. At the rapture event he meets his bride in the air to escort her back to heaven, decidedly Jewish fashion. Here though, he sets his foot on Mount Olivet (Zech 14:4), an earthquake happens at that moment as he ushers in an entirely new age, a one-thousand year period known as the Millennial Reign of Christ, which gives way to eternity.

Pentecostal believers refer to the rapture as the blessed hope. The rapture is not a frightening event to be used as a scare tactic. It is a wonderful event. That's why Paul says, "Therefore, encourage one another with these words" (1 Thess 4:18, NIV). This trumpet alarms only the unprepared. For you and I who are watching and waiting, it is a hopeful horn.

A Tale of the Undoing of Death

> *Revelation 5:4, 5*
>
> *I cried hard because no one was found worthy to open the scroll or see inside it. Then one of the elders said to me, "Stop crying and look! The one who is called both the 'Lion from the Tribe of Judah' and 'King David's Great Descendant' has won the victory. He will open the book and its seven seals."*

Sin entered the world with cold chills of remorse and disregard. The demerit swept through the small, new humanity of two. They had shooed the gentle Lamb away from the stock of the Knowing Tree. In order to reach its high branches the aid of a helping Serpent was enlisted, and sampling its forbidden produce, the shutter of a rebellious wind ripped the pathetic shingling off our despot race leaving gaping holes in its wake. We are undone. An undertow of separation pulls relentlessly. Ripples of hate course over our drowning souls. Calamity hastens the death sting; still the wretched fingers stretch and reach.

One of the two great trees is sampled. We own a generic wisdom, a house-brand knowledge. We know good and evil. But it is a counterfeiter's treasure, a fool's gold. Father Adam and Mother Eve would feign grasp the branches of Everlasting Life had not the Good Gardner marked it off with the improvised barbed wire of a thorny Vine, his hand-crafted ring of briers. And shortly the wind, so immense, scorches, drives back, detaches and isolates. Like a mighty cataclysmic black hole sucking, the vortex of evil assails every resistance. We are sealed. Adam, your lips have moistened the envelope. Death is done. Only the dead can undo it. But, alas, only the living can do anything. The dead cannot do or undo. The dead cannot be or not be. The dead cannot live. Eve, you have sealed our fate. We are sealed.

Before us continually, the erect reminder, the verdict, stamped with the hot wax of judgment. Guarded by the Serpent, the deed stands encased, enthroned, and the snake seems to stare us down. The very best we can do is to caress our weakly, cracked fingernails under the visible brink of just one of the seven, strong seals. We can but slightly displace the glue so as to crinkle a peeled edge. But that is only from the very best of the sons of Adam and the daughters of Eve. Most of us are perpetually distanced and never within reach to even attempt release. We are like jailed inmates slinging a sewing needle that is dangled on a flimsy thread, hoping to prick the seal with the pointed edge whenever Snake Eyes turns his awful gaze away. But the wind is too great. An industrial-strength fan pushes a Hollywood hurricane right at our futile attempt. Our dark fate is sealed.

From our darkened corner see, emerging, the brilliant Lamb, draped in thorns and pierced clean through. *"But I thought he was killed,"* voices one of our number. Indeed, he was. He died the most severe, cruel death. The wind held him up, pinned against the Vine trellis. He was tacked until his own wind expired. Remember how the Serpent sneered. *"How, then, does he stand before us?"* chimes the questioner. He died, the undoing of life. But he was life's Author, its Creator. So, though he died, he aroused, and lives now. And since he was dead but lives now, he is the undoing of death.

The voice of the Lamb is clear and commanding. The seals shrivel by his authority. With each break a mighty torrent of counterattacks is launched against the culprit Serpent. He is slung like an annoying hair. Satan and his sycophants subdued. Adam and his ancestry accommodated. Christ and his crown coronated.

Wormwood Words

> Revelation 8:11
>
> *The name of the star is Wormwood. A third of the waters turned bitter, and many people died from the waters that had become bitter.*

The plants from which we derive Wormwood are named *Artemisia absinthium*, and also Mugwort, *Atemisis vulgaris*. It is a metaphor in the Bible for things that are so bitter they can't be tolerated. For examples consider the poisonous pot of stew that Elisha cured (2 Kgs 4:38-41); Hosea's hemlock (Hos 10:4); and the bitter poison of Deuteronomy 29:18.

It is at least interesting to note some of the interpretations for wormwood. One view from the science world is that an asteroid striking the world, or a comet colliding with our planet, could produce chemical changes in the atmosphere which would produce nitric-acid rain. The "bitter" effects would be detrimental upon earth's water supply.

One theory has the Vatican involved in a cover-up. Yeah, they have suppressed secret files about a satellite pointed toward Hale-Bopp Comet. In correspondence with the United Nations and NASA they already know this to be Wormwood. I'm not convinced. It sure sounds hyped up.

Possibly the most intriguing theory centers on the idea of a nuclear reactor. A nuclear detonation would definitely poison the water supply. The Chernobyl disaster in Ukraine is pointed to as a possible fulfillment of this prophecy because the name Chernobyl translates as "wormwood."

My personal view is that this prophecy has not been fulfilled. Rather, I see the stage set. The Lord is conditioning the planet to receive fulfillment. (I might also add that the enemy uses tactics to condition us too. For example, QR Codes, and microchip implants.) As part of the stage-setting there are intentional "coincidences." This has been so historically, but especially in the modern era, i.e. - Henry Kissinger's name adding up to 666; or the theory that sees Barak Obama embedded in Jesus' words of Luke 18:10. And honestly, I don't know if we can discern accurately which events are from the Lord and which ones are dastardly and evil. They come fast and furious and it seems there are new discoveries every day.

But it has always been this way. In 1973 Basil Clarke interpreted Geoffrey of Monmouth's "Vita Merlini" (Life of Merlyn) which located Wormwood in Welsh in the middle of the 6th Century. We must always be watchful and waiting. Each generation is without excuse. One thing is certain, nothing will occur without clearance from the Air Traffic Controller of heaven.

Faithful to the End

Revelation 9:20, 21

The people who lived through these terrible troubles did not turn away from the idols they had made, and they did not stop worshiping demons. They kept on worshiping idols that were made of gold, silver, bronze, stone, and wood. Not one of these idols could see, hear, or walk. No one stopped murdering or practicing witchcraft or being immoral or stealing.

There is a school of thought that has the Revelation as purely, mythical fantasy. They cite apocalyptic literature from the era which was along the lines of science fiction of our day. Some say the Revelation is nothing more than a clever slam against mighty Rome, along the lines of other apocalyptic pieces like the Book of Enoch; the Apocalypse of Bar; or the Apocalypse of Ezra. But these pieces are pseudonymous, whereas John clearly claims to be the author of the Revelation, the same one who wrote the gospel of John and the three letters by the same name. And they are fictitious; but the Revelation makes no claim to be fictional. In fact John has seen real visions of Jesus Christ. Two places in the Revelation he claims to speak truth on behalf of Christ, (Rev 1:3; 22:18). Furthermore, the other works are rambling and confusing; but John's Revelation follows an order and purpose. There's a succession of sevens that flow in a progression.

The relevant Revelation is not just for the first century. One primary difference between the book of the Revelation and other first-century apocalyptic works is the call to holiness and righteousness. The concern of John is not that his nation has been suppressed by a world power called Rome; rather he speaks as a spokesman for God who is dismayed by the fact humanity will not give up sinful practices. They hold to their sins stubbornly in spite of obvious judgment. The message of Revelation? Jesus is coming back soon. He will judge sin. The tribulation believers are encouraged to embrace faith and remain faithful to the end.

And Nothing but the Truth

Revelation 11:3

My two witnesses will wear sackcloth, while I let them preach for one thousand two hundred sixty days.

The truth, the whole truth, and nothing but the truth. Just who are these two witnesses? Doubtless you have heard the handful of theories that abound about them.

Some say it could be Moses and Elijah, because Elijah stopped the rain in his earthly ministry, and Moses turned the water to blood. There are similarities. On this theory they are continuing to do the same kinds of things in the Revelation.

Some say it could be the Old Testament and the New Testament, God's two great covenants, literally a living, breathing representation of the Word of God. But these are humans who die and are resurrected. That's problematic.

Some say it could be Enoch and Elijah because they are the only ones who did not die in Scripture. "Man is destined to die once, and after that to face judgment" (Heb 9:27, NIV). So it couldn't be Moses, this would make him die twice.

Bryan T. Huie has written extensively about his very interesting theory. His view docks mainly upon verse 4 about the olive trees and lamp stands. He has done an impressive amount of studying Scriptures in their contextual setting, both exegetically and culturally. He thinks the two witnesses are actually the revamped divided kingdom, the Northern Tribes and the Southern Tribes. In his theory the lost 10 tribes become a representation of the called-out gentiles from around the world. He goes to great lengths to describe Moses' 72 (Num 11:24-27), and Jesus' 72 (Luke 18:1-20), combining (72+72) to fulfill the 144,000 sealed ones in the Revelation. On his view the two witnesses are actually 144,000 witnesses who are martyred on the streets of Jerusalem. A worldwide party ensues to celebrate their deaths. But 3 1/2 days later they are resurrected and raptured to join the heavenly party. Whew! Though much of Huie's work appears to be sound, the weakness is this theory dabbles into date-setting and speculative symbolism. The 72 is multiplied by 2,000 (years that have passed) to arrive at 144,000.

All of these theories are intriguing. I find myself wondering about the intentional wording of John who describes 42 months in verse two, but switches to 1,260 days in verse 3. On first glance it is just a poetic way of saying the same thing because the ancient Jewish calendar of 360-day years fits. In other words, 1,260 days is 3 1/2 years: 42 months is 3 1/2 years. Oh, okay, they are both saying the same thing. But a day is one complete revolution of the earth on its axis; and a month is lunar, one complete resolution of the moon around the earth; and a year is one complete resolution of the earth around the sun. In a covenant agreement in which seasons are monitored by divinity, the two designations are the same. However, in a time when sun is blackened and moon is blood-red, with cataclysmic disasters occurring on earth, severe quakes that may even tilt its axis, all bets are off on the orbit God set spinning at creation. The birth of the new heaven and new earth may cause it to undergo contractions. Could the day and month spin differently at this time than they have to date? Is it the intersection of two realms? The two realities might be the fulfillment of 2 Peter 3:8, 9 and Psalm 90:3, 4.

But I digress badly!

The point of Revelation 11:1-14 is to show the absolute, unquestioned authority of God. The enemy can resist, kick and scream, but God wins. His two witnesses will speak the truth, the whole truth, and nothing but the truth. God's Word is authoritative. The same Word that wins in the end, wins in your life today!

It's On like Donkey Kong

Revelation 12:7-10

A war broke out in heaven. Michael and his angels were fighting against the dragon and its angels. But the dragon lost the battle. It and its angels were forced out of their places in heaven and were thrown down to the earth. Yes, that old snake and his angels were thrown out of heaven! That snake, who fools everyone on earth, is known as the devil and Satan. Then I heard a voice from heaven shout, "Our God has shown his saving power, and his kingdom has come! God's own Chosen One has shown his authority. Satan accused our people in the presence of God day and night. Now he has been thrown out!"

Ever seen a fight break out? You know, maybe on the elementary school playground, or in later grades with big high school kids in an out-of-sight breezeway. Sometimes a fight is depicted in the prison yard on TV. Who knows? Maybe you have even been the one fighting.

Here in Revelation 12 there is a pre-brawl tension that hangs in the atmosphere sort of like the kinetic static hovering before a lightning strike. You can sense it, a real uneasiness. John describes a brawl that literally is *in* the atmosphere. The taunting smirk, arrogance, smack talking, a circling brush, a push, a shove - and then it's on, it's on, like Donkey Kong!

This is a furious exchange of blows on a supernatural level. Michael, one of God's high ranking warrior-angels, goes to blows with Satan. It is a concise cease and desist order. The menace is hurled from the heavens. It mirrors his being cast out of paradise in a prehistoric event. Not much has changed with the passage of time.

Ezekiel speaks entirely past tense of Satan humbled (Ezek 28:12-18). Jesus saw Satan hurled from the heavens (Luke 18:10). He seems to speak of it as a real time event that he witnessed as his disciples ministered. Isaiah references what seems to be the prehistoric episode; but at moments it feels futuristic (Isa 14:12-15). And here in the Revelation we see the heavens, the very planetary alignments and stars, depicting Lucifer hurled to the ground. Are these separate events? Or are they a description of one singular event happening simultaneously as time collapses upon itself? One thing is clear. God is in absolute control. Satan and his imps are powerless before him.

The Restoration of All Things

Revelation 21:3-7

I heard a loud voice shout from the throne: God's home is now with his people. He will live with them, and they will be his own. Yes, God will make his home among his people. He will wipe all tears from their eyes, and there will be no more death, suffering, crying, or pain. These things of the past are gone forever.

Then the one sitting on the throne said: I am making everything new. Write down what I have said. My words are true and can be trusted. Everything is finished. I am Alpha and Omega, the beginning and the end. I will freely give water from the life-giving fountain to everyone who is thirsty. All who win the victory will be given these blessings. I will be their God, and they will be my people.

In the restoration of all things life will be as it was meant to be in the beginning. I'm not sure it is correct to say creation is set to default, factory settings. No, because this is not reformation, or revival. I'm not sure if our minds are ready to grasp, "Good morning, Lord. How are you?" Can you imagine not having the least hint of a sinful thought? A world completely absent of anything violent, devoid of lust, and emptied of jealousy. A New Jerusalem, the holy city, is come down from God in heaven.

We have spent our entire lives sojourning toward the bridegroom. Like Rebekah of old, we have never seen him with our eyes. We have only responded to the invitation of his servant, whether preacher, evangelist, missionary, or just a good friend, "Will you choose to do what's right for my Master?" Now, our hope is actualized, our faith is fruitful. We can embrace eternity with confidence. At the end of all things we find all things unending.

Alpha and Omega

> Revelation 22:13
>
> *I am Alpha and Omega, the first and the last, the beginning and the end.*

What a perfect ending to God's perfect book, the Bible. Jesus is speaking here, to John, the recorder. Fitting, after all, it is his Revelation. There is one Revelation. The book is not Revelations. This is incorrect. It is the Revelation of Jesus Christ.

Alpha is the first letter of the Greek alphabet. Omega is the last. It is like saying I am the A and the Z. The One who is the living Word is the complete alphabet that every word is based upon. You can't make one word without letters. Jesus, the living Word, encompasses all the letters. He is all-sufficient, entirely complete, very fulfillment.

The late conservative scholar, J. Vernon McGee, pastored Church of the Open Door in Los Angeles for twenty-one years, and was well-known for his radio teaching ministry. He wrote that Jesus "is the only alphabet you can use to reach God, my friend. The only language God speaks and understands is the language where Jesus is the Alpha and Omega and all the letters in between. He is the 'A' and the 'Z,' and the 'ABC.'"[xxxiv]

In the text of the original language the letter "alpha" is spelled out as a word; however, the omega is simply relegated to the first letter. To illustrate, if you were to attempt to translate it into English, what John wrote might be rendered as, "He is the Āye and the Z." Dr. McGee said the reason for this is Christ is the beginning and the end. The beginning is completed. Therefore, "Āye" could be spelled out. But the "Z" wasn't spelled out because the end is still being lived out in real time. Oh, to be sure, the work was accomplished with the death of Jesus on the cross, and his resurrection from the tomb. But one day he will carry out the finality of God's program. McGee then cites Hebrews 13:8, "Jesus Christ, the same yesterday, and to day, and for ever" (KJV). In Christ's attributes he is consistently the same. "He is immutable. Since he is the beginning and the ending, he encompasses all time and eternity."

APPENDIX A
Cross-Off List by Groups Numbered

1. Faith of Our Patriarchs (38)
- Creation
- Teeming with Life
- Temptation
- Observations Early On
- The Nephilim
- Noah's Flood
- Shem
- Orientation
- Is This What Faith Looks Like?
- The Posture of Prayer
- The Hot Coals and the Knife
- Choose What's Right
- Right Where God Wants You to Be
- Missed It By That Much
- The Fun in Dysfunction
- Anointed and Annoyed
- Was it Right?
- A Super-Race?
- Immaculate Integrity
- A Predestination of My Choosing
- Close Family Bonds
- Don't Let the Left Hand Know
- Parting Is Such Sweet Sorrow
- The Way and That
- O-M-T
- Silence the Croakers
- A Yellow Jersey
- No Bones about It
- God-Speak Human Jibberish
- Remember to Forget
- Ghetto Spirituality
- Keeper of the Flame
- Limitless Mercy
- Diamonds in the Rough
- The Devil's Workshop
- Something Different
- Redeeming a Culture of Arts
- Apex of Human Experience

2. Law and Allegiance (24)
- A Living Aroma
- The Trickle Down of Leadership
- Wired to Worship
- Every Last Vestige
- Capital Casualty
- A True Social Security
- Foreshadowing a Blessing
- The Need to Be Needed
- A Vow of the Heart
- Can You Imagine?
- You No Good Rapscallion
- Caleb's Different Spirit
- Glory Incognito
- Donkeys, Dogs and Discernment
- Audience of One
- Arouse the Nostalgia of Almighty
- The Purple Lineage
- The Glory Hole
- Golfers and Gates Giving Testimony
- Reverent Worship
- Not on My Watch
- The Compassionate Heart of God
- Loose Shoe, Loose Shoe
- Warfare

3. Trust in War Times (44)
- The Scarlet Cord
- Achan's Ache
- Lumberjacks and Waterboys
- Divine Intervention
- Ponds and Prayer
- A Sharp Attack on Dullness
- Housewife Gone Covert
- Deflected Accolades
- He Intervenes
- The Punch Lineage
- Old Testament Theophany
- The Blessing of Integrity
- Remember Wally Pipp
- You Are Alright
- A Really Special Friend
- Give Me a Sign
- Common Sense Isn't Common
- Irony of Two Desperate Kings
- The Storyline of Humanity
- The Bygones Backfired
- I'll Run No Matter What
- Dumb, Dumber and Dumbest
- Steps of Trepidation

- Singing the Blues
- My Oh My, Micaiah
- Christian Voodoo?
- Doubly Blessed
- Elisha Room
- No Guarantees
- What's in a Name?
- On Another Level
- Be Careful Little Eyes What You See
- Oh, the Music!
- A Tribute to My Friend Jap
- Running Interference
- In a Word
- Hezekiah's Hesitation
- Testing, Testing, 1, 2, 3
- A Slam on the Worship Wars
- Open and Honest Prayer
- No Easy Undertaking
- Great Projects in Bite-Sized Chunks
- A Sudden Flash of Inspiration
- Such Reverence

4. Prophets and Poets Believing (62)
- Nashty and Vashti
- Esther's Keen Sense
- Holy Trinity Inferred
- I Didn't Even Know
- Confessions of a Techie-Schizo
- Beauty
- A Hen and a Pig and a Sacrifice
- The Instant Message God
- Oh, I Get It
- The Absence of I
- The First Mistletoe
- The Dis-Ease of Disease
- Fulcrum and Counterweights
- Within
- Code Talkers
- Eat Mor Chikin
- Unity
- Hanging Harps and Hope
- Impassioned Plea
- My Heart's Keeping
- Bait Christian
- My Friend's Advice
- Five Mississippi
- Disarming Antagonists
- That's What Friends are For
- Use It or Lose It
- Coach

- Thirty Second Tune-Up
- Wordly Wisdom
- Right in the Happy Middle
- Praise to Whom Praise is Due
- Fly a Kite
- Save Some Kick
- Boring!
- Snow White and the Seven Grieves
- Greatest Joy
- Before the Ice Cream Melts
- I Wait
- Migration to Salvation
- A Flood of Mercy
- Interstate Isaiah
- He's An Early Almond
- Job Posting: Prophet
- The Weeping Prophet
- The Diaspora – Figs Gone Figurative
- Creative Genius
- Optical Omnipotent
- The Silence of Madmen
- New Morning, New Mercy
- Second Addam's Family
- Insight on Predestination
- Resolve Rests
- Bethlehem Bakery
- Trust and Timing
- He Welcomes Our Wrestling
- Up on the Camelback
- Our Crooning Crown
- The Desired of All Nations
- Again, What's in a Name?
- Last Joshua
- Riders on the Storm
- Jesus and Jimmy the Greek

5. A New Living Hope (58)
- Bethlehem Remembered
- The Trellis of Your Faith
- Stunning Beauty of Nature
- Scariest Verse in the Bible
- A-S-K
- Healed Emphatically
- Clarity of Assignment
- Feather Light Burdens
- Separation Stories
- Eternity – What If?
- The True You of You
- And He Healed Them All
- The Amazing Mind Reader
- Catch and Release

- [ ] Small Huddles
- [ ] Keep Fiddling Away
- [ ] Catcalling and Raucous Bellowing
- [ ] A Very Taxing Burden
- [ ] A Literal Underground Church
- [ ] Do Well by God
- [ ] Table Fellowship
- [ ] Jesus Barabbas or Jesus Christ?
- [ ] A Downpour in the Desert
- [ ] A Really Clever Impostor?
- [ ] Incompatible Capacities
- [ ] Thread-Breadth Window
- [ ] To Coin a Phrase
- [ ] Mary Mother
- [ ] He Has Staked His Claim
- [ ] 71 Mustang Fastback
- [ ] What Does it Mean to Pray?
- [ ] Fruitful Consequences
- [ ] Listen to How You Listen
- [ ] Afterlife
- [ ] The Glory of Humility
- [ ] To the Day
- [ ] Living Logos
- [ ] Eternal Wind
- [ ] Seeker Sensitive Worshiper
- [ ] Aching, Yearning, Longing
- [ ] A Little Dirt Don't Hurt
- [ ] Doubting Thomas, I Doubt It
- [ ] Lazarus, A Mob Hit
- [ ] Judas, Dine In or Carry Out?
- [ ] Purely Incarnational
- [ ] The High Priestly Prayer
- [ ] Taser versus Transformer
- [ ] The Symbol of the Cross
- [ ] The Breath of God
- [ ] Pneumatic Uplift
- [ ] Heavenly Languages
- [ ] Upwardly Mobile
- [ ] The Holy Spirit's Prompting
- [ ] Way
- [ ] The Right Stuff
- [ ] Shepherd Savior
- [ ] This Was a Misunderstanding
- [ ] Shake the Snake

6. Letters that Show Loyalty (60)
- [ ] Luther's Gate
- [ ] The Christian Hokey Pokey
- [ ] The Golf Clap of Heaven
- [ ] I've Stepped in Sticker Patch
- [ ] Devotion Stew
- [ ] Rockabilly Red Boots
- [ ] One Form of Identification
- [ ] Real. Comforter. Genes
- [ ] Money and Love Growing Like Trees
- [ ] Beauty in Diversity
- [ ] No Air Boxing
- [ ] Discernment
- [ ] Unclean, Unclean!
- [ ] Loyalty
- [ ] Veritable Law Couriers
- [ ] That's Just Wrong
- [ ] Duped by the Mundane
- [ ] The God-Filled Life
- [ ] The Man in the Moon
- [ ] Good Stock
- [ ] Our Dream
- [ ] Emptied Excellence
- [ ] Further Up, Further In
- [ ] Feature Presentation
- [ ] Love Struck
- [ ] A Really Happy Life
- [ ] If Only
- [ ] Good Use of the Time
- [ ] Military Fatigues
- [ ] It's All about You
- [ ] Celestial Super-Band
- [ ] Recipe for Zero Joy
- [ ] A Nameless Verse
- [ ] 100% Pure
- [ ] A Model on Mentoring
- [ ] Investigative Journalism
- [ ] Used and Amused
- [ ] New Digs
- [ ] From His Vantage Point
- [ ] Pistachios, Profiles and Peace
- [ ] Solid Food
- [ ] New and Improved
- [ ] This Can't Be Faith
- [ ] Substantive Faith
- [ ] Faith that Lives
- [ ] The Courage to Encourage
- [ ] Wavy Wishfulness
- [ ] Nearness
- [ ] How Valuable is Faith!
- [ ] Open Heavens
- [ ] Steady as She Goes
- [ ] Lamp Shining in a Dark Place
- [ ] Is Salvation a Fixed Invitation List?
- [ ] Disappearing Trick
- [ ] God's Kids and Devil's Kids
- [ ] A Loving Father and a Willing Son

- ❏ Gnostic Know-It-Alls
- ❏ Exercise Inside and Out
- ❏ Jester in the Holy Court
- ❏ Attitude

7. Apocalyptic Assurance (24)
- ❏ Finiteness Hits a Wall
- ❏ Generational Goodness
- ❏ It's God's Fault
- ❏ Dem Dry Bones
- ❏ Gog Me with a Span
- ❏ The Dead Sea Lives
- ❏ Divided Land, Unified Hearts
- ❏ Watch Out for the Freshman Fifteen
- ❏ A Word on Hostile Environments
- ❏ Determinant Resolve
- ❏ Daniel's Deliverance
- ❏ Literal Lions and Reverie Rams
- ❏ Crossing the Delaware
- ❏ Apocalyptic Endurance
- ❏ Glorious Age
- ❏ Hocus Pocus, Help Us Focus
- ❏ A Hopeful Horn
- ❏ A Tale of the Undoing of Death
- ❏ Wormwood Words
- ❏ Faithful to the End
- ❏ And Nothing but the Truth
- ❏ It's On Like Donkey Kong
- ❏ The Restoration of All Things
- ❏ Alpha and Omega

APPENDIX B
Literary Genres with Group Number

Storytelling
Immaculate Integrity (1)
You No Good Rapscallion (2)
Achan's Ache (3)
The Scarlet Cord (3)
Remember Wally Pipp (3)
A Sudden Flash of Inspiration (3)
My Oh My, Micaiah (3)
No Easy Undertaking (3)
Snow White and the Seven Grieves (4)
A-S-K (5)
The Courage to Encourage (6)
Steady as She Goes (6)
A Tale of the Undoing of Death (7)
Determinant Resolve (7)

Humor
You No Good rapscallion (2)
Confessions of a Techie-Schizo (4)
A Hen and a Pig and a Sacrifice (4)
The Need to Be Needed (2)
Dumb, Dumber and Dumbest (3)
Testing, Testing, 1, 2, 3 (3)
The Christian Hokey Pokey (6)
No Air Boxing (6)
Watch Out for the Freshmen Fifteen (7)

Real-life Anecdotes
Immaculate Integrity (1)
Was It Right? (1)
Five Mississippi (4)
You No Good Rapscallion (2)
Confessions of Techie-Schizo (4)

Incarnation
The First Mistletoe (4)
Bethlehem Bakery (4)
The Desired of All Nations (4)
Bethlehem Remembered (5)
Purely Incarnational (5)
Mary Mother (5)

New or Recent Concepts
Interstate Isaiah (4)
Insight on Predestination (4)
Jesus Bar. or Jesus Christ? (5)
Lazarus, a Mob Hit (5)
Devotion Stew (6)

Poetry or Songs
In a Word (3)
Within (4)
My Heart's Keeping (4)
My Friend's Advice (4)
I Wait (4)
Bethlehem Remembered (5)
Eternal Wind (5)
Pneumatic Uplift (5)
The Golf Clap of Heaven (6)
Our Dream (6)
Love Struck (6)
If Only (6)
A Nameless Verse (6)

Prayer
The Posture of Prayer (1)
Ponds and Prayer (3)

Open and Honest Prayer (3)
The High Priestly Prayer (5)
What Does It Mean to Pray? (5)
Devotion Stew (6)

Pun Titles
The Fun in Dysfunction (1)
O-M-T (1)
A Sharp Attack on Dullness (3)
The Punch Lineage (3)
The Dis-ease of Disease (4)
Wordly Wisdom (4)
Snow White and the 7 Grieves (4)
The Diaspora - Figs Figurative (4)
Second Addams Family (4)
Riders on the Storm (4)
A Literal Underground Church (5)
Doubting Thomas, I Doubt It (5)
Judas, Dine In or Carry Out? (5)
Real. Comforter. Genes (6)
Military Fatigues (6)
Gnostic Know-It-Alls (6)
Jester in the Holy Court (6)
Gog Me with a Span (7)
Hocus Pocus, Help Us Focus (7)
The Dead Sea Lives (7)
Divided Land, Unified Hearts (7)

Alliteration Titles
Anointed and Annoyed (1)
Immaculate Integrity (1)
Capital Casualty (2)
Donkeys, Dogs and Discernment (2)
Golfers and Gates Giving Testimony (2)
Achan's Ache (3)
Ponds and Prayer (3)
Wordly Wisdom (4)
Hanging Harps and Hope (4)
Optical Omnipotent (4)

New Morning, New Mercy (4)
Resolve Rests (4)
Bethlehem Bakery (4)
Trust and Timing (4)
Mary Mother (5)
Living Logos (5)
Taser versus Transformer (5)
Shepherd Savior (6)
Emptied Excellence (6)
Pistachios, Profiles & Peace (6)
Wavy Wishfulness (6)
Literary Lions and Reverie (7)
A Hopeful Horn (7)
Wormwood Words (7)

Faith
Is This What Faith? (1)
God-Speak (1)
Luther's Gate (6)
This Can't Be Faith (6)
How Valuable is Faith! (6)
Faith that Lives (6)
Substantive Faith (6)
It's All about You (6)
The Trellis of Your Faith (5)
Wavy Wishfulness (6)
Faithful to the End (7)

Family
Immaculate Integrity (1)
Close Family Bonds (1)
The Blessing of Integrity (3)
The Glory of Humility (5)
Parting is Such Sweet (1)
The Fun in Dysfunction (1)
Dumb, Dumber, Dumbest (3)
Coach (4)
Confessions of a Techie (4)
Praise to Whom Praise (4)
Fly a Kite (4)
Before the Ice Cream (4)
Up on the Camelback (4)
Riders on the Storm (4)

Money and Love Growing Like Trees (6)
The God-filled Life (6)
A Loving Father and a Willing Son (6)
Watch Out for the Freshman Fifteen (7)

Predestination and Free-Will
A Predestination of My Choosing (1)
Insight on Predestination (4)
Is Salvation a Fixed Invitation List? (6)

The Importance of Names
What's in a Name? (3)
Again, What's in a Name? (4)

Sports Analogies
A Yellow Jersey (1)
Immaculate Integrity (1)
Golfers and Gates Giving Testimony (2)
Remember Wally Pipp (3)
I'll Run No Matter What (3)
Nashty and Vashti (4)
Five Mississippi (4)
Coach (4)
Save Some Kick (4)
Riders on the Storm (4)
Jesus and Jimmy the Greek (4)
Clarity of Assignment (5)
Catch and Release (5)
Small Huddles (5)
The Golf Clap of Heaven (6)
No Air Boxing (6)
The Courage to Encourage (6)
Steady as She Goes (6)
Exercise Inside and Out (6)

Women in Ministry
Housewife Gone Covert (2)
Boring! (4)
Praise to Whom Praise Is Due (4)

Friendship
A Really Special Friend (3)
A Tribute to My Friend Jap (3)
That's What Friends are For (4)
My Friend's Advice (4)

History
Warfare (2)
Divine Intervention (3)
Golfers and Gates Giving (2)
A Really Special Friend (3)
Code Talkers (4)
Migration to Salvation (4)
Resolve Rests (4)
Crossing the Delaware (7)

Care of the Earth
Teeming with Life (1)
Before the Ice Cream Melts (4)
Creative Genius (4)
Stunning Beauty of Nature (5)
New Digs (6)
The Dead Sea Lives (7)
Divided Land, Unified Hearts (7)

Jewish Culture and History
The Fun in Dysfunction (1)
Anointed and Annoyed (1)
A Super-Race? (1)
Limitless Mercy (1)
A True Social Security (2)
Foreshadowing a Blessing (2)
Arouse the Nostalgia (2)
The Purple Lineage (2)
Lumberjacks and Waterboys (2)
The Punch Lineage (3)
Nashty and Vashti (4)
Esther's Keen Sense (4)
Migration to Salvation (4)
Interstate Isaiah (4)
A Flood of Mercy (4)
The Weeping Prophet (4)
The Diaspora – Figs (4)
New Morning, New Mercy (5)
The Desired of All Nations (5)
Watch Out for Freshman (7)

GLOSSARY OF SELECTED TERMS

Anachronistic – Imposing current beliefs, views and practices upon cultures, customs, traditions and literature from a previous period of time.

Anthropology – From the Greek word *anthropos*, "man", the science that deals with the origins, physical and cultural development, biological characteristics, and social customs and beliefs of humankind.

Doxology – A hymn or ascription of words containing praise to God.

Eschaton – From the Greek word, *eskatos*, end of the world, end of time, climax of history. In conservative, biblical exegesis, the glorious Day of the Lord. The eternal age.

Glossalalia – Incomprehensible speech in a heavenly language, tongues.

Idiom – An expression that is not understandable simply with the usual definition or grammar of words, but which takes on meaning when used in a certain language, dialect, or culture of a particular people.

Imprimatur – A license granted by a bishop certifying the Roman Catholic Church's endorsement or approval of a book or Bible version.

Incarnation – The act of God becoming man, that is, Jesus Christ becoming a human baby.

Masoretes – The group of scholars and scribes from the 9th Century BC, primarily from the Sons of Asher, and partly from the Sons of Naphtali, who were responsible for devising the vowel system in the Hebrew language, which became very important for preservation and accuracy.

Midrash – A story about Hebrew Scripture, the word means to investigate or interpret, a form of Hebrew Rabbinic literature, best thought of as commentaries on the Scriptures.

Second Temple – The time period from approximately 520 BC when the temple was rebuilt upon the return of the Jews from Babylon, extending to 70 AD when Titus, the Roman General, attacked Jerusalem.

Sitz im Leben – A German, theological word that translates "life setting," basically the idea of providing a context in which to house a written work or life encounter.

Talmud – A collection of 63 tractates that give the opinions of thousands of Rabbis on law, ethics, philosophy, customs, history, theology, lore and other topics. It is over 6,200 pages in print and is considered as second only to Torah by Judaic Rabbis. Contains two parts, the Mishnah, completed around 200 CE, and the Gemara, completed around 500 CE.

Tetragrammaton – The designation for God's name among the Jewish people. It is made up of four letters, all consonants, Y-H-W-H.

Theology – A combination of two Greek words, *theos* (God) and *logos* (reason), it means to think deeply about God.

Theophany – A manifestation of God to man, visible, though perhaps not material.

Transliteration – To bring one word, letter by letter, out of one language and into another in the strictest way, preserving the closest alphabetic representation.

Worship Wars – the designation for the ongoing and often divisive discussion centered on the use of contemporary methods of music, media, lighting and styles in worship as opposed to more traditional approaches.

Xenolalia – The ability to speak in a language which the individual has not learned.

GENERAL INDEX

A

AARON...58, 59, 60, 61, 70, 72, 78, 82, 167, 274, 317
ABELARD, PETER 330
ABIGAIL............................120, 121
ABIMELECH 37, 112, 113, 114
ABRAHAM....*34, 35, 36, 37, 44, 45, 50, 89,* 114, 187, 247, *282, 294,* 297, 317, *334, 335*
ABSALOM 77, 123, 124
accountability...51, 95, 96, 156, 196, 230, 310, 313
ACHAN 104, 187
ACHSAH.................................108
ADAM ...31, 32, 33, 36, 48, 55, *115,* 184, 195, 197, 198, 209, 246, 247, 261, 262, 330, 353, 356, 357
ADDAMS, CHARLES 197
ADLER, MORTIMER J. 249
ADONIJAH 140
advice ...69, 85, 106, 141, 170, 171, 172, 229, 325, 347
agreement 103, 118, 183, 187, 194, 195, 197, 319
AHIMAAZ................................124
allegory 112
Almighty..*36, 47, 60, 73, 83, 87, 93, 115, 122, 130, 133, 182,* 257, *334*
ALTSCHULER, ERIC 339
ambush................................275, 344
America...6, 21, 74, 173, 174, 312, 325, 347

American 27, 97, 109, 134, 166, 172, 176, 237, 300, 312, 322, 351, 352
AMNON....................................123
AMON 134
Anarchist.................................247
Anathoth.................................191
ANDREW.................................229
anger... 43, 156, 181, 187, 298, 302
animal-life................................34
anointing.............. 63, 132, 167, 335
ANSELM 330
anthropology 123
anthropomorphism 67
Antichrist 207, 247
apocalypse 24, 350, 355
apocalyptic 358
appease 330
appropriateness 62, 322
ARISTOTLE 236
Ark of the Covenant...... 59, 60, 122, 164
armor.......................................307
aroma 47, 56, 68, 73
ARTAXERXES 208
artist 61, 139
ASAPH............................. 138, 161
ASHER....................................110
Assemblies of God 181
Assyria 134, 188, 189, 203
atonement 81, 221, 319, 330
Atonement Theories............ 81, 330
attitude 38, 95, 160, 222, 335
AULEN, GUSTAF......................331
authenticity 128, 131, 167, 327, 345
Author of Life............................252

373

authority....38, 41, 47, 74, *137*, 206, 220, 245, 247, 357, 360
AVNI, GIDEON 108

B

Babylon.75, 90, 105, 143, 167, 192, 193, 197, 208, 209, 347
Barabbas 237
BARABBAS 236, 237
BATHSHEBA 122, 123
beauty 113, 123, 158, 159, 163, 217, 309, 340
belief 22, 32, 81, 182, 243, 269, 270, 286, 323, 330, 339, 351, 354
believe 43, 51, 56, 61, 69, 79, 84, 91, 111, 115, 120, 131, 165, 183, 194, 195, 198, 199, 240, 246, 247, 255, 257, 258, 264, 266, 274, 282, 287, 288, 308, 310, 313, 314, 322, 341, 345, 354
believer 59, 86, 91, 145, 284
Bema Seat 135
BENJAMIN *48*, 109, 344
BERMES, GEZA 339
Bethel 55, *115*
Bethlehem 202, 203, 209, 215, 236, 365, 368
betrayal 233, 260, 261
Bible.. 19, 24, 25, 27, 33, 44, 45, 51, 52, 55, 64, 67, 68, 73, 74, 77, 84, 86, 88, 90, 92, 95, 96, 97, 103, 111, 126, 132, 133, *136*, 143, 145, 161, 165, 166, 173, 180, 182, 186, 191, 198, 199, 200, 220, 221, 228, 229, 236, 237, 249, 272, 283, 284, 289, 292, 294, 296, 300, 312, 313, 316, 325, 326, 327, 334, 339, 344, 345, 346, 351, 353, 354, 357, 362, 365

BILHAH 43, 45, 347
BISHOP, BUDDY 170
bitterness *39*, 55, *67*
black magic 203, 240
bless 41, 42, 49, 75, 89, 96, 167, 207, 208, 220, 235, 251
blessed ... 19, 21, *39*, *41*, 49, *50*, *60*, 75, *76*, 113, 117, 123, 124, *131*, *133*, 140, 158, 175, 177, 184, 191, 192, 198, 223, 235, 236, 245, 250, 251, 255, 256, 294, *298*, 347, 348, 355
blessing .. *38*, *39*, 42, *45*, *49*, *50*, 75, *80*, 115, *116*, 167, *189*, *236*, 251, 271, 361
blind.. 227, 231, 232, 257, 258, 353, 354
BOAZ .. 97, 113, 114, 163, 164, 215
body 50, 77, 78, 126, 180, 182, 235, 253, 259, 273, 290, 292, 294, 301, 315, 332, 333
bones 25, 44, 54, 55, 134
BONHOEFFER, DIETRICH 259, 261, 403
BOYD, GREG 200
Bread of Life 56, *115*, 202, 236, 261
breastplate 60
*breath*33, 47, 55, 68, 163, 195, 217, 267, 308, 343
BRODSKY, HAROLD 346
broken 45, 48, 54, 55, 164, 189, 197, 210, 211, 255, 256, 275, 282, 343
brokenness 236, 256
BRYANT, DEZ 153
BUCER, MARTIN 199
burdens 70, 71, 222, 243, 319
BUSH, GEORGE W. 97, 190

C

CAESAR 245, 327

CAIN 32
CALEB 80, 108, 120
Calvary *36, 83*, 255
CALVIN, JOHN 199
Calvinism 199
care of the earth.. 31, 183, 194, 195, 217, 218, 315, 346
careful obedience 114, 126, 192, 235, 324, 325
caregivers 227
CARETTO, CARLO 291
CARLISLE, FRANK E. 339
CATHY, DAN 166
CATHY, TRUETT 166
chaos 69, 129
character..... 20, 48, 50, 62, 83, 108, 159, 205, 210, 237, 244, 251, 283, 285, 292, 315, 348, 355
CHARETTE, BLAINE 300
charisma 204, 319
chief priests 259, 264
CHRIST ..22, 37, 40, 41, 45, 55, 57, 60, 63, 70, 81, 83, 86, 89, 94, 112, 114, 121, 123, 135, 137, 142, 145, 164, 166, 170, 187, 188, 203, 215, 220, 221, 223, 226, 233, 234, 236, 238, 245, 250, 251, 253, 257, 258, 259, 263, 264, 283, 286, 287, 288, 290, 293, 294, 296, 297, 298, 299, 300, 302, 306, 307, 308, 309, 314, 315, 319, 325, 326, 331, 332, 333, 334, 341, 343, 346, 354, 355, 357, 358, 363, 366, 368
CHRIST JESUS.297, 299, 307, 309
Christian .21, 24, 25, 27, 31, 37, 59, 62, 70, 84, 88, 91, 92, 93, 99, 128, 131, 145, 169, 170, 172, 173, 184, 219, 233, 234, 239, 248, 277, 282, 284, 285, 286, 290, 291, 304, 305, 306, 307, 313, 314, 317, 323, 325, 331, 334, 354, 365, 366, 368
Christianity ... 63, 68, 170, 189, 234, 239, 261, 290, 296, 332
Christus Victor Theory 36, 331
Church.... 21, 22, 25, 32, 48, 56, 68, 73, 77, 79, 87, 88, 92, 93, 110, 111, 115, 116, 117, 120, 123, 125, 138, 140, 159, 161, 173, 175, 178, 181, 182, 184, 192, 199, 226, 230, 233, 234, 237, 248, 255, 263, 264, 274, 275, 276, 289, 293, 297, 298, 308, 310, 312, 315,317, 318, 326, 330, 331, 332, 333, 335, 352, 354, 362, 369
circumcision 112, 187
clarity 176, 221, 222, 285
CLARKE, BASIL 358
coach.. 54, 175, 221, 274, 276, 291, 322, 325
COLE, NEIL 230
commitment.. 46, 71, 118, 124, 132, 182, 259, 318, 348
communication 156, 157
communion 261
community .. 43, 58, 68, 71, 92, 128, 134, 180, 184, 290, 313
compassion 122, 236, 256
confession 40, 79, 156, 163, 164, 177, 281, 287, 288, 304, 342, 350, 351
conscience 52, 53, 156, 185
consequences 39, 75, 81, 249, 272, 342
conspiracy 123, 191
consubstantiation 256
conviction 62
COOK, J.W. 153
COSBY, BILL 334
Costa Rica 161, 218
counselor 68, 84, 246

375

courage........71, 204, 296, 315, 322
covenant.60, 79, 83, 112, 115, 118, 164, 197, 198, 266, 319
cowboy 139
creation...31, 32, 36, 37, 57, 69, 91, 126, 138, 179, 194, 196, 223, 257, 262, 263, 265, 266, 267, 273, 315, 319, 330, 343, 360
creativity .61, 62, 63, 148, 285, 304, 334
creator 148, 160, 300, 356
crisis 69, 84, 122, 351
cross........36, 55, 60, 80, 81, 89, 96, 103, 127, *137*, 145, 147, 182, 197, 211, *220*, 221, 225, 226, 246, 247, 252, 254, 261, 264, 266, 268, 301, 306, 329, 330, 331, 334, 343, 352, 363
crucifixion..189, 234, 264, 265, 266, 267, 268
culture.....34, 43, 44, 52, 62, 63, 97, 110, 111, 134, 135, 255, 275, 313, 314, 343, 349
curses.....45, 73, 89, 123, 183, 184, 191, 198, 341, 351
cymbals 138, 204

D

Dad...35, *44*, *49*, *50*, *116*, 117, *125*, *140*, 143, *179*, 205, 226, 229, 250, 251, 282, *283*, 289, *298*, *313*, 325, 329, 341
DAN.....................................63, 110
DANIEL.24, 26, 135, 136, 161, 207, 252, 347, 348, 349, 350, 351, 367
DAVID.......60, 77, 94, 95, 109, 114, 117, *118*, 119, *120*, 121, 122, 123, 125, 126, *135*, *136*, 137, 138, 140, 141, 143, 157, 159, 162, 163, 167, 168, 188, 202, 204, 211, 215, 231, 247, 355
Day of Atonement......................330
Day of Pentecost262, 269, 270, 343
Dead Sea 345
death 36, 37, 44, 45, 53, 55, 70, 71, 76, 78, 81, 86, 92, 94, 121, 124, 126, 140, 141, 191, 195, 224, 229, 241, 242, 259, 260, 264, 265, 268, 272, 273, 274, 282, 287, 309, 316, 319, 329, 330, 331, 332, 334, 335, 340, 356
DEBORAH 110
decisions 39, 126, 146, 272, 293, 298, 326, 342
DEFFINBAUGH, BOB 108
deity...................................240, 265
deliverance. 54, 136, 154, 187, 194, 208, 209, 255, 351
demons 141, 220, 221
Desired of all Nations 207
desperate 121
destroy ...32, 33, 75, 105, 112, 187, 226, 250, 287, 329, 333, 341
devil....61, 224, 239, 247, 261, 276, 282, 287, 316, 329, 330, 331, 341, 350, 360
devotion................ 46, 99, 114, 165
difference 52, 62, 85, 273
DINAH 42, 43, 45, 112
discernment. 86, 141, 235, 249, 291
disciples *38*, 206, 220, 221, 224, 226, 228, 229, 230, 231, 232, 235, 236, *241*, *242*, *243*, *244*, *245*, 248, 252, 254, 255, 257, 258, 260, 261, 262, 263, 267, 327, 329, 332, 343, 361
discipline 70, 75, 79, 147, 178, 183, 190, 206, 217, 254, 258, 285, 288, 291, 293, 323, 328
disciplines............ 25, 284, 291, 318

disease 163, 172, 193, 221, 229, 251, 274, 354
distributed 236, 255, 256
divinity.................................... 56, 265
DOBSON, JAMES 93
Doctrine of the Two Kingdoms..... 92
Dome of the Rock 59
dreams.... 46, 47, 58, 137, 180, 182, 297, 340
DUROCHER, LEO 321
dysfunction 40, 43, 312

E

earth .31, 32, 33, 35, 37, 40, 42, 50, 62, 63, 64, 88, 91, 136, 139, 140, 158, 162, 183, 184, 187, 188, 189, 193, 194, 195, 199, 205, 206, 210, 211, 217, 218, 222, 241, 245, 246, 248, 251, 255, 262, 263, 264, 270, 299, 304, 309, 315, 316, 331, 343, 345, 348, 354, 357, 360, *See* Care of the Earth
Eden 140, 198, 315
EDERSHEIM, ALFRED 207
Edom 96, 98, 197, 198, 199, 200, 201
Egypt 37, 38, 47, 48, 50, 51, 53, 54, 56, 57, 60, 71, 72, 81, 82, 90, 92, 94, 96, 103, 112, 134, 161, 188, 189, 193, 194, 206, 215, 274
EHUD 109
El Salvador 161, 217
elect 199
ELIJAH 127, 128, 131, 132, 241, 242, 243, 359
ELIMELECH 114
ELISHA....... 85, 128, 132, 133, 134, 148, 204, 357, 365
Emmanuel 245

emotions. 45, 54, 79, 117, 131, 227, 253, 254, 285, 301
encourage 23, 25, 181, 311, 322
encouragement 23, 50, *115*, *117*, *118*, 140, 192, 219, 291, 310, 352, 355
endurance 283, 307
enemies................... 60, 79, 80, 160
enemy .. 43, 56, 78, 85, 98, 99, 106, 108, 110, 111, 119, 122, 129, 137, 143, 199, 202, 276, 331, 332, 341, 344, 352, 357, 360
ENOCH 358, 359
Ephesus 270
EPHRAIM..................... *49*, 346, 347
ESAU 38, 39, 49, 197, 199, 200, 201, 286, 328
Eschaton 202, 263, 266, 353
ESTHER........................... 154, 155
eternity *36*, 40, 51, 96, *115*, *137*, 160, *161*, 179, 184, 192, 202, *203*, *221*, *224*, 250, *256*, 266, 286, 289, 308, *315*, 316, 321, 329, 340, 353, 355, 362, 363
ethics.................................. 31, 166
ethos 252, 253
evangelist... 68, 110, 174, 220, 226, 298, 333
EVE 31, 32, *33*, *36*, *48*, *55*, *115*, 198, 261, 262, 293, 330, *334*, 356
evil.... 33, 34, 44, 45, 47, 49, 61, 81, 96, 112, 134, 142, 171, 172, 195, 203, 204, 220, 232, 240, 256, 261, 263, 283, 329, 332, 341, 356, 358
evolution............................ 183, 194
executive branch 74, 347
existence *35*, *42*, *164*, *170*, *178*, *286*, *294*, *304*, *311*, *317*
expression........... 52, 139, 225, 308

EZEKIEL...24, 26, 55, 70, 339, 340, 341, 342, 343, 344, 345, 346, 347, 350, 361
EZRA..26, 144, 145, 146, 149, 209, 358

F

face.33, 41, 47, 64, 83, 86, 97, 127, 130, 156, 197, 225, 244, 275, 288, 320
faith...19, 21, 23, 24, 25, 29, 35, 37, *40*, 42, 46, 49, *56*, 59, *68*, *80*, *81*, *92*, 93, 108, *120*, 128, *131*, 143, 145, 168, 185, 186, 188, 204, 216, 217, 218, 223, 227, 228, *233*, 237, *239*, *240*, *244*, 248, 250, 258, 259, 264, 266, 272, 281, *282*, 283, *285*, *286*, *287*, *288*, *289*, *290*, 299, *305*, 306, 307, *308*, *309*, 310, *311*, *312*, *313*, 314, 317, 319, 320, 321, 322, 323, 324, 326, 327, 333, *334*, 335, 348, 350, 353, 359, 362, 364, 365, 366, 369, 403
faith building 204
faith looks like ...204, 282, 290, 319, 320
faith, hope and love 306
faithful 107, 108, *116*, 117, 125, 134, 136, 192, 210, *235*, 236, 275, 291, 332, 341, 349, 350, 358, 359, 367
faithfulness*118*, 125, 148, 164, 192, 197, 350
false prophets 127, 129, 134, 233
family 21, 22, 33, 37, 39, 40, 42, 43, 44, 46, 48, 50, 54, 59, 62, 71, 72, 73, 77, 78, 84, 88, 91, 96, 97, 98, 103, 105, *116*, 117, *118*, 122, 126, 127, 137, 138, 141, 146, 148, 153, 154, 164, 165, 173,
175, 178, 182, 183, 191, 197, 198, *202*, 207, 208, 210, 219, 224, 228, 234, 246, 247, 251, 289, 290, 292, 293, 297, 298, 304, 322, 325, 339, 341, 342
farmer..223
father 20, 37, 38, 39, *43*, 44, 45, 46, 48, 49, 50, 71, 74, 87, 96, 97, 103, 108, 113, 114, 115, *116*, 117, *118*, *120*, 123, 134, 141, 156, 176, 191, 197, 237, 238, 246, *282*, 297, 298, 310, 317, 325, 329, 330, 341, 356, 403
Father... *35*, *36*, *37*, *38*, *39*, *89*, 112, *115*, 120, 121, 123, *136*, 144, 155, 157, *161*, 162, 182, 183, 184, 188, 195, 206, 216, 220, 228, 237, 238, *240*, 246, 248, 254, 256, 257, 262, 263, 268, *284*, 293, 306, 307, *316*, 329, 330, 331, 332, 366, 369
fatigues......................................307
fellowship 230, 257, 318
fine arts 62
flame 58, 59
flood 33, 34, 37, 187, 238
foreshadowing..............55, 75, 255
forget.. 57, 59, 60, 68, 95, 103, 128, 133, 141, 174, 314, 319
forgiveness... 47, 77, 123, 155, 227, 238, 239, 240, 286, 289, 315, 329
foundation 31, 36, 39, 60, 104, 286, 315
free will 32, 327
freedom. *32*, 42, *47*, *73*, *81*, *92*, *304*
friend 64, 68, 71, 75, 77, 80, 84, 88, 106, 117, 118, 120, 123, 139, 140, 142, 145, 156, 170, 171, 172, 173, 177, 178, 182, 183, 217, 227, 239, 240, 241, 250, 251, 265, 273, 276, 286, 301,

307, 309, 314, 317, 318, 320, 321, 323, 327, 333, 335, 362, 364
friendship 22, 90, 155, 173, 219, 227, 228, 265, 270, 289, 291, 327, 342, 347, 349

G

GAD 49, 88, 110
GAEBELEIN, ARNO *38*
GEHRIG, LOU 117
genealogy 246, 317
generational curses 32, 341
Gentiles 186, 221, 222, 286, 326
genuine 68, 222, 240, 310
GEOFFREY of MONMOUTH 358
Gethsemane 230, 254, 256
Gibeonites 106
GIDEON ... 111, 112, 113, 114, *119, 256*
gifts 19, 22, 23, 39, 48, 108, 133, 139, 140, 148, 158, 159, 175, 192, 205, 234, 282, 292, 306, 324, 352
global warming 183, 184
glorious 32, 138, 243, 263, 266, 301, 304, 345, 353
glorious Day 263
glory .. 63, 64, 82, 90, 112, 139, 188, 189, 226, 251, 254, 308, 309, 323, 332, 340
Gnosticism 332
GOD . 21, 27, 31, 32, 33, 34, 35, 36, 37, 38, 40, 41, 42, 43, 45, 46, 47, 48, 49, 51, 52, 53, 54, 56, 57, 58, 60, 62, 63, 64, 67, 68, 69, 70, 71, 72, 73, 74, 75, 76, 77, 80, 81, 82, 83, 84, 86, 87, 88, 89, 91, 92, 93, 94, 95, 96, 98, 99, 104, 105, 106, 107, 109, 110, 111, 112, 113, 114, *115*, 116, *118, 119, 120*,
121, 122, 123, 124, 126, 127, 128, 129, 130, 131, 132, 134, 135, *136, 137*, 138, 139, 140, 142, 143, 144, 145, 146, 147, 148, 149, 150, 155, 156, 157, 158, 159, 160, 161, 162, 163, 164, 165, 166, 168, 169, 170, 175, 176, 177, 178, 179, 180, 181, 182, 183, 184, 186, 187, 188, 189, 190, 192, 193, 194, 195, 197, 198, 199, 200, 201, 203, 204, 205, 206, 208, 209, 210, 217, 218, 219, 220, 223, 226, 227, 228, 229, 230, 231, 232, 234, 235, 237, 238, 239, 240, 241, 242, 243, 244, 245, 246, 247, 248, 250, 251, 252, 253, 254, 255, 256, 257, 259, 261, 264, 265, 266, 267, 269, 272, 274, 275, 276, 281, 282, 283, 284, 285, 286, 287, 288, 290, 291, 292, 293, 294, 295, 296, 297, 299, 300, 304, 306, 307, 308, 309, 310, 311, 312, 313, 314, 315, 316, 318, 319, 320, 321, 322, 323, 324, 325, 326, 327, 328, 329, 330, 331, 332, 333, 334, 335, 339, 340, 341, 342, 343, 344, 345, 346, 347, 348, 349, 350, 351, 352, 353, 354, 355, 359, 360, 361, 362, 363, 364, 365, 366, 367, 369, 372, 403
GOLIATH *118*, 137, 138
good . 33, 35, 36, 37, 40, 41, 47, 51, 58, 61, 69, 76, 80, 87, 96, 98, 124, 127, 128, 133, 134, 142, 159, 161, 162, 163, 169, 172, 177, 180, 183, 185, 188, 189, 190, 197, 204, 223, 226, 229, 234, 236, 238, 241, 261, 272, 282, 284, 296, 298, 302, 304,

305, 306, 311, 312, 313, 314, 319, 320, 321, 322, 334
gospel.....56, 81, 92, 189, 222, 256, 259, 274, 306, 309
Governmental Theory 331
grace.....21, 22, 35, 60, 87, 92, 124, 156, 178, 180, 187, 192, 211, 221, 281, 282, 284, 289, 290
GRAHAM, BILLY 350
grams..273
GRANT, ULYSSES S. 98
Great White Throne Judgment ..135
Greek Classics..........................327
GRENZ, STANLEY J. 58
GRIFFITH, ANDY 59
guilty 57, 68, 125, 140, 160

H

HABAKKUK 204
HAGAR 37, 44
HAGGAI......................26, 206, 208
HAMMURABI..............................57
harp 138, 204
healing 56, 123, 143, 189, 204, 220, 221, 227, 228, 239, 257, 318
heart .19, 35, 39, 46, 47, 48, 53, 55, 60, 63, 70, 72, 78, 96, 98, 104, 109, 111, 114, 117, *122*, 123, 124, 130, 132, 134, *135*, 142, 144, 145, 146, 147, 149, 150, 155, 156, 163, 164, 169, 173, *175*, 179, 181, 187, 195, 197, 205, 211, 219, 228, 229, 248, 253, 255, 259, *261*, 264, 266, 271, 283, 285, 287, 289, 297, 299, 307, 308, 309, *311*, 312, 313, 318, 320, 323, 326, 327, 331, 347, 349
heaven..60, 91, 127, 128, 131, 134, 137, 161, 192, 206, 220, 226, 236, 245, 246, 248, 251, 264,

267, 283, 286, 298, 300, 301, 308, 309, 315, 316, 326, 329, 335, 354, 358, 360, 362
heavenly Father 120, 195, 254, 329
Hebrew.....51, 68, 72, 93, 120, 134, 161, 165, 190, 196, 204, 207, 237, 294, 317
hell.....161, 224, 226, 239, 286, 328
HEMAN 138, 139
HERODOTUS 236
HEZEKIAH 134, 142, 143, 144
high priest.....60, 68, 124, 164, 271, 319
HITLER, ADOLF................119, 261
holiness 57, 71, 74, 137, 358
holistic 253, 333
holy... 24, 36, 52, 58, 59, 60, 62, 70, 72, 77, 78, 89, 93, 95, 115, 127, 130, 134, 143, 156, 158, 163, 166, 188, 202, 233, 236, 238, 240, 245, 253, 254, 260, 298, 301, 306, 312, 316, 326, 327, 332, 333, 334, 339
Holy of holies........................60, 61
Holy Spirit......*63*, *85*, *115*, 293, 330, 335
HOLY SPIRIT...148, 149, 155, 248, 262, 263, 269, 270, 271, 276, 292, 293
honesty...46, 70, 79, 142, 145, 146, 176, 222, 228, 244, 298, 305, 325
honor..21, 106, 111, 116, 165, 250, 251
hope .22, 25, 40, 42, 50, 55, 63, 86, 107, *117*, 122, 138, 139, 166, 168, 178, 184, 185, 189, 194, 196, 197, 199, 204, 219, 225, 229, 238, 244, 249, 255, 256, 260, 276, 282, 283, 285, 296, 304, 306, 307, 320, 322, 325, 333, 342, 356, 362

House of Bread 202
HOWARD, BOBBIE 318
HOWARD, JAMES E. *116*, 250, 289, 318
HOWARD, NICHOLAS 22, 125, 153, 175, 183, 209, 296, 347
HOWARD, STEFANIE 7, 20, 22, 125, 133, 149, 157, 175, 177, 178, 183, 298, 299, 302, 311
HOWARD, TIM 267
HOWARD, ZAKARY ... 22, 125, 153, 175, 179, 183, 205, 209, 296, 347
HUIE, BRYAN T. 359
human history 45, 47, 134, 155, 183, 257
human nature 75, 156
humanity 31, 33, 40, 45, 51, 63, 113, 122, 123, 135, *136*, 160, 164, 166, 184, 187, 188, 189, 199, 202, 247, 259, 282, 294, 306, 315, 316, 328, 330, 331, 342, 343, 356, 359
humility 47, 172, 192, 222, 251, 300, 350
HYBELS, BILL 305
hypocrisy 156

I

identity 41, 220, 261, 286, 287
idol 60, 61, 90
idolatry 111, 134, 342, 358
improvisation 138
inauguration 140
Incarnation .. 41, 162, 188, 245, 258, 368, 371
integrity ... 46, 68, 87, 108, 111, 114, *116*, 117, 133, 142, 161, 167, 205, 275, 302
intellect 90, 253, 301, 330
Interstate Isaiah 188, 189

intimacy 256
Iraq 203
irony 43, 57, 122, 124, 256, 300
IRWIN, JAMES 297
Isaac 36, 37, *89*, *334*
ISAAC 36, 37, 38, 39, 44, 49, *50*
ISAIAH 26, *36*, 41, *74*, 75, *136*, 143, 144, 168, 181, *182*, 183, 184, 185, 186, 187, 188, 189, *202*, 220, 221, 228, 238, 246, 255, *286*, 347, 361, 365, 368
ISHMAEL *37*, *38*
Israel 25, *38*, *39*, *40*, *41*, *42*, *43*, *48*, *49*, *55*, *56*, *58*, *60*, *63*, *70*, *71*, *74*, *75*, *79*, *80*, *81*, *82*, *86*, *88*, *94*, *96*, *97*, 98, *103*, 104, 106, 107, 108, 109, 111, 113, 114, 122, *130*, 137, 138, *141*, *161*, *164*, *182*, 184, 186, 188, 189, 190, 192, 194, 198, 199, 200, 203, 204, 207, 209, 210, 221, 222, 227, *245*, 250, *274*, *288*, *290*, 330, 342, 343, 344, 345, 346, 355
Israeli Antiquities Authority 108
Israelites. 53, 54, 56, 57, 58, 61, 72, 76, 79, 81, 82, 86, 87, 91, 98, 103, 106, 108, 109, 128, 130, 189, 197, 202, 222, 274

J

JACKSON, KEITH 54
Jacob 38
JACOB ... 38, 39, 40, 41, 42, 43, 45, 48, 49, 50, *89*, 112, 199, 200, 201, 204, 250, 286, 328, 355
JAEL 110
JAMES ... 38, 69, 77, 180, 221, 230, 241, 300, 320, 321, 322, 323
JAPHETH 44
JEDUTHAN 138
JEFFERSON, THOMAS 92

JEREMIAH ...26, 49, 134, 190, 191, 192, 193, 194, 195, 196, 197, 199, 201, 351
Jericho 104, 231
Jerusalem 60, 94, 123, 134, 135, 141, 142, 146, 148, 167, 168, 185, 186, 188, 189, 193, 200, 208, 209, 210, 211, 215, 247, 252, 266, 271, 275, 326, 350, 359, 362, 372
JESSE 114, *118*
JESUS 21, 22, 24, *36*, *38*, *43*, *48*, *49*, *55*, 56, *60*, *68*, 77, *81*, *83*, *86*, *88*, *89*, *91*, *93*, *98*, *103*, 109, 112, 113, 114, 115, *127*, *128*, *136*, *137*, 139, 149, 150, *156*, *161*, 162, *170*, 173, *178*, *182*, 186, 187, 188, 189, *202*, 204, 206, 207, 208, 209, 210, 211, 215, 219, 220, 221, 222, 223, 224, 226, 227, 228, 229, 230, 231, 232, 233, 235, 236, 237, 238, 239, 240, *241*, 242, *243*, *244*, *245*, 246, 247, 248, 249, 250, 252, 253, 254, 255, 256, 257, 258, 259, 260, 261, 262, 263, 264, 265, 266, 267, 268, 269, *272*, *274*, *275*, *282*, 283, *284*, *286*, *287*, 288, 289, *290*, 292, 293, 299, *300*, 301, *304*, 306, 307, *309*, *314*, *316*, *317*, 318, 319, 320, 321, 323, 324, 325, 326, 327, 329, 330, 331, 332, 333, *334*, *335*, 340, 341, 343, 349, 353, 354, 355, 358, 359, 361, 362, 363, 365, 366, 368
JESUS BARABBAS 236, 237
JESUS CHRIST *36*, *48*, *83*, *86*, 109, *115*, *161*, 162, *182*, 186, 188, 189, 221, 237, *239*, *240*, 259, 269, *274*, *284*, *286*, *288*, *290*, 307, 318, 319, 323, *333*, 358, 362
Jewish 40, 42, 44, 59, 74, 87, 89, 114, 148, 154, 162, 186, 193, 197, 206, 207, 233, 242, 245, 246, 252, 260, 271, 275, 290, 294, 326, 330, 351, 355, 360, 372
Jews . 51, 54, 60, 75, 106, 143, 154, 186, 187, 188, 192, 193, 197, 199, 200, 208, 246, 261, 275, 281, 286, 326, 347, 355, 372
JOAB 123, 124, 140
JOB 26, 55, 155, 191, 350, 365
JOHN 26, *36*, *38*, *55*, 77, *85*, *98*, 109, 112, *161*, 162, 165, 173, 184, 188, 199, 208, 221, 230, 238, *240*, *241*, *243*, 248, 252, 253, 254, 255, 256, 257, 258, 259, 260, 262, 263, 264, 265, 266, 267, 271, *275*, 287, 293, 300, 320, 323, 325, 328, 329, 330, 332, 333, 339, 340, 352, 355, 358, 360, 361, 362
JONAH 203
JONATHAN118, 119, *120*, 137, 138
JOSEPH45, *46*, *47*, *48*, *49*, *50*, 113, 190, 346, 347
JOSHUA. 56, 86, 95, 103, 104, 105, 106, 107, 108, 197, 209, 237, 344, 365
JOSIAH 55, 95, 134
JOTHAM 112, 113
Judah 113, 134, 142, 143, 188, 192, 195
JUDAH ... 44, 45, 48, 49, 50, 55, *63*, *126*, *130*, *141*, 193, 202, 215, 317
JUDAS 260, 261, 262, 264
Judea 215, 258
judgement 45, 126

judgment.50, 55, 69, 121, 124, 135, 136, 191, 192, 196, 197, 199, 200, 201, 203, 204, 206, 220, 229, 234, 262, 334, 342, 356, 359
judicial branch 74, 347
justice 51, 55, 57, 71, 81, 93, 96, 123, 163, 204, 302
JUSTIN 57

K

KENDALL, THOMAS *33*
KIERKEGAARD, SOREN *36*
KILCHER, EIVIN 147
KILCHER, OTTO 146
kindness 196, 206, 319, 322
king ... 27, 37, 45, 49, 52, 53, 57, 74, 86, 89, 94, 95, 96, 109, 111, 112, 113, 114, 116, 121, 122, 123, 124, 128, 129, 130, 131, 134, 135, 138, 141, 142, 143, 144, 145, 148, 153, 154, 158, 162, 168, 180, 181, 193, 195, 207, 208, 209, 210, 215, 229, 265, 275, 276, 300, 317, 318, 326, 347, 348, 355
kingdom 38, 112, 113, 124, 137, 141, 220, 222, 223, 241, 245, 265, 276, 300
kingdom of God 112
kingdom of heaven *137*, 220
kingship 111, 113, 114
KINISON, SAM 333
KISSINGER, HENRY 358
knowledge 254, 259, 261, 332, 351, 352, 356

L

LABAN *37*
LABRIOLI, JIM 334

ladies 181
LaGASSE, EMERILE 257
lamb *31, 36, 54, 55, 72, 88, 103*, 136, 191, 220, 221, *316*, 330, 348, 356
Lamb of God 261
Lamb's Book of Life *136*, 220
lamp 58, 59, 133, 134, 326, 327
language 37, 41, 56, 63, 85, 90, 93, 180, 184, 240, 275
Laodicea 353
laugh 44, 48, 315, 322, 334, 335
law.... 20, 24, 43, 44, 45, 46, 57, 74, 92, 95, 97, 107, 108, 113, 114, 154, 169, 170, 220, 273, 282, 289, 326, 331, 350
Law... 57, 65, 86, 94, 114, 134, 149, 186, 228, 239, 241, 242, 275, 282, 288, 294, 364, 366
LAZARUS 221, 258, 259, 260
leader 53, 68, 74, 78, 79, 86, 87, 130, 132, 233, 275, 310
leaders 51, 68, 72, 74, 97, 183, 184, 228, 229, 231, 240, 245, 271, 282, 326
leadership 25, 68, 72, 73, 86, 95, 106, 107, 110, 123, 126, 176, 195, 197
LEAH *40, 43, 45, 50*, 347
legacy 117
legislative branch 74, 347
LEIBUSH, R. MEIR 346
LEVI ... 42, 43, 50, *76, 94*, 112, 140, 346, 347
Levite 204
LEVOISIER, ANTOINE 273
LEWIS, C.S. 64, 239, 301, 403
life..... 23, 25, 31, 32, 33, 34, 39, 44, 46, 47, 48, 49, 50, 51, 53, 55, 58, 60, 68, 72, 73, 77, 79, 81, 88, 90, 92, 95, 96, 104, 109, 111, 113, 114, 116, 120, 121, 122, 124,

383

126, 127, 132, 133, 136, 140,
142, 143, 156, 162, 170, 171,
173, 174, 176, 177, 178,
179,191, 192, 194, 195, 196,
197, 199, 202, 204, 205, 206,
215, 218, 222, 224, 226, 231,
237, 240, 254, 255, 256, 257,
258, 259, 260, 264, 265, 267,
268, 272, 273, 276, 284, 287,
290, 291, 296, 297, 298, 300,
304, 305, 308, 310, 313, 314,
315, 316, 321, 322, 323, 324,
325, 326, 328, 329, 330, 331,
332, 333, 343, 348, 353, 356,
360
listening 91, 98, 157, 223, 224, 227,
235, 291, 292, 348
living water..83, 238, 239, 265, 293,
346
logos 178, 252, 253, 301
LONG, LUZ 119
Lord ..25, *34*, *35*, *38*, *45*, *51*, *52*, *56*,
58, *61*, *63*, *67*, *69*, *70*, *75*, *78*, *79*,
80, *82*, *83*, *84*, *86*, *92*, *93*, *94*,
118, *126*, *128*, *130*, *131*, *132*,
134, 138, 140, *141*, 142, 143,
161, *163*, *172*, *176*, *178*, *181*,
182, 183, 186, 188, 189, 204,
206, 238, *239*, 271, *274*, *275*,
283, *289*, *297*, *298*, *304*, *312*,
318, 322, 324, *333*
*LORD*22, 23, 25, 31, 32, 33, 34, 35,
37, 51, 53, *74*, *91*, *93*, *94*, *95*, *96*,
98, 99, 104, 106, 107, 109, 111,
112, 113, 115, 117, *119*, *120*,
121, 123, 125, 126, 136, 144,
145, 146, 157, 158, 160, 164,
167, 168, 185, 187, 188, 190,
191, 192, 193, 194, 196, 197,
198, 200, 201, 202, 203, 205,
206, 208, 210, 219, 220, 226,
228, 229, 230, 231, 236, *242*,
245, 246, 251, 252, 253, 260,
265, 266, 267, 268, 269, 271,
272, 273, *276*, 283, *284*, *287*,
288, *289*, 290, 292, 297, 300,
306, 307, 308, *309*, *315*, 319,
325, 327, 328, 333, 341, 342,
343, 344, 346, 347, 350, 352,
354, 355, 357, 358, 362
LOT 34, 37, 44
love... 31, 36, 40, 42, 50, 69, 95, 96,
113, 116, 123, 135, 139, 159,
168, 175, 178, 181, 185, 187,
188, 206, 207, 217, 220, 225,
231, 241, 242, 246, 248, 250,
259, 261, 265, 266, 281, 282,
283, 285, 287, 289, 290, 296,
298, 299, 302, 303, 306, 307,
308, 310, 311, 312, 313, 316,
317, 319, 324, 325, 326, 329,
330, 334, 343, 350, 351
LOWRY, MARK 246
loyalty. 48, 114, 141, 168, 172, 266,
293, 302, 348
LUKE.. 26, 112, 137, 206, 220, 227,
228, 245, 246, 247, 248, 249,
250, 251, 258, 358, 359, 361
LUTHER, MARTIN 87, 92, 199, 281
lyre 204

M

MACARTHUR, JOHN 293
MADISON,JAMES 107
MAHER, BILL 334
maker 48, 72
MALACHI 201
MANASSEH. 49, *88*, 110, 134, 346,
347
manuscripts 327
MARK 56, 57, 93, 131, 189, 220,
228, 238, 239, 241, 242, 243,
244

Marriage Supper of the Lamb .. 121, 354
MARTIN, SAM 173
MARY 245, 246
master 37, 40, 46, 63, 160, 275, 315
MATTHEW ... 26, 77, 114, 215, 217, 220, 221, 222, 223, 224, 226, 227, 228, 229, 231, 232, 233, 234, 235, 236, 243, 246
MAYS, WILLIE 321, 322
McDOUGALL, DUNCAN 273
McGEE, J. VERNON 362
meaningful prayer 126, 199, 248, 325
mentor 132, 138, 139, 160, 175, 298, 310, 313, 323, 325
MEPHIBOSHETH 119
mercy 59, 60, 96, 124, 161, 162, 187, 192, 196, 197, 204, 313, 314, 328, 364, 365
MEREDITH, DON 54
Messiah 93, *115*, 184, 187, 236, 237, 240, 241, 242, 246
metamorphosis 259
MEYER, FREDERICK B. 226
mid-tribulation rapture 354
MILLER, JANICE 253
MILTON, JOHN 339
mind .. 36, 49, 53, 56, 57, 61, 72, 74, 80, 83, 97, 98, 130, 140, 157, 178, 183, 190, 191, 198, 228, 229, 233, 240, 244, 257, 276, 282, 285, 301, 302, 307, 317, 322, 323
ministry ... 20, 22, 23, 59, 68, 73, 77, 86, 108, 110, *116*, 124, 132, 133, 137, 173, 174, 178, 181, 190, 192, 203, 230, 235, 255, 276, 295, 306, 310, 318, 332, 333, 335, 348, 353, 359, 362

miracle 55, 84, 91, 127, 143, 228, 236, 240, 244, 255, 257, 294, 326
miracles 56, 91, 132, 220, 239, 248, 255, 335
missionary 21, 68, 98, 124, 174, 259, 335, 349, 362
mistrust 45
Moab 83, 84, 96, 196
Mom *43*, *48*, *103*, *116*, 117, *172*, 251, *283*, 297, *298*
money 37, 74, 97, 125, 126, 176, 234, 235, 289
MONROE, JAMES 352
Moral Exemplar Theory 330
morality 36, 97, 331
MORDECAI 154
MORRISON, JIM 210
MOSES .. 50, 51, 52, 53, 54, 56, 57, 60, 61, 63, 64, 70, 71, 72, 73, 78, 79, 80, 82, 83, 86, 88, 90, 95, 98, 134, *136*, 163, 187, 198, 239, 241, 242, 243, 287, 294, 340, 351, 359
motives 135, 177, 205
movie 62
music 62, 63, 77, 130, 138, 139, 231, 285, 313
musicians 138
mysteries 223
mystery ... 32, 33, 40, 41, 49, 59, 60, 61, 70, 112, *136*, 157, 166, 210, 261, 285, 308, 309, 317, 331, 352

N

NABAL 120, 121
NAHUM 203
name 39, 40, 41, 51, 62, 71, 79, 96, 97, 98, 110, 114, 116, 120, 135, 137, 139, 145, 159, 160, 164,

385

188, 192, 195, 196, 197, 199, 200, 204, 208, 220, 236, 237, 244, 246, 250, 258, 259, 263, 286, 290, 313, 314, 317, 325, 331, 334, 341, 346, 357, 358, 372
NAOMI 97, 113, 114, 215
NAPHTALI 40, 110
narrative.... 23, 62, 78, 81, 112, 123, 141, 264, 326
NASH, STEVE 153
NATHAN 122
nature ... 23, 43, 164, 177, 217, 218, 240, 266, 284, 315, 322
Nazis 119
NEBUCHADNEZZAR 195
NEE, WATCHMAN 145, 146
NEHEMIAH .. 26, 147, 148, 149, 209
neighbors 42, 58, 92
Nephilim 32, 33
NEUFELD, THOMAS R. YODER
.... 335
New Jerusalem 346, 347
Ninevah 203
NOAH *33, 34, 44*, 187, 350
NORTHRUP, DARY 227

O

OBADIAH . 127, 128, 198, 199, 200, 201
OBAMA, BARAK 358
OBED 114
obedience 70, 75, 83, 117, 138, 145, 183, 191, 220, 234, 235, 285, 311, 321, 328, 350
obey .. 35, 55, 58, 75, 82, 86, 91, 93, 94, 126, 134, 182, 284, 287, 294, 297, 298
Old Testament 78, 81, 114, 115, 187, 199, 201, 294, 319, 331, 341, 359

Olympics 118, 166
orientation 35, 290
ORIGEN 237, 330
OSBORNE, GRANT 354
OSTEEN, JOHN 173
OTHNIEL 108
OWENS, JESSE 118

P

pagan 78, 196, 330
PAGANINI, NICCOLO 231
PAINE, THOMAS 351
panoramic 75, 135, 188
PASCAL, BLAISE 253
Passover 54, 72, 87, 143, 235, 260, 348
past 57, 104, 186, 284
pastor ... 20, 21, 50, 62, 68, 87, 106, *116*, 123, 137, 139, 173, 177, 180, 191, 226, 227, 267, 286, 298, *309*, 325, 335
pastors . 46, 59, 110, 124, 157, 162, 276, 310
pathos 252, 301
patience 117, 199, 225, 304, 321, 327, 328, 342
PAUL 55, 59, 64, 69, 85, 93, 162, 172, 186, 187, 200, 201, 205, 208, 226, 246, 250, 252, 253, 263, 270, 272, 275, 276, 277, 281, 282, 286, 287, 290, 291, 293, 294, 295, 302, 305, 306, 307, 308, 309, 310, 313, 314, 326, 327, 328, 331, 333, 355
peace 61, 72, 98, 106, 123, 136, 159, 161, 162, 163, 167, 185, 187, 188, 199, 208, 210, 224, 225, 238, 246, 252, 283, 302, 304, 307, 317, 318, 366
Penal Substitution Theory 36, 81, 195, 331

Pentecost............................88, 267
Pentecostal...25, 87, 123, 138, 204, 269, 270, 333, 354, 355
Pentecostal theology 354
PEREZ...................................49, 187
Persians......................................153
PETER 26, *36*, *38*, *83*, *85*, 162, 193, 220, 221, 228, 229, 230, 232, *241*, *242*, 260, 263, 267, 268, 269, 271, *275*, 301, 323, 324, 326, 327, 328, 330, 350, 360
PETERSON, EUGENE......237, 247, 300, 325
PHARAOH.......................*46*, *52*, *53*
Pharisees..228, 232, 233, 242, 244, 258, 261, 264
Philistines 37, 78, 137
physical state......................186, 194
PILATE 112, 236, 237, 265
PIPP, WALLY 117, 364, 368
PLATO.................................236, 327
POREE, ANTHONY....................286
post-tribulation rapture...............354
posture.........................35, 131, 232
power....*80*, *95*, *131*, *132*, *137*, *141*, *163*, *216*, *231*, *241*, 247, 263, 265, *266*, 297, 300, *304*, *310*, *313*, *314*, *316*, 343, 346, 358, 360
praise..79, 104, 112, 138, 139, 158, 164, 177, 178, 187, 232, 240, 253, 283, 290, 297, 301, 308, 323, 355
pray.46, 52, 69, 74, 79, 86, 89, 126, 145, 156, 161, 163, 172, 186, 252, 284, 304, 306, 307, 313
prayer 19, 24, 42, 46, 53, 59, 61, 62, 69, 74, 85, 88, 99, 106, 107, 108, 111, 113, 118, 119, 120, 122, 123, 127, 131, 133, 134, 140, 143, 145, 146, 147, 149, 154, 156, 157, 161, 164, 166, 168, 172, 175, 176, 177, 178, 185, 191, 192, 199, 204, 205, 219, 229, 230, 248, 249, 251, 256, 263, 264, 268, 271, 291, 292, 293, 297, 304, 306, 311, 323, 324, 333, 335, 341, 349, 350
preacher.....................................148
predestination........ 39, *47*, 199, *286*, 327, 328
presence 60, 63, 64, 80, 83, 86, 91, 164, 196, 255, 256, 310
pressure 92, 122, 180
pre-tribulation rapture 354
pride ... 79, 126, 143, 144, 181, 202, 203, 205
priesthood of the believer 86
promise 44, 89, 103, 178, 180, 187, 282, 294, 297, 298, 324
Promised Land ... 58, 74, 75, 82, 87, 111, 197, 198, 209, 344
promises............ 187, 189, 190, 287
prophecy 24, 50, 55, 75, 77, 122, 141, 186, 191, 202, 204, 211, 251, 252, 275, 343, 357
prophet... 49, 55, 85, 110, 111, 112, *116*, 121, 122, 126, 127, 128, 129, 132, 134, 141, 143, 191, 192, 193, 195, 198, 203, 204, 220, 228, 238
prophetic 85, 184, 190, 192, 326
prophets 77, 86, 128, 129, 130, 132, 134, 188, 192, 197, 199, 200, 206, 225, 282, 326, 342, 344
prosperity 304, 333
providence............................. 47, 49
provision........ 55, 83, 177, 228, 230
psalmist............................. 138, 156
psyche................................. 50, 156
purposeful Bible reading... 126, 199, 325, 345

387

Q

quantum physics 200

R

RACHEL *40, 43, 45,* 215, 347
ransom 330, 331
Ransom Theory 36, 330
rapture 88, 184, 354
reassurance 43
REBEKAH .. *37, 40, 44, 49, 50,* 200, 201, 362
redemption.... 45, 50, 189, 206, 319, 346, 348
REDPATH, ALLEN 226
reformation 331, 362
Reformed 199, 286
Reformed theology 328
relationship 48, 69, 88, 93, 106, 132, 146, 149, 198, 219, 220, 248, 257, 284, 325
relief ministry 256
religious elite 257, 259
remember . 56, 57, 60, 96, 103, 132, 277, 288, 314, 321
renewal 143, 259, 315
repentance 145, 146
resolution 349, 360
resolve 141, 202, 349, 350
responsibility . 34, 57, 58, 61, 68, 86, 95, 313, 319
rest 41, 48, 55, 62, 63, 75, 80, 91, 133, 160, 174, 222, 223
restoration 45, 87, 123, 206, 221, 261, 362
resurrection 24, 64, 86, 88, 255, 258, 265, 267, 308, 309, 333, 340, 343, 363
REUBEN *45, 49, 50, 88,* 110
revelation ... 120, 126, 149, 166, 254
reverence *73, 93, 115,* 147, 149

revival 56, 110, 362
Revolutionary War 352
reward 88, 191, 192, 193, 240, 250, 251, 297, 298
REXROAT, STEPHEN 23
right .. 37, 38, 41, 43, 45, 46, 47, 49, 52, 56, 58, 61, 62, 70, 73, 75, 76, 78, 79, 81, 84, 85, 92, 95, 97, 103, 127, 130, 131, 133, 141, 161, 164, 170, 172, 174, 176, 177, 178, 240, 243, 244, 245, 273, 275, 276, 286, 287, 288, 294, 295, 296, 297, 300, 301, 302, 304, 310, 316
righteousness . 34, 94, 98, 114, 117, 124, 126, *136,* 161, 162, 272, 281, 317, 318, 331, 358
Robert's Rules of Order 73
ROBERTS, JERRY 174
ROBERTS, KEENAN *46*
ROBERTS, MAMIE 174
ROEVER, AL 207
Roman Road to Salvation 188
Rome 245, 275, 358, 359
ROSEN, STEVEN A 108
ROSS, BILL 170
ROSS, BOB 61
RUTH 97, 113, 114, 215

S

Sabbath 87, 228, 257
sacred 34, 58, 59, 63, 70, 73, 76, 77, 82, 182
sacrifice .. 36, 67, 68, 69, 77, 78, 87, 147, 159, 163, 202, 329, 330
salvation . 72, 80, 93, 103, 126, 140, 146, 166, 184, 186, 188, 198, 199, 201, 209, 237, 243, 244, 247, 256, 264, 265, 281, 282, 286, 287, 288, 290, 294, 307,

309, 313, 315, 316, 318, 319, 327, 328, 341
Samaritans 221, 255
SAMSON 78, 339
SAMUEL...26, *49*, 77, *94*, 112, 114, *115*, *116*, *118*, *119*, *120*, 121, 122, 123, 124, 125, *127*, 207
SARAH 44
Satan 126, 206, 220, 228, 247, 260, 287, 329, 330, 334, 357, 360, 361
Satanic...................................256
Satisfaction Theory 330
SAUL ..94, 114, *118*, 121, 122, 127, 204, 207, 271
Savior .86, 146, 206, 215, 246, 274, 290, 300, 331, 366
SCOTT, E.P. 349
scripture.. 19, 20, 23, 24, 31, 41, 44, 51, 57, 60, 63, 64, 67, 75, 89, 90, 92, 94, 108, 111, 119, 120, 121, 127, 134, 144, 145, 166, 173, 174, 181, 184, 187, 192, 199, 200, 205, 210, 215, 222, 232, 236, 237, 239, 241, 242, 256, 263, 270, 281, 284, 285, 291, 315, 319, 323, 326, 327, 333, 334, 335, 345, 351, 354, 359
Second Temple..........................345
SEINFELD, JERRY 259
self-confidence.........................322
separation.47, 71, 77, 92, 223, 224, 307
serpent.............................31, 32, 248
servant 35, 37, 45, 80, 85, 156, 159, 182, 189, 231, 234, 235, 245, 304, 324
SHADDICK, DAVID 117
SHECHEM........42, 43, 44, 112, 113
Shem 34
SHEM 44, 51
SHEMEI 140

sign............ *119*, *120*, *143*, *256*, *318*
silence. 53, 129, 196, 233, 238, 291
SIMEON 42, 43, 50, 112
simplicity...................... 70, 311, 313
sin..... 31, 32, 34, 36, 43, 62, 68, 77, 78, 90, 104, 109, 123, 145, 146, 155, 181, 182, 184, 189, 202, 221, 226, 227, 231, 238, 247, 257, 262, 282, 283, 284, 289, 294, 311, 312, 317, 325, 327, 328, 329, 330, 331, 332, 335, 340, 341, 342, 350, 354, 359
sinful nature.............................. 328
sinners........................ 62, 107, 145
sins. 44, 68, 83, 156, 161, 181, 182, 183, 239, 240, 269, 319
smell................................ 47, 56, 67
Sodom and Gomorrah......... *44*, *115*
SOLOMON 55, 72, 94, 140, 141, 143, 163, 164, 179
Son... 36, 81, 94, 96, 118, 123, 161, 182, 195, 229, 231, 232, 237, 238, 239, 241, 243, 265, 274, 286, 316, 329, 330, 331, 332, 341
sorcery 203
soul... 142, 144, 148, 226, 253, 273, 293, 301, 333
sovereignty............................. 47, 87
speaking in tongues 269
spirit 68, 80, 84, 121, 127, 130, 143, 160, 168, 175, 204, 215, 226, 228, 240, 253, 254, 255, 272, 291, 292, 293, 294, 332, 333, 341, 348
SPIRIT.... 22, 31, 35, 43, 46, 47, 55, 63, 64, 67, 70, 84, 88, 108, 115, 124, 125, 128, 130, 131, 133, 144, 155, 159, 168, 172, 181, 187, 202, 206, 208, 211, 216, 217, 238, 248, 253, 254, 267, 268, 269, 270, 274, 283, 284,

288, 291, 292, 304, 306, 308, 309, 311, 313, 314, 316, 317, 320, 326, 328, 353, 369, 403
spiritual ...25, 35, 43, 62, 63, 67, 68, 83, 84, 118, 121, 137, 229, 239, 254, 284, 295, 298, 316, 318, 321, 340
spirituality..........58, 62, 92, 318, 333
SPURGEON, CHARLES HADDON 108
STEDMAN, RAY C. *33*
STEVENS, RAY............................49
STEWART, PAYNE.....................91
story 37, 40, 42, 49, 55, 78, 84, 109, 112, 114, 115, 116, 118, 140, 145, 157, 195, 203, 223, 224, 225, 226, 227, 234, 257, 309, 322, 349, 403
strength...50, 70, 78, 121, 177, 185, 205, 226, 230, 251, 283, 302, 323, 340, 351, 356
struggle...25, 40, 67, 110, 179, 206, 237, 250, 276
struggles 40, 267
substance ...25, 147, 226, 273, 288, 318, 320, 323
substitution 331
Substitutionary Atonement......... *See* Penal Substitution Theory
SUETONIUS..............................327
supernatural.........................32, 166

T

tabernacle..60, 76, 81, 88, 138, 229
table fellowship 236, 256
TACITUS 327
TAMAR................................44, 45
teamwork 167
TEBOW, TIM 334
temple.78, 134, 138, 142, 143, 144, 149, 159, 160, 163, 188, 200,

204, 206, 208, 229, 247, 252, 264, 271, 275, 339, 345, 346, 347, 372
temptation 25, 32, 97, 158, 235, 247, 329
Ten Commandments.............57, 67
test 36, 70, 143, 144, 175, 230, 232, 244, 264
The Blessed Hope..................... 355
The Diaspora............................. 193
theology 58, 62, 199, 227, 286, 294, 327, 330, 335
theophany *115*, 155
theories 81, 330, 331, 359, 360
THOMAS 33, 92, 258, 259, 263
thoughts 24, 47, 172, 183, 205, 240, 285
THUCYDIDES................... 236, 327
time .. 25, 33, 35, 36, 38, 39, 40, 42, 43, 45, 48, 49, 50, 51, 52, 53, 54, 56, 60, 64, 70, 72, 73, 75, 78, 79, 86, 87, 89, 91, 92, 95, 97, 103, 124, 125, 127, 129, 130, 132, 134, 139, 141, 142, 143, 156, 157, 159, 160, 162, 163, 164, 170, 174, 175, 176, 178, 179, 183, 186, 187, 188, 189, 190, 191, 203, 204, 215, 225, 234, 237, 238, 242, 245, 256, 257, 272, 273, 275, 282, 283, 284, 286, 287, 294, 295, 301, 305, 306, 307, 309, 310, 311, 314, 318, 321, 322, 327, 333, 334
timing... 82, 140, 176, 203, 204, 222
TITUS. 26, 200, 310, 311, 312, 313, 314
tongues 268
Torah.... 93, 95, 110, 165, 168, 246, 282
transfiguration 229
transubstantiation...................... 256
Trinity *115*, 254, *316*

trust...25, 35, 37, 40, 56, 75, 81, 83, 92, 96, 104, 121, 126, 129, 142, 169, 172, 176, 177, 185, 186, 187, 191, 203, 204, 229, 268, 282, 286, 299, 320, 321, 322, 323, 327, 329, 348
truth 19, 44, 106, 128, 130, 131, 158, 160, 161, 162, 166, 175, 183, 216, 238, 243, 244, 254, 259, 261, 263, 290, 293, 331, 341, 347, 358, 359, 360
TWAIN, MARK............................166

U

unfaithful 94, 197, 258
unity 167, 309, 340
URIAH 122

V

VAN DOREN, CHARLES 249
VAN IMPE, JACK 252
VANDER LAAN, RAY 93
view screen............53, 57, 228, 301
vision 58, 63, 130, 188, 190, 193, 297
visions................................129, 339

W

wait .44, 61, 86, 127, 137, 145, 155, 159, 184, 185, 187, 191, 323
WALLACE, JIM............................93
war......24, 40, 75, 78, 89, 106, 122, 141, 165, 201, 210, 344, 355, 360
WASHINGTON, GEORGE 351
WEAVER, JASPER 139
WESLEY, CHARLES.................309
WILDER, THORNTON *48*

will 24, 25, 33, 35, 36, 37, 38, 39, 41, 42, 44, 46, 47, 48, 49, 50, 51, 52, 53, 54, 56, 57, 58, 60, 61, 62, 63, 67, 68, 69, 70, 73, 74, 75, 76, 77, 80, 81, 82, 83, 85, 86, 88, 89, 91, 93, 94, 95, 96, 97, 98, 103, 104, 105, 109, 110, 111, 112, 113, 114, 115, 116, 117, 118, 119, 121, 122, 123, 125, 126, 127, 129, 130, 131, 132, 133, 135, 136, 137, 141, 144, 156, 160, 161, 164, 166, 170, 173, 174, 175, 176, 177, 178, 179, 181, 182, 183, 185, 186, 187, 188, 189, 191, 192, 193, 194, 195, 196, 202, 203, 204, 205, 206, 215, 217, 218, 220, 222, 223, 224, 225, 226, 228, 230, 231, 232, 233, 234, 238, 239, 241, 243, 245, 252, 253, 255, 257, 258, 260, 261, 262, 263, 264, 265, 266, 267, 272, 275, 276, 284, 285, 286, 287, 288, 291, 293, 294, 296, 297, 301, 304, 305, 307, 309, 310, 312, 313, 315, 317, 319, 320, 321, 322, 323, 324, 326, 328, 329, 332, 334, 340, 341, 353, 354, 355, 358, 359, 360
WILLARD, DALLAS........... 216, 403
WILLIAMS, RALPH 335
witchcraft 57, 203, 358
woman.............................. *See EVE*
Word..... 27, 87, 107, 109, 142, 149, 161, 178, 252, 285, 287, 332, 348, 352, 359, 360, 362, 365, 367, 368, 370
work 74, 76, 95, 128, 129, 139, 141, 161, 172, 181, 202, 205, 233, 239, 244, 300, 302, 306, 307, 326

world .31, 33, 36, 38, 48, 57, 60, 70, 81, 90, 92, 96, 97, 104, 111, 112, 121, 162, 164, 179, 180, 186, 188, 189, 216, 218, 223, 226, 237, 242, 256, 257, 258, 261, 263, 264, 265, 266, 272, 273, 285, 287, 308, 309, 313, 327, 328, 357

World War II 119, 165, 173, 202

worship .60, 69, 76, 92, 93, 94, 114, 115, 117, 139, 144, 162, 163, 178, 182, 184, 189, 229, 248, 254, 275, 290, 339, 347, 349, 364

worthy 98, 268, 301, 310, 355

wrestle 25, *32*, 36, 41, 42, *43*, 49, 59, 92, 200, 204, 205, 261, 262, 288, 302

wrestling 25, 193, 206, 250

Y

YAHWEH 40, 51, *136*
Year of Jubilee 73, 74, 75
YESHUA 86, 237

Z

ZADOK 124
ZASPEL, FRED G. 344
ZEBULUN 110
ZECHARIAH 26, 208
ZEDEKIAH 129, 130, 193, 195
ZEPHENIAH 206
ZERAH 49
ZERUBBABEL 208
ZIKLAG 121
ZILPAH 43, 45, 347
ZWINGLI, ULRICH 199

SCRIPTURE INDEX

Genesis
  1:1, 34, 320
  1:2, 31
  2:6, 7, 257
  2:15, 31
  3:1-7, 32
  3:15, 248
  4:7, 32
  6:1-8, 32
  7:1, 33
  11:10, 34
  12:3, 89
  13:12, 13, 18, 34
  14:8, 317
  15:1, 297
  15:2-6, 35
  18, 115
  18: 27, 28, 35
  22:6-8, 36
  24:25-31, 42
  24:49, 37
  25:23, 200
  25:28, 201
  25:30, 197
  26:1, 2, 37
  27:30-36, 38
  30:8, 40
  32:24-32, 41
  33:9, 199
  38:24-26, 44
  40:20-22, 45
  42:6-9, 47
  44:27-31, 48
  48:14, 49
  49:28-33, 49

Exodus
  2:12, 50
  3:14, 51
  8:9, 10, 52
  8:20, 89
  9:5-7, 53
  12:46, 54
  14:15, 56
  17:14-16, 56
  20:13, 250
  22:6-8, 57
  26:34, 59
  27:20, 21, 58
  28:29, 60
  32:24, 61
  35:30-35, 63
  40:34-38, 63

Leviticus
  3:16, 67
  4:3, 68
  9:24, 69
  10:5-7, 70
  24:14, 71
  25:10, 73
  26, 191
  26:33-35, 75

Numbers
  1:49-51, 76
  6:9-11, 77
  7:11, 78

10:35, 36, 79
11:24-27, 359
12:3, 136
14:24, 80
20:1-11, 82
22:22-32, 83
27:17-23, 86
28:6, 87

Deuteronomy
4:41-43, 88
9:21, 90
11:18-21, 91
13:4, 93
17:15-19, 94
24:19-22, 95
25:5-10, 96
27-29, 198
28, 191
29:18, 357
30:14, 287
32:30, 98
33:2, 294

Joshua
1:8, 95
2:17-21, 103
7:20-22, 104
8:3-22, 344
9:14, 106
10:42, 107

Judges
1:15, 108
3:15, 16, 109
4:9, 109
8:23, 111
9:15, 112

13:17-19, 41
20:29-46, 344

Ruth
4:13-22, 113

1 Samuel
8:7, 112
9:20, 207
10:3, 114
12:3, 115
12:24, 117
16:23, 204
17:18, 118
20:14, 118
20:37, 38, 119
25:25, 120
30:6, 121

2 Samuel
8:7, 94
12:11, 12, 122
12:23, 123
14:14, 123
18:23, 124
18:33, 123
22:11, 211
24:10, 125

1 Kings
13:1, 55
13:17-20, 126
13:23, 126
19:13, 127
22:19, 128

2 Kings
1:15, 131

2:9, 132
3:15, 204
4:10, 133
4:38-41, 357
6:8-12, 148
23:25, 26, 134

1 Chronicles
4:1-8, 135
14:15, 136
20:6, 7, 137
25:1, 138, 204
29:13, 14, 139

2 Chronicles
10:15-19, 141
21:20, 142
31:20, 21, 142
32:31, 143

Ezra
3:13, 144
8:22, 23, 145
10:13, 14, 146

Nehemiah
6:3, 147
6:12, 13, 148
6:15, 148
8:12, 149

Esther
1:10-12, 153
4:11-14, 154

Job
33:1-4, 155, 156

Psalms
1:1, 2, 107
2:4, 335
18:10, 211
19:12,13, 155
22:1, 123
25:15, 354
27:7-10, 156
34:20, 211
48:1, 2, 158
50:14, 159
51, 122
68:17, 294
70:5, 160
73:17, 160
79:8, 9, 162
80:15, 161
80:19, 161
85:10, 161
90:3, 4, 360
90:10, 174
94:19, 162
97:2, 163
103:1, 164
104:3, 211
110:4, 317
119:11, 109
119:105, 165
127:2, 166
133:1-3, 167
139:1, 4, 228
144:5, 168

Proverbs
2:7-20, 272
3:3, 168
4:27, 229
11:6, 169

12:15, 170
15:1, 172
15:24, 268
15:28, 171, 172
16:32, 172
17:17, 173
17:21, 120
17:28, 172
19:27, 174
20:5, 175
20:7, 117
23:7, 175
25:9-11, 176
25:11, 20
27:17, 313
30:7, 8, 176
30:7-8, 177
31:31, 177

Ecclesiastes
3:14, 178
9:11, 12, 179

Song of Solomon
3:11, 181

Isaiah
1:18, 181
7:14, 188, 246
9:6, 41, 162, 188, 210, 246
11:3, 182
11:16, 188
14:12-15, 361
19: 23, 24, 189
24:36, 183
28:16, 286
29:13, 228
30:31, 185

32:2, 238
33:8, 189
33:22, 74, 347
35:6, 238
35:8, 189
40:3, 189
43:19, 20, 238
49:2-23, 185
52:7, 98
52:14, 189, 255
53:5, 189, 211, 221
54:7-10, 187
55:9, 136
61:1, 168
62:10, 189
64:6, 136
65:2, 75
66:18, 189
66:18-21, 188

Jeremiah
1:11, 12, 190
11:18-23, 191
13:17, 192
13:23, 192
14:2, 192
15:6, 192
22:15, 134
23:7, 8, 194
24:2, 193
24:8-10, 193
29:16-20, 193
33:1-3, 20, 25, 194
39:5-7, 195
48:2, 196
49:7-22, 199

Lamentations
3:21-24, 196
3:23, 124
4:1-22, 134

Ezekiel
1:15-17, 339
14:14, 20, 350
16:44, 341
18:2, 341
18:20, 340
28:12-18, 361
33:18, 342
37:3-6, 343
38:17, 18, 344
47:8, 9, 345
48:29, 346

Daniel
1:14-17, 347
2:10, 11, 348
3:17, 18, 349
6:10, 350
9:3-5, 350
9:24-27, 252
10:18, 19, 351
11:37, 207

Hosea
2:18, 266
6:7, 197
10:4, 357

Joel
2:28, 238
3:10, 201

Amos
1:11, 12, 201

Obadiah
1:1-4, 198
1:6, 200
1:10, 12, 200
1:12, 199
1:18, 200

Jonah
1:17, 203

Micah
5:2, 202

Nahum
1:7, 8, 203

Habakkuk
2:4, 204
3:19, 205

Zephaniah
3:17, 206

Haggai
2:3-9, 206

Zechariah
1:1, 208
3:8, 209
9:9, 266
9:9, 10, 209
12:10, 211
14:4, 355

Malachi
1:2, 3, 201

Matthew
1:1, 114
2:1, 215
2:23, 77
6:3, 49, 216
6:30, 217
7:7, 219
7:21-23, 220
8:17, 220
10:5, 6, 221
10:16, 43
11:28-30, 222
12:36, 52
13:7, 223
13:42, 224
15:8, 228
15:16, 242
15:29-31, 227
16:8, 228
16:18, 353
16:23, 228
16:24-26, 226
17:1-9, 230
17:13, 243
17:24, 25, 229
18:18, 137
18:20, 230
20:25-28, 231
20:29, 30, 231
22:17, 232
24:8-11, 233
25:15, 25, 28, 234
26:26, 235
27:17, 236
27:42, 247
28:18-20, 189

Mark
1:2-4, 238
1:35, 230
2:1-8, 239
2:8, 228
5:33, 93
5:37-42, 230
6:6, 56
6:39, 40, 230
7:6, 228
8:17, 242
9:1-13, 241
10:25-27, 243
10:27, 341
10:45, 330
12:13-17, 43, 44, 244
13:42-46, 230
16:14, 56
16:15-18, 189
16:17, 137

Luke
1:28, 245
1:33, 112
2:35, 211, 246
3:38, 246
4:9, 247
5:16, 248
5:22, 228
6:8, 228
6:12, 248
6:43, 249
8:18, 249
9:18, 248
9:19, 230
10:18-20, 206
10:19, 137
11:1, 248

11:29-32, 207
12:4, 249
14:10, 250
16:24, 162
18:1-20, 359
18:10, 358, 361
19:41, 42, 252
22:39, 248

John
1:1, 252, 332
1:14, 332
1:27, 98
3:8, 253, 320
3:16, 96, 208, 330
4:23, 24, 254
4:32, 255
6:55, 255
8:40, 254
8:41-46, 282
9:5-7, 257
9:32, 257
10:10, 250, 287, 304, 329
11:14-16, 258
12:9-11, 259
13:21-30, 260
13:35, 329
14:3, 254
14:6, 162
14:12, 248
15:13, 265
16:18-22, 262
17:11-20, 263
18:3-6, 264
18:36, 112
19:6-8, 265
19:35-37, 55
20:26, 340

21:18, 19, 267

Acts
2:1-4, 263
2:3, 269
2:4, 268
2:13, 270
2:38, 39, 269
3:3, 4, 270
3:15, 260
4:13, 242
7:52, 53, 294
9:1, 2, 271
17:31-34, 272
20:28, 274
25:8, 275
28:3, 276

Romans
1:16, 17, 281
1:20, 266
2:29, 187
3:23, 282
4:16, 282
5:1-5, 283
6:23, 282
7:17, 283
8:5, 284
8:17, 128
8:22, 184, 263
9:10-18, 199
9:13, 328
9:33, 285
10:8-10, 287
10:13, 201, 341
12:15, 132
13:8, 289
13:14, 288

14:1, 289

1 Corinthians
1:30, 226
4:2, 59
6:19, 208
9:26, 27, 290
9:27, 291
12:10, 291
13:13, 306
15:2, 333
15:31, 226
15:45, 247
15:55, 301

2 Corinthians
2:11, 276
5:10, 135
5:17, 315, 319
7:1, 292
11:1-6, 293

Galatians
3:18-20, 294
5:16, 284, 328
6:3, 295
6:9, 295

Ephesians
1:21, 137
1:22, 137
3:19, 296
3:20, 21, 297
4:11, 20, 192
4:29, 172
5:18, 115, 128, 270
5:25, 298
5:27, 355

6:1-4, 297

Philippians
1:3, 172
1:21-24, 251
2:5-7, 299
2:12, 93
4:8, 301, 307
4:11-13, 302
4:13, 302

Colossians
1:3-5, 306
1:9-11, 304
1:15, 257
3:2, 304
4:5, 6, 305

1 Thessalonians
1:2, 3, 306
3:1-12, 307
4:16-18, 354
4:18, 355
5:8, 307
5:14, 15, 321

2 Thessalonians
2:3, 247

1 Timothy
1:2, 162
2:1, 2, 74
3:1, 69
3:16, 308
4:8, 333
5:1, 310

2 Timothy
    1:2, 162
    4:5, 348

Titus
    1:1, 310
    1:15, 16, 311
    2:2-7, 312
    3:5, 313

Philemon
    17-19, 314

Hebrews
    1:2, 294
    1:10-12, 315
    2:14, 316
    2:14-18, 316
    2:18, 316
    4:12, 109
    4:13, 51
    4:15, 32
    4:16, 60
    5: 6, 10, 317
    5:11-14, 318
    6:9-12, 306
    6:20, 317
    7:1, 10, 11, 15, 17, 317
    8:12, 13, 319
    9:27, 359
    10:37-39, 319
    11:1, 320
    12:1, 128
    13:2, 295
    13:8, 363
    13:15, 79

James
    1:5, 166
    1:5-8, 322
    2:14-17, 320
    2:20, 321
    3:1, 69
    4:5, 317

1 Peter
    1:3, 162
    1:7, 323
    3:1-2, 7, 324
    4:11, 349
    5:2, 3, 324
    5:8, 350

2 Peter
    1:18-21, 326
    3:8, 193
    3:8, 9, 360
    3:8, 9, 15, 327
    3:9, 75

1 John
    1:1, 332
    2:17, 328
    3:10, 329
    4:10, 329

2 John
    1:2, 162
    1:7, 332

3 John
    1:2, 333

Jude
    1:17, 18, 333

1:20, 335

Revelation
1:3, 358
2:7, 353
2:12, 109
3:17, 18, 353
3:20, 173
4:1, 354
5:4, 5, 355
7:11, 340
8:11, 357
9:20, 21, 358
11:1-14, 360
11:3, 359
12:7-10, 360
13:8, 330
19:11-14, 210
21:3-7, 361
21:5, 263
22:13, 362
22:18, 358

END NOTES

[i] Soren Kierkagaard, *Fear and Trembling* (New York: Cambridge University Press, 2006), 46.
[ii] Stanley J. Grenz, *Theology for the Community of God* (Grand Rapids: Broadman and Holman Publishers, 1994), 6, 7.
[iii] C.S. Lewis, *The Lion, the Witch and the Wardrobe* (New York: HarperCollins, 1950), 182.
[iv] *Alaska: The Last Frontier*, Discovery Channel, 10/9/12.
[v] J.M. Cook, *The Persians* (London: Folio Society, 2003), 592 pp.
[vi] Online http://www.brainyquote.com/quotes/m/marktwain153875.html
[vii] Richmond Times Dispatch, Associated Press Release, September 21, 2012, online http://www2.timesdispatch.com/news/2012/sep/21/tdmain10-chick-fil-a-muddies-controversy-ar-2222122/
[viii] This story was shared by Joel Osteen about his father during the July 22, 2012 television broadcast of *Joel Osteen Ministries*.
[ix] John F. Haught, *The Promise of Nature: Ecology and Cosmic Purpose* (Eugene, OR: Wipf & Stock Publishers, 2004), 160 pp.
[xx] Tim LaHaye and Jerry B. Jenkins, *Are We Living in the End Times?* (Carol Stream, IL: Tyndale House, 2011), 432 pp.
[xi] Greg Boyd, *God of the Possible: A Biblical Introduction to the Open View of God* (Grand Rapids: Baker Books, 2000), 110.
[xii] Stephen Davis, *Jim Morrison: Life, Death, Legend* (New York: Penguin Group, 2004), 35.
[xiii] Dallas Willard, *The Spirit of the Disciplines: Understanding How God Changes Lives* (San Francisco: HarperCollins, 1991), 152.
[xiv] "The Secret of Guidance" by F.B. Meyer, A companion volume to "Light on Life's Duties", Fleming H. Revell Company, New York. http://www.ccel.org/ccel/meyer/guidance/guidance.htm
[xv] Alan Redpath, *The Making of a Man of God* (Grand Rapids: Revell, 1962), 79.
[xvi] Neil Cole, *Organic Church: Growing Faith Where Life Happens* (San Francisco: Jossey-Bass, 2005), 100-2.
[xvii] C.S. Lewis, *Mere Christianity*, (New York: HarperCollins, 1952), 68.
[xviii] Mortimer J. Adler and Charles Van Doren, *How To Read a Book* (New York: Touchstone, 1940), 430 pp.
[xix] Janice Miller, *This Blue Planet: Finding God in the Wonders of Nature* (Chicago: Moody, 1994), 151.
[xx] Dietrich Bonhoeffer, *Ethics* (Touchstone: New York, 1995), 42-3.

[xxi] Ibid, Bonhoeffer, *Ethics*, 51.
[xxii] William Byron Forbush, ed. *Fox's Book of Martyrs: A History of the Lives, Sufferings and Deaths of the Early Christian and Protestant Martyrs* (Grand Rapids: Zondervan, 1967), 4.
[xxiii] Martin Luther, Autobiographical Fragment, written in 1545, available online
http://www.brenthobbs.com/index_files/15fcc3a851f7033dd0e49c8b8d19a8a3-109.php
[xxiv] Reuben P. Job and Norman Shawchuck, *A Guide to Prayer for Ministers and Other Servants*, (Nashville: Upper Room Books, 1983), 226.
[xxv] C.S. Lewis, *The Last Battle,* (New York: HarperCollins, 1956) 181-205.
[xxvi] Bill Hybels and Mark Mittelberg, *Becoming a Contagious Christian*, (Grand Rapids: Zondervan, 1994), 46.
[xxvii] Eugene Peterson, *A Long Obedience in the Same Direction*, ed. 2 (Downer's Grove: InterVarsity Press, 2000), 43.
[xxviii] Amanda Lorber Youtube channel, "My Response to 'Religulous'"
http://www.youtube.com/user/superrfr3ak?feature=results_main
[xxix] Thomas R. Yoder Neufeld, *Recovering Jesus: The Witness of the New Testament* (Grand Rapids: Brazos Press, 2007), 327.
[xxx] Online http://www.biblicalstudies.com/bstudy/eschatology/ezekiel.htm
[xxxi] Robert J. Morgan, *Then Sings My Soul: 150 of the World's Greatest Hymn Stories* (Nashville: Thomas Nelson, 2003), 77.
[xxxii] Lynne Cheney, *When Washington Crossed the Delaware: A Wintertime Story for Young Patriots* (New York: Simon & Schuster, 2004), 40 pp.
[xxxiii] Darrell L. Guder, et tel, *Missional Church: A Vision for the Sending of the Church in North America* (Grand Rapids: Eerdmans, 1998), 78.
[xxxiv] Online http://www.jesus.org/is-jesus-god/names-of-jesus/the-alpha-and-omega.html

www.ingramcontent.com/pod-product-compliance
Lightning Source LLC
LaVergne TN
LVHW051822080426
835512LV00018B/2677